Praise for *Advances in Fi\.*

In his new book *Advances in Financial Machine Learning*, noted financial scholar Marcos López de Prado strikes a well-aimed karate chop at the naive and often statistically overfit techniques that are so prevalent in the financial world today. He points out that not only are business-as-usual approaches largely impotent in today's high-tech finance, but in many cases they are actually prone to lose money. But López de Prado does more than just expose the mathematical and statistical sins of the finance world. Instead, he offers a technically sound roadmap for finance professionals to join the wave of machine learning. What is particularly refreshing is the author's empirical approach—his focus is on real-world data analysis, not on purely theoretical methods that may look pretty on paper but which, in many cases, are largely ineffective in practice. The book is geared to finance professionals who are already familiar with statistical data analysis techniques, but it is well worth the effort for those who want to do real state-of-the-art work in the field."

Dr. David H. Bailey, former Complex Systems Lead,
Lawrence Berkeley National Laboratory. Co-discoverer of the
BBP spigot algorithm

"Finance has evolved from a compendium of heuristics based on historical financial statements to a highly sophisticated scientific discipline relying on computer farms to analyze massive data streams in real time. The recent highly impressive advances in machine learning (ML) are fraught with both promise and peril when applied to modern finance. While finance offers up the nonlinearities and large data sets upon which ML thrives, it also offers up noisy data and the human element which presently lie beyond the scope of standard ML techniques. To err is human, but if you really want to f**k things up, use a computer. Against this background, Dr. López de Prado has written the first comprehensive book describing the application of modern ML to financial modeling. The book blends the latest technological developments in ML with critical life lessons learned from the author's decades of financial experience in leading academic and industrial institutions. I highly recommend this exciting book to both prospective students of financial ML and the professors and supervisors who teach and guide them."

Prof. Peter Carr, Chair of the Finance and Risk Engineering
Department, NYU Tandon School of Engineering

"Marcos is a visionary who works tirelessly to advance the finance field. His writing is comprehensive and masterfully connects the theory to the application. It is not often you find a book that can cross that divide. This book is an essential read for both practitioners and technologists working on solutions for the investment community."

Landon Downs, President and Cofounder, 1QBit

"Academics who want to understand modern investment management need to read this book. In it, Marcos López de Prado explains how portfolio managers use machine learning to derive, test, and employ trading strategies. He does this from a very unusual combination of an academic perspective and extensive experience in industry, allowing him to both explain in detail what happens in industry and to explain how it works. I suspect that some readers will find parts of the book that they do not understand or that they disagree with, but everyone interested in understanding the application of machine learning to finance will benefit from reading this book."

Prof. David Easley, Cornell University. Chair of the
NASDAQ-OMX Economic Advisory Board

"For many decades, finance has relied on overly simplistic statistical techniques to identify patterns in data. Machine learning promises to change that by allowing researchers to use modern nonlinear and highly dimensional techniques, similar to those used in scientific fields like DNA analysis and astrophysics. At the same time, applying those machine learning algorithms to model financial problems would be dangerous. Financial problems require very distinct machine learning solutions. Dr. López de Prado's book is the first one to characterize what makes standard machine learning tools fail when applied to the field of finance, and the first one to provide practical solutions to unique challenges faced by asset managers. Everyone who wants to understand the future of finance should read this book."

Prof. Frank Fabozzi, EDHEC Business School. Editor of
The Journal of Portfolio Management

"This is a welcome departure from the knowledge hoarding that plagues quantitative finance. López de Prado defines for all readers the next era of finance: industrial scale scientific research powered by machines."

John Fawcett, Founder and CEO, Quantopian

"Marcos has assembled in one place an invaluable set of lessons and techniques for practitioners seeking to deploy machine learning techniques in finance. If machine learning is a new and potentially powerful weapon in the arsenal of quantitative finance, Marcos's insightful book is laden with useful advice to help keep a curious practitioner from going down any number of blind alleys, or shooting oneself in the foot."

Ross Garon, Head of Cubist Systematic Strategies. Managing
Director, Point72 Asset Management

"The first wave of quantitative innovation in finance was led by Markowitz optimization. Machine Learning is the second wave, and it will touch every aspect of finance. López de Prado's *Advances in Financial Machine Learning* is essential for readers who want to be ahead of the technology rather than being replaced by it."

Prof. Campbell Harvey, Duke University. Former President of
the American Finance Association

"The complexity inherent to financial systems justifies the application of sophisticated mathematical techniques. *Advances in Financial Machine Learning* is an exciting book that unravels a complex subject in clear terms. I wholeheartedly recommend this book to anyone interested in the future of quantitative investments."

Prof. John C. Hull, University of Toronto. Author of
Options, Futures, and other Derivatives

"Prado's book clearly illustrates how fast this world is moving, and how deep you need to dive if you are to excel and deliver top of the range solutions and above the curve performing algorithms... Prado's book is clearly at the bleeding edge of the machine learning world."

Irish Tech News

"Financial data is special for a key reason: The markets have only one past. There is no 'control group', and you have to wait for true out-of-sample data. Consequently, it is easy to fool yourself, and with the march of Moore's Law and the new machine learning, it's easier than ever. López de Prado explains how to avoid falling for these common mistakes. This is an excellent book for anyone working, or hoping to work, in computerized investment and trading."

Dr. David J. Leinweber, Former Managing Director, First Quadrant.
Author of *Nerds on Wall Street: Math, Machines and Wired Markets*

"In his new book, Dr. López de Prado demonstrates that financial machine learning is more than standard machine learning applied to financial datasets. It is an important field of research in its own right. It requires the development of new mathematical tools and approaches, needed to address the nuances of financial datasets. I strongly recommend this book to anyone who wishes to move beyond the standard Econometric toolkit."

Dr. Richard R. Lindsey, Managing Partner, Windham Capital Management.
Former Chief Economist, U.S. Securities and Exchange Commission

"Dr. Lopez de Prado, a well-known scholar and an accomplished portfolio manager who has made several important contributions to the literature on machine learning (ML) in finance, has produced a comprehensive and innovative book on the subject. He has illuminated numerous pitfalls awaiting anyone who wishes to use ML in earnest, and he has provided much needed blueprints for doing it successfully. This timely book, offering a good balance of theoretical and applied findings, is a must for academics and practitioners alike."

Prof. Alexander Lipton, Connection Science Fellow, Massachusetts
Institute of Technology. *Risk*'s Quant of the Year (2000)

"How does one make sense of todays' financial markets in which complex algorithms route orders, financial data is voluminous, and trading speeds are measured in nanoseconds? In this important book, Marcos López de Prado sets out a new paradigm for investment management built on machine learning. Far from being a "black box" technique, this book clearly explains the tools and process of financial machine learning. For academics and practitioners alike, this book fills an important gap in our understanding of investment management in the machine age."

Prof. Maureen O'Hara, Cornell University. Former President of
the American Finance Association

"Marcos López de Prado has produced an extremely timely and important book on machine learning. The author's academic and professional first-rate credentials shine through the pages of this book—indeed, I could think of few, if any, authors better suited to explaining both the theoretical and the practical aspects of this new and (for most) unfamiliar subject. Both novices and experienced professionals will find insightful ideas, and will understand how the subject can be applied in novel and useful ways. The Python code will give the novice readers a running start and will allow them to gain quickly a hands-on appreciation of the subject. Destined to become a classic in this rapidly burgeoning field."

Prof. Riccardo Rebonato, EDHEC Business School. Former
Global Head of Rates and FX Analytics at PIMCO

"A tour de force on practical aspects of machine learning in finance, brimming with ideas on how to employ cutting-edge techniques, such as fractional differentiation and quantum computers, to gain insight and competitive advantage. A useful volume for finance and machine learning practitioners alike."

Dr. Collin P. Williams, Head of Research, D-Wave Systems

Advances in Financial Machine Learning

Advances in Financial Machine Learning

MARCOS LÓPEZ DE PRADO

For general information on our other products and services or for technical support, please contact our Customer Care Department within the United States at (800) 762-2974, outside the United States at (317) 572-3993, or fax (317) 572-4002.

Wiley publishes in a variety of print and electronic formats and by print-on-demand. Some material included with standard print versions of this book may not be included in e-books or in print-on-demand. If this book refers to media such as a CD or DVD that is not included in the version you purchased, you may download this material at http://booksupport.wiley.com. For more information about Wiley products, visit www.wiley.com.

ISBN 978-1-119-48208-6 (Hardcover)
ISBN 978-1-119-48211-6 (ePDF)
ISBN 978-1-119-48210-9 (ePub)

Printed in the United States of America

V10003129_081418

Dedicated to the memory of my coauthor and friend,
Professor Jonathan M. Borwein, FRSC, FAAAS,
FBAS, FAustMS, FAA, FAMS, FRSNSW
(1951–2016)

There are very few things which we know, which are not capable of being reduced to a mathematical reasoning. And when they cannot, it's a sign our knowledge of them is very small and confused. Where a mathematical reasoning can be had, it's as great a folly to make use of any other, as to grope for a thing in the dark, when you have a candle standing by you.

—*Of the Laws of Chance*, Preface (1692)
John Arbuthnot (1667–1735)

Contents

About the Author

Dr. Marcos López de Prado manages multibillion-dollar funds using machine learning (ML) and supercomputing technologies. He founded Guggenheim Partners' Quantitative Investment Strategies (QIS) business, where he developed high-capacity strategies that consistently delivered superior risk-adjusted returns. After managing up to $13 billion in assets, Marcos acquired QIS and spunout that business from Guggenheim in 2018.

Since 2011, Marcos has been a research fellow at Lawrence Berkeley National Laboratory (U.S. Department of Energy, Office of Science). One of the top-10 most read authors in finance (SSRN's rankings), he has published dozens of scientific articles on ML and supercomputing in the leading academic journals, and he holds multiple international patent applications on algorithmic trading.

Marcos earned a PhD in Financial Economics (2003), a second PhD in Mathematical Finance (2011) from Universidad Complutense de Madrid, and is a recipient of Spain's National Award for Academic Excellence (1999). He completed his post-doctoral research at Harvard University and Cornell University, where he teaches a Financial ML course at the School of Engineering. Marcos has an Erdős #2 and an Einstein #4 according to the American Mathematical Society.

For additional details, visit www.QuantResearch.org

Preamble

CHAPTER 1

Financial Machine Learning as a Distinct Subject

1.1 MOTIVATION

Machine learning (ML) is changing virtually every aspect of our lives. Today ML algorithms accomplish tasks that until recently only expert humans could perform. As it relates to finance, this is the most exciting time to adopt a disruptive technology that will transform how everyone invests for generations. This book explains scientifically sound ML tools that have worked for me over the course of two decades, and have helped me to manage large pools of funds for some of the most demanding institutional investors.

Books about investments largely fall in one of two categories. On one hand we find books written by authors who have not practiced what they teach. They contain extremely elegant mathematics that describes a world that does not exist. Just because a theorem is true in a logical sense does not mean it is true in a physical sense. On the other hand we find books written by authors who offer explanations absent of any rigorous academic theory. They misuse mathematical tools to describe actual observations. Their models are overfit and fail when implemented. Academic investigation and publication are divorced from practical application to financial markets, and many applications in the trading/investment world are not grounded in proper science.

A first motivation for writing this book is to cross the proverbial divide that separates academia and the industry. I have been on both sides of the rift, and I understand how difficult it is to cross it and how easy it is to get entrenched on one side. Virtue is in the balance. This book will not advocate a theory merely because of its mathematical beauty, and will not propose a solution just because it appears to work. My goal is to transmit the kind of knowledge that only comes from experience, formalized in a rigorous manner.

A second motivation is inspired by the desire that finance serves a purpose. Over the years some of my articles, published in academic journals and newspapers, have expressed my displeasure with the current role that finance plays in our society. Investors are lured to gamble their wealth on wild hunches originated by charlatans and encouraged by mass media. One day in the near future, ML will dominate finance, science will curtail guessing, and investing will not mean gambling. I would like the reader to play a part in that revolution.

A third motivation is that many investors fail to grasp the complexity of ML applications to investments. This seems to be particularly true for discretionary firms moving into the "quantamental" space. I am afraid their high expectations will not be met, not because ML failed, but because they used ML incorrectly. Over the coming years, many firms will invest with off-the-shelf ML algorithms, directly imported from academia or Silicon Valley, and my forecast is that they will lose money (to better ML solutions). Beating the wisdom of the crowds is harder than recognizing faces or driving cars. With this book my hope is that you will learn how to solve some of the challenges that make finance a particularly difficult playground for ML, like backtest overfitting. Financial ML is a subject in its own right, related to but separate from standard ML, and this book unravels it for you.

1.2 THE MAIN REASON FINANCIAL MACHINE LEARNING PROJECTS USUALLY FAIL

The rate of failure in quantitative finance is high, particularly so in financial ML. The few who succeed amass a large amount of assets and deliver consistently exceptional performance to their investors. However, that is a rare outcome, for reasons explained in this book. Over the past two decades, I have seen many faces come and go, firms started and shut down. In my experience, there is one critical mistake that underlies all those failures.

1.2.1 The Sisyphus Paradigm

Discretionary portfolio managers (PMs) make investment decisions that do not follow a particular theory or rationale (if there were one, they would be systematic PMs). They consume raw news and analyses, but mostly rely on their judgment or intuition. They may rationalize those decisions based on some story, but there is always a story for every decision. Because nobody fully understands the logic behind their bets, investment firms ask them to work independently from one another, in silos, to ensure diversification. If you have ever attended a meeting of discretionary PMs, you probably noticed how long and aimless they can be. Each attendee seems obsessed about one particular piece of anecdotal information, and giant argumentative leaps are made without fact-based, empirical evidence. This does not mean that discretionary PMs cannot be successful. On the contrary, a few of them are. The point is, they cannot naturally work as a team. Bring 50 discretionary PMs together, and they will influence one another until eventually you are paying 50 salaries for the work of one. Thus it makes sense for them to work in silos so they interact as little as possible.

Wherever I have seen that formula applied to quantitative or ML projects, it has led to disaster. The boardroom's mentality is, let us do with quants what has worked with discretionary PMs. Let us hire 50 PhDs and demand that each of them produce an investment strategy within six months. This approach always backfires, because each PhD will frantically search for investment opportunities and eventually settle for (1) a false positive that looks great in an overfit backtest or (2) standard factor investing, which is an overcrowded strategy with a low Sharpe ratio, but at least has academic support. Both outcomes will disappoint the investment board, and the project will be cancelled. Even if 5 of those PhDs identified a true discovery, the profits would not suffice to cover for the expenses of 50, so those 5 will relocate somewhere else, searching for a proper reward.

1.2.2   The Meta-Strategy Paradigm

If you have been asked to develop ML strategies on your own, the odds are stacked against you. It takes almost as much effort to produce one true investment strategy as to produce a hundred, and the complexities are overwhelming: data curation and processing, HPC infrastructure, software development, feature analysis, execution simulators, backtesting, etc. Even if the firm provides you with shared services in those areas, you are like a worker at a BMW factory who has been asked to build an entire car by using all the workshops around you. One week you need to be a master welder, another week an electrician, another week a mechanical engineer, another week a painter . . . You will try, fail, and circle back to welding. How does that make sense?

Every successful quantitative firm I am aware of applies the meta-strategy paradigm (López de Prado [2014]). Accordingly, this book was written as a research manual for teams, not for individuals. Through its chapters you will learn how to set up a research factory, as well as the various stations of the assembly line. The role of each quant is to specialize in a particular task, to become the best there is at it, while having a holistic view of the entire process. This book outlines the factory plan, where teamwork yields discoveries at a predictable rate, with no reliance on lucky strikes. This is how Berkeley Lab and other U.S. National Laboratories routinely make scientific discoveries, such as adding 16 elements to the periodic table, or laying out the groundwork for MRIs and PET scans.[1] No particular individual is responsible for these discoveries, as they are the outcome of team efforts where everyone contributes. Of course, setting up these financial laboratories takes time, and requires people who know what they are doing and have done it before. But what do you think has a higher chance of success, this proven paradigm of organized collaboration or the Sisyphean alternative of having every single quant rolling their immense boulder up the mountain?

---

[1] Berkeley Lab, http://www.lbl.gov/about.

1.3 BOOK STRUCTURE

This book disentangles a web of interconnected topics and presents them in an ordered fashion. Each chapter assumes that you have read the previous ones. Part 1 will help you structure your financial data in a way that is amenable to ML algorithms. Part 2 discusses how to do research with ML algorithms on that data. Here the emphasis is on doing research and making an actual discovery through a scientific process, as opposed to searching aimlessly until some serendipitous (likely false) result pops up. Part 3 explains how to backtest your discovery and evaluate the probability that it is false.

These three parts give an overview of the entire process, from data analysis to model research to discovery evaluation. With that knowledge, Part 4 goes back to the data and explains innovative ways to extract informative features. Finally, much of this work requires a lot of computational power, so Part 5 wraps up the book with some useful HPC recipes.

1.3.1 Structure by Production Chain

Mining gold or silver was a relatively straightforward endeavor during the 16th and 17th centuries. In less than a hundred years, the Spanish treasure fleet quadrupled the amount of precious metals in circulation throughout Europe. Those times are long gone, and today prospectors must deploy complex industrial methods to extract microscopic bullion particles out of tons of earth. That does not mean that gold production is at historical lows. On the contrary, nowadays miners extract 2,500 metric tons of microscopic gold every year, compared to the average annual 1.54 metric tons taken by the Spanish conquistadors throughout the entire 16th century![2] Visible gold is an infinitesimal portion of the overall amount of gold on Earth. *El Dorado* was always there . . . if only Pizarro could have exchanged the sword for a microscope.

The discovery of investment strategies has undergone a similar evolution. If a decade ago it was relatively common for an individual to discover macroscopic alpha (i.e., using simple mathematical tools like econometrics), currently the chances of that happening are quickly converging to zero. Individuals searching nowadays for macroscopic alpha, regardless of their experience or knowledge, are fighting overwhelming odds. The only true alpha left is microscopic, and finding it requires capital-intensive industrial methods. Just like with gold, microscopic alpha does not mean smaller overall profits. Microscopic alpha today is much more abundant than macroscopic alpha has ever been in history. There is a lot of money to be made, but you will need to use heavy ML tools.

Let us review some of the stations involved in the chain of production within a modern asset manager.

---

[2] http://www.numbersleuth.org/worlds-gold/.

1.3.1.1 Data Curators

This is the station responsible for collecting, cleaning, indexing, storing, adjusting, and delivering all data to the production chain. The values could be tabulated or hierarchical, aligned or misaligned, historical or real-time feeds, etc. Team members are experts in market microstructure and data protocols such as FIX. They must develop the data handlers needed to understand the context in which that data arises. For example, was a quote cancelled and replaced at a different level, or cancelled without replacement? Each asset class has its own nuances. For instance, bonds are routinely exchanged or recalled; stocks are subjected to splits, reverse-splits, voting rights, etc.; futures and options must be rolled; currencies are not traded in a centralized order book. The degree of specialization involved in this station is beyond the scope of this book, and Chapter 1 will discuss only a few aspects of data curation.

1.3.1.2 Feature Analysts

This is the station responsible for transforming raw data into informative signals. These informative signals have some predictive power over financial variables. Team members are experts in information theory, signal extraction and processing, visualization, labeling, weighting, classifiers, and feature importance techniques. For example, feature analysts may discover that the probability of a sell-off is particularly high when: (1) quoted offers are cancelled-replaced with market sell orders, and (2) quoted buy orders are cancelled-replaced with limit buy orders deeper in the book. Such a finding is not an investment strategy on its own, and can be used in alternative ways: execution, monitoring of liquidity risk, market making, position taking, etc. A common error is to believe that feature analysts develop strategies. Instead, feature analysts collect and catalogue libraries of findings that can be useful to a multiplicity of stations. Chapters 2–9 and 17–19 are dedicated to this all-important station.

1.3.1.3 Strategists

In this station, informative features are transformed into actual investment algorithms. A strategist will parse through the libraries of features looking for ideas to develop an investment strategy. These features were discovered by different analysts studying a wide range of instruments and asset classes. The goal of the strategist is to make sense of all these observations and to formulate a general theory that explains them. Therefore, the strategy is merely the experiment designed to test the validity of this theory. Team members are data scientists with a deep knowledge of financial markets and the economy. Remember, the theory needs to explain a large collection of important features. In particular, a theory must identify the economic mechanism that causes an agent to lose money to us. Is it a behavioral bias? Asymmetric information? Regulatory constraints? Features may be discovered by a black box, but the strategy is developed in a white box. Gluing together a number of catalogued features does not constitute a theory. Once a strategy is finalized, the strategists will prepare code that utilizes the full algorithm and submit that prototype to the backtesting team described below. Chapters 10 and 16 are dedicated to this station, with the understanding that it would be unreasonable for a book to reveal specific investment strategies.

1.3.1.4 Backtesters

This station assesses the profitability of an investment strategy under various scenarios. One of the scenarios of interest is how the strategy would perform if history repeated itself. However, the historical path is merely one of the possible outcomes of a stochastic process, and not necessarily the most likely going forward. Alternative scenarios must be evaluated, consistent with the knowledge of the weaknesses and strengths of a proposed strategy. Team members are data scientists with a deep understanding of empirical and experimental techniques. A good backtester incorporates in his analysis meta-information regarding how the strategy came about. In particular, his analysis must evaluate the probability of backtest overfitting by taking into account the number of trials it took to distill the strategy. The results of this evaluation will not be reused by other stations, for reasons that will become apparent in Chapter 11. Instead, backtest results are communicated to management and not shared with anyone else. Chapters 11–16 discuss the analyses carried out by this station.

1.3.1.5 Deployment Team

The deployment team is tasked with integrating the strategy code into the production line. Some components may be reused by multiple strategies, especially when they share common features. Team members are algorithm specialists and hardcore mathematical programmers. Part of their job is to ensure that the deployed solution is logically identical to the prototype they received. It is also the deployment team's responsibility to optimize the implementation sufficiently, such that production latency is minimized. As production calculations often are time sensitive, this team will rely heavily on process schedulers, automation servers (Jenkins), vectorization, multithreading, multiprocessing, graphics processing unit (GPU-NVIDIA), distributed computing (Hadoop), high-performance computing (Slurm), and parallel computing techniques in general. Chapters 20–22 touch on various aspects interesting to this station, as they relate to financial ML.

1.3.1.6 Portfolio Oversight

Once a strategy is deployed, it follows a *cursus honorum*, which entails the following stages or lifecycle:

1. **Embargo:** Initially, the strategy is run on data observed after the end date of the backtest. Such a period may have been reserved by the backtesters, or it may be the result of implementation delays. If embargoed performance is consistent with backtest results, the strategy is promoted to the next stage.
2. **Paper trading:** At this point, the strategy is run on a live, real-time feed. In this way, performance will account for data parsing latencies, calculation latencies, execution delays, and other time lapses between observation and positioning. Paper trading will take place for as long as it is needed to gather enough evidence that the strategy performs as expected.
3. **Graduation:** At this stage, the strategy manages a real position, whether in isolation or as part of an ensemble. Performance is evaluated precisely, including attributed risk, returns, and costs.

4. **Re-allocation:** Based on the production performance, the allocation to graduated strategies is re-assessed frequently and automatically in the context of a diversified portfolio. In general, a strategy's allocation follows a concave function. The initial allocation (at graduation) is small. As time passes, and the strategy performs as expected, the allocation is increased. Over time, performance decays, and allocations become gradually smaller.

5. **Decommission**: Eventually, all strategies are discontinued. This happens when they perform below expectations for a sufficiently extended period of time to conclude that the supporting theory is no longer backed by empirical evidence.

In general, it is preferable to release new variations of a strategy and run them in parallel with old versions. Each version will go through the above lifecycle, and old strategies will receive smaller allocations as a matter of diversification, while taking into account the degree of confidence derived from their longer track record.

1.3.2 Structure by Strategy Component

Many investment managers believe that the secret to riches is to implement an extremely complex ML algorithm. They are setting themselves up for a disappointment. If it was as easy as coding a state-of-the art classifier, most people in Silicon Valley would be billionaires. A successful investment strategy is the result of multiple factors. Table 1.1 summarizes what chapters will help you address each of the challenges involved in developing a successful investment strategy.

Throughout the book, you will find many references to journal articles I have published over the years. Rather than repeating myself, I will often refer you to one of them, where you will find a detailed analysis of the subject at hand. All of my cited papers can be downloaded for free, in pre-print format, from my website: www.QuantResearch.org.

1.3.2.1 Data
- Problem: Garbage in, garbage out.
- Solution: Work with unique, hard-to-manipulate data. If you are the only user of this data, whatever its value, it is all for you.
- How:
  - Chapter 2: Structure your data correctly.
  - Chapter 3: Produce informative labels.
  - Chapters 4 and 5: Model non-IID series properly.
  - Chapters 17–19: Find predictive features.

1.3.2.2 Software
- Problem: A specialized task requires customized tools.
- Solution: Develop your own classes. Using popular libraries means more competitors tapping the same well.

TABLE 1.1 Overview of the Challenges Addressed by Every Chapter

Part	Chapter	Fin. data	Software	Hardware	Math	Meta-Strat	Overfitting
1	2	X	X				
1	3	X	X				
1	4	X	X				
1	5	X	X		X		
2	6		X				
2	7		X			X	X
2	8		X			X	
2	9		X			X	
3	10		X			X	
3	11		X		X		X
3	12		X		X		X
3	13		X		X		X
3	14		X		X		X
3	15		X		X		X
3	16		X		X	X	X
4	17	X	X		X		
4	18	X	X		X		
4	19	X	X				
5	20		X	X	X		
5	21		X	X	X		
5	22		X	X	X		

- How:
  - Chapters 2–22: Throughout the book, for each chapter, we develop our own functions. For your particular problems, you will have to do the same, following the examples in the book.

1.3.2.3 Hardware

- Problem: ML involves some of the most computationally intensive tasks in all of mathematics.
- Solution: Become an HPC expert. If possible, partner with a National Laboratory to build a supercomputer.
- How:
  - Chapters 20 and 22: Learn how to think in terms of multiprocessing architectures. Whenever you code a library, structure it in such a way that functions can be called in parallel. You will find plenty of examples in the book.
  - Chapter 21: Develop algorithms for quantum computers.

1.3.2.4 Math

- Problem: Mathematical proofs can take years, decades, and centuries. No investor will wait that long.

- Solution: Use experimental math. Solve hard, intractable problems, not by proof but by experiment. For example, Bailey, Borwein, and Plouffe [1997] found a spigot algorithm for π (pi) without proof, against the prior perception that such mathematical finding would not be possible.
- How:
  - Chapter 5: Familiarize yourself with memory-preserving data transformations.
  - Chapters 11–15: There are experimental methods to assess the value of your strategy, with greater reliability than a historical simulation.
  - Chapter 16: An algorithm that is optimal in-sample can perform poorly out-of-sample. There is no mathematical proof for investment success. Rely on experimental methods to lead your research.
  - Chapters 17 and 18: Apply methods to detect structural breaks, and quantify the amount of information carried by financial series.
  - Chapter 20: Learn queuing methods for distributed computing so that you can break apart complex tasks and speed up calculations.
  - Chapter 21: Become familiar with discrete methods, used among others by quantum computers, to solve intractable problems.

1.3.2.5   *Meta-Strategies*
- Problem: Amateurs develop individual strategies, believing that there is such a thing as a magical formula for riches. In contrast, professionals develop methods to mass-produce strategies. The money is not in making a car, it is in making a car factory.
- Solution: Think like a business. Your goal is to run a research lab like a factory, where true discoveries are not born out of inspiration, but out of methodic hard work. That was the philosophy of physicist Ernest Lawrence, the founder of the first U.S. National Laboratory.
- How:
  - Chapters 7–9: Build a research process that identifies features relevant across asset classes, while dealing with multi-collinearity of financial features.
  - Chapter 10: Combine multiple predictions into a single bet.
  - Chapter 16: Allocate funds to strategies using a robust method that performs well out-of-sample.

1.3.2.6   *Overfitting*
- Problem: Standard cross-validation methods fail in finance. Most discoveries in finance are false, due to multiple testing and selection bias.
- Solution:
  - Whatever you do, always ask yourself in what way you may be overfitting. Be skeptical about your own work, and constantly challenge yourself to prove that you are adding value.

○ Overfitting is unethical. It leads to promising outcomes that cannot be delivered. When done knowingly, overfitting is outright scientific fraud. The fact that many academics do it does not make it right: They are not risking anyone's wealth, not even theirs.

○ It is also a waste of your time, resources, and opportunities. Besides, the industry only pays for out-of-sample returns. You will only succeed *after* you have created substantial wealth for your investors.

• How:
○ Chapters 11–15: There are three backtesting paradigms, of which historical simulation is only one. Each backtest is always overfit to some extent, and it is critical to learn to quantify by how much.

○ Chapter 16: Learn robust techniques for asset allocation that do not overfit in-sample signals at the expense of out-of-sample performance.

1.3.3 Structure by Common Pitfall

Despite its many advantages, ML is no panacea. The flexibility and power of ML techniques have a dark side. When misused, ML algorithms will confuse statistical flukes with patterns. This fact, combined with the low signal-to-noise ratio that characterizes finance, all but ensures that careless users will produce false discoveries at an ever-greater speed. This book exposes some of the most pervasive errors made by ML experts when they apply their techniques on financial datasets. Some of these pitfalls are listed in Table 1.2, with solutions that are explained in the indicated chapters.

1.4 TARGET AUDIENCE

This book presents advanced ML methods specifically designed to address the challenges posed by financial datasets. By "advanced" I do not mean extremely difficult to grasp, or explaining the latest reincarnation of deep, recurrent, or convolutional neural networks. Instead, the book answers questions that senior researchers, who have experience applying ML algorithms to financial problems, will recognize as critical. If you are new to ML, and you do not have experience working with complex algorithms, this book may not be for you (yet). Unless you have confronted in practice the problems discussed in these chapters, you may have difficulty understanding the utility of solving them. Before reading this book, you may want to study several excellent introductory ML books published in recent years. I have listed a few of them in the references section.

The core audience of this book is investment professionals with a strong ML background. My goals are that you monetize what you learn in this book, help us modernize finance, and deliver actual value for investors.

This book also targets data scientists who have successfully implemented ML algorithms in a variety of fields outside finance. If you have worked at Google and have applied deep neural networks to face recognition, but things do not seem to

TABLE 1.2   Common Pitfalls in Financial ML

#	Category	Pitfall	Solution	Chapter
1	Epistemological	The Sisyphus paradigm	The meta-strategy paradigm	1
2	Epistemological	Research through backtesting	Feature importance analysis	8
3	Data processing	Chronological sampling	The volume clock	2
4	Data processing	Integer differentiation	Fractional differentiation	5
5	Classification	Fixed-time horizon labeling	The triple-barrier method	3
6	Classification	Learning side and size simultaneously	Meta-labeling	3
7	Classification	Weighting of non-IID samples	Uniqueness weighting; sequential bootstrapping	4
8	Evaluation	Cross-validation leakage	Purging and embargoing	7, 9
9	Evaluation	Walk-forward (historical) backtesting	Combinatorial purged cross-validation	11, 12
10	Evaluation	Backtest overfitting	Backtesting on synthetic data; the deflated Sharpe ratio	10–16

work so well when you run your algorithms on financial data, this book will help you. Sometimes you may not understand the financial rationale behind some structures (e.g., meta-labeling, the triple-barrier method, fracdiff), but bear with me: Once you have managed an investment portfolio long enough, the rules of the game will become clearer to you, along with the meaning of these chapters.

1.5   REQUISITES

Investment management is one of the most multi-disciplinary areas of research, and this book reflects that fact. Understanding the various sections requires a practical knowledge of ML, market microstructure, portfolio management, mathematical finance, statistics, econometrics, linear algebra, convex optimization, discrete math, signal processing, information theory, object-oriented programming, parallel processing, and supercomputing.

Python has become the *de facto* standard language for ML, and I have to assume that you are an experienced developer. You must be familiar with scikit-learn (sklearn), pandas, numpy, scipy, multiprocessing, matplotlib and a few other libraries.

Code snippets invoke functions from these libraries using their conventional prefix, pd for pandas, np for numpy, mpl for matplotlib, etc. There are numerous books on each of these libraries, and you cannot know enough about the specifics of each one. Throughout the book we will discuss some issues with their implementation, including unresolved bugs to keep in mind.

1.6   FAQs

How can ML algorithms be useful in finance?

Many financial operations require making decisions based on pre-defined rules, like option pricing, algorithmic execution, or risk monitoring. This is where the bulk of automation has taken place so far, transforming the financial markets into ultra-fast, hyper-connected networks for exchanging information. In performing these tasks, machines were asked to follow the rules as fast as possible. High-frequency trading is a prime example. See Easley, López de Prado, and O'Hara [2013] for a detailed treatment of the subject.

The algorithmization of finance is unstoppable. Between June 12, 1968, and December 31, 1968, the NYSE was closed every Wednesday, so that back office could catch up with paperwork. Can you imagine that? We live in a different world today, and in 10 years things will be even better. Because the next wave of automation does not involve following rules, but making judgment calls. As emotional beings, subject to fears, hopes, and agendas, humans are not particularly good at making fact-based decisions, particularly when those decisions involve conflicts of interest. In those situations, investors are better served when a machine makes the calls, based on facts learned from hard data. This not only applies to investment strategy development, but to virtually every area of financial advice: granting a loan, rating a bond, classifying a company, recruiting talent, predicting earnings, forecasting inflation, etc. Furthermore, machines will comply with the law, always, when programmed to do so. If a dubious decision is made, investors can go back to the logs and understand exactly what happened. It is much easier to improve an algorithmic investment process than one relying entirely on humans.

How can ML algorithms beat humans at investing?

Do you remember when people were certain that computers would never beat humans at chess? Or *Jeopardy!*? Poker? Go? Millions of years of evolution (a genetic algorithm) have fine-tuned our ape brains to survive in a hostile 3-dimensional world where the laws of nature are static. Now, when it comes to identifying subtle patterns in a high-dimensional world, where the rules of the game change every day, all that fine-tuning turns out to be detrimental. An ML algorithm can spot patterns in a 100-dimensional world as easily as in our familiar 3-dimensional one. And while we all laugh when we see an algorithm make a silly mistake, keep in mind, algorithms have been around only a fraction of our millions of years. Every day they get better at this, we do not. Humans are slow learners, which puts us at a disadvantage in a fast-changing world like finance.

Does that mean that there is no space left for human investors?

Not at all. No human is better at chess than a computer. And no computer is better at chess than a human supported by a computer. Discretionary PMs are at a disadvantage when betting against an ML algorithm, but it is possible that the best results are achieved by combining discretionary PMs with ML algorithms. This is what has come to be known as the "quantamental" way. Throughout the book you will find techniques that can be used by quantamental teams, that is, methods that allow you to combine human guesses (inspired by fundamental variables) with mathematical forecasts. In particular, Chapter 3 introduces a new technique called meta-labeling, which allows you to add an ML layer on top of a discretionary one.

How does financial ML differ from econometrics?

Econometrics is the application of classical statistical methods to economic and financial series. The essential tool of econometrics is multivariate linear regression, an 18th-century technology that was already mastered by Gauss before 1794 (Stigler [1981]). Standard econometric models do not learn. It is hard to believe that something as complex as 21st-century finance could be grasped by something as simple as inverting a covariance matrix.

Every empirical science must build theories based on observation. If the statistical toolbox used to model these observations is linear regression, the researcher will fail to recognize the complexity of the data, and the theories will be awfully simplistic, useless. I have no doubt in my mind, econometrics is a primary reason economics and finance have not experienced meaningful progress over the past 70 years (Calkin and López de Prado [2014a, 2014b]).

For centuries, medieval astronomers made observations and developed theories about celestial mechanics. These theories never considered non-circular orbits, because they were deemed unholy and beneath God's plan. The prediction errors were so gross, that ever more complex theories had to be devised to account for them. It was not until Kepler had the temerity to consider non-circular (elliptical) orbits that all of the sudden a much simpler general model was able to predict the position of the planets with astonishing accuracy. What if astronomers had never considered non-circular orbits? Well . . . what if economists finally started to consider non-linear functions? Where is our Kepler? Finance does not have a *Principia* because no Kepler means no Newton.

Financial ML methods do not replace theory. They guide it. An ML algorithm learns patterns in a high-dimensional space without being specifically directed. Once we understand what features are predictive of a phenomenon, we can build a theoretical explanation, which can be tested on an independent dataset. Students of economics and finance would do well enrolling in ML courses, rather than econometrics. Econometrics may be good enough to succeed in financial academia (for now), but succeeding in business requires ML.

What do you say to people who dismiss ML algorithms as black boxes?

If you are reading this book, chances are ML algorithms are white boxes to you. They are transparent, well-defined, crystal-clear, pattern-recognition functions. Most people do not have your knowledge, and to them ML is like a magician's box: "Where did that rabbit come from? How are you tricking us, witch?" People mistrust what they do not understand. Their prejudices are rooted in ignorance, for which the Socratic remedy is simple: education. Besides, some of us enjoy using our brains, even though neuroscientists still have not figured out exactly how they work (a black box in itself).

From time to time you will encounter Luddites, who are beyond redemption. Ned Ludd was a weaver from Leicester, England, who in 1779 smashed two knitting frames in an outrage. With the advent of the industrial revolution, mobs infuriated by mechanization sabotaged and destroyed all machinery they could find. Textile workers ruined so much industrial equipment that Parliament had to pass laws making "machine breaking" a capital crime. Between 1811 and 1816, large parts of England were in open rebellion, to the point that there were more British troops fighting Luddites than there were fighting Napoleon on the Iberian Peninsula. The Luddite rebellion ended with brutal suppression through military force. Let us hope that the black box movement does not come to that.

Why don't you discuss specific ML algorithms?

The book is agnostic with regards to the particular ML algorithm you choose. Whether you use convolutional neural networks, AdaBoost, RFs, SVMs, and so on, there are many shared generic problems you will face: data structuring, labeling, weighting, stationary transformations, cross-validation, feature selection, feature importance, overfitting, backtesting, etc. In the context of financial modeling, answering these questions is non-trivial, and framework-specific approaches need to be developed. That is the focus of this book.

What other books do you recommend on this subject?

To my knowledge, this is the first book to provide a complete and systematic treatment of ML methods specific for finance: starting with a chapter dedicated to financial data structures, another chapter for labeling of financial series, another for sample weighting, time series differentiation, . . . all the way to a full part devoted to the proper backtesting of investment strategies. To be sure, there are a handful of prior publications (mostly journal articles) that have applied standard ML to financial series, but that is not what this book offers. My goal has been to address the unique nuisances that make financial ML modeling particularly challenging. Like any new subject, it is fast evolving, and the book will be updated as major advances take place. Please contact me at mldp@quantresearch.org if there is any particular topic you would like to see treated in future editions. I will gladly add those chapters, while acknowledging the names of those readers who suggested them.

I do not understand some of the sections and chapters. What should I do?

My advice is that you start by reading the references listed at the end of the chapter. When I wrote the book, I had to assume the reader was familiar with the existing literature, or this book would lose its focus. If after reading those references the sections still do not make sense, the likely reason is that they are related to a problem well understood by investment professionals (even if there is no mention of it in the literature). For example, Chapter 2 will discuss effective methods to adjust futures prices for the roll, a problem known to most practitioners, even though it is rarely addressed in textbooks. I would encourage you to attend one of my regular seminars, and ask me your question at the end of my talk.

Why is the book so fixated on backtest overfitting?

There are two reasons. First, backtest overfitting is arguably the most important open problem in all of mathematical finance. It is our equivalent to "P versus NP" in computer science. If there was a precise method to prevent backtest overfitting, we would be able to take backtests to the bank. A backtest would be almost as good as cash, rather than a sales pitch. Hedge funds would allocate funds to portfolio managers with confidence. Investors would risk less, and would be willing to pay higher fees. Regulators would grant licenses to hedge fund managers on the basis of reliable evidence of skill and knowledge, leaving no space for charlatans. In my opinion, an investments book that does not address this issue is not worth your time. Why would you read a book that deals with CAPM, APT, asset allocation techniques, risk management, etc. when the empirical results that support those arguments were selected without determining their false discovery probabilities?

The second reason is that ML is a great weapon in your research arsenal, and a dangerous one to be sure. If backtest overfitting is an issue in econometric analysis, the flexibility of ML makes it a constant threat to your work. This is particularly the case in finance, because our datasets are shorter, with lower signal-to-noise ratio, and we do not have laboratories where we can conduct experiments while controlling for all environmental variables (López de Prado [2015]). An ML book that does not tackle these concerns can be more detrimental than beneficial to your career.

What is the mathematical nomenclature of the book?

When I started to write this book, I thought about assigning one symbol to each mathematical variable or function through all the chapters. That would work well if this book dealt with a single subject, like stochastic optimal control. However this book deals with a wide range of mathematical subjects, each with its own conventions. Readers would find it harder to consult references unless I also followed literature standards, which means that sometimes we must re-use symbols. To prevent any confusion, every chapter explains the nomenclature as it is being used. Most of the math is accompanied by a code snippet, so in case of doubt, please always follow the code.

Who wrote Chapter 22?

A popular perception is that ML is a new fascinating technology invented or perfected at IBM, Google, Facebook, Amazon, Netflix, Tesla, etc. It is true that technology firms have become heavy users of ML, especially in recent years. Those firms sponsored some of the most publicized recent ML achievements (like *Jeopardy!* or Go), which may have reinforced that perception.

However, the reader may be surprised to learn that, in fact, U.S. National Laboratories are among the research centers with the longest track record and experience in using ML. These centers utilized ML before it was cool, and they applied it successfully for many decades to produce astounding scientific discoveries. If predicting what movies Netflix should recommend you to watch next is a worthy endeavor, so it is to understand the rate of expansion of the universe, or forecasting what coastlines will be most impacted by global warming, or preventing a cataclysmic failure of our national power grid. These are just some of the amazing questions that institutions like Berkeley Lab work on every day, quietly but tirelessly, with the help of ML.

In Chapter 22, Drs. Horst Simon and Kesheng Wu offer the perspective of a deputy director and a project leader at a major U.S. National Laboratory specializing in large-scale scientific research involving big data, high-performance computing, and ML. Unlike traditional university settings, National Laboratories achieve scientific breakthroughs by putting together interdisciplinary teams that follow well-devised procedures, with strong division of labor and responsibilities. That kind of research model by production chain was born at Berkeley Lab almost 90 years ago and inspired the meta-strategy paradigm explained in Sections 1.2.2 and 1.3.1.

1.7 ACKNOWLEDGMENTS

Dr. Horst Simon, who is the deputy director of Lawrence Berkeley National Laboratory, accepted to co-author Chapter 22 with Dr. Kesheng Wu, who leads several projects at Berkeley Lab and the National Energy Research Scientific Computing Center (NERSC).[3] ML requires extreme amounts of computing power, and my research would not have been possible without their generous support and guidance. In that chapter, Horst and Kesheng explain how Berkeley Lab satisfies the supercomputing needs of researchers worldwide, and the instrumental role played by ML and big data in today's scientific breakthroughs.

Prof. Riccardo Rebonato was the first to read this manuscript and encouraged me to publish it. My many conversations with Prof. Frank Fabozzi on these topics were instrumental in shaping the book in its current form. Very few people in academia have Frank's and Riccardo's industry experience, and very few people in the industry have Riccardo's and Frank's academic pedigree.

Over the past two decades, I have published nearly a hundred works on this book's subject, including journal articles, books, chapters, lectures, source code, etc. In my latest count, these works were co-authored with more than 30 leading experts in this field, including Prof. David H. Bailey (15 articles), Prof. David Easley (8 articles), Prof. Maureen O'Hara (8 articles), and Prof. Jonathan M. Borwein (6 articles). This book is to a great extent also theirs, for it would not have been possible without their support, insights, and continuous exchange of ideas over the years. It would take too long to give them proper credit, so instead I have published the following link where you can find our collective effort: http://www.quantresearch.org/Co-authors.htm.

Last but not least, I would like to thank some of my research team members for proofreading the book and helping me produce some of the figures: Diego Aparicio,

[3] http://www.nersc.gov/about.

Dr. Lee Cohn, Dr. Michael Lewis, Dr. Michael Lock, Dr. Yaxiong Zeng, and Dr. Zhibai Zhang.

EXERCISES

1.1 Are you aware of firms that have attempted to transition from discretionary investments to ML-led investments, or blending them into what they call "quantamental" funds?

(a) Have they succeeded?

(b) What are the cultural difficulties involved in this transition?

1.2 What is the most important open problem in mathematical finance? If this problem was resolved, how could:

(a) regulators use it to grant investment management licenses?

(b) investors use it to allocate funds?

(c) firms use it to reward researchers?

1.3 According to *Institutional Investor*, only 17% of hedge fund assets are managed by quantitative firms. That is about $500 billion allocated in total across all quantitative funds as of June 2017, compared to $386 billion a year earlier. What do you think is driving this massive reallocation of assets?

1.4 According to *Institutional Investor*'s Rich List, how many quantitative investment firms are placed within the top 10 most profitable firms? How does that compare to the proportion of assets managed by quantitative funds?

1.5 What is the key difference between econometric methods and ML? How would economics and finance benefit from updating their statistical toolkit?

1.6 Science has a very minimal understanding of how the human brain (or any brain) works. In this sense, the brain is an absolute black box. What do you think causes critics of financial ML to disregard it as a black box, while embracing discretionary investing?

1.7 You read a journal article that describes an investment strategy. In a backtest, it achieves an annualized Sharpe ratio in excess of 2, with a confidence level of 95%. Using their dataset, you are able to reproduce their result in an independent backtest. Why is this discovery likely to be false?

1.8 Investment advisors are plagued with conflicts of interest while making decisions on behalf of their investors.

(a) ML algorithms can manage investments without conflict of interests. Why?

(b) Suppose that an ML algorithm makes a decision that leads to a loss. The algorithm did what it was programmed to do, and the investor agreed to the terms of the program, as verified by forensic examination of the computer logs. In what sense is this situation better for the investor, compared to a loss caused by a discretionary PM's poor judgment? What is the investor's recourse in each instance?

(c) Would it make sense for financial advisors to benchmark their decisions against the decisions made by such neutral agents?

REFERENCES

Bailey, D., P. Borwein, and S. Plouffe (1997): "On the rapid computation of various polylogarithmic constants." *Mathematics of Computation*, Vol. 66, No. 218, pp. 903–913.

Calkin, N. and M. López de Prado (2014a): "Stochastic flow diagrams." *Algorithmic Finance*, Vol. 3, No. 1, pp. 21–42.

Calkin, N. and M. López de Prado (2014b): "The topology of macro financial flows: An application of stochastic flow diagrams." *Algorithmic Finance*, Vol. 3, No. 1, pp. 43–85.

Easley, D., M. López de Prado, and M. O'Hara (2013): *High-Frequency Trading*, 1st ed. Risk Books.

López de Prado, M. (2014): "Quantitative meta-strategies." *Practical Applications, Institutional Investor Journals*, Vol. 2, No. 3, pp. 1–3.

López de Prado, M. (2015): "The Future of Empirical Finance." *Journal of Portfolio Management*, Vol. 41, No. 4, pp. 140–144.

Stigler, Stephen M. (1981): "Gauss and the invention of least squares." *Annals of Statistics*, Vol. 9, No. 3, pp. 465–474.

BIBLIOGRAPHY

Abu-Mostafa, Y., M. Magdon-Ismail, and H. Lin (2012): *Learning from Data*, 1st ed. AMLBook.

Akansu, A., S. Kulkarni, and D. Malioutov (2016): *Financial Signal Processing and Machine Learning*, 1st ed. John Wiley & Sons-IEEE Press.

Aronson, D. and T. Masters (2013): *Statistically Sound Machine Learning for Algorithmic Trading of Financial Instruments: Developing Predictive-Model-Based Trading Systems Using TSSB*, 1st ed. CreateSpace Independent Publishing Platform.

Boyarshinov, V. (2012): *Machine Learning in Computational Finance: Practical Algorithms for Building Artificial Intelligence Applications*, 1st ed. LAP LAMBERT Academic Publishing.

Cerniglia, J., F. Fabozzi, and P. Kolm (2016): "Best practices in research for quantitative equity strategies." *Journal of Portfolio Management*, Vol. 42, No. 5, pp. 135–143.

Chan, E. (2017): *Machine Trading: Deploying Computer Algorithms to Conquer the Markets*, 1st ed. John Wiley & Sons.

Gareth, J., D. Witten, T. Hastie, and R. Tibshirani (2013): *An Introduction to Statistical Learning: with Applications in R*, 1st ed. Springer.

Geron, A. (2017): *Hands-On Machine Learning with Scikit-Learn and TensorFlow: Concepts, Tools, and Techniques to Build Intelligent Systems*, 1st ed. O'Reilly Media.

Gyorfi, L., G. Ottucsak, and H. Walk (2012): *Machine Learning for Financial Engineering*, 1st ed. Imperial College Press.

Hackeling, G. (2014): *Mastering Machine Learning with Scikit-Learn*, 1st ed. Packt Publishing.

Hastie, T., R. Tibshirani, and J. Friedman (2016): *The Elements of Statistical Learning*, 2nd ed. Springer-Verlag.

Hauck, T. (2014): *Scikit-Learn Cookbook*, 1st ed. Packt Publishing.

McNelis, P. (2005): *Neural Networks in Finance*, 1st ed. Academic Press.

Raschka, S. (2015): *Python Machine Learning*, 1st ed. Packt Publishing.

PART 1

Data Analysis

CHAPTER 2

Financial Data Structures

2.1 MOTIVATION

In this chapter we will learn how to work with unstructured financial data, and from that to derive a structured dataset amenable to ML algorithms. In general, you do not want to consume someone else's processed dataset, as the likely outcome will be that you discover what someone else already knows or will figure out soon. Ideally your starting point is a collection of unstructured, raw data that you are going to process in a way that will lead to informative features.

2.2 ESSENTIAL TYPES OF FINANCIAL DATA

Financial data comes in many shapes and forms. Table 2.1 shows the four essential types of financial data, ordered from left to right in terms of increasing diversity. Next, we will discuss their different natures and applications.

2.2.1 Fundamental Data

Fundamental data encompasses information that can be found in regulatory filings and business analytics. It is mostly accounting data, reported quarterly. A particular aspect of this data is that it is reported with a lapse. You must confirm exactly when each data point was released, so that your analysis uses that information only after it was publicly available. A common beginner's error is to assume that this data was published at the end of the reporting period. That is never the case.

For example, fundamental data published by Bloomberg is indexed by the last date included in the report, which precedes the date of the release (often by 1.5 months). In other words, Bloomberg is assigning those values to a date when they were not known. You could not believe how many papers are published every year using misaligned

TABLE 2.1   The Four Essential Types of Financial Data

Fundamental Data	Market Data	Analytics	Alternative Data
• Assets	• Price/yield/implied	• Analyst	• Satellite/CCTV
• Liabilities	volatility	recommendations	images
• Sales	• Volume	• Credit ratings	• Google searches
• Costs/earnings	• Dividend/coupons	• Earnings	• Twitter/chats
• Macro variables	• Open interest	expectations	• Metadata
• …	• Quotes/cancellations	• News sentiment	• …
	• Aggressor side	• …	
	• …		

fundamental data, especially in the factor-investing literature. Once you align the data correctly, a substantial number of findings in those papers cannot be reproduced.

A second aspect of fundamental data is that it is often backfilled or reinstated. "Backfilling" means that missing data is assigned a value, even if those values were unknown at that time. A "reinstated value" is a corrected value that amends an incorrect initial release. A company may issue multiple corrections for a past quarter's results long after the first publication, and data vendors may overwrite the initial values with their corrections. The problem is, the corrected values were not known on that first release date. Some data vendors circumvent this problem by storing multiple release dates and values for each variable. For example, we typically have three values for a single quarterly GDP release: the original released value and two monthly revisions. Still, it is very common to find studies that use the final released value and assign it to the time of the first release, or even to the last day in the reporting period. We will revisit this mistake, and its implications, when we discuss backtesting errors in Chapter 11.

Fundamental data is extremely regularized and low frequency. Being so accessible to the marketplace, it is rather unlikely that there is much value left to be exploited. Still, it may be useful in combination with other data types.

2.2.2   Market Data

Market data includes all trading activity that takes place in an exchange (like CME) or trading venue (like MarketAxess). Ideally, your data provider has given you a raw feed, with all sorts of unstructured information, like FIX messages that allow you to fully reconstruct the trading book, or the full collection of BWIC (bids wanted in competition) responses. Every market participant leaves a characteristic footprint in the trading records, and with enough patience, you will find a way to anticipate a competitor's next move. For example, TWAP algorithms leave a very particular footprint that is used by predatory algorithms to front-run their end-of-day trading (usually hedging) activity (Easley, López de Prado, and O'Hara [2011]). Human GUI traders often trade in round lots, and you can use this fact to estimate what percentage of the volume is coming from them at a given point in time, then associate it with a particular market behavior.

One appealing aspect of FIX data is that it is not trivial to process, unlike fundamental data. It is also very abundant, with over 10 TB being generated on a daily basis. That makes it a more interesting dataset for strategy research.

2.2.3 Analytics

You could think of analytics as derivative data, based on an original source, which could be fundamental, market, alternative, or even a collection of other analytics. What characterizes analytics is not the content of the information, but that it is not readily available from an original source, and that it has been processed for you in a particular way. Investment banks and research firms sell valuable information that results from in-depth analyses of companies' business models, activities, competition, outlook, etc. Some specialized firms sell statistics derived from alternative data, for example, the sentiment extracted from news reports and social media.

A positive aspect of analytics is that the signal has been extracted for you from a raw source. The negative aspects are that analytics may be costly, the methodology used in their production may be biased or opaque, and you will not be the sole consumer.

2.2.4 Alternative Data

Kolanovic and Krishnamachari [2017] differentiate among alternative data produced by individuals (social media, news, web searches, etc.), business processes (transactions, corporate data, government agencies, etc.), and sensors (satellites, geolocation, weather, CCTV, etc.). Some popular satellite image or video feeds include monitoring of tankers, tunnel traffic activity, or parking lot occupancies.

What truly characterizes alternative data is that it is primary information, that is, information that has not made it to the other sources. Before Exxon Mobile reported increased earnings, before its market price shot up, before analysts wrote their commentary of their latest filings, before all of that, there were movements of tankers and drillers and pipeline traffic. They happened months before those activities were reflected in the other data types. Two problematic aspects of alternative data are their cost and privacy concerns. All that spy craft is expensive, and the surveilled company may object, not to mention bystanders.

Alternative data offers the opportunity to work with truly unique, hard-to-process datasets. Remember, data that is hard to store, manipulate, and operate is always the most promising. You will recognize that a dataset *may be* useful if it annoys your data infrastructure team. Perhaps your competitors did not try to use it for logistic reasons, gave up midway, or processed it incorrectly.

2.3 BARS

In order to apply ML algorithms on your unstructured data, we need to parse it, extract valuable information from it, and store those extractions in a regularized format. Most ML algorithms assume a table representation of the extracted data.

Finance practitioners often refer to those tables' rows as "bars." We can distinguish between two categories of bar methods: (1) standard bar methods, which are common in the literature, and (2) more advanced, information-driven methods, which sophisticated practitioners use although they cannot be found (yet) in journal articles. In this section, we will discuss how to form those bars.

2.3.1 Standard Bars

Some bar construction methods are very popular in the financial industry, to the point that most data vendors' APIs offer several of them. The purpose of these methods is to transform a series of observations that arrive at irregular frequency (often referred to as "inhomogeneous series") into a homogeneous series derived from regular sampling.

2.3.1.1 Time Bars
Time bars are obtained by sampling information at fixed time intervals, e.g., once every minute. The information collected usually includes:

- Timestamp
- Volume-weighted average price (VWAP)
- Open (i.e., first) price
- Close (i.e., last) price
- High price
- Low price
- Volume traded, etc.

Although time bars are perhaps the most popular among practitioners and academics, they should be avoided for two reasons. First, markets do not process information at a constant time interval. The hour following the open is much more active than the hour around noon (or the hour around midnight in the case of futures). As biological beings, it makes sense for humans to organize their day according to the sunlight cycle. But today's markets are operated by algorithms that trade with loose human supervision, for which CPU processing cycles are much more relevant than chronological intervals (Easley, López de Prado, and O'Hara [2011]). This means that time bars oversample information during low-activity periods and undersample information during high-activity periods. Second, time-sampled series often exhibit poor statistical properties, like serial correlation, heteroscedasticity, and non-normality of returns (Easley, López de Prado, and O'Hara [2012]). GARCH models were developed, in part, to deal with the heteroscedasticity associated with incorrect sampling. As we will see next, forming bars as a subordinated process of trading activity avoids this problem in the first place.

2.3.1.2 Tick Bars
The idea behind tick bars is straightforward: The sample variables listed earlier (timestamp, VWAP, open price, etc.) will be extracted each time a pre-defined number

of transactions takes place, e.g., 1,000 ticks. This allows us to synchronize sampling with a proxy of information arrival (the speed at which ticks are originated).

Mandelbrot and Taylor [1967] were among the first to realize that sampling as a function of the number of transactions exhibited desirable statistical properties: "Price changes over a fixed number of transactions may have a Gaussian distribution. Price changes over a fixed time period may follow a stable Paretian distribution, whose variance is infinite. Since the number of transactions in any time period is random, the above statements are not necessarily in disagreement."

Ever since Mandelbrot and Taylor's paper, multiple studies have confirmed that sampling as a function of trading activity allows us to achieve returns closer to IID Normal (see Ané and Geman [2000]). This is important, because many statistical methods rely on the assumption that observations are drawn from an IID Gaussian process. Intuitively, we can only draw inference from a random variable that is invariant, and tick bars allow for better inference than time bars.

When constructing tick bars, you need to be aware of outliers. Many exchanges carry out an auction at the open and an auction at the close. This means that for a period of time, the order book accumulates bids and offers without matching them. When the auction concludes, a large trade is published at the clearing price, for an outsized amount. This auction trade could be the equivalent of thousands of ticks, even though it is reported as one tick.

2.3.1.3   Volume Bars

One problem with tick bars is that order fragmentation introduces some arbitrariness in the number of ticks. For example, suppose that there is one order sitting on the offer, for a size of 10. If we buy 10 lots, our one order will be recorded as one tick. If instead on the offer there are 10 orders of size 1, our one buy will be recorded as 10 separate transactions. In addition, matching engine protocols can further split one fill into multiple artificial partial fills, as a matter of operational convenience.

Volume bars circumvent that problem by sampling every time a pre-defined amount of the security's units (shares, futures contracts, etc.) have been exchanged. For example, we could sample prices every time a futures contract exchanges 1,000 units, regardless of the number of ticks involved.

It is hard to imagine these days, but back in the 1960s vendors rarely published volume data, as customers were mostly concerned with tick prices. After volume started to be reported as well, Clark [1973] realized that sampling returns by volume achieved even better statistical properties (i.e., closer to an IID Gaussian distribution) than sampling by tick bars. Another reason to prefer volume bars over time bars or tick bars is that several market microstructure theories study the interaction between prices and volume. Sampling as a function of one of these variables is a convenient artifact for these analyses, as we will find out in Chapter 19.

2.3.1.4   Dollar Bars

Dollar bars are formed by sampling an observation every time a pre-defined market value is exchanged. Of course, the reference to dollars is meant to apply to the currency in which the security is denominated, but nobody refers to euro bars, pound bars, or yen bars (although gold bars would make for a fun pun).

Let me illustrate the rationale behind dollar bars with a couple of examples. First, suppose that we wish to analyze a stock that has exhibited an appreciation of 100% over a certain period of time. Selling $1,000 worth of that stock at the end of the period requires trading half the number of shares it took to buy $1,000 worth of that stock at the beginning. In other words, the number of shares traded is a function of the actual value exchanged. Therefore, it makes sense sampling bars in terms of dollar value exchanged, rather than ticks or volume, particularly when the analysis involves significant price fluctuations. This point can be verified empirically. If you compute tick bars and volume bars on E-mini S&P 500 futures for a given bar size, the number of bars per day will vary wildly over the years. That range and speed of variation will be reduced once you compute the number of dollar bars per day over the years, for a constant bar size. Figure 2.1 plots the exponentially weighted average number of bars per day when we apply a fixed bar size on tick, volume, and dollar sampling methods.

A second argument that makes dollar bars more interesting than time, tick, or volume bars is that the number of outstanding shares often changes multiple times over the course of a security's life, as a result of corporate actions. Even after adjusting for splits and reverse splits, there are other actions that will impact the amount of ticks and volumes, like issuing new shares or buying back existing shares (a very common practice since the Great Recession of 2008). Dollar bars tend to be robust in the face of those actions. Still, you may want to sample dollar bars where the size of the bar is not kept constant over time. Instead, the bar size could be adjusted dynamically as a function of the free-floating market capitalization of a company (in the case of stocks), or the outstanding amount of issued debt (in the case of fixed-income securities).

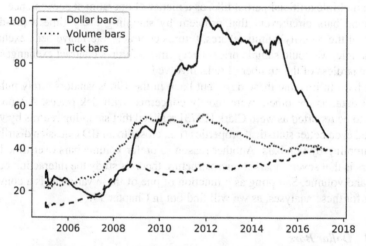

FIGURE 2.1   Average daily frequency of tick, volume, and dollar bars

2.3.2   Information-Driven Bars

The purpose of information-driven bars is to sample more frequently when new information arrives to the market. In this context, the word "information" is used in a market microstructural sense. As we will see in Chapter 19, market microstructure theories confer special importance to the persistence of imbalanced signed volumes, as that phenomenon is associated with the presence of informed traders. By synchronizing sampling with the arrival of informed traders, we may be able to make decisions before prices reach a new equilibrium level. In this section we will explore how to use various indices of information arrival to sample bars.

2.3.2.1   Tick Imbalance Bars

Consider a sequence of ticks $\{(p_t, v_t)\}_{t=1,\dots,T}$, where p_t is the price associated with tick t and v_t is the volume associated with tick t. The so-called tick rule defines a sequence $\{b_t\}_{t=1,\dots,T}$ where

$$b_t = \begin{cases} b_{t-1} & \text{if } \Delta p_t = 0 \\ \dfrac{|\Delta p_t|}{\Delta p_t} & \text{if } \Delta p_t \neq 0 \end{cases}$$

with $b_t \in \{-1, 1\}$, and the boundary condition b_0 is set to match the terminal value b_T from the immediately preceding bar. The idea behind tick imbalance bars (TIBs) is to sample bars whenever tick imbalances exceed our expectations. We wish to determine the tick index, T, such that the accumulation of signed ticks (signed according to the tick rule) exceeds a given threshold. Next, let us discuss the procedure to determine T.

First, we define the tick imbalance at time T as

$$\theta_T = \sum_{t=1}^{T} b_t$$

Second, we compute the expected value of θ_T at the beginning of the bar, $E_0[\theta_T] = E_0[T](P[b_t = 1] - P[b_t = -1])$, where $E_0[T]$ is the expected size of the tick bar, $P[b_t = 1]$ is the unconditional probability that a tick is classified as a buy, and $P[b_t = -1]$ is the unconditional probability that a tick is classified as a sell. Since $P[b_t = 1] + P[b_t = -1] = 1$, then $E_0[\theta_T] = E_0[T](2P[b_t = 1] - 1)$. In practice, we can estimate $E_0[T]$ as an exponentially weighted moving average of T values from prior bars, and $(2P[b_t = 1] - 1)$ as an exponentially weighted moving average of b_t values from prior bars.

Third, we define a tick imbalance bar (TIB) as a T^*-contiguous subset of ticks such that the following condition is met:

$$T^* = \arg\min_{T} \left\{ |\theta_T| \geq E_0[T] \left| 2P[b_t = 1] - 1 \right| \right\}$$

where the size of the expected imbalance is implied by $|2P[b_t = 1] - 1|$. When θ_T is more imbalanced than expected, a low T will satisfy these conditions. Accordingly, TIBs are produced more frequently under the presence of informed trading (asymmetric information that triggers one-side trading). In fact, we can understand TIBs as buckets of trades containing equal amounts of information (regardless of the volumes, prices, or ticks traded).

2.3.2.2 Volume/Dollar Imbalance Bars

The idea behind volume imbalance bars (VIBs) and dollar imbalance bars (DIBs) is to extend the concept of tick imbalance bars (TIBs). We would like to sample bars when volume or dollar imbalances diverge from our expectations. Based on the same notions of tick rule and boundary condition b_0 as we discussed for TIBs, we will define a procedure to determine the index of the next sample, T.

First, we define the imbalance at time T as

$$\theta_T = \sum_{t=1}^{T} b_t v_t$$

where v_t may represent either the number of securities traded (VIB) or the dollar amount exchanged (DIB). Your choice of v_t is what determines whether you are sampling according to the former or the latter.

Second, we compute the expected value of θ_T at the beginning of the bar

$$E_0[\theta_T] = E_0\left[\sum_{t|b_t=1}^{T} v_t\right] - E_0\left[\sum_{t|b_t=-1}^{T} v_t\right] = E_0[T](P[b_t = 1]E_0[v_t|b_t = 1]$$

$$-P[b_t = -1]E_0[v_t|b_t = -1])$$

Let us denote $v^+ = P[b_t = 1]E_0[v_t|b_t = 1]$, $v^- = P[b_t = -1]E_0[v_t|b_t = -1]$, so that $E_0[T]^{-1}E_0[\sum_t v_t] = E_0[v_t] = v^+ + v^-$. You can think of v^+ and v^- as decomposing the initial expectation of v_t into the component contributed by buys and the component contributed by sells. Then

$$E_0[\theta_T] = E_0[T](v^+ - v^-) = E_0[T](2v^+ - E_0[v_t])$$

In practice, we can estimate $E_0[T]$ as an exponentially weighted moving average of T values from prior bars, and $(2v^+ - E_0[v_t])$ as an exponentially weighted moving average of $b_t v_t$ values from prior bars.

Third, we define VIB or DIB as a T^*-contiguous subset of ticks such that the following condition is met:

$$T^* = \arg\min_T \{|\theta_T| \geq E_0[T]|2v^+ - E_0[v_t]|\}$$

where the size of the expected imbalance is implied by $|2v^+ - E_0[v_t]|$. When θ_T is more imbalanced than expected, a low T will satisfy these conditions. This is the information-based analogue of volume and dollar bars, and like its predecessors, it addresses the same concerns regarding tick fragmentation and outliers. Furthermore, it also addresses the issue of corporate actions, because the above procedure does not rely on a constant bar size. Instead, the bar size is adjusted dynamically.

2.3.2.3   Tick Runs Bars

TIBs, VIBs, and DIBs monitor order flow imbalance, as measured in terms of ticks, volumes, and dollar values exchanged. Large traders will sweep the order book, use iceberg orders, or slice a parent order into multiple children, all of which leave a trace of runs in the $\{b_t\}_{t=1,\ldots,T}$ sequence. For this reason, it can be useful to monitor the *sequence* of buys in the overall volume, and take samples when that sequence diverges from our expectations.

First, we define the length of the current run as

$$\theta_T = \max \left\{ \sum_{t|b_t=1}^{T} b_t, - \sum_{t|b_t=-1}^{T} b_t \right\}$$

Second, we compute the expected value of θ_T at the beginning of the bar

$$E_0[\theta_T] = E_0[T]\max\{P[b_t = 1], 1 - P[b_t = 1]\}$$

In practice, we can estimate $E_0[T]$ as an exponentially weighted moving average of T values from prior bars, and $P[b_t = 1]$ as an exponentially weighted moving average of the proportion of buy ticks from prior bars.

Third, we define a tick runs bar (TRB) as a T^*-contiguous subset of ticks such that the following condition is met:

$$T^* = \arg \min_{T} \{\theta_T \geq E_0[T]\max\{P[b_t = 1], 1 - P[b_t = 1]\}\}$$

where the expected count of ticks from runs is implied by $\max\{P[b_t = 1], 1 - P[b_t = -1]\}$. When θ_T exhibits more runs than expected, a low T will satisfy these conditions. Note that in this definition of runs we allow for sequence breaks. That is, instead of measuring the length of the longest sequence, we count the number of ticks of each side, without offsetting them (no imbalance). In the context of forming bars, this turns out to be a more useful definition than measuring sequence lengths.

2.3.2.4   Volume/Dollar Runs Bars

Volume runs bars (VRBs) and dollar runs bars (DRBs) extend the above definition of runs to volumes and dollars exchanged, respectively. The intuition is that we wish to sample bars whenever the volumes or dollars traded by one side exceed our expectation for a bar. Following our customary nomenclature for the tick rule, we need to determine the index T of the last observation in the bar.

First, we define the volumes or dollars associated with a run as

$$\theta_T = \max \left\{ \sum_{t|b_t=1}^{T} b_t v_t, - \sum_{t|b_t=-1}^{T} b_t v_t \right\}$$

where v_t may represent either number of securities traded (VRB) or dollar amount exchanged (DRB). Your choice of v_t is what determines whether you are sampling according to the former or the latter.

Second, we compute the expected value of θ_T at the beginning of the bar,

$$E_0[\theta_T] = E_0[T]\max\{P[b_t = 1]E_0[v_t|b_t = 1], (1 - P[b_t = 1])E_0[v_t|b_t = -1]\}$$

In practice, we can estimate $E_0[T]$ as an exponentially weighted moving average of T values from prior bars, $P[b_t = 1]$ as an exponentially weighted moving average of the proportion of buy ticks from prior bars, $E_0[v_t|b_t = 1]$ as an exponentially weighted moving average of the buy volumes from prior bars, and $E_0[v_t|b_t = -1]$ as an exponentially weighted moving average of the sell volumes from prior bars.

Third, we define a volume runs bar (VRB) as a T^*-contiguous subset of ticks such that the following condition is met:

$$T^* = \arg \min_{T}\{\theta_T \geq E_0[T]\max\{P[b_t = 1]E_0[v_t|b_t = 1],$$

$$(1 - P[b_t = 1])E_0[v_t|b_t = -1]\}\}$$

where the expected volume from runs is implied by $\max\{P[b_t = 1]E_0[v_t|b_t = 1]$, $(1 - P[b_t = 1])E_0[v_t|b_t = -1]\}$. When θ_T exhibits more runs than expected, or the volume from runs is greater than expected, a low T will satisfy these conditions.

2.4   DEALING WITH MULTI-PRODUCT SERIES

Sometimes we are interested in modelling a time series of instruments, where the weights need to be dynamically adjusted over time. Other times we must deal with products that pay irregular coupons or dividends, or that are subject to corporate actions. Events that alter the nature of the time series under study need to be treated properly, or we will inadvertently introduce a structural break that will mislead our research efforts (more on this in Chapter 17). This problem appears in many guises: when we model spreads with changing weights, or baskets of securities where dividends/coupons must be reinvested, or baskets that must be rebalanced, or when an index's constituents are changed, or when we must replace an expired/matured contract/security with another, etc.

Futures are a case in point. In my experience, people struggle unnecessarily when manipulating futures, mainly because they do not know how to handle the roll well. The same can be said of strategies based on spreads of futures, or baskets of stocks or bonds. In the next section, I'll show you one way to model a basket of securities as if it was a single cash product. I call it the "ETF trick" because the goal is to transform any complex multi-product dataset into a single dataset that resembles a total-return ETF. Why is this useful? Because your code can always assume that you only trade cashlike products (non-expiring cash instruments), regardless of the complexity and composition of the underlying series.

2.4.1   The ETF Trick

Suppose we wish to develop a strategy that trades a spread of futures. A few nuisances arise from dealing with a spread rather than an outright instrument. First, the spread is characterized by a vector of weights that changes over time. As a result, the spread itself may converge even if prices do not change. When that happens, a model trading that series will be misled to believe that PnL (the net mark-to-market value of profits and losses) has resulted from that weight-induced convergence. Second, spreads can acquire negative values, because they do not represent a price. This can often be problematic, as most models assume positive prices. Third, trading times will not align exactly for all constituents, so the spread is not always tradeable at the last levels published, or with zero latency risk. Also, execution costs must be considered, like crossing the bid-ask spread.

One way to avoid these issues is to produce a time series that reflects the value of $1 invested in a spread. Changes in the series will reflect changes in PnL, the series will be strictly positive (at worst, infinitesimal), and the implementation shortfall will be taken into account. This will be the series used to model, generate signals, and trade, as if it were an ETF.

Suppose that we are given a history of bars, as derived from any of the methods explained in Section 2.3. These bars contain the following columns:

- $o_{i,t}$ is the raw open price of instrument $i = 1, \dots, I$ at bar $t = 1, \dots, T$.
- $p_{i,t}$ is the raw close price of instrument $i = 1, \dots, I$ at bar $t = 1, \dots, T$.
- $\varphi_{i,t}$ is the USD value of one point of instrument $i = 1, \dots, I$ at bar $t = 1, \dots, T$. This includes foreign exchange rate.
- $v_{i,t}$ is the volume of instrument $i = 1, \dots, I$ at bar $t = 1, \dots, T$.
- $d_{i,t}$ is the carry, dividend, or coupon paid by instrument i at bar t. This variable can also be used to charge margin costs, or costs of funding.

where all instruments $i = 1, \dots, I$ were tradeable at bar $t = 1, \dots, T$. In other words, even if some instruments were not tradeable over the entirety of the time interval $[t - 1, t]$, at least they were tradeable at times $t - 1$ and t (markets were open and able to execute orders at those instants). For a basket of futures characterized by an allocations vector ω_t rebalanced (or rolled) on bars $B \subseteq \{1, \ldots, T\}$, the \$1 investment value $\{K_t\}$ is derived as

$$h_{i,t} = \begin{cases} \dfrac{\omega_{i,t} K_t}{o_{i,t+1} \varphi_{i,t} \sum_{i=1}^{I} |\omega_{i,t}|} & \text{if } t \in B \\ h_{i,t-1} & \text{otherwise} \end{cases}$$

$$\delta_{i,t} = \begin{cases} p_{i,t} - o_{i,t} & \text{if } (t-1) \in B \\ \Delta p_{i,t} & \text{otherwise} \end{cases}$$

$$K_t = K_{t-1} + \sum_{i=1}^{I} h_{i,t-1} \varphi_{i,t} \left(\delta_{i,t} + d_{i,t} \right)$$

and $K_0 = 1$ in the initial AUM. Variable $h_{i,t}$ represents the holdings (number of securities or contracts) of instrument i at time t. Variable $\delta_{i,t}$ is the change of market value between $t-1$ and t for instrument i. Note that profits or losses are being reinvested whenever $t \in B$, hence preventing the negative prices. Dividends $d_{i,t}$ are already embedded in K_t, so there is no need for the strategy to know about them. The purpose of $\omega_{i,t} \left(\sum_{i=1}^{I} |\omega_{i,t}| \right)^{-1}$ in $h_{i,t}$ is to de-lever the allocations. For series of futures, we may not know $p_{i,t}$ of the new contract at a roll time t, so we use $o_{i,t+1}$ as the closest in time.

Let τ_i be the transaction cost associated with trading \$1 of instrument i, e.g., $\tau_i = 1E - 4$ (one basis point). There are three additional variables that the strategy needs to know for every observed bar t:

1. **Rebalance costs:** The variable cost $\{c_t\}$ associated with the allocation rebalance is $c_t = \sum_{i=1}^{I} (|h_{i,t-1}| p_{i,t} + |h_{i,t}| o_{i,t+1}) \varphi_{i,t} \tau_i$, $\forall t \in B$. We do not embed c_t in K_t, or shorting the spread will generate fictitious profits when the allocation is rebalanced. In your code, you can treat $\{c_t\}$ as a (negative) dividend.

2. **Bid-ask spread:** The cost $\{\tilde{c}_t\}$ of buying or selling one unit of this virtual ETF is $\tilde{c}_t = \sum_{i=1}^{I} |h_{i,t-1}| p_{i,t} \varphi_{i,t} \tau_i$. When a unit is bought or sold, the strategy must charge this cost $\tilde{c}_t$, which is the equivalent to crossing the bid-ask spread of this virtual ETF.

3. **Volume:** The volume traded $\{v_t\}$ is determined by the least active member in the basket. Let $v_{i,t}$ be the volume traded by instrument i over bar t. The number of tradeable basket units is $v_t = \min_i \left\{ \dfrac{v_{i,t}}{|h_{i,t-1}|} \right\}$.

Transaction costs functions are not necessarily linear, and those non-linear costs can be simulated by the strategy based on the above information. Thanks to the ETF trick, we can model a basket of futures (or a single futures) as if it was a single non-expiring cash product.

matches the price at the start of the raw series. In a backward roll, the price at the end of the rolled series matches the price at the end of the raw series.

SNIPPET 2.2   FORM A GAPS SERIES, DETRACT IT FROM PRICES

```
def getRolledSeries(pathIn,key):
    series=pd.read_hdf(pathIn,key='bars/ES_10k')
    series['Time']=pd.to_datetime(series['Time'],format='%Y%m%d%H%M%S%f')
    series=series.set_index('Time')
    gaps=rollGaps(series)
    for fld in ['Close','VWAP']:series[fld]-=gaps
    return series
#————————————————————————————————————
def rollGaps(series,dictio={'Instrument':'FUT_CUR_GEN_TICKER','Open':'PX_OPEN', \
    'Close':'PX_LAST'},matchEnd=True):
    # Compute gaps at each roll, between previous close and next open
    rollDates=series[dictio['Instrument']].drop_duplicates(keep='first').index
    gaps=series[dictio['Close']]*0
    iloc=list(series.index)
    iloc=[iloc.index(i)-1 for i in rollDates] # index of days prior to roll
    gaps.loc[rollDates[1:]]=series[dictio['Open']].loc[rollDates[1:]]- \
        series[dictio['Close']].iloc[iloc[1:]].values
    gaps=gaps.cumsum()
    if matchEnd:gaps-=gaps.iloc[-1] # roll backward
    return gaps
```

Rolled prices are used for simulating PnL and portfolio mark-to-market values. However, raw prices should still be used to size positions and determine capital consumption. Keep in mind, rolled prices can indeed become negative, particularly in futures contracts that sold off while in contango. To see this, run Snippet 2.2 on a series of Cotton #2 futures or Natural Gas futures.

In general, we wish to work with non-negative rolled series, in which case we can derive the price series of a \$1 investment as follows: (1) Compute a time series of rolled futures prices, (2) compute the return (r) as rolled price change divided by the previous raw price, and (3) form a price series using those returns (i.e., $(1+r)$.cumprod()). Snippet 2.3 illustrates this logic.

SNIPPET 2.3   NON-NEGATIVE ROLLED PRICE SERIES

```
raw=pd.read_csv(filePath,index_col=0,parse_dates=True)
gaps=rollGaps(raw,dictio={'Instrument':'Symbol','Open':'Open','Close':'Close'})
rolled=raw.copy(deep=True)
for fld in ['Open','Close']:rolled[fld]-=gaps
rolled['Returns']=rolled['Close'].diff()/raw['Close'].shift(1)
rolled['rPrices']=(1+rolled['Returns']).cumprod()
```

2.5   SAMPLING FEATURES

So far we have learned how to produce a continuous, homogeneous, and structured dataset from a collection of unstructured financial data. Although you could attempt to apply an ML algorithm on such a dataset, in general that would not be a good idea, for a couple of reasons. First, several ML algorithms do not scale well with sample size (e.g., SVMs). Second, ML algorithms achieve highest accuracy when they attempt to learn from relevant examples. Suppose that you wish to predict whether the next 5% absolute return will be positive (a 5% rally) or negative (a 5% sell-off). At any random time, the accuracy of such a prediction will be low. However, if we ask a classifier to predict the sign of the next 5% absolute return after certain catalytic conditions, we are more likely to find informative features that will help us achieve a more accurate prediction. In this section we discuss ways of sampling bars to produce a features matrix with relevant training examples.

2.5.1   Sampling for Reduction

As we have mentioned earlier, one reason for sampling features from a structured dataset is to reduce the amount of data used to fit the ML algorithm. This operation is also referred to as *downsampling*. This is often done by either sequential sampling at a constant step size (linspace sampling), or by sampling randomly using a uniform distribution (uniform sampling).

The main advantage of linspace sampling is its simplicity. The disadvantages are that the step size is arbitrary, and that outcomes may vary depending on the seed bar. Uniform sampling addresses these concerns by drawing samples uniformly across the entire set of bars. Still, both methods suffer the criticism that the sample does not necessarily contain the subset of most relevant observations in terms of their predictive power or informational content.

2.5.2   Event-Based Sampling

Portfolio managers typically place a bet after some event takes place, such as a structural break (Chapter 17), an extracted signal (Chapter 18), or microstructural phenomena (Chapter 19). These events could be associated with the release of some macroeconomic statistics, a spike in volatility, a significant departure in a spread away from its equilibrium level, etc. We can characterize an event as significant, and let the ML algorithm learn whether there is an accurate prediction function under those circumstances. Perhaps the answer is no, in which case we would redefine what constitutes an event, or try again with alternative features. For illustration purposes, let us discuss one useful event-based sampling method.

2.5.2.1   The CUSUM Filter

The CUSUM filter is a quality-control method, designed to detect a shift in the mean value of a measured quantity away from a target value. Consider IID observations $\{y_t\}_{t=1,...,T}$ arising from a locally stationary process. We define the cumulative sums

$$S_t = \max\left\{0, S_{t-1} + y_t - \mathrm{E}_{t-1}\left[y_t\right]\right\}$$

with boundary condition $S_0 = 0$. This procedure would recommend an action at the first t satisfying $S_t \geq h$, for some threshold h (the filter size). Note that $S_t = 0$ whenever $y_t \leq \mathrm{E}_{t-1}[y_t] - S_{t-1}$. This zero floor means that we will skip some downward deviations that otherwise would make S_t negative. The reason is, the filter is set up to identify a sequence of upside divergences from any reset level zero. In particular, the threshold is activated when

$$S_t \geq h \Leftrightarrow \exists \tau \in [1, t] \left|\sum_{i=\tau}^{t} \left(y_i - \mathrm{E}_{i-1}\left[y_t\right]\right)\right| \geq h$$

This concept of run-ups can be extended to include run-downs, giving us a symmetric CUSUM filter:

$$S_t^+ = \max\left\{0, S_{t-1}^+ + y_t - \mathrm{E}_{t-1}\left[y_t\right]\right\}, \ S_0^+ = 0$$

$$S_t^- = \min\left\{0, S_{t-1}^- + y_t - \mathrm{E}_{t-1}\left[y_t\right]\right\}, \ S_0^- = 0$$

$$S_t = \max\left\{S_t^+, -S_t^-\right\}$$

Lam and Yam [1997] propose an investment strategy whereby alternating buy-sell signals are generated when an absolute return h is observed relative to a prior high or low. Those authors demonstrate that such strategy is equivalent to the so-called "filter trading strategy" studied by Fama and Blume [1966]. Our use of the CUSUM filter is different: We will sample a bar t if and only if $S_t \geq h$, at which point S_t is reset. Snippet 2.4 shows an implementation of the symmetric CUSUM filter, where $\mathrm{E}_{t-1}[y_t] = y_{t-1}$.

SNIPPET 2.4 THE SYMMETRIC CUSUM FILTER

```
def getTEvents(gRaw,h):
    tEvents,sPos,sNeg=[],0,0
    diff=gRaw.diff()
    for i in diff.index[1:]:
        sPos,sNeg=max(0,sPos+diff.loc[i]),min(0,sNeg+diff.loc[i])
        if sNeg<-h:
            sNeg=0;tEvents.append(i)
        elif sPos>h:
            sPos=0;tEvents.append(i)
    return pd.DatetimeIndex(tEvents)
```

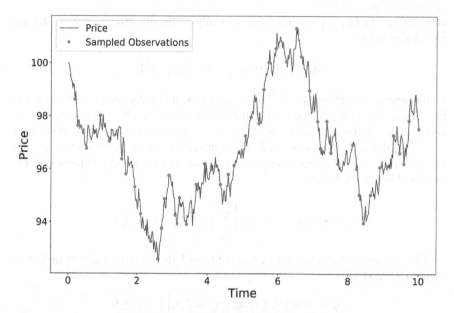

FIGURE 2.3 CUSUM sampling of a price series

The function getTEvents receives two arguments: the raw time series we wish to filter (gRaw) and the threshold, h. One practical aspect that makes CUSUM filters appealing is that multiple events are not triggered by gRaw hovering around a threshold level, which is a flaw suffered by popular market signals such as Bollinger bands. It will require a full run of length h for gRaw to trigger an event. Figure 2.3 illustrates the samples taken by a CUSUM filter on a price series.

Variable S_t could be based on any of the features we will discuss in Chapters 17–19, like structural break statistics, entropy, or market microstructure measurements. For example, we could declare an event whenever SADF departs sufficiently from a previous reset level (to be defined in Chapter 17). Once we have obtained this subset of event-driven bars, we will let the ML algorithm determine whether the occurrence of such events constitutes actionable intelligence.

EXERCISES

2.1 On a series of E-mini S&P 500 futures tick data:
  (a) Form tick, volume, and dollar bars. Use the ETF trick to deal with the roll.
  (b) Count the number of bars produced by tick, volume, and dollar bars on a weekly basis. Plot a time series of that bar count. What bar type produces the most stable weekly count? Why?
  (c) Compute the serial correlation of returns for the three bar types. What bar method has the lowest serial correlation?

(d) Partition the bar series into monthly subsets. Compute the variance of returns for every subset of every bar type. Compute the variance of those variances. What method exhibits the smallest variance of variances?

(e) Apply the Jarque-Bera normality test on returns from the three bar types. What method achieves the lowest test statistic?

2.2 On a series of E-mini S&P 500 futures tick data, compute dollar bars and dollar imbalance bars. What bar type exhibits greater serial correlation? Why?

2.3 On dollar bar series of E-mini S&P 500 futures and Eurostoxx 50 futures:

(a) Apply Section 2.4.2 to compute the $\{\hat{\omega}_t\}$ vector used by the ETF trick. (Hint: You will need FX values for EUR/USD at the roll dates.)

(b) Derive the time series of the S&P 500/Eurostoxx 50 spread.

(c) Confirm that the series is stationary, with an ADF test.

2.4 Form E-mini S&P 500 futures dollar bars:

(a) Compute Bollinger bands of width 5% around a rolling moving average. Count how many times prices cross the bands out (from within the bands to outside the bands).

(b) Now sample those bars using a CUSUM filter, where $\{y_t\}$ are returns and $h = 0.05$. How many samples do you get?

(c) Compute the rolling standard deviation of the two-sampled series. Which one is least heteroscedastic? What is the reason for these results?

2.5 Using the bars from exercise 4:

(a) Sample bars using the CUSUM filter, where $\{y_t\}$ are absolute returns and $h = 0.05$.

(b) Compute the rolling standard deviation of the sampled bars.

(c) Compare this result with the results from exercise 4. What procedure delivered the least heteroscedastic sample? Why?

REFERENCES

Ané, T. and H. Geman (2000): "Order flow, transaction clock and normality of asset returns." *Journal of Finance*, Vol. 55, pp. 2259–2284.

Bailey, David H., and M. López de Prado (2012): "Balanced baskets: A new approach to trading and hedging risks." *Journal of Investment Strategies (Risk Journals)*, Vol. 1, No. 4 (Fall), pp. 21–62.

Clark, P. K. (1973): "A subordinated stochastic process model with finite variance for speculative prices." *Econometrica*, Vol. 41, pp. 135–155.

Easley, D., M. López de Prado, and M. O'Hara (2011): "The volume clock: Insights into the high frequency paradigm." *Journal of Portfolio Management*, Vol. 37, No. 2, pp. 118–128.

Easley, D., M. López de Prado, and M. O'Hara (2012): "Flow toxicity and liquidity in a high frequency world." *Review of Financial Studies*, Vol. 25, No. 5, pp. 1457–1493.

Fama, E. and M. Blume (1966): "Filter rules and stock market trading." *Journal of Business*, Vol. 40, pp. 226–241.

Kolanovic, M. and R. Krishnamachari (2017): "Big data and AI strategies: Machine learning and alternative data approach to investing." White paper, JP Morgan, Quantitative and Derivatives Strategy. May 18.

Lam, K. and H. Yam (1997): "CUSUM techniques for technical trading in financial markets." *Financial Engineering and the Japanese Markets*, Vol. 4, pp. 257–274.

López de Prado, M. and D. Leinweber (2012): "Advances in cointegration and subset correlation hedging methods." *Journal of Investment Strategies (Risk Journals)*, Vol. 1, No. 2 (Spring), pp. 67–115.

Mandelbrot, B. and M. Taylor (1967): "On the distribution of stock price differences." *Operations Research*, Vol. 15, No. 5, pp. 1057–1062.

CHAPTER 3

Labeling

3.1 MOTIVATION

In Chapter 2 we discussed how to produce a matrix X of financial features out of an unstructured dataset. Unsupervised learning algorithms can learn the patterns from that matrix X, for example whether it contains hierarchical clusters. On the other hand, supervised learning algorithms require that the rows in X are associated with an array of labels or values y, so that those labels or values can be predicted on unseen features samples. In this chapter we will discuss ways to label financial data.

3.2 THE FIXED-TIME HORIZON METHOD

As it relates to finance, virtually all ML papers label observations using the fixed-time horizon method. This method can be described as follows. Consider a features matrix X with I rows, $\{X_i\}_{i=1,...,I}$, drawn from some bars with index $t = 1, ..., T$, where $I \leq T$. Chapter 2, Section 2.5 discussed sampling methods that produce the set of features $\{X_i\}_{i=1,...,I}$. An observation X_i is assigned a label $y_i \in \{-1, 0, 1\}$,

$$
y_i = \begin{cases} -1 & \text{if } r_{t_{i,0}, t_{i,0}+h} < -\tau \\ 0 & \text{if } |r_{t_{i,0}, t_{i,0}+h}| \leq \tau \\ 1 & \text{if } r_{t_{i,0}, t_{i,0}+h} > \tau \end{cases}
$$

where τ is a pre-defined constant threshold, $t_{i,0}$ is the index of the bar immediately after X_i takes place, $t_{i,0} + h$ is the index of the h-th bar after $t_{i,0}$, and $r_{t_{i,0}, t_{i,0}+h}$ is the price return over a bar horizon h,

$$
r_{t_{i,0}, t_{i,0}+h} = \frac{p_{t_{i,0}+h}}{p_{t_{i,0}}} - 1
$$

Because the literature almost always works with time bars, h implies a fixed-time horizon. The bibliography section lists multiple ML studies, of which Dixon et al. [2016] is a recent example of this labeling method. Despite its popularity, there are several reasons to avoid this approach in most cases. First, as we saw in Chapter 2, time bars do not exhibit good statistical properties. Second, the same threshold τ is applied regardless of the observed volatility. Suppose that $\tau = 1E-2$, where sometimes we label an observation as $y_i = 1$ subject to a realized bar volatility of $\sigma_{t_{i,0}} = 1E-4$ (e.g., during the night session), and sometimes $\sigma_{t_{i,0}} = 1E-2$ (e.g., around the open). The large majority of labels will be 0, even if return $r_{t_{i,0},t_{i,0}+h}$ was predictable and statistically significant.

In other words, it is a very common error to label observations according to a fixed threshold on time bars. Here are a couple of better alternatives. First, label per a varying threshold $\sigma_{t_{i,0}}$, estimated using a rolling exponentially weighted standard deviation of returns. Second, use volume or dollar bars, as their volatilities are much closer to constant (homoscedasticity). But even these two improvements miss a key flaw of the fixed-time horizon method: the path followed by prices. Every investment strategy has stop-loss limits, whether they are self-imposed by the portfolio manager, enforced by the risk department, or triggered by a margin call. It is simply unrealistic to build a strategy that profits from positions that would have been stopped-out by the exchange. That virtually no publication accounts for that when labeling observations tells you something about the current state of the investment literature.

3.3   COMPUTING DYNAMIC THRESHOLDS

As argued in the previous section, in practice we want to set profit taking and stop-loss limits that are a function of the risks involved in a bet. Otherwise, sometimes we will be aiming too high ($\tau \gg \sigma_{t_{i,0}}$), and sometimes too low ($\tau \ll \sigma_{t_{i,0}}$), considering the prevailing volatility.

Snippet 3.1 computes the daily volatility at intraday estimation points, applying a span of span0 days to an exponentially weighted moving standard deviation. See the pandas documentation for details on the pandas.Series.ewm function.

SNIPPET 3.1   DAILY VOLATILITY ESTIMATES

```
def getDailyVol(close,span0=100):
    # daily vol, reindexed to close
    df0=close.index.searchsorted(close.index-pd.Timedelta(days=1))
    df0=df0[df0>0]
    df0=pd.Series(close.index[df0-1], index=close.index[close.shape[0]-df0.shape[0]:])
    df0=close.loc[df0.index]/close.loc[df0.values].values-1 # daily returns
    df0=df0.ewm(span=span0).std()
    return df0
```

We can use the output of this function to set default profit taking and stop-loss limits throughout the rest of this chapter.

3.4   THE TRIPLE-BARRIER METHOD

Here I will introduce an alternative labeling method that I have not found in the literature. If you are an investment professional, I think you will agree that it makes more
sense. I call it the triple-barrier method because it labels an observation according to
the first barrier touched out of three barriers. First, we set two horizontal barriers and
one vertical barrier. The two horizontal barriers are defined by profit-taking and stop-
loss limits, which are a dynamic function of estimated volatility (whether realized
or implied). The third barrier is defined in terms of number of bars elapsed since the
position was taken (an expiration limit). If the upper barrier is touched first, we label
the observation as a 1. If the lower barrier is touched first, we label the observation
as a -1. If the vertical barrier is touched first, we have two choices: the sign of the
return, or a 0. I personally prefer the former as a matter of realizing a profit or loss
within limits, but you should explore whether a 0 works better in your particular
problems.

You may have noticed that the triple-barrier method is path-dependent. In order to
label an observation, we must take into account the entire path spanning $[t_{i,0}, t_{i,0} + h]$,
where h defines the vertical barrier (the expiration limit). We will denote $t_{i,1}$ the time
of the first barrier touch, and the return associated with the observed feature is $r_{t_{i,0},t_{i,1}}$.
For the sake of clarity, $t_{i,1} \leq t_{i,0} + h$ and the horizontal barriers are not necessarily
symmetric.

Snippet 3.2 implements the triple-barrier method. The function receives four
arguments:

- `close`: A pandas series of prices.
- `events`: A pandas dataframe, with columns,
  - `t1`: The timestamp of vertical barrier. When the value is `np.nan`, there will
    not be a vertical barrier.
  - `trgt`: The unit width of the horizontal barriers.
- `ptSl`: A list of two non-negative float values:
  - `ptSl[0]`: The factor that multiplies `trgt` to set the width of the upper barrier.
    If 0, there will not be an upper barrier.
  - `ptSl[1]`: The factor that multiplies `trgt` to set the width of the lower barrier.
    If 0, there will not be a lower barrier.
- `molecule`: A list with the subset of event indices that will be processed by a
  single thread. Its use will become clear later on in the chapter.

SNIPPET 3.2   TRIPLE-BARRIER LABELING METHOD

```
def applyPtSlOnT1(close,events,ptSl,molecule):
    # apply stop loss/profit taking, if it takes place before t1 (end of event)
    events_=events.loc[molecule]
    out=events_[['t1']].copy(deep=True)
```

```
if ptSl[0]>0:pt=ptSl[0]*events_['trgt']
else:pt=pd.Series(index=events.index) # NaNs
if ptSl[1]>0:sl=-ptSl[1]*events_['trgt']
else:sl=pd.Series(index=events.index) # NaNs
for loc,t1 in events_['t1'].fillna(close.index[-1]).iteritems():
    df0=close[loc:t1] # path prices
    df0=(df0/close[loc]-1)*events_.at[loc,'side'] # path returns
    out.loc[loc,'sl']=df0[df0<sl[loc]].index.min() # earliest stop loss.
    out.loc[loc,'pt']=df0[df0>pt[loc]].index.min() # earliest profit taking.
return out
```

The output from this function is a pandas dataframe containing the timestamps (if any) at which each barrier was touched. As you can see from the previous description, the method considers the possibility that each of the three barriers may be disabled. Let us denote a barrier configuration by the triplet [pt,sl,t1], where a 0 means that the barrier is inactive and a 1 means that the barrier is active. The possible eight configurations are:

- Three useful configurations:
  - [1,1,1]: This is the standard setup, where we define three barrier exit conditions. We would like to realize a profit, but we have a maximum tolerance for losses and a holding period.
  - [0,1,1]: In this setup, we would like to exit after a number of bars, unless we are stopped-out.
  - [1,1,0]: Here we would like to take a profit as long as we are not stopped-out. This is somewhat unrealistic in that we are willing to hold the position for as long as it takes.
- Three less realistic configurations:
  - [0,0,1]: This is equivalent to the fixed-time horizon method. It may still be useful when applied to volume-, dollar-, or information-driven bars, and multiple forecasts are updated within the horizon.
  - [1,0,1]: A position is held until a profit is made or the maximum holding period is exceeded, without regard for the intermediate unrealized losses.
  - [1,0,0]: A position is held until a profit is made. It could mean being locked on a losing position for years.
- Two illogical configurations:
  - [0,1,0]: This is an aimless configuration, where we hold a position until we are stopped-out.
  - [0,0,0]: There are no barriers. The position is locked forever, and no label is generated.

Figure 3.1 shows two alternative configurations of the triple-barrier method. On the left, the configuration is [1,1,0], where the first barrier touched is the lower horizontal one. On the right, the configuration is [1,1,1], where the first barrier touched is the vertical one.

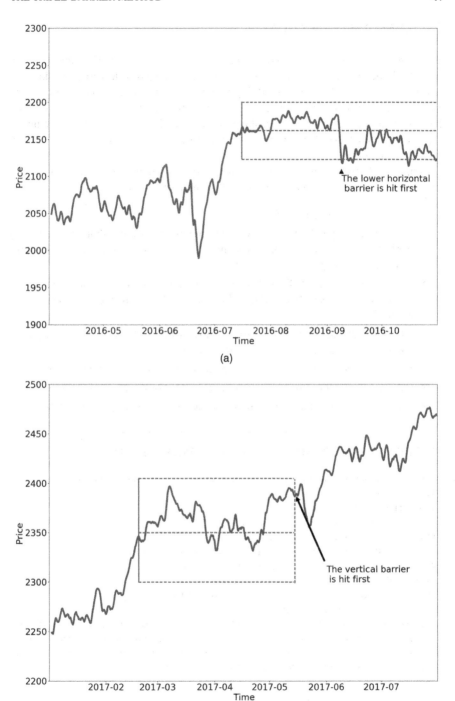

FIGURE 3.1   Two alternative configurations of the triple-barrier method

3.5   LEARNING SIDE AND SIZE

In this section we will discuss how to label examples so that an ML algorithm can learn both the side and the size of a bet. We are interested in learning the side of a bet when we do not have an underlying model to set the sign of our position (long or short). Under such circumstance, we cannot differentiate between a profit-taking barrier and a stop-loss barrier, since that requires knowledge of the side. Learning the side implies that either there are no horizontal barriers or that the horizontal barriers must be symmetric.

Snippet 3.3 implements the function getEvents, which finds the time of the first barrier touch. The function receives the following arguments:

- close: A pandas series of prices.
- tEvents: The pandas timeindex containing the timestamps that will seed every triple barrier. These are the timestamps selected by the sampling procedures discussed in Chapter 2, Section 2.5.
- ptSl: A non-negative float that sets the width of the two barriers. A 0 value means that the respective horizontal barrier (profit taking and/or stop loss) will be disabled.
- t1: A pandas series with the timestamps of the vertical barriers. We pass a False when we want to disable vertical barriers.
- trgt: A pandas series of targets, expressed in terms of absolute returns.
- minRet: The minimum target return required for running a triple barrier search.
- numThreads: The number of threads concurrently used by the function.

SNIPPET 3.3   GETTING THE TIME OF FIRST TOUCH

```
def getEvents(close,tEvents,ptSl,trgt,minRet,numThreads,t1=False):
    #1) get target
    trgt=trgt.loc[tEvents]
    trgt=trgt[trgt>minRet] # minRet
    #2) get t1 (max holding period)
    if t1 is False:t1=pd.Series(pd.NaT,index=tEvents)
    #3) form events object, apply stop loss on t1
    side_=pd.Series(1.,index=trgt.index)
    events=pd.concat({'t1':t1,'trgt':trgt,'side':side_}, \
        axis=1).dropna(subset=['trgt'])
    df0=mpPandasObj(func=applyPtSlOnT1,pdObj=('molecule',events.index), \
        numThreads=numThreads,close=close,events=events,ptSl=[ptSl,ptSl])
    events['t1']=df0.dropna(how='all').min(axis=1) # pd.min ignores nan
    events=events.drop('side',axis=1)
    return events
```

Suppose that $I = 1E6$ and $h = 1E3$, then the number of conditions to evaluate is up to one billion on a single instrument. Many ML tasks are computationally expensive unless you are familiar with multi-threading, and this is one of them. Here is where parallel computing comes into play. Chapter 20 discusses a few multiprocessing functions that we will use throughout the book.

Function `mpPandasObj` calls a multiprocessing engine, which is explained in depth in Chapter 20. For the moment, you simply need to know that this function will execute `applyPtSlOnT1` in parallel. Function `applyPtSlOnT1` returns the timestamps at which each barrier is touched (if any). Then, the time of the first touch is the earliest time among the three returned by `applyPtSlOnT1`. Because we must learn the side of the bet, we have passed `ptSl = [ptSl, ptSl]` as argument, and we arbitrarily set the side to be always long (the horizontal barriers are symmetric, so the side is irrelevant to determining the time of the first touch). The output from this function is a pandas dataframe with columns:

- `t1`: The timestamp at which the first barrier is touched.
- `trgt`: The target that was used to generate the horizontal barriers.

Snippet 3.4 shows one way to define a vertical barrier. For each index in `tEvents`, it finds the timestamp of the next price bar at or immediately after a number of days `numDays`. This vertical barrier can be passed as optional argument `t1` in `getEvents`.

SNIPPET 3.4   ADDING A VERTICAL BARRIER

```
t1=close.index.searchsorted(tEvents+pd.Timedelta(days=numDays))
t1=t1[t1<close.shape[0]]
t1=pd.Series(close.index[t1],index=tEvents[:t1.shape[0]]) # NaNs at end
```

Finally, we can label the observations using the `getBins` function defined in Snippet 3.5. The arguments are the `events` dataframe we just discussed, and the `close` pandas series of prices. The output is a dataframe with columns:

- `ret`: The return realized at the time of the first touched barrier.
- `bin`: The label, $\{-1, 0, 1\}$, as a function of the sign of the outcome. The function can be easily adjusted to label as 0 those events when the vertical barrier was touched first, which we leave as an exercise.

SNIPPET 3.5   LABELING FOR SIDE AND SIZE

```
def getBins(events,close):
    #1) prices aligned with events
    events_=events.dropna(subset=['t1'])
    px=events_.index.union(events_['t1'].values).drop_duplicates()
    px=close.reindex(px,method='bfill')
```

```
#2) create out object
out=pd.DataFrame(index=events_.index)
out['ret']=px.loc[events_['t1'].values].values/px.loc[events_.index]-1
out['bin']=np.sign(out['ret'])
return out
```

3.6 META-LABELING

Suppose that you have a model for setting the side of the bet (long or short). You just need to learn the size of that bet, which includes the possibility of no bet at all (zero size). This is a situation that practitioners face regularly. We often know whether we want to buy or sell a product, and the only remaining question is how much money we should risk in such a bet. We do not want the ML algorithm to learn the side, just to tell us what is the appropriate size. At this point, it probably does not surprise you to hear that no book or paper has so far discussed this common problem. Thankfully, that misery ends here. I call this problem meta-labeling because we want to build a secondary ML model that learns how to use a primary exogenous model.

Rather than writing an entirely new getEvents function, we will make some adjustments to the previous code, in order to handle meta-labeling. First, we accept a new side optional argument (with default None), which contains the side of our bets as decided by the primary model. When side is not None, the function understands that meta-labeling is in play. Second, because now we know the side, we can effectively discriminate between profit taking and stop loss. The horizontal barriers do not need to be symmetric, as in Section 3.5. Argument ptSl is a list of two non-negative float values, where ptSl[0] is the factor that multiplies trgt to set the width of the upper barrier, and ptSl[1] is the factor that multiplies trgt to set the width of the lower barrier. When either is 0, the respective barrier is disabled. Snippet 3.6 implements these enhancements.

SNIPPET 3.6 EXPANDING getEvents TO INCORPORATE META-LABELING

```
def getEvents(close,tEvents,ptSl,trgt,minRet,numThreads,t1=False,side=None):
    #1) get target
    trgt=trgt.loc[tEvents]
    trgt=trgt[trgt>minRet] # minRet
    #2) get t1 (max holding period)
    if t1 is False:t1=pd.Series(pd.NaT,index=tEvents)
    #3) form events object, apply stop loss on t1
    if side is None:side_,ptSl_=pd.Series(1.,index=trgt.index),[ptSl[0],ptSl[0]]
    else:side_,ptSl_=side.loc[trgt.index],ptSl[:2]
    events=pd.concat({'t1':t1,'trgt':trgt,'side':side_}, \
        axis=1).dropna(subset=['trgt'])
    df0=mpPandasObj(func=applyPtSlOnT1,pdObj=('molecule',events.index), \
        numThreads=numThreads,close=inst['Close'],events=events,ptSl=ptSl_)
```

```
events['t1']=df0.dropna(how='all').min(axis=1) # pd.min ignores nan
if side is None:events=events.drop('side',axis=1)
return events
```

Likewise, we need to expand the getBins function, so that it handles meta-labeling. Snippet 3.7 implements the necessary changes.

SNIPPET 3.7 EXPANDING getBins TO INCORPORATE META-LABELING

```
def getBins(events,close):
    '''
    Compute event's outcome (including side information, if provided).
    events is a DataFrame where:
    —events.index is event's starttime
    —events['t1'] is event's endtime
    —events['trgt'] is event's target
    —events['side'] (optional) implies the algo's position side
    Case 1: ('side' not in events): bin in (-1,1) <—label by price action
    Case 2: ('side' in events): bin in (0,1) <—label by pnl (meta-labeling)
    '''
    #1) prices aligned with events
    events_=events.dropna(subset=['t1'])
    px=events_.index.union(events_['t1'].values).drop_duplicates()
    px=close.reindex(px,method='bfill')
    #2) create out object
    out=pd.DataFrame(index=events_.index)
    out['ret']=px.loc[events_['t1'].values].values/px.loc[events_.index]-1
    if 'side' in events_:out['ret']*=events_['side'] # meta-labeling
    out['bin']=np.sign(out['ret'])
    if 'side' in events_:out.loc[out['ret']<=0,'bin']=0 # meta-labeling
    return out
```

Now the possible values for labels in out['bin'] are {0,1}, as opposed to the previous feasible values {−1,0,1}. The ML algorithm will be trained to decide whether to take the bet or pass, a purely binary prediction. When the predicted label is 1, we can use the probability of this secondary prediction to derive the size of the bet, where the side (sign) of the position has been set by the primary model.

3.7 HOW TO USE META-LABELING

Binary classification problems present a trade-off between type-I errors (false positives) and type-II errors (false negatives). In general, increasing the true positive rate of a binary classifier will tend to increase its false positive rate. The receiver operating

POSITIVES   NEGATIVES

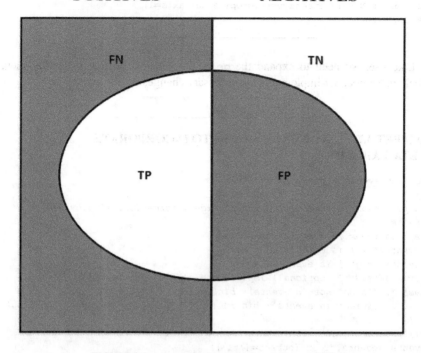

FIGURE 3.2   A visualization of the "confusion matrix"

characteristic (ROC) curve of a binary classifier measures the cost of increasing the
true positive rate, in terms of accepting higher false positive rates.

Figure 3.2 illustrates the so-called "confusion matrix." On a set of observations,
there are items that exhibit a condition (positives, left rectangle), and items that do not
exhibit a condition (negative, right rectangle). A binary classifier predicts that some
items exhibit the condition (ellipse), where the TP area contains the true positives
and the TN area contains the true negatives. This leads to two kinds of errors: false
positives (FP) and false negatives (FN). "Precision" is the ratio between the TP area
and the area in the ellipse. "Recall" is the ratio between the TP area and the area
in the left rectangle. This notion of recall (aka true positive rate) is in the context
of classification problems, the analogous to "power" in the context of hypothesis
testing. "Accuracy" is the sum of the TP and TN areas divided by the overall set of
items (square). In general, decreasing the FP area comes at a cost of increasing the
FN area, because higher precision typically means fewer calls, hence lower recall.
Still, there is some combination of precision and recall that maximizes the overall
efficiency of the classifier. The F1-score measures the efficiency of a classifier as the
harmonic average between precision and recall (more on this in Chapter 14).

Meta-labeling is particularly helpful when you want to achieve higher F1-scores.
First, we build a model that achieves high recall, even if the precision is not
particularly high. Second, we correct for the low precision by applying meta-labeling
to the positives predicted by the primary model.

Meta-labeling will increase your F1-score by filtering out the false positives, where the majority of positives have already been identified by the primary model. Stated differently, the role of the secondary ML algorithm is to determine whether a positive from the primary (exogenous) model is true or false. It is *not* its purpose to come up with a betting opportunity. Its purpose is to determine whether we should act or pass on the opportunity that has been presented.

Meta-labeling is a very powerful tool to have in your arsenal, for four additional reasons. First, ML algorithms are often criticized as black boxes (see Chapter 1). Meta-labeling allows you to build an ML system on top of a white box (like a fundamental model founded on economic theory). This ability to transform a fundamental model into an ML model should make meta-labeling particularly useful to "quantamental" firms. Second, the effects of overfitting are limited when you apply meta-labeling, because ML will not decide the side of your bet, only the size. Third, by decoupling the side prediction from the size prediction, meta-labeling enables sophisticated strategy structures. For instance, consider that the features driving a rally may differ from the features driving a sell-off. In that case, you may want to develop an ML strategy exclusively for long positions, based on the buy recommendations of a primary model, and an ML strategy exclusively for short positions, based on the sell recommendations of an entirely different primary model. Fourth, achieving high accuracy on small bets and low accuracy on large bets will ruin you. As important as identifying good opportunities is to size them properly, so it makes sense to develop an ML algorithm solely focused on getting that critical decision (sizing) right. We will retake this fourth point in Chapter 10. In my experience, meta-labeling ML models can deliver more robust and reliable outcomes than standard labeling models.

3.8 THE QUANTAMENTAL WAY

You may have read in the press that many hedge funds are embracing the quantamental approach. A simple Google search will show reports that many hedge funds, including some of the most traditional ones, are investing tens of millions of dollars in technologies designed to combine human expertise with quantitative methods. It turns out, meta-labeling is exactly what these people have been waiting for. Let us see why.

Suppose that you have a series of features that you believe can forecast some prices, you just do not know how. Since you do not have a model to determine the side of each bet, you need to learn both side and size. You apply what you have learned in Section 3.5, and produce some labels based on the triple-barrier method with symmetric horizontal barriers. Now you are ready to fit your algorithm on a training set, and evaluate the accuracy of your forecasts on a testing set. Alternatively, you could do the following:

1. Use your forecasts from the primary model, and generate meta-labels. Remember, horizontal barriers do not need to be symmetric in this case.
2. Fit your model again on the same training set, but this time using the meta-labels you just generated.
3. Combine the "sides" from the first ML model with the "sizes" from the second ML model.

You can always add a meta-labeling layer to any primary model, whether that is an ML algorithm, an econometric equation, a technical trading rule, a fundamental analysis, etc. That includes forecasts generated by a human, solely based on his intuition. In that case, meta-labeling will help us figure out when we should pursue or dismiss a discretionary PM's call. The features used by such meta-labeling ML algorithm could range from market information to biometric statistics to psychological assessments. For example, the meta-labeling ML algorithm could find that discretionary PMs tend to make particularly good calls when there is a structural break (Chapter 17), as they may be quicker to grasp a change in the market regime. Conversely, it may find that PMs under stress, as evidenced by fewer hours of sleep, fatigue, change in weight, etc. tend to make inaccurate predictions.[1] Many professions require regular psychological exams, and an ML meta-labeling algorithm may find that those scores are also relevant to assess our current degree of confidence on a PM's predictions. Perhaps none of these factors affect discretionary PMs, and their brains operate independently from their emotional being, like cold calculating machines. My guess is that this is not the case, and therefore meta-labeling should become an essential ML technique for every discretionary hedge fund. In the near future, every discretionary hedge fund will become a quantamental firm, and meta-labeling offers them a clear path to make that transition.

3.9 DROPPING UNNECESSARY LABELS

Some ML classifiers do not perform well when classes are too imbalanced. In those circumstances, it is preferable to drop extremely rare labels and focus on the more common outcomes. Snippet 3.8 presents a procedure that recursively drops observations associated with extremely rare labels. Function dropLabels recursively eliminates those observations associated with classes that appear less than a fraction minPct of cases, unless there are only two classes left.

SNIPPET 3.8 DROPPING UNDER-POPULATED LABELS

```
def dropLabels(events,minPtc=.05):
    # apply weights, drop labels with insufficient examples
    while True:
        df0=events['bin'].value_counts(normalize=True)
        if df0.min()>minPct or df0.shape[0]<3:break
        print 'dropped label',df0.argmin(),df0.min()
        events=events[events['bin']!=df0.argmin()]
    return events
```

[1] You are probably aware of at least one large hedge fund that monitors the emotional state of their research analysts on a daily basis.

Incidentally, another reason you may want to drop unnecessary labels is this known sklearn bug: https://github.com/scikit-learn/scikit-learn/issues/8566. This sort of bug is a consequence of very fundamental assumptions in sklearn implementation, and resolving them is far from trivial. In this particular instance, the error stems from sklearn's decision to operate with standard numpy arrays rather than structured arrays or pandas objects. It is unlikely that there will be a fix by the time you are reading this chapter, or in the near future. In later chapters, we will study ways to circumvent these sorts of implementation errors, by building your own classes and expanding sklearn's functionality.

EXERCISES

3.1 Form dollar bars for E-mini S&P 500 futures:

   (a) Apply a symmetric CUSUM filter (Chapter 2, Section 2.5.2.1) where the threshold is the standard deviation of daily returns (Snippet 3.1).

   (b) Use Snippet 3.4 on a pandas series t1, where numDays = 1.

   (c) On those sampled features, apply the triple-barrier method, where ptSl = [1,1] and t1 is the series you created in point 1.b.

   (d) Apply getBins to generate the labels.

3.2 From exercise 1, use Snippet 3.8 to drop rare labels.

3.3 Adjust the getBins function (Snippet 3.5) to return a 0 whenever the vertical barrier is the one touched first.

3.4 Develop a trend-following strategy based on a popular technical analysis statistic (e.g., crossing moving averages). For each observation, the model suggests a side, but not a size of the bet.

   (a) Derive meta-labels for ptSl = [1,2] and t1 where numDays = 1. Use as trgt the daily standard deviation as computed by Snippet 3.1.

   (b) Train a random forest to decide whether to trade or not. Note: The decision is whether to trade or not, {0,1}, since the underlying model (the crossing moving average) has decided the side, {−1,1}.

3.5 Develop a mean-reverting strategy based on Bollinger bands. For each observation, the model suggests a side, but not a size of the bet.

   (a) Derive meta-labels for ptSl = [0,2] and t1 where numDays = 1. Use as trgt the daily standard deviation as computed by Snippet 3.1.

   (b) Train a random forest to decide whether to trade or not. Use as features: volatility, serial correlation, and the crossing moving averages from exercise 2.

   (c) What is the accuracy of predictions from the primary model (i.e., if the secondary model does not filter the bets)? What are the precision, recall, and F1-scores?

   (d) What is the accuracy of predictions from the secondary model? What are the precision, recall, and F1-scores?

BIBLIOGRAPHY

Ahmed, N., A. Atiya, N. Gayar, and H. El-Shishiny (2010): "An empirical comparison of machine learning models for time series forecasting." *Econometric Reviews*, Vol. 29, No. 5–6, pp. 594–621.

Ballings, M., D. van den Poel, N. Hespeels, and R. Gryp (2015): "Evaluating multiple classifiers for stock price direction prediction." *Expert Systems with Applications*, Vol. 42, No. 20, pp. 7046–7056.

Bontempi, G., S. Taieb, and Y. Le Borgne (2012): "Machine learning strategies for time series forecasting." *Lecture Notes in Business Information Processing*, Vol. 138, No. 1, pp. 62–77.

Booth, A., E. Gerding and F. McGroarty (2014): "Automated trading with performance weighted random forests and seasonality." *Expert Systems with Applications*, Vol. 41, No. 8, pp. 3651–3661.

Cao, L. and F. Tay (2001): "Financial forecasting using support vector machines." *Neural Computing & Applications*, Vol. 10, No. 2, pp. 184–192.

Cao, L., F. Tay and F. Hock (2003): "Support vector machine with adaptive parameters in financial time series forecasting." *IEEE Transactions on Neural Networks*, Vol. 14, No. 6, pp. 1506–1518.

Cervelló-Royo, R., F. Guijarro, and K. Michniuk (2015): "Stock market trading rule based on pattern recognition and technical analysis: Forecasting the DJIA index with intraday data." *Expert Systems with Applications*, Vol. 42, No. 14, pp. 5963–5975.

Chang, P., C. Fan and J. Lin (2011): "Trend discovery in financial time series data using a case-based fuzzy decision tree." *Expert Systems with Applications*, Vol. 38, No. 5, pp. 6070–6080.

Kuan, C. and L. Tung (1995): "Forecasting exchange rates using feedforward and recurrent neural networks." *Journal of Applied Econometrics*, Vol. 10, No. 4, pp. 347–364.

Creamer, G. and Y. Freund (2007): "A boosting approach for automated trading." *Journal of Trading*, Vol. 2, No. 3, pp. 84–96.

Creamer, G. and Y. Freund (2010): "Automated trading with boosting and expert weighting." *Quantitative Finance*, Vol. 10, No. 4, pp. 401–420.

Creamer, G., Y. Ren, Y. Sakamoto, and J. Nickerson (2016): "A textual analysis algorithm for the equity market: The European case." *Journal of Investing*, Vol. 25, No. 3, pp. 105–116.

Dixon, M., D. Klabjan, and J. Bang (2016): "Classification-based financial markets prediction using deep neural networks." *Algorithmic Finance*, forthcoming (2017). Available at SSRN: https://ssrn.com/abstract=2756331.

Dunis, C., and M. Williams (2002): "Modelling and trading the euro/US dollar exchange rate: Do neural network models perform better?" *Journal of Derivatives & Hedge Funds*, Vol. 8, No. 3, pp. 211–239.

Feuerriegel, S. and H. Prendinger (2016): "News-based trading strategies." *Decision Support Systems*, Vol. 90, pp. 65–74.

Hsu, S., J. Hsieh, T. Chih, and K. Hsu (2009): "A two-stage architecture for stock price forecasting by integrating self-organizing map and support vector regression." *Expert Systems with Applications*, Vol. 36, No. 4, pp. 7947–7951.

Huang, W., Y. Nakamori, and S. Wang (2005): "Forecasting stock market movement direction with support vector machine." *Computers & Operations Research*, Vol. 32, No. 10, pp. 2513–2522.

Kara, Y., M. Boyacioglu, and O. Baykan (2011): "Predicting direction of stock price index movement using artificial neural networks and support vector machines: The sample of the Istanbul Stock Exchange." *Expert Systems with Applications*, Vol. 38, No. 5, pp. 5311–5319.

Kim, K. (2003): "Financial time series forecasting using support vector machines." *Neurocomputing*, Vol. 55, No. 1, pp. 307–319.

Krauss, C., X. Do, and N. Huck (2017): "Deep neural networks, gradient-boosted trees, random forests: Statistical arbitrage on the S&P 500." *European Journal of Operational Research*, Vol. 259, No. 2, pp. 689–702.

Laborda, R. and J. Laborda (2017): "Can tree-structured classifiers add value to the investor?" *Finance Research Letters*, Vol. 22 (August), pp. 211–226.

Nakamura, E. (2005): "Inflation forecasting using a neural network." *Economics Letters*, Vol. 86, No. 3, pp. 373–378.

Olson, D. and C. Mossman (2003): "Neural network forecasts of Canadian stock returns using accounting ratios." *International Journal of Forecasting*, Vol. 19, No. 3, pp. 453–465.

Patel, J., S. Sha, P. Thakkar, and K. Kotecha (2015): "Predicting stock and stock price index movement using trend deterministic data preparation and machine learning techniques." *Expert Systems with Applications*, Vol. 42, No. 1, pp. 259–268.

Patel, J., S. Sha, P. Thakkar, and K. Kotecha (2015): "Predicting stock market index using fusion of machine learning techniques." *Expert Systems with Applications*, Vol. 42, No. 4, pp. 2162–2172.

Qin, Q., Q. Wang, J. Li, and S. Shuzhi (2013): "Linear and nonlinear trading models with gradient boosted random forests and application to Singapore Stock Market." *Journal of Intelligent Learning Systems and Applications*, Vol. 5, No. 1, pp. 1–10.

Sorensen, E., K. Miller, and C. Ooi (2000): "The decision tree approach to stock selection." *Journal of Portfolio Management*, Vol. 27, No. 1, pp. 42–52.

Theofilatos, K., S. Likothanassis, and A. Karathanasopoulos (2012): "Modeling and trading the EUR/USD exchange rate using machine learning techniques." *Engineering, Technology & Applied Science Research*, Vol. 2, No. 5, pp. 269–272.

Trafalis, T. and H. Ince (2000): "Support vector machine for regression and applications to financial forecasting." *Neural Networks*, Vol. 6, No. 1, pp. 348–353.

Trippi, R. and D. DeSieno (1992): "Trading equity index futures with a neural network." *Journal of Portfolio Management*, Vol. 19, No. 1, pp. 27–33.

Tsai, C. and S. Wang (2009): "Stock price forecasting by hybrid machine learning techniques." *Proceedings of the International Multi-Conference of Engineers and Computer Scientists*, Vol. 1, No. 1, pp. 755–760.

Tsai, C., Y. Lin, D. Yen, and Y. Chen (2011): "Predicting stock returns by classifier ensembles." *Applied Soft Computing*, Vol. 11, No. 2, pp. 2452–2459.

Wang, J. and S. Chan (2006): "Stock market trading rule discovery using two-layer bias decision tree." *Expert Systems with Applications*, Vol. 30, No. 4, pp. 605–611.

Wang, Q., J. Li, Q. Qin, and S. Ge (2011): "Linear, adaptive and nonlinear trading models for Singapore Stock Market with random forests." Proceedings of the 9th IEEE International Conference on Control and Automation, pp. 726–731.

Wei, P. and N. Wang (2016): "Wikipedia and stock return: Wikipedia usage pattern helps to predict the individual stock movement." Proceedings of the 25th International Conference Companion on World Wide Web, Vol. 1, pp. 591–594.

Żbikowski, K. (2015): "Using volume weighted support vector machines with walk forward testing and feature selection for the purpose of creating stock trading strategy." *Expert Systems with Applications*, Vol. 42, No. 4, pp. 1797–1805.

Zhang, G., B. Patuwo, and M. Hu (1998): "Forecasting with artificial neural networks: The state of the art." *International Journal of Forecasting*, Vol. 14, No. 1, pp. 35–62.

Zhu, M., D. Philpotts and M. Stevenson (2012): "The benefits of tree-based models for stock selection." *Journal of Asset Management*, Vol. 13, No. 6, pp. 437–448.

Zhu, M., D. Philpotts, R. Sparks, and J. Stevenson, Maxwell (2011): "A hybrid approach to combining CART and logistic regression for stock ranking." *Journal of Portfolio Management*, Vol. 38, No. 1, pp. 100–109.

CHAPTER 4

Sample Weights

4.1 MOTIVATION

Chapter 3 presented several new methods for labeling financial observations. We introduced two novel concepts, the triple-barrier method and meta-labeling, and explained how they are useful in financial applications, including quantamental investment strategies. In this chapter you will learn how to use sample weights to address another problem ubiquitous in financial applications, namely that observations are not generated by independent and identically distributed (IID) processes. Most of the ML literature is based on the IID assumption, and one reason many ML applications fail in finance is because those assumptions are unrealistic in the case of financial time series.

4.2 OVERLAPPING OUTCOMES

In Chapter 3 we assigned a label y_i to an observed feature X_i, where y_i was a function of price bars that occurred over an interval $[t_{i,0}, t_{i,1}]$. When $t_{i,1} > t_{j,0}$ and $i < j$, then y_i and y_j will both depend on a common return $r_{t_{j,0}, \min\{t_{i,1}, t_{j,1}\}}$, that is, the return over the interval $[t_{j,0}, \min\{t_{i,1}, t_{j,1}\}]$. The implication is that the series of labels, $\{y_i\}_{i=1,\dots,I}$, are not IID whenever there is an overlap between any two consecutive outcomes, $\exists i \, | t_{i,1} > t_{i+1,0}$.

Suppose that we circumvent this problem by restricting the bet horizon to $t_{i,1} \leq t_{i+1,0}$. In this case there is no overlap, because every feature outcome is determined before or at the onset of the next observed feature. That would lead to coarse models where the features' sampling frequency would be limited by the horizon used to determine the outcome. On one hand, if we wished to investigate outcomes that lasted a month, features would have to be sampled with a frequency up to monthly. On the other hand, if we increased the sampling frequency to let's say daily, we would be forced to reduce the outcome's horizon to one day. Furthermore, if we wished to apply a path-dependent labeling technique, like the triple-barrier method, the sampling frequency would be subordinated to the first barrier's touch. No matter what you do, restricting the outcome's horizon to eliminate overlaps is a terrible solution. We must allow $t_{i,1} > t_{i+1,0}$, which brings us back to the problem of overlapping outcomes described earlier.

This situation is characteristic of financial applications. Most non-financial ML researchers can assume that observations are drawn from IID processes. For example, you can obtain blood samples from a large number of patients, and measure their cholesterol. Of course, various underlying common factors will shift the mean and standard deviation of the cholesterol distribution, but the samples are still independent: There is one observation per subject. Suppose you take those blood samples, and someone in your laboratory spills blood from each tube into the following nine tubes to their right. That is, tube 10 contains blood for patient 10, but also blood from patients 1 through 9. Tube 11 contains blood from patient 11, but also blood from patients 2 through 10, and so on. Now you need to determine the features predictive of high cholesterol (diet, exercise, age, etc.), without knowing for sure the cholesterol level of each patient. That is the equivalent challenge that we face in financial ML, with the additional handicap that the spillage pattern is non-deterministic and unknown. Finance is not a plug-and-play subject as it relates to ML applications. Anyone who tells you otherwise will waste your time and money.

There are several ways to attack the problem of non-IID labels, and in this chapter we will address it by designing sampling and weighting schemes that correct for the undue influence of overlapping outcomes.

4.3   NUMBER OF CONCURRENT LABELS

Two labels y_i and y_j are concurrent at t when both are a function of at least one common return, $r_{t-1,t} = \frac{p_t}{p_{t-1}} - 1$. The overlap does not need to be perfect, in the sense of both labels spanning the same time interval. In this section we are going to compute the number of labels that are a function of a given return, $r_{t-1,t}$. First, for each time point $t = 1, \ldots, T$, we form a binary array, $\{1_{t,i}\}_{i=1,\ldots,I}$, where $1_{t,i} \in \{0, 1\}$. Variable $1_{t,i} = 1$ if and only if $[t_{i,0}, t_{i,1}]$ overlaps with $[t-1, t]$ and $1_{t,i} = 0$ otherwise. Recall that the labels' spans $\{[t_{i,0}, t_{i,1}]\}_{i=1,\ldots,I}$ are defined by the t1 object introduced in Chapter 3. Second, we compute the number of labels concurrent at t, $c_t = \sum_{i=1}^{I} 1_{t,i}$. Snippet 4.1 illustrates an implementation of this logic.

SNIPPET 4.1   ESTIMATING THE UNIQUENESS OF A LABEL

```
def mpNumCoEvents(closeIdx,t1,molecule):
    '''
    Compute the number of concurrent events per bar.
    +molecule[0] is the date of the first event on which the weight will be computed
    +molecule[-1] is the date of the last event on which the weight will be computed
```

```
Any event that starts before t1[molecule].max() impacts the count.
'''
#1) find events that span the period [molecule[0],molecule[-1]]
t1=t1.fillna(closeIdx[-1]) # unclosed events still must impact other weights
t1=t1[t1>=molecule[0]] # events that end at or after molecule[0]
t1=t1.loc[:t1[molecule].max()] # events that start at or before t1[molecule].max()
#2) count events spanning a bar
iloc=closeIdx.searchsorted(np.array([t1.index[0],t1.max()]))
count=pd.Series(0,index=closeIdx[iloc[0]:iloc[1]+1])
for tIn,tOut in t1.iteritems():count.loc[tIn:tOut]+=1.
return count.loc[molecule[0]:t1[molecule].max()]
```

4.4   AVERAGE UNIQUENESS OF A LABEL

In this section we are going to estimate a label's uniqueness (non-overlap) as its average uniqueness over its lifespan. First, the uniqueness of a label i at time t is $u_{t,i} = 1_{t,i} c_t^{-1}$. Second, the average uniqueness of label i is the average $u_{t,i}$ over the label's lifespan, $\bar{u}_i = \left(\sum_{t=1}^{T} u_{t,i} \right) \left(\sum_{t=1}^{T} 1_{t,i} \right)^{-1}$. This average uniqueness can also be interpreted as the reciprocal of the harmonic average of c_t over the event's lifespan. Figure 4.1 plots the histogram of uniqueness values derived from an object t1. Snippet 4.2 implements this calculation.

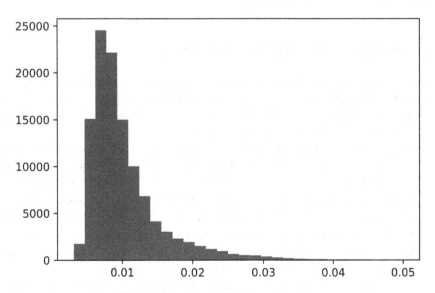

FIGURE 4.1   Histogram of uniqueness values

SNIPPET 4.2   ESTIMATING THE AVERAGE UNIQUENESS OF A LABEL

```
def mpSampleTW(t1,numCoEvents,molecule):
    # Derive average uniqueness over the event's lifespan
    wght=pd.Series(index=molecule)
    for tIn,tOut in t1.loc[wght.index].iteritems():
        wght.loc[tIn]=(1./numCoEvents.loc[tIn:tOut]).mean()
    return wght
#-----------------------------------------------------------
numCoEvents=mpPandasObj(mpNumCoEvents,('molecule',events.index),numThreads, \
        closeIdx=close.index,t1=events['t1'])
numCoEvents=numCoEvents.loc[~numCoEvents.index.duplicated(keep='last')]
numCoEvents=numCoEvents.reindex(close.index).fillna(0)
out['tW']=mpPandasObj(mpSampleTW,('molecule',events.index),numThreads, \
        t1=events['t1'],numCoEvents=numCoEvents)
```

Note that we are making use again of the function mpPandasObj, which speeds up calculations via multiprocessing (see Chapter 20). Computing the average uniqueness associated with label i, $\bar{u}_i$, requires information that is not available until a future time, events['t1']. This is not a problem, because $\{\bar{u}_i\}_{i=1,...,I}$ are used on the training set in combination with label information, and not on the testing set. These $\{\bar{u}_i\}_{i=1,...,I}$ are not used for forecasting the label, hence there is no information leakage. This procedure allows us to assign a uniqueness score between 0 and 1 for each observed feature, in terms of non-overlapping outcomes.

4.5   BAGGING CLASSIFIERS AND UNIQUENESS

The probability of not selecting a particular item i after I draws with replacement on a set of I items is $(1 - I^{-1})^I$. As the sample size grows, that probability converges to the asymptotic value $\lim_{I \to \infty} (1 - I^{-1})^I = e^{-1}$. That means that the number of unique observations drawn is expected to be $(1 - e^{-1}) \approx \frac{2}{3}$.

Suppose that the maximum number of non-overlapping outcomes is $K \leq I$. Following the same argument, the probability of not selecting a particular item i after I draws with replacement on a set of I items is $(1 - K^{-1})^I$. As the sample size grows, that probability can be approximated as $(1 - K^{-1})^{K \frac{I}{K}} \approx e^{-\frac{I}{K}}$. The number of times a particular item is sampled follows approximately a Poisson distribution with mean $\frac{I}{K} \geq 1$. The implication is that incorrectly assuming IID draws leads to oversampling.

When sampling with replacement (bootstrap) on observations with $I^{-1} \sum_{i=1}^{I} \bar{u}_i \ll 1$, it becomes increasingly likely that in-bag observations will be (1) redundant to each other, and (2) very similar to out-of-bag observations.

Redundancy of draws makes the bootstrap inefficient (see Chapter 6). For example, in the case of a random forest, all trees in the forest will essentially be very similar copies of a single overfit decision tree. And because the random sampling makes out-of-bag examples very similar to the in-bag ones, out-of-bag accuracy will be grossly inflated. We will address this second issue in Chapter 7, when we study cross-validation under non-IID observations. For the moment, let us concentrate on the first issue, namely bagging under observations where $I^{-1} \sum_{i=1}^{I} \bar{u}_i \ll 1$.

A first solution is to drop overlapping outcomes before performing the bootstrap. Because overlaps are not perfect, dropping an observation just because there is a partial overlap will result in an extreme loss of information. I do not advise you to follow this solution.

A second and better solution is to utilize the average uniqueness, $I^{-1} \sum_{i=1}^{I} \bar{u}_i$, to reduce the undue influence of outcomes that contain redundant information. Accordingly, we could sample only a fraction `out['tW'].mean()` of the observations, or a small multiple of that. In sklearn, the `sklearn.ensemble.BaggingClassifier` class accepts an argument `max_samples`, which can be set to `max_samples=out['tW'].mean()`. In this way, we enforce that the in-bag observations are not sampled at a frequency much higher than their uniqueness. Random forests do not offer that `max_samples` functionality, however, a solution is to bag a large number of decision trees. We will discuss this solution further in Chapter 6.

4.5.1 Sequential Bootstrap

A third and better solution is to perform a sequential bootstrap, where draws are made according to a changing probability that controls for redundancy. Rao et al. [1997] propose sequential resampling with replacement until K distinct original observations appear. Although interesting, their scheme does not fully apply to our financial problem. In the following sections we introduce an alternative method that addresses directly the problem of overlapping outcomes.

First, an observation X_i is drawn from a uniform distribution, $i \sim U[1, I]$, that is, the probability of drawing any particular value i is originally $\delta_i^{(1)} = I^{-1}$. For the second draw, we wish to reduce the probability of drawing an observation X_j with a highly overlapping outcome. Remember, a bootstrap allows sampling with repetition, so it is still possible to draw X_i again, but we wish to reduce its likelihood, since there is an overlap (in fact, a perfect overlap) between X_i and itself. Let us denote as φ the sequence of draws so far, which may include repetitions. Until now, we know that $\varphi^{(1)} = \{i\}$. The uniqueness of j at time t is $u_{t,j}^{(2)} = 1_{t,j} \left(1 + \sum_{k \in \varphi^{(1)}} 1_{t,k} \right)^{-1}$, as that is the uniqueness that results from adding alternative j's to the existing sequence of draws $\varphi^{(1)}$. The average uniqueness of j is the average $u_{t,j}^{(2)}$ over j's lifespan,

$\bar{u}_j^{(2)} = \left(\sum_{t=1}^{T} u_{t,j} \right) \left(\sum_{t=1}^{T} 1_{t,j} \right)^{-1}$. We can now make a second draw based on the updated probabilities $\left\{ \delta_j^{(2)} \right\}_{j=1,\ldots,I}$,

$$\delta_j^{(2)} = \bar{u}_j^{(2)} \left(\sum_{k=1}^{I} \bar{u}_k^{(2)} \right)^{-1}$$

where $\left\{ \delta_j^{(2)} \right\}_{j=1,\ldots,I}$ are scaled to add up to 1, $\sum_{j=1}^{I} \delta_j^{(2)} = 1$. We can now do a second draw, update $\varphi^{(2)}$ and re-evaluate $\left\{ \delta_j^{(3)} \right\}_{j=1,\ldots,I}$. The process is repeated until I draws have taken place. This sequential bootstrap scheme has the advantage that overlaps (even repetitions) are still possible, but decreasingly likely. The sequential bootstrap sample will be much closer to IID than samples drawn from the standard bootstrap method. This can be verified by measuring an increase in $I^{-1} \sum_{i=1}^{I} \bar{u}_i$, relative to the standard bootstrap method.

4.5.2 Implementation of Sequential Bootstrap

Snippet 4.3 derives an indicator matrix from two arguments: the index of bars (barIx), and the pandas Series t1, which we used multiple times in Chapter 3. As a reminder, t1 is defined by an index containing the time at which the features are observed, and a values array containing the time at which the label is determined. The output of this function is a binary matrix indicating what (price) bars influence the label for each observation.

SNIPPET 4.3 BUILD AN INDICATOR MATRIX

```
import pandas as pd,numpy as np
#————————————————————————————————————
def getIndMatrix(barIx,t1):
    # Get indicator matrix
    indM=pd.DataFrame(0,index=barIx,columns=range(t1.shape[0]))
    for i,(t0,t1) in enumerate(t1.iteritems()):indM.loc[t0:t1,i]=1.
    return indM
```

Snippet 4.4 returns the average uniqueness of each observed feature. The input is the indicator matrix built by getIndMatrix.

SNIPPET 4.4   COMPUTE AVERAGE UNIQUENESS

```
def getAvgUniqueness(indM):
    # Average uniqueness from indicator matrix
    c=indM.sum(axis=1) # concurrency
    u=indM.div(c,axis=0) # uniqueness
    avgU=u[u>0].mean() # average uniqueness
    return avgU
```

Snippet 4.5 gives us the index of the features sampled by sequential bootstrap. The inputs are the indicator matrix (indM) and an optional sample length (sLength), with a default value of as many draws as rows in indM.

SNIPPET 4.5   RETURN SAMPLE FROM SEQUENTIAL BOOTSTRAP

```
def seqBootstrap(indM,sLength=None):
    # Generate a sample via sequential bootstrap
    if sLength is None:sLength=indM.shape[1]
    phi=[]
    while len(phi)<sLength:
        avgU=pd.Series()
        for i in indM:
            indM_=indM[phi+[i]] # reduce indM
            avgU.loc[i]=getAvgUniqueness(indM_).iloc[-1]
        prob=avgU/avgU.sum() # draw prob
        phi+=[np.random.choice(indM.columns,p=prob)]
    return phi
```

4.5.3   A Numerical Example

Consider a set of labels $\{y_i\}_{i=1,2,3}$, where label y_1 is a function of return $r_{0,3}$, label y_2 is a function of return $r_{2,4}$ and label y_3 is a function of return $r_{4,6}$. The outcomes' overlaps are characterized by this indicator matrix $\{1_{t,i}\}$,

$$\{1_{t,i}\} = \begin{bmatrix} 1 & 0 & 0 \\ 1 & 0 & 0 \\ 1 & 1 & 0 \\ 0 & 1 & 0 \\ 0 & 0 & 1 \\ 0 & 0 & 1 \end{bmatrix}$$

The procedure starts with $\varphi^{(0)} = \emptyset$, and a uniform distribution of probability, $\delta_i = \frac{1}{3}$, $\forall i = 1, 2, 3$. Suppose that we randomly draw a number from $\{1, 2, 3\}$, and 2 is selected. Before we make a second draw on $\{1, 2, 3\}$ (remember, a bootstrap samples with repetition), we need to adjust the probabilities. The set of observations drawn so far is $\varphi^{(1)} = \{2\}$. The average uniqueness for the first feature is $\bar{u}_1^{(2)} = \left(1 + 1 + \frac{1}{2}\right)\frac{1}{3} = \frac{5}{6} < 1$, and for the second feature is $\bar{u}_2^{(2)} = \left(\frac{1}{2} + \frac{1}{2}\right)\frac{1}{2} = \frac{1}{2} < 1$. The probabilities for the second draw are $\delta^{(2)} = \left\{\frac{5}{14}, \frac{3}{14}, \frac{6}{14}\right\}$. Two points are worth mentioning: (1) The lowest probability goes to the feature that was picked in the first draw, as that would exhibit the highest overlap; and (2) among the two possible draws outside $\varphi^{(1)}$, the greater probability goes to $\delta_3^{(2)}$, as that is the label with no overlap to $\varphi^{(1)}$. Suppose that the second draw selects number 3. We leave as an exercise the update of the probabilities $\delta^{(3)}$ for the third and final draw. Snippet 4.6 runs a sequential bootstrap on the $\{1_{t,i}\}$ indicator matrix in this example.

SNIPPET 4.6 EXAMPLE OF SEQUENTIAL BOOTSTRAP

```
def main():
    t1=pd.Series([2,3,5],index=[0,2,4]) # t0,t1 for each feature obs
    barIx=range(t1.max()+1) # index of bars
    indM=getIndMatrix(barIx,t1)
    phi=np.random.choice(indM.columns,size=indM.shape[1])
    print phi
    print 'Standard uniqueness:',getAvgUniqueness(indM[phi]).mean()
    phi=seqBootstrap(indM)
    print phi
    print 'Sequential uniqueness:',getAvgUniqueness(indM[phi]).mean()
    return
```

4.5.4 Monte Carlo Experiments

We can evaluate the efficiency of the sequential bootstrap algorithm through experimental methods. Snippet 4.7 lists the function that generates a random t1 series for a number of observations numObs (I). Each observation is made at a random number, drawn from a uniform distribution, with boundaries 0 and numBars, where numBars is the number of bars (T). The number of bars spanned by the observation is determined by drawing a random number from a uniform distribution with boundaries 0 and maxH.

SNIPPET 4.7 GENERATING A RANDOM T1 SERIES

```
def getRndT1(numObs,numBars,maxH):
    # random t1 Series
    t1=pd.Series()
```

```
for i in xrange(numObs):
    ix=np.random.randint(0,numBars)
    val=ix+np.random.randint(1,maxH)
    t1.loc[ix]=val
return t1.sort_index()
```

Snippet 4.8 takes that random `t1` series, and derives the implied indicator matrix, `indM`. This matrix is then subjected to two procedures. In the first one, we derive the average uniqueness from a standard bootstrap (random sampling with replacement). In the second one, we derive the average uniqueness by applying our sequential bootstrap algorithm. Results are reported as a dictionary.

SNIPPET 4.8   UNIQUENESS FROM STANDARD AND SEQUENTIAL BOOTSTRAPS

```
def auxMC(numObs,numBars,maxH):
    # Parallelized auxiliary function
    t1=getRndT1(numObs,numBars,maxH)
    barIx=range(t1.max()+1)
    indM=getIndMatrix(barIx,t1)
    phi=np.random.choice(indM.columns,size=indM.shape[1])
    stdU=getAvgUniqueness(indM[phi]).mean()
    phi=seqBootstrap(indM)
    seqU=getAvgUniqueness(indM[phi]).mean()
    return {'stdU':stdU,'seqU':seqU}
```

These operations have to be repeated over a large number of iterations. Snippet 4.9 implements this Monte Carlo using the multiprocessing techniques discussed in Chapter 20. For example, it will take about 6 hours for a 24-cores server to carry out a Monte Carlo of 1E6 iterations, where numObs=10, numBars=100, and maxH=5. Without parallelization, a similar Monte Carlo experiment would have taken about 6 days.

SNIPPET 4.9   MULTI-THREADED MONTE CARLO

```
import pandas as pd,numpy as np
from mpEngine import processJobs,processJobs_
#
def mainMC(numObs=10,numBars=100,maxH=5,numIters=1E6,numThreads=24):
    # Monte Carlo experiments
    jobs=[]
    for i in xrange(int(numIters)):
        job={'func':auxMC,'numObs':numObs,'numBars':numBars,'maxH':maxH}
        jobs.append(job)
```

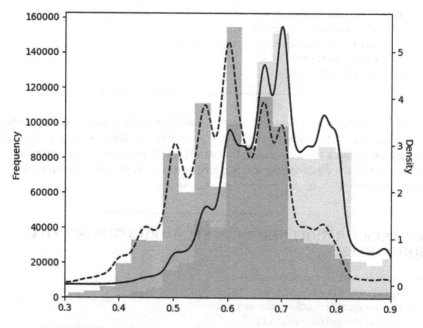

FIGURE 4.2   Monte Carlo experiment of standard vs. sequential bootstraps

```
if numThreads==1:out=processJobs_(jobs)
else:out=processJobs(jobs,numThreads=numThreads)
print pd.DataFrame(out).describe()
return
```

Figure 4.2 plots the histogram of the uniqueness from standard bootstrapped samples (left) and the sequentially bootstrapped samples (right). The median of the average uniqueness for the standard method is 0.6, and the median of the average uniquenes for the sequential method is 0.7. A one-sided t-test on the difference of means yields a vanishingly small probability. Statistically speaking, samples from the sequential bootstrap method have an expected uniqueness that exceeds that of the standard bootstrap method, at any reasonable confidence level.

4.6   RETURN ATTRIBUTION

In the previous section we learned a method to bootstrap samples closer to IID. In this section we will introduce a method to weight those samples for the purpose of training an ML algorithm. Highly overlapping outcomes would have disproportionate weights if considered equal to non-overlapping outcomes. At the same time, labels associated with large absolute returns should be given more importance than labels with negligible absolute returns. In short, we need to weight observations by some function of both uniqueness and absolute return.

When labels are a function of the return sign ($\{-1, 1\}$ for standard labeling or $\{0, 1\}$ for meta-labeling), the sample weights can be defined in terms of the sum of the attributed returns over the event's lifespan, $\left[t_{i,0}, t_{i,1}\right]$,

$$\tilde{w}_i = \left| \sum_{t=t_{i,0}}^{t_{i,1}} \frac{r_{t-1,t}}{c_t} \right|$$

$$w_i = \tilde{w}_i I \left(\sum_{j=1}^{I} \tilde{w}_j \right)^{-1}$$

hence $\sum_{i=1}^{I} w_i = I$. We have scaled these weights to add up to I, since libraries (including sklearn) usually define algorithmic parameters assuming a default weight of 1.

The rationale for this method is that we wish to weight an observation as a function of the absolute log returns that can be attributed uniquely to it. However, this method will not work if there is a "neutral" (return below threshold) case. For that case, lower returns should be assigned higher weights, not the reciprocal. The "neutral" case is unnecessary, as it can be implied by a "-1" or "1" prediction with low confidence. This is one of several reasons I would generally advise you to drop "neutral" cases. Snippet 4.10 implements this method.

SNIPPET 4.10   DETERMINATION OF SAMPLE WEIGHT BY ABSOLUTE RETURN ATTRIBUTION

```
def mpSampleW(t1,numCoEvents,close,molecule):
    # Derive sample weight by return attribution
    ret=np.log(close).diff() # log-returns, so that they are additive
    wght=pd.Series(index=molecule)
    for tIn,tOut in t1.loc[wght.index].iteritems():
        wght.loc[tIn]=(ret.loc[tIn:tOut]/numCoEvents.loc[tIn:tOut]).sum()
    return wght.abs()
#——————————————————————————————
out['w']=mpPandasObj(mpSampleW,('molecule',events.index),numThreads, \
        t1=events['t1'],numCoEvents=numCoEvents,close=close)
out['w']*=out.shape[0]/out['w'].sum()
```

4.7 TIME DECAY

Markets are adaptive systems (Lo [2017]). As markets evolve, older examples are less relevant than the newer ones. Consequently, we would typically like sample weights to decay as new observations arrive. Let $d[x] \geq 0, \forall x \in \left[0, \sum_{i=1}^{I} \bar{u}_i\right]$ be the time-decay factors that will multiply the sample weights derived in the previous section. The final weight has no decay, $d\left[\sum_{i=1}^{I} \bar{u}_i\right] = 1$, and all other weights will be adjusted relative to that. Let $c \in (-1, 1]$ be a user-defined parameter that determines the decay function as follows: For $c \in [0, 1]$, then $d[1] = c$, with linear decay; for $c \in (-1, 0)$, then $d\left[-c \sum_{i=1}^{I} \bar{u}_i\right] = 0$, with linear decay between $\left[-c \sum_{i=1}^{I} \bar{u}_i, \sum_{i=1}^{I} \bar{u}_i\right]$ and $d[x] = 0 \; \forall x \leq -c \sum_{i=1}^{I} \bar{u}_i$. For a linear piecewise function $d = \max\{0, a + bx\}$, such requirements are met by the following boundary conditions:

1. $d = a + b \sum_{i=1}^{I} \bar{u}_i = 1 \Rightarrow a = 1 - b \sum_{i=1}^{I} \bar{u}_i$.
2. Contingent on c:

   (a) $d = a + b0 = c \Rightarrow b = (1 - c)\left(\sum_{i=1}^{I} \bar{u}_i\right)^{-1}, \forall c \in [0, 1]$

   (b) $d = a - bc \sum_{i=1}^{I} \bar{u}_i = 0 \Rightarrow b = \left[(c + 1)\sum_{i=1}^{I} \bar{u}_i\right]^{-1}, \forall c \in (-1, 0)$

Snippet 4.11 implements this form of time-decay factors. Note that time is not meant to be chronological. In this implementation, decay takes place according to cumulative uniqueness, $x \in \left[0, \sum_{i=1}^{I} \bar{u}_i\right]$, because a chronological decay would reduce weights too fast in the presence of redundant observations.

SNIPPET 4.11   IMPLEMENTATION OF TIME-DECAY FACTORS

```
def getTimeDecay(tW,clfLastW=1.):
    # apply piecewise-linear decay to observed uniqueness (tW)
    # newest observation gets weight=1, oldest observation gets weight=clfLastW
    clfW=tW.sort_index().cumsum()
    if clfLastW>=0:slope=(1.-clfLastW)/clfW.iloc[-1]
    else:slope=1./((clfLastW+1)*clfW.iloc[-1])
    const=1.-slope*clfW.iloc[-1]
    clfW=const+slope*clfW
    clfW[clfW<0]=0
    print const,slope
    return clfW
```

It is worth discussing a few interesting cases:

- $c = 1$ means that there is no time decay.
- $0 < c < 1$ means that weights decay linearly over time, but every observation still receives a strictly positive weight, regardless of how old.

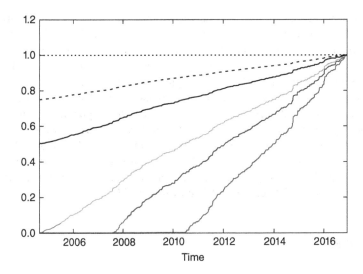

FIGURE 4.3   Piecewise-linear time-decay factors

- $c = 0$ means that weights converge linearly to zero, as they become older.
- $c < 0$ means that the oldest portion cT of the observations receive zero weight (i.e., they are erased from memory).

Figure 4.3 shows the decayed weights, out['w']*df, after applying the decay factors for $c \in \{1, .75, .5, 0, -.25, -.5\}$. Although not necessarily practical, the procedure allows the possibility of generating weights that increase as they get older, by setting $c > 1$.

4.8   CLASS WEIGHTS

In addition to sample weights, it is often useful to apply class weights. Class weights are weights that correct for underrepresented labels. This is particularly critical in classification problems where the most important classes have rare occurrences (King and Zeng [2001]). For example, suppose that you wish to predict liquidity crisis, like the flash crash of May 6, 2010. These events are rare relative to the millions of observations that take place in between them. Unless we assign higher weights to the samples associated with those rare labels, the ML algorithm will maximize the accuracy of the most common labels, and flash crashes will be deemed to be outliers rather than rare events.

ML libraries typically implement functionality to handle class weights. For example, sklearn penalizes errors in samples of class[j], $j=1,...,J$, with weighting class_weight[j] rather than 1. Accordingly, higher class weights on label j will force the algorithm to achieve higher accuracy on j. When class weights do not add up to J, the effect is equivalent to changing the regularization parameter of the classifier.

In financial applications, the standard labels of a classification algorithm are $\{-1, 1\}$, where the zero (or neutral) case will be implied by a prediction with probability only slightly above 0.5 and below some neutral threshold. There is no reason for favoring accuracy of one class over the other, and as such a good default is to assign class_weight='balanced'. This choice re-weights observations so as to simulate that all classes appeared with equal frequency. In the context of bagging classifiers, you may want to consider the argument class_weight='balanced_subsample', which means that class_weight='balanced' will be applied to the in-bag bootstrapped samples, rather than to the entire dataset. For full details, it is helpful to read the source code implementing class_weight in sklearn. Please also be aware of this reported bug: https://github.com/scikit-learn/scikit-learn/issues/4324.

EXERCISES

4.1 In Chapter 3, we denoted as t1 a pandas series of timestamps where the first barrier was touched, and the index was the timestamp of the observation. This was the output of the getEvents function.

   (a) Compute a t1 series on dollar bars derived from E-mini S&P 500 futures tick data.

   (b) Apply the function mpNumCoEvents to compute the number of overlapping outcomes at each point in time.

   (c) Plot the time series of the number of concurrent labels on the primary axis, and the time series of exponentially weighted moving standard deviation of returns on the secondary axis.

   (d) Produce a scatterplot of the number of concurrent labels (x-axis) and the exponentially weighted moving standard deviation of returns (y-axis). Can you appreciate a relationship?

4.2 Using the function mpSampleTW, compute the average uniqueness of each label. What is the first-order serial correlation, AR(1), of this time series? Is it statistically significant? Why?

4.3 Fit a random forest to a financial dataset where $I^{-1} \sum_{i=1}^{I} \bar{u}_i \ll 1$.

   (a) What is the mean out-of-bag accuracy?

   (b) What is the mean accuracy of k-fold cross-validation (without shuffling) on the same dataset?

   (c) Why is out-of-bag accuracy so much higher than cross-validation accuracy? Which one is more correct / less biased? What is the source of this bias?

4.4 Modify the code in Section 4.7 to apply an exponential time-decay factor.

4.5 Consider you have applied meta-labels to events determined by a trend-following model. Suppose that two thirds of the labels are 0 and one third of the labels are 1.

   (a) What happens if you fit a classifier without balancing class weights?

(b) A label 1 means a true positive, and a label 0 means a false positive. By applying balanced class weights, we are forcing the classifier to pay more attention to the true positives, and less attention to the false positives. Why does that make sense?

(c) What is the distribution of the predicted labels, before and after applying balanced class weights?

4.6 Update the draw probabilities for the final draw in Section 4.5.3.

4.7 In Section 4.5.3, suppose that number 2 is picked again in the second draw. What would be the updated probabilities for the third draw?

REFERENCES

Rao, C., P. Pathak and V. Koltchinskii (1997): "Bootstrap by sequential resampling." *Journal of Statistical Planning and Inference*, Vol. 64, No. 2, pp. 257–281.

King, G. and L. Zeng (2001): "Logistic Regression in Rare Events Data." Working paper, Harvard University. Available at https://gking.harvard.edu/files/0s.pdf.

Lo, A. (2017): *Adaptive Markets*, 1st ed. Princeton University Press.

BIBLIOGRAPHY

Sample weighting is a common topic in the ML learning literature. However the practical problems discussed in this chapter are characteristic of investment applications, for which the academic literature is extremely scarce. Below are some publications that tangentially touch some of the issues discussed in this chapter.

Efron, B. (1979): "Bootstrap methods: Another look at the jackknife." *Annals of Statistics*, Vol. 7, pp. 1–26.

Efron, B. (1983): "Estimating the error rote of a prediction rule: Improvement on cross-validation." *Journal of the American Statistical Association*, Vol. 78, pp. 316–331.

Bickel, P. and D. Freedman (1981): "Some asymptotic theory for the bootstrap." *Annals of Statistics*, Vol. 9, pp. 1196–1217.

Gine, E. and J. Zinn (1990): "Bootstrapping general empirical measures." *Annals of Probability*, Vol. 18, pp. 851–869.

Hall, P. and E. Mammen (1994): "On general resampling algorithms and their performance in distribution estimation." *Annals of Statistics*, Vol. 24, pp. 2011–2030.

Mitra, S. and P. Pathak (1984): "The nature of simple random sampling." *Annals of Statistics*, Vol. 12, pp. 1536–1542.

Pathak, P. (1964): "Sufficiency in sampling theory." *Annals of Mathematical Statistics*, Vol. 35, pp. 795–808.

Pathak, P. (1964): "On inverse sampling with unequal probabilities." *Biometrika*, Vol. 51, pp. 185–193.

Praestgaard, J. and J. Wellner (1993): "Exchangeably weighted bootstraps of the general empirical process." *Annals of Probability*, Vol. 21, pp. 2053–2086.

Rao, C., P. Pathak and V. Koltchinskii (1997): "Bootstrap by sequential resampling." *Journal of Statistical Planning and Inference*, Vol. 64, No. 2, pp. 257–281.

CHAPTER 5

Fractionally Differentiated Features

5.1 MOTIVATION

It is known that, as a consequence of arbitrage forces, financial series exhibit low signal-to-noise ratios (López de Prado [2015]). To make matters worse, standard stationarity transformations, like integer differentiation, further reduce that signal by removing memory. Price series have memory, because every value is dependent upon a long history of previous levels. In contrast, integer differentiated series, like returns, have a memory cut-off, in the sense that history is disregarded entirely after a finite sample window. Once stationarity transformations have wiped out all memory from the data, statisticians resort to complex mathematical techniques to extract whatever residual signal remains. Not surprisingly, applying these complex techniques on memory-erased series likely leads to false discoveries. In this chapter we introduce a data transformation method that ensures the stationarity of the data while preserving as much memory as possible.

5.2 THE STATIONARITY VS. MEMORY DILEMMA

It is common in finance to find non-stationary time series. What makes these series non-stationary is the presence of memory, i.e., a long history of previous levels that shift the series' mean over time. In order to perform inferential analyses, researchers need to work with invariant processes, such as returns on prices (or changes in log-prices), changes in yield, or changes in volatility. These data transformations make the series stationary, at the expense of removing all memory from the original series (Alexander [2001], chapter 11). Although stationarity is a necessary property for inferential purposes, it is rarely the case in signal processing that we wish all memory to be erased, as that memory is the basis for the model's predictive power. For example, equilibrium (stationary) models need some memory to assess how far the price process has drifted away from the long-term expected value in order to generate a forecast. The dilemma is that returns are stationary, however memory-less, and prices have memory, however they are non-stationary. The question arises: What is the minimum amount of differentiation that makes a price series stationary while preserving as much memory as possible? Accordingly, we would like to generalize the notion of returns to consider *stationary series where not all memory is erased.* Under this framework, returns are just one kind of (and in most cases suboptimal) price transformation among many other possibilities.

Part of the importance of cointegration methods is their ability to model series with memory. But why would the particular case of zero differentiation deliver best outcomes? Zero differentiation is as arbitrary as 1-step differentiation. There is a wide region between these two extremes (fully differentiated series on one hand, and zero differentiated series on the other) that can be explored through fractional differentiation for the purpose of developing a highly predictive ML model.

Supervised learning algorithms typically require stationary features. The reason is that we need to map a previously unseen (unlabeled) observation to a collection of labeled examples, and infer from them the label of that new observation. If the features are not stationary, we cannot map the new observation to a large number of known examples. But stationarity does not ensure predictive power. Stationarity is a necessary, non-sufficient condition for the high performance of an ML algorithm. The problem is, there is a trade-off between stationarity and memory. We can always make a series more stationary through differentiation, but it will be at the cost of erasing some memory, which will defeat the forecasting purpose of the ML algorithm. In this chapter, we will study one way to resolve this dilemma.

5.3   LITERATURE REVIEW

Virtually all the financial time series literature is based on the premise of making non-stationary series stationary through integer transformation (see Hamilton [1994] for an example). This raises two questions: (1) Why would integer 1 differentiation (like the one used for computing returns on log-prices) be optimal? (2) Is over-differentiation one reason why the literature has been so biased in favor of the efficient markets hypothesis?

The notion of fractional differentiation applied to the predictive time series analysis dates back at least to Hosking [1981]. In that paper, a family of ARIMA processes was generalized by permitting the degree of differencing to take fractional values. This was useful because fractionally differenced processes exhibit long-term persistence and antipersistence, hence enhancing the forecasting power compared to the standard ARIMA approach. In the same paper, Hosking states: "Apart from a passing reference by Granger (1978), fractional differencing does not appear to have been previously mentioned in connection with time series analysis."

After Hosking's paper, the literature on this subject has been surprisingly scarce, adding up to eight journal articles written by only nine authors: Hosking, Johansen, Nielsen, MacKinnon, Jensen, Jones, Popiel, Cavaliere, and Taylor. See the references for details. Most of those papers relate to technical matters, such as fast algorithms for the calculation of fractional differentiation in continuous stochastic processes (e.g., Jensen and Nielsen [2014]).

Differentiating the stochastic process is a computationally expensive operation. In this chapter we will take a practical, alternative, and novel approach to recover stationarity: We will generalize the difference operator to non-integer steps.

5.4   THE METHOD

Consider the backshift operator, B, applied to a matrix of real-valued features $\{X_t\}$, where $B^k X_t = X_{t-k}$ for any integer $k \geq 0$. For example, $(1 - B)^2 = 1 - 2B + B^2$, where $B^2 X_t = X_{t-2}$, so that $(1 - B)^2 X_t = X_t - 2X_{t-1} + X_{t-2}$. Note that $(x + y)^n = \sum_{k=0}^{n} \binom{n}{k} x^k y^{n-k} = \sum_{k=0}^{n} \binom{n}{k} x^{n-k} y^k$, for n a positive integer. For a real number d, $(1 + x)^d = \sum_{k=0}^{\infty} \binom{d}{k} x^k$, the binomial series.

In a fractional model, the exponent d is allowed to be a real number, with the following formal binomial series expansion:

$$(1 - B)^d = \sum_{k=0}^{\infty} \binom{d}{k} (-B)^k = \sum_{k=0}^{\infty} \frac{\prod_{i=0}^{k-1}(d - i)}{k!} (-B)^k$$

$$= \sum_{k=0}^{\infty} (-B)^k \prod_{i=0}^{k-1} \frac{d - i}{k - i}$$

$$= 1 - dB + \frac{d(d - 1)}{2!} B^2 - \frac{d(d - 1)(d - 2)}{3!} B^3 + \cdots$$

5.4.1   Long Memory

Let us see how a real (non-integer) positive d preserves memory. This arithmetic series consists of a dot product

$$\tilde{X}_t = \sum_{k=0}^{\infty} \omega_k X_{t-k}$$

with weights ω

$$\omega = \left\{ 1, -d, \frac{d(d - 1)}{2!}, -\frac{d(d - 1)(d - 2)}{3!}, \ldots, (-1)^k \prod_{i=0}^{k-1} \frac{d - i}{k!}, \ldots \right\}$$

and values X

$$X = \left\{ X_t, X_{t-1}, X_{t-2}, X_{t-3}, \ldots, X_{t-k}, \ldots \right\}$$

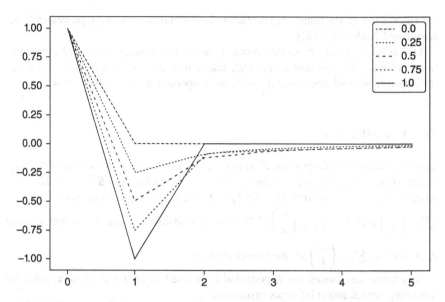

FIGURE 5.1 ω_k (y-axis) as k increases (x-axis). Each line is associated with a particular value of $d \in [0,1]$, in 0.1 increments.

When d is a positive integer number, $\prod_{i=0}^{k-1} \frac{d-i}{k!} = 0, \forall k > d$, and memory beyond that point is cancelled. For example, $d = 1$ is used to compute returns, where $\prod_{i=0}^{k-1} \frac{d-i}{k!} = 0, \forall k > 1$, and $\omega = \{1, -1, 0, 0, \dots\}$.

5.4.2   Iterative Estimation

Looking at the sequence of weights, ω, we can appreciate that for $k = 0, \dots, \infty$, with $\omega_0 = 1$, the weights can be generated iteratively as:

$$\omega_k = -\omega_{k-1} \frac{d - k + 1}{k}$$

Figure 5.1 plots the sequence of weights used to compute each value of the fractionally differentiated series. The legend reports the value of d used to generate each sequence, the x-axis indicates the value of k, and the y-axis shows the value of ω_k. For example, for $d = 0$, all weights are 0 except for $\omega_0 = 1$. That is the case where the differentiated series coincides with the original one. For $d = 1$, all weights are 0 except for $\omega_0 = 1$ and $\omega_1 = -1$. That is the standard first-order integer differentiation, which is used to derive log-price returns. Anywhere in between these two cases, all weights after $\omega_0 = 1$ are negative and greater than -1.

Figure 5.2 plots the sequence of weights where $d \in [1, 2]$, at increments of 0.1. For $d > 1$, we observe $\omega_1 < -1$ and $\omega_k > 0$, $\forall k \geq 2$.

Snippet 5.1 lists the code used to generate these plots.

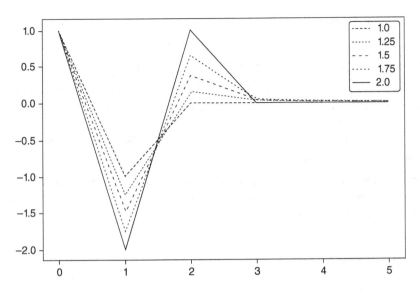

FIGURE 5.2 ω_k (y-axis) as k increases (x-axis). Each line is associated with a particular value of $d \in$ [1,2], in 0.1 increments.

SNIPPET 5.1 WEIGHTING FUNCTION

```
def getWeights(d,size):
    # thres>0 drops insignificant weights
    w=[1.]
    for k in range(1,size):
        w_=-w[-1]/k*(d-k+1)
        w.append(w_)
    w=np.array(w[::-1]).reshape(-1,1)
    return w
#————————————————————————————————
def plotWeights(dRange,nPlots,size):
    w=pd.DataFrame()
    for d in np.linspace(dRange[0],dRange[1],nPlots):
        w_=getWeights(d,size=size)
        w_=pd.DataFrame(w_,index=range(w_.shape[0])[::-1],columns=[d])
        w=w.join(w_,how='outer')
    ax=w.plot()
    ax.legend(loc='upper left');mpl.show()
    return
#————————————————————————————————
if __name__=='__main__':
    plotWeights(dRange=[0,1],nPlots=11,size=6)
    plotWeights(dRange=[1,2],nPlots=11,size=6)
```

5.4.3   Convergence

Let us consider the convergence of the weights. From the above result, we can see that for $k > d$, if $\omega_{k-1} \neq 0$, then $\left|\frac{\omega_k}{\omega_{k-1}}\right| = \left|\frac{d-k+1}{k}\right| < 1$, and $\omega_k = 0$ otherwise. Consequently, the weights converge asymptotically to zero, as an infinite product of factors within the unit circle. Also, for a positive d and $k < d + 1$, we have $\frac{d-k+1}{k} \geq 0$, which makes the initial weights alternate in sign. For a non-integer d, once $k \geq d + 1$, ω_k will be negative if int[d] is even, and positive otherwise. Summarizing, $\lim_{k \to \infty} \omega_k = 0^-$ (converges to zero from the left) when int[d] is even, and $\lim_{k \to \infty} \omega_k = 0^+$ (converges to zero from the right) when Int[d] is odd. In the special case $d \in (0, 1)$, this means that $-1 < \omega_k < 0, \forall k > 0$. This alternation of weight signs is necessary to make $\{\tilde{X}_t\}_{t=1,\dots,T}$ stationary, as memory wanes or is offset over the long run.

5.5   IMPLEMENTATION

In this section we will explore two alternative implementations of fractional differentiation: the standard "expanding window" method, and a new method that I call "fixed-width window fracdiff" (FFD).

5.5.1   Expanding Window

Let us discuss how to fractionally differentiate a (finite) time series in practice. Suppose a time series with T real observations, $\{X_t\}$, $t = 1, \dots, T$. Because of data limitations, the fractionally differentiated value $\tilde{X}_T$ cannot be computed on an infinite series of weights. For instance, the last point $\tilde{X}_T$ will use weights $\{\omega_k\}$, $k = 0, \dots, T - 1$, and $\tilde{X}_{T-l}$ will use weights $\{\omega_k\}$, $k = 0, \dots, T - l - 1$. This means that the initial points will have a different amount of memory compared to the final points. For each l, we can determine the relative weight-loss, $\lambda_l = \frac{\sum_{j=T-l}^{T} |\omega_j|}{\sum_{i=0}^{T-1} |\omega_i|}$. Given a tolerance level $\tau \in [0, 1]$, we can determine the value l^* such that $\lambda_{l^*} \leq \tau$ and $\lambda_{l^*+1} > \tau$. This value l^* corresponds to the first results $\{\tilde{X}_t\}_{t=1,\dots,l^*}$ where the weight-loss is beyond the acceptable threshold, $\lambda_t > \tau$ (e.g., $\tau = 0.01$).

From our earlier discussion, it is clear that λ_{l^*} depends on the convergence speed of $\{\omega_k\}$, which in turn depends on $d \in [0, 1]$. For $d = 1$, $\omega_k = 0$, $\forall k > 1$, and $\lambda_l = 0$, $\forall l > 1$, hence it suffices to drop $\tilde{X}_1$. As $d \to 0^+$, l^* increases, and a larger portion of the initial $\{\tilde{X}_t\}_{t=1,\dots,l^*}$ needs to be dropped in order to keep the weight-loss $\lambda_{l^*} \leq \tau$. Figure 5.3 plots the E-mini S&P 500 futures trade bars of size 1E4, rolled forward, fractionally differentiated, with parameters ($d = .4, \tau = 1$) on the top and parameters ($d = .4, \tau = 1E - 2$) on the bottom.

The negative drift in both plots is caused by the negative weights that are added to the initial observations as the window is expanded. When we do not control for weight loss, the negative drift is extreme, to the point that only that trend is visible. The negative drift is somewhat more moderate in the right plot, after controlling

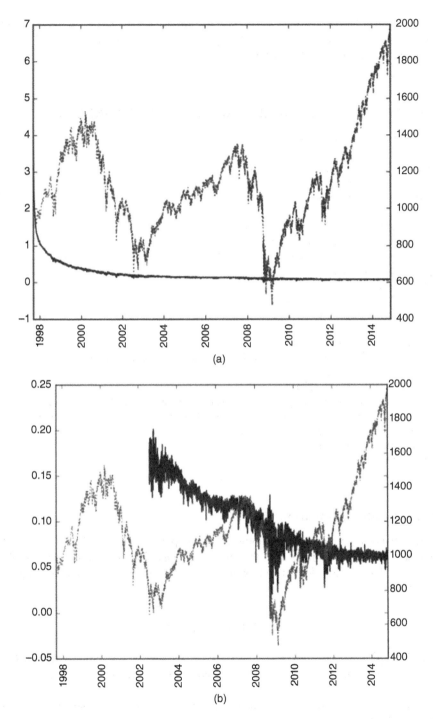

FIGURE 5.3   Fractional differentiation without controlling for weight loss (top plot) and after control-ling for weight loss with an expanding window (bottom plot)

for the weight loss, however, it is still substantial, because values $\{\tilde{X}_t\}_{t=l^*+1,\ldots,T}$ are computed on an expanding window. This problem can be corrected by a fixed-width window, implemented in Snippet 5.2.

SNIPPET 5.2   STANDARD FRACDIFF (EXPANDING WINDOW)

```
def fracDiff(series,d,thres=.01):
    '''
    Increasing width window, with treatment of NaNs
    Note 1: For thres=1, nothing is skipped.
    Note 2: d can be any positive fractional, not necessarily bounded [0,1].
    '''
    #1) Compute weights for the longest series
    w=getWeights(d,series.shape[0])
    #2) Determine initial calcs to be skipped based on weight-loss threshold
    w_=np.cumsum(abs(w))
    w_/=w_[-1]
    skip=w_[w_>thres].shape[0]
    #3) Apply weights to values
    df={}
    for name in series.columns:
        seriesF,df_=series[[name]].fillna(method='ffill').dropna(),pd.Series()
        for iloc in range(skip,seriesF.shape[0]):
            loc=seriesF.index[iloc]
            if not np.isfinite(series.loc[loc,name]):continue # exclude NAs
            df_[loc]=np.dot(w[-(iloc+1):,:].T,seriesF.loc[:loc])[0,0]
        df[name]=df_.copy(deep=True)
    df=pd.concat(df,axis=1)
    return df
```

5.5.2   Fixed-Width Window Fracdiff

Alternatively, fractional differentiation can be computed using a fixed-width window, that is, dropping the weights after their modulus ($|\omega_k|$) falls below a given threshold value (τ). This is equivalent to finding the first l^* such that $|\omega_{l^*}| \geq \tau$ and $|\omega_{l^*+1}| \leq \tau$, setting a new variable $\tilde{\omega}_k$

$$\tilde{\omega}_k = \begin{cases} \omega_k & \text{if } k \leq l^* \\ 0 & \text{if } k > l^* \end{cases}$$

and $\tilde{X}_t = \sum_{k=0}^{l^*} \tilde{\omega}_k X_{t-k}$, for $t = T - l^* + 1, \ldots, T$. Figure 5.4 plots E-mini S&P 500 futures trade bars of size 1E4, rolled forward, fractionally differentiated ($d = .4, \tau = 1E-5$).

This procedure has the advantage that the same vector of weights is used across all estimates of $\{\tilde{X}_t\}_{t=l^*,\ldots,T}$, hence avoiding the negative drift caused by an

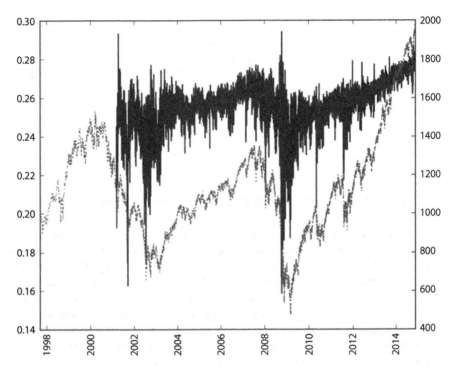

FIGURE 5.4 Fractional differentiation after controlling for weight loss with a fixed-width window

expanding window's added weights. The result is a driftless blend of level plus noise, as expected. The distribution is no longer Gaussian, as a result of the skewness and excess kurtosis that comes with memory, however it is stationary. Snippet 5.3 presents an implementation of this idea.

SNIPPET 5.3 THE NEW FIXED-WIDTH WINDOW FRACDIFF METHOD

```
def getWeights_FFD(d,thres):
    w,k=[1.],1
    while True:
        w_=-w[-1]/k*(d-k+1)
        if abs(w_)<thres:break
        w.append(w_);k+=1
    return np.array(w[::-1]).reshape(-1,1)
#---------------------------------------------------------------------------
def fracDiff_FFD(series,d,thres=1e-5):
    # Constant width window (new solution)
    w,width,df=getWeights_FFD(d,thres),len(w)-1,{}
```

```
for name in series.columns:
    seriesF,df_=series[[name]].fillna(method='ffill').dropna(),pd.Series()
    for iloc1 in range(width,seriesF.shape[0]):
        loc0,loc1=seriesF.index[iloc1-width],seriesF.index[iloc1]
        if not np.isfinite(series.loc[loc1,name]):continue # exclude NAs
        df_[loc1]=np.dot(w.T,seriesF.loc[loc0:loc1])[0,0]
    df[name]=df_.copy(deep=True)
df=pd.concat(df,axis=1)
return df
```

5.6 STATIONARITY WITH MAXIMUM MEMORY PRESERVATION

Consider a series $\{X_t\}_{t=1,\ldots,T}$. Applying the fixed-width window fracdiff (FFD) method on this series, we can compute the minimum coefficient d^* such that the resulting fractionally differentiated series $\{\tilde{X}_t\}_{t=l^*,\ldots,T}$ is stationary. This coefficient d^* quantifies the amount of memory that needs to be removed to achieve stationarity. If $\{X_t\}_{t=l^*,\ldots,T}$ is already stationary, then $d^* = 0$. If $\{X_t\}_{t=l^*,\ldots,T}$ contains a unit root, then $d^* < 1$. If $\{X_t\}_{t=l^*,\ldots,T}$ exhibits explosive behavior (like in a bubble), then $d^* > 1$. A case of particular interest is $0 < d^* \ll 1$, when the original series is "mildly non-stationary." In this case, although differentiation is needed, a full integer differentiation removes excessive memory (and predictive power).

Figure 5.5 illustrates this concept. On the right y-axis, it plots the ADF statistic computed on E-mini S&P 500 futures log-prices, rolled forward using the ETF trick

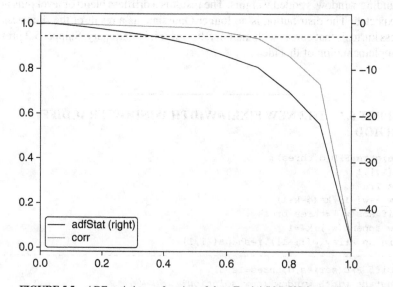

FIGURE 5.5 ADF statistic as a function of d, on E-mini S&P 500 futures log-prices

(see Chapter 2), downsampled to daily frequency, going back to the contract's inception. On the x-axis, it displays the d value used to generate the series on which the ADF statistic was computed. The original series has an ADF statistic of -0.3387, while the returns series has an ADF statistic of -46.9114. At a 95% confidence level, the test's critical value is -2.8623. The ADF statistic crosses that threshold in the vicinity of $d = 0.35$. The left y-axis plots the correlation between the original series ($d = 0$) and the differentiated series at various d values. At $d = 0.35$ the correlation is still very high, at 0.995. This confirms that the procedure introduced in this chapter has been successful in achieving stationarity without giving up too much memory. In contrast, the correlation between the original series and the returns series is only 0.03, hence showing that the standard integer differentiation wipes out the series' memory almost entirely.

Virtually all finance papers attempt to recover stationarity by applying an integer differentiation $d = 1 \gg 0.35$, which means that most studies have over-differentiated the series, that is, they have removed much more memory than was necessary to satisfy standard econometric assumptions. Snippet 5.4 lists the code used to produce these results.

SNIPPET 5.4 FINDING THE MINIMUM D VALUE THAT PASSES THE ADF TEST

```
def plotMinFFD():
    from statsmodels.tsa.stattools import adfuller
    path,instName='./','ES1_Index_Method12'
    out=pd.DataFrame(columns=['adfStat','pVal','lags','nObs','95% conf','corr'])
    df0=pd.read_csv(path+instName+'.csv',index_col=0,parse_dates=True)
    for d in np.linspace(0,1,11):
        df1=np.log(df0[['Close']]).resample('1D').last() # downcast to daily obs
        df2=fracDiff_FFD(df1,d,thres=.01)
        corr=np.corrcoef(df1.loc[df2.index,'Close'],df2['Close'])[0,1]
        df2=adfuller(df2['Close'],maxlag=1,regression='c',autolag=None)
        out.loc[d]=list(df2[:4])+[df2[4]['5%']]+[corr] # with critical value
    out[['adfStat','corr']].plot(secondary_y='adfStat')
    mpl.axhline(out['95% conf'].mean(),linewidth=1,color='r',linestyle='dotted')
    mpl.savefig(path+instName+'_testMinFFD.png')
    return
```

The example on E-mini futures is by no means an exception. Table 5.1 shows the ADF statistics after applying FFD(d) on various values of d, for 87 of the most liquid futures worldwide. In all cases, the standard $d = 1$ used for computing returns implies over-differentiation. In fact, in all cases stationarity is achieved with $d < 0.6$. In some cases, like orange juice (JO1 Comdty) or live cattle (LC1 Comdty) no differentiation at all was needed.

TABLE 5.1   ADF Statistic on FFD(d) for Some of the Most Liquid Futures Contracts

	0	0.1	0.2	0.3	0.4	0.5	0.6	0.7	0.8	0.9	1
AD1 Curncy	-1.7253	-1.8665	-2.2801	-2.9743	-3.9590	-5.4450	-7.7387	-10.3412	-15.7255	-22.5170	-43.8281
BO1 Comdty	-0.7039	-1.0021	-1.5848	-2.4038	-3.4284	-4.8916	-7.0604	-9.5089	-14.4065	-20.4393	-38.0683
BP1 Curncy	-1.0573	-1.4963	-2.3223	-3.4641	-4.8976	-6.9157	-9.8833	-13.1575	-19.4238	-26.6320	-43.3284
BTS1 Comdty	-1.7987	-2.1428	-2.7600	-3.7019	-4.8522	-6.2412	-7.8115	-9.4645	-11.0334	-12.4470	-13.6410
BZ1 Index	-1.6569	-1.8766	-2.3948	-3.2145	-4.2821	-5.9431	-8.3329	-10.9046	-15.7006	-20.7224	-29.9510
C 1 Comdty	-1.7870	-2.1273	-2.9539	-4.1642	-5.7307	-7.9577	-11.1798	-14.6946	-20.9925	-27.6602	-39.3576
CC1 Comdty	-2.3743	-2.9503	-4.1694	-5.8997	-8.0868	-10.9871	-14.8206	-18.6154	-24.1738	-29.0285	-34.8580
CD1 Curncy	-1.6304	-2.0557	-2.7284	-3.8380	-5.2341	-7.3172	-10.3738	-13.8263	-20.2897	-27.6242	-43.6794
CF1 Index	-1.5539	-1.9387	-2.7421	-3.9235	-5.5085	-7.7585	-11.0571	-14.6829	-21.4877	-28.9810	-44.5059
CL1 Comdty	-0.3795	-0.7164	-1.3359	-2.2018	-3.2603	-4.7499	-6.9504	-9.4531	-14.4936	-20.8392	-41.1169
CN1 Comdty	-0.8798	-0.8711	-1.1020	-1.4626	-1.9732	-2.7508	-3.9217	-5.2944	-8.4257	-12.7300	-42.1411
CO1 Comdty	-0.5124	-0.8468	-1.4247	-2.2402	-3.2566	-4.7022	-6.8601	-9.2836	-14.1511	-20.2313	-39.2207
CT1 Comdty	-1.7604	-2.0728	-2.7529	-3.7853	-5.1397	-7.1123	-10.0137	-13.1851	-19.0603	-25.4513	-37.5703
DM1 Index	-0.1929	-0.5718	-1.2414	-2.1127	-3.1765	-4.6695	-6.8852	-9.4219	-14.6726	-21.5411	-49.2663
DU1 Comdty	-0.3365	-0.4572	-0.7647	-1.1447	-1.6132	-2.2759	-3.3389	-4.5689	-7.2101	-10.9025	-42.9012
DX1 Curncy	-1.5768	-1.9458	-2.7358	-3.8423	-5.3101	-7.3507	-10.3569	-13.6451	-19.5832	-25.8907	-37.2623
EC1 Comdty	-0.2727	-0.6650	-1.3359	-2.2112	-3.3112	-4.8320	-7.0777	-9.6299	-14.8258	-21.4634	-44.6452
EC1 Curncy	-1.4733	-1.9344	-2.8507	-4.1588	-5.8240	-8.1834	-11.6278	-15.4095	-22.4317	-30.1482	-45.6373
ED1 Comdty	-0.4084	-0.5350	-0.7948	-1.1772	-1.6633	-2.3818	-3.4601	-4.7041	-7.4373	-11.3175	-46.4487
EE1 Curncy	-1.2100	-1.6378	-2.4216	-3.5470	-4.9821	-7.0166	-9.9962	-13.2920	-19.5047	-26.5158	-41.4672
EO1 Comdty	-0.7903	-0.8917	-1.0551	-1.3465	-1.7302	-2.3500	-3.3068	-4.5136	-7.0157	-10.6463	-45.2100

EO1 Index	−0.6561	−1.0567	−1.7409	−2.6774	−3.8543	−5.5096	−7.9133	−10.5674	−15.6442	−21.3066	−35.1397
ER1 Comdty	−0.1970	−0.3442	−0.6334	−1.0363	−1.5327	−2.2378	−3.2819	−4.4647	−7.1031	−10.7389	−40.0407
ES1 Index	−0.3387	−0.7206	−1.3324	−2.2252	−3.2733	−4.7976	−7.0436	−9.6095	−14.8624	−21.6177	−46.9114
FA1 Index	−0.5292	−0.8526	−1.4250	−2.2359	−3.2500	−4.6902	−6.8272	−9.2410	−14.1664	−20.3733	−41.9705
FC1 Comdty	−1.8846	−2.1853	−2.8808	−3.8546	−5.1483	−7.0226	−9.6889	−12.5679	−17.8160	−23.0530	−31.6503
FV1 Comdty	−0.7257	−0.8515	−1.0596	−1.4304	−1.8312	−2.5302	−3.6296	−4.9499	−7.8292	−12.0467	−49.1508
G 1 Comdty	0.2326	0.0026	−0.4686	−1.0590	−1.7453	−2.6761	−4.0336	−5.5624	−8.8575	−13.3277	−42.9177
GC1 Comdty	−2.2221	−2.3544	−2.7467	−3.4140	−4.4861	−6.0632	−8.4803	−11.2152	−16.7111	−23.1750	−39.0715
GX1 Index	−1.5418	−1.7749	−2.4666	−3.4417	−4.7321	−6.6155	−9.3667	−12.5240	−18.6291	−25.8116	−43.3610
HG1 Comdty	−1.7372	−2.1495	−2.8323	−3.9090	−5.3257	−7.3805	−10.4121	−13.7669	−19.8902	−26.5819	−39.3267
HI1 Index	−1.8289	−2.0432	−2.6203	−3.5233	−4.7514	−6.5743	−9.2733	−12.3722	−18.5308	−25.9762	−45.3396
HO1 Comdty	−1.6024	−1.9941	−2.6619	−3.7131	−5.1772	−7.2468	−10.3326	−13.6745	−19.9728	−26.9772	−40.9824
IB1 Index	−2.3912	−2.8254	−3.5813	−4.8774	−6.5884	−9.0665	−12.7381	−16.6706	−23.6752	−30.7986	−43.0687
IK1 Comdty	−1.7373	−2.3000	−2.7764	−3.7101	−4.8686	−6.3504	−8.2195	−9.8636	−11.7882	−13.3983	−14.8391
IR1 Comdty	−2.0622	−2.4188	−3.1736	−4.3178	−5.8119	−7.9816	−11.2102	−14.7956	−21.6158	−29.4555	−46.2683
JA1 Comdty	−2.4701	−2.7292	−3.3925	−4.4658	−5.9236	−8.0270	−11.2082	−14.7198	−21.2681	−28.4380	−42.1937
JB1 Comdty	−0.2081	−0.4319	−0.8490	−1.4289	−2.1160	−3.0932	−4.5740	−6.3061	−9.9454	−15.0151	−47.6037
JE1 Curncy	−0.9268	−1.2078	−1.7565	−2.5398	−3.5545	−5.0270	−7.2096	−9.6808	−14.6271	−20.7168	−37.6954
JG1 Comdty	−1.7468	−1.8071	−2.0654	−2.5447	−3.2237	−4.3418	−6.0690	−8.0537	−12.3908	−18.1881	−44.2884
JO1 Comdty	−3.0052	−3.3099	−4.2639	−5.7291	−7.5686	−10.1683	−13.7068	−17.3054	−22.7853	−27.7011	−33.4658
JY1 Curncy	−1.2616	−1.5891	−2.2042	−3.1407	−4.3715	−6.1600	−8.8261	−11.8449	−17.8275	−25.0700	−44.8394
KC1 Comdty	−0.7786	−1.1172	−1.7723	−2.7185	−3.8875	−5.5651	−8.0217	−10.7422	−15.9423	−21.8651	−35.3354
L 1 Comdty	−0.0805	−0.2228	−0.6144	−1.0751	−1.6335	−2.4186	−3.5676	−4.8749	−7.7528	−11.7669	−44.0349

At a 95% confidence level, the ADF test's critical value is −2.8623. All of the log-price series achieve stationarity at $d < 0.6$, and the great majority are stationary at $d < 0.3$.

5.7 CONCLUSION

To summarize, most econometric analyses follow one of two paradigms:

1. **Box-Jenkins:** Returns are stationary, however memory-less.
2. **Engle-Granger:** Log-prices have memory, however they are non-stationary. Cointegration is the trick that makes regression work on non-stationary series, so that memory is preserved. However the number of cointegrated variables is limited, and the cointegrating vectors are notoriously unstable.

In contrast, the FFD approach introduced in this chapter shows that there is no need to give up all of the memory in order to gain stationarity. And there is no need for the cointegration trick as it relates to ML forecasting. Once you become familiar with FFD, it will allow you to achieve stationarity without renouncing to memory (or predictive power).

In practice, I suggest you experiment with the following transformation of your features: First, compute a cumulative sum of the time series. This guarantees that some order of differentiation is needed. Second, compute the FFD(d) series for various $d \in [0, 1]$. Third, determine the minimum d such that the p-value of the ADF statistic on FFD(d) falls below 5%. Fourth, use the FFD(d) series as your predictive feature.

EXERCISES

5.1 Generate a time series from an IID Gaussian random process. This is a memory-less, stationary series:
(a) Compute the ADF statistic on this series. What is the p-value?
(b) Compute the cumulative sum of the observations. This is a non-stationary series without memory.
   (i) What is the order of integration of this cumulative series?
   (ii) Compute the ADF statistic on this series. What is the p-value?
(c) Differentiate the series twice. What is the p-value of this over-differentiated series?

5.2 Generate a time series that follows a sinusoidal function. This is a stationary series with memory.
(a) Compute the ADF statistic on this series. What is the p-value?
(b) Shift every observation by the same positive value. Compute the cumulative sum of the observations. This is a non-stationary series with memory.
   (i) Compute the ADF statistic on this series. What is the p-value?
   (ii) Apply an expanding window fracdiff, with $\tau = 1E - 2$. For what minimum d value do you get a p-value below 5%?
   (iii) Apply FFD, with $\tau = 1E - 5$. For what minimum d value do you get a p-value below 5%?

5.3 Take the series from exercise 2.b:

  (a) Fit the series to a sine function. What is the R-squared?

  (b) Apply FFD($d = 1$). Fit the series to a sine function. What is the R-squared?

  (c) What value of d maximizes the R-squared of a sinusoidal fit on FFD(d). Why?

5.4 Take the dollar bar series on E-mini S&P 500 futures. Using the code in Snippet 5.3, for some $d \in [0, 2]$, compute `fracDiff_FFD(fracDiff_FFD(series,d),-d)`. What do you get? Why?

5.5 Take the dollar bar series on E-mini S&P 500 futures.

  (a) Form a new series as a cumulative sum of log-prices.

  (b) Apply FFD, with $\tau = 1E - 5$. Determine for what minimum $d \in [0, 2]$ the new series is stationary.

  (c) Compute the correlation of the fracdiff series to the original (untransformed) series.

  (d) Apply an Engel-Granger cointegration test on the original and fracdiff series. Are they cointegrated? Why?

  (e) Apply a Jarque-Bera normality test on the fracdiff series.

5.6 Take the fracdiff series from exercise 5.

  (a) Apply a CUSUM filter (Chapter 2), where h is twice the standard deviation of the series.

  (b) Use the filtered timestamps to sample a features' matrix. Use as one of the features the fracdiff value.

  (c) Form labels using the triple-barrier method, with symmetric horizontal barriers of twice the daily standard deviation, and a vertical barrier of 5 days.

  (d) Fit a bagging classifier of decision trees where:

    (i) The observed features are bootstrapped using the sequential method from Chapter 4.

    (ii) On each bootstrapped sample, sample weights are determined using the techniques from Chapter 4.

REFERENCES

Alexander, C. (2001): *Market Models*, 1st edition. John Wiley & Sons.

Hamilton, J. (1994): *Time Series Analysis*, 1st ed. Princeton University Press.

Hosking, J. (1981): "Fractional differencing." *Biometrika*, Vol. 68, No. 1, pp. 165–176.

Jensen, A. and M. Nielsen (2014): "A fast fractional difference algorithm." *Journal of Time Series Analysis*, Vol. 35, No. 5, pp. 428–436.

López de Prado, M. (2015): "The Future of Empirical Finance." *Journal of Portfolio Management*, Vol. 41, No. 4, pp. 140–144. Available at https://ssrn.com/abstract=2609734.

BIBLIOGRAPHY

Cavaliere, G., M. Nielsen, and A. Taylor (2017): "Quasi-maximum likelihood estimation and bootstrap inference in fractional time series models with heteroskedasticity of unknown form." *Journal of Econometrics*, Vol. 198, No. 1, pp. 165–188.

Johansen, S. and M. Nielsen (2012): "A necessary moment condition for the fractional functional central limit theorem." *Econometric Theory*, Vol. 28, No. 3, pp. 671–679.

Johansen, S. and M. Nielsen (2012): "Likelihood inference for a fractionally cointegrated vector autoregressive model." *Econometrica*, Vol. 80, No. 6, pp. 2267–2732.

Johansen, S. and M. Nielsen (2016): "The role of initial values in conditional sum-of-squares estimation of nonstationary fractional time series models." *Econometric Theory*, Vol. 32, No. 5, pp. 1095–1139.

Jones, M., M. Nielsen and M. Popiel (2015): "A fractionally cointegrated VAR analysis of economic voting and political support." *Canadian Journal of Economics*, Vol. 47, No. 4, pp. 1078–1130.

Mackinnon, J. and M. Nielsen, M. (2014): "Numerical distribution functions of fractional unit root and cointegration tests." *Journal of Applied Econometrics*, Vol. 29, No. 1, pp. 161–171.

PART 2

Modelling

CHAPTER 6

Ensemble Methods

6.1 MOTIVATION

In this chapter we will discuss two of the most popular ML ensemble methods.[1] In the references and footnotes you will find books and articles that introduce these techniques. As everywhere else in this book, the assumption is that you have already used these approaches. The goal of this chapter is to explain what makes them effective, and how to avoid common errors that lead to their misuse in finance.

6.2 THE THREE SOURCES OF ERRORS

ML models generally suffer from three errors:[2]

1. **Bias:** This error is caused by unrealistic assumptions. When bias is high, the ML algorithm has failed to recognize important relations between features and outcomes. In this situation, the algorithm is said to be "underfit."
2. **Variance:** This error is caused by sensitivity to small changes in the training set. When variance is high, the algorithm has overfit the training set, and that is why even minimal changes in the training set can produce wildly different predictions. Rather than modelling the general patterns in the training set, the algorithm has mistaken noise with signal.

---

[1] For an introduction to ensemble methods, please visit: http://scikit-learn.org/stable/modules/ensemble.html.

[2] I would not typically cite Wikipedia, however, on this subject the user may find some of the illustrations in this article useful: https://en.wikipedia.org/wiki/Bias%E2%80%93variance_tradeoff.

3. **Noise:** This error is caused by the variance of the observed values, like unpredictable changes or measurement errors. This is the irreducible error, which cannot be explained by any model.

Consider a training set of observations $\{x_i\}_{i=1,\ldots,n}$ and real-valued outcomes $\{y_i\}_{i=1,\ldots,n}$. Suppose a function $f[x]$ exists, such that $y = f[x] + \varepsilon$, where ε is white noise with $\mathrm{E}[\varepsilon_i] = 0$ and $\mathrm{E}[\varepsilon_i^2] = \sigma_\varepsilon^2$. We would like to estimate the function $\hat{f}[x]$ that best fits $f[x]$, in the sense of making the variance of the estimation error $\mathrm{E}[(y_i - \hat{f}[x_i])^2]$ minimal (the mean squared error cannot be zero, because of the noise represented by σ_ε^2). This mean-squared error can be decomposed as

$$\mathrm{E}\left[(y_i - \hat{f}[x_i])^2\right] = \underbrace{\left(\mathrm{E}[\hat{f}[x_i] - f[x_i]]\right)^2}_{bias} + \underbrace{\mathrm{V}[\hat{f}[x_i]]}_{variance} + \underbrace{\sigma_\varepsilon^2}_{noise}$$

An ensemble method is a method that combines a set of weak learners, all based on the same learning algorithm, in order to create a (stronger) learner that performs better than any of the individual ones. Ensemble methods help reduce bias and/or variance.

6.3 BOOTSTRAP AGGREGATION

Bootstrap aggregation (bagging) is an effective way of reducing the variance in forecasts. It works as follows: First, generate N training datasets by random sampling *with replacement*. Second, fit N estimators, one on each training set. These estimators are fit independently from each other, hence the models can be fit in parallel. Third, the ensemble forecast is the *simple* average of the individual forecasts from the N models. In the case of categorical variables, the probability that an observation belongs to a class is given by the proportion of estimators that classify that observation as a member of that class (majority voting). When the base estimator can make forecasts with a prediction probability, the bagging classifier may derive a mean of the probabilities.

If you use sklearn's `BaggingClassifier` class to compute the out-of-bag accuracy, you should be aware of this bug: https://github.com/scikit-learn/scikit-learn/issues/8933. One workaround is to rename the labels in integer sequential order.

6.3.1 Variance Reduction

Bagging's main advantage is that it reduces forecasts' variance, hence helping address overfitting. The variance of the bagged prediction ($\varphi_i[c]$) is a function of the number of bagged estimators (N), the average variance of a single estimator's prediction ($\bar{\sigma}$), and the average correlation among their forecasts ($\bar{\rho}$):

$$V\left[\frac{1}{N}\sum_{i=1}^{N}\varphi_i[c]\right] = \frac{1}{N^2}\sum_{i=1}^{N}\left(\sum_{j=1}^{N}\sigma_{i,j}\right) = \frac{1}{N^2}\sum_{i=1}^{N}\left(\sigma_i^2 + \sum_{j\neq i}^{N}\sigma_i\sigma_j\rho_{i,j}\right)$$

$$= \frac{1}{N^2}\sum_{i=1}^{N}\left(\bar{\sigma}^2 + \underbrace{\sum_{j\neq i}^{N}\bar{\sigma}^2\bar{\rho}}_{\substack{=(N-1)\bar{\sigma}^2\bar{\rho} \\ \text{for a fixed } i}}\right) = \frac{\bar{\sigma}^2 + (N-1)\bar{\sigma}^2\bar{\rho}}{N}$$

$$= \bar{\sigma}^2\left(\bar{\rho} + \frac{1-\bar{\rho}}{N}\right)$$

where $\sigma_{i,j}$ is the covariance of predictions by estimators i,j; $\sum_{i=1}^{N}\bar{\sigma}^2 = \sum_{i=1}^{N}\sigma_i^2 \Leftrightarrow \bar{\sigma}^2 = N^{-1}\sum_{i=1}^{N}\sigma_i^2$; and $\sum_{j\neq i}^{N}\bar{\sigma}^2\bar{\rho} = \sum_{j\neq i}^{N}\sigma_i\sigma_j\rho_{i,j} \Leftrightarrow \bar{\rho} = (\bar{\sigma}^2 N(N-1))^{-1}\sum_{j\neq i}^{N}\sigma_i\sigma_j\rho_{i,j}$.

The equation above shows that bagging is only effective to the extent that $\bar{\rho} < 1$; as $\bar{\rho} \to 1 \Rightarrow V[\frac{1}{N}\sum_{i=1}^{N}\varphi_i[c]] \to \bar{\sigma}^2$. One of the goals of sequential bootstrapping (Chapter 4) is to produce samples as independent as possible, thereby reducing $\bar{\rho}$, which should lower the variance of bagging classifiers. Figure 6.1 plots the standard deviation of the bagged prediction as a function of $N \in [5, 30]$, $\bar{\rho} \in [0, 1]$ and $\bar{\sigma} = 1$.

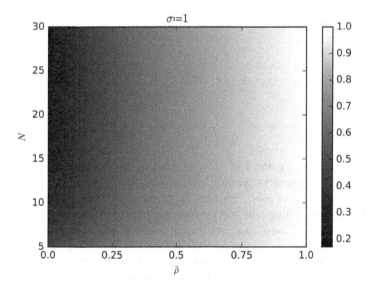

FIGURE 6.1 Standard deviation of the bagged prediction

6.3.2   Improved Accuracy

Consider a bagging classifier that makes a prediction on k classes by majority voting among N independent classifiers. We can label the predictions as $\{0,1\}$, where 1 means a correct prediction. The accuracy of a classifier is the probability p of labeling a prediction as 1. On average we will get Np predictions labeled as 1, with variance $Np(1-p)$. Majority voting makes the correct prediction when the most forecasted class is observed. For example, for $N = 10$ and $k = 3$, the bagging classifier made a correct prediction when class A was observed and the cast votes were $[A, B, C] = [4,3,3]$. However, the bagging classifier made an incorrect prediction when class A was observed and the cast votes were $[A, B, C] = [4,1,5]$. A sufficient condition is that the sum of these labels is $X > \frac{N}{2}$. A necessary (non-sufficient) condition is that $X > \frac{N}{k}$, which occurs with probability

$$
P\left[X > \frac{N}{k}\right] = 1 - P\left[X \le \frac{N}{k}\right] = 1 - \sum_{i=0}^{\left\lfloor N/k \right\rfloor} \binom{N}{i} p^i (1-p)^{N-i}
$$

The implication is that for a sufficiently large N, say $N > p(p - \frac{1}{k})^{-2}$, then $p > \frac{1}{k} \Rightarrow P[X > \frac{N}{k}] > p$, hence the bagging classifier's accuracy exceeds the average accuracy of the individual classifiers. Snippet 6.1 implements this calculation.

SNIPPET 6.1   ACCURACY OF THE BAGGING CLASSIFIER

```
from scipy.misc import comb
N,p,k=100,1./3,3.
p_=0
for i in xrange(0,int(N/k)+1):
    p_+=comb(N,i)*p**i*(1-p)**(N-i)
print p,1-p_
```

This is a strong argument in favor of bagging any classifier in general, when computational requirements permit it. However, unlike boosting, bagging cannot improve the accuracy of poor classifiers: If the individual learners are poor classifiers ($p \ll \frac{1}{k}$), majority voting will still perform poorly (although with lower variance). Figure 6.2 illustrates these facts. Because it is easier to achieve $\bar{p} \ll 1$ than $p > \frac{1}{k}$, bagging is more likely to be successful in reducing variance than in reducing bias.

For further analysis on this topic, the reader is directed to Condorcet's Jury Theorem. Although the theorem is derived for the purposes of majority voting in political

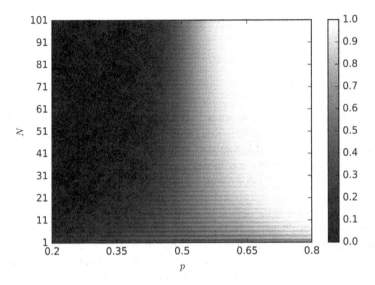

FIGURE 6.2   Accuracy of a bagging classifier as a function of the individual estimator's accuracy (P), the number of estimators (N), and $k = 2$

science, the problem addressed by this theorem shares similarities with the above discussion.

6.3.3   Observation Redundancy

In Chapter 4 we studied one reason why financial observations cannot be assumed to be IID. Redundant observations have two detrimental effects on bagging. First, the samples drawn with replacement are more likely to be virtually identical, even if they do not share the same observations. This makes $\bar{\rho} \approx 1$, and bagging will not reduce variance, regardless of N. For example, if each observation at t is labeled according to the return between t and $t + 100$, we should sample 1% of the observations per bagged estimator, but not more. Chapter 4, Section 4.5 recommended three alternative solutions, one of which consisted of setting `max_samples=out['tW'].mean()` in sklearn's implementation of the bagging classifier class. Another (better) solution was to apply the sequential bootstrap method.

The second detrimental effect from observation redundancy is that out-of-bag accuracy will be inflated. This happens because random sampling with replacement places in the training set samples that are very similar to those out-of-bag. In such a case, a proper stratified k-fold cross-validation without shuffling before partitioning will show a much lower testing-set accuracy than the one estimated out-of-bag. For this reason, it is advisable to set `StratifiedKFold(n_splits=k, shuffle=False)` when using that sklearn class, cross-validate the bagging classifier, and ignore the out-of-bag accuracy results. A low number k is preferred to a high one, as excessive partitioning would again place in the testing set samples too similar to those used in the training set.

6.4 RANDOM FOREST

Decision trees are known to be prone to overfitting, which increases the variance of the forecasts.[3] In order to address this concern, the random forest (RF) method was designed to produce ensemble forecasts with lower variance.

RF shares some similarities with bagging, in the sense of training independently individual estimators over bootstrapped subsets of the data. The key difference with bagging is that random forests incorporate a second level of randomness: When optimizing each node split, only a random subsample (without replacement) of the attributes will be evaluated, with the purpose of further decorrelating the estimators.

Like bagging, RF reduces forecasts' variance without overfitting (remember, as long as $\bar{\rho} < 1$). A second advantage is that RF evaluates feature importance, which we will discuss in depth in Chapter 8. A third advantage is that RF provides out-of-bag accuracy estimates, however in financial applications they are likely to be inflated (as discussed in Section 6.3.3). But like bagging, RF will not necessarily exhibit lower bias than individual decision trees.

If a large number of samples are redundant (non-IID), overfitting will still take place: Sampling randomly with replacement will build a large number of essentially identical trees ($\bar{\rho} \approx 1$), where each decision tree is overfit (a flaw for which decision trees are notorious). Unlike bagging, RF always fixes the size of the bootstrapped samples to match the size of the training dataset. Let us review ways we can address this RF overfitting problem in sklearn. For illustration purposes, I will refer to sklearn's classes; however, these solutions can be applied to any implementation:

1. Set a parameter `max_features` to a lower value, as a way of forcing discrepancy between trees.

2. Early stopping: Set the regularization parameter `min_weight_fraction_leaf` to a sufficiently large value (e.g., 5%) such that out-of-bag accuracy converges to out-of-sample (k-fold) accuracy.

3. Use `BaggingClassifier` on `DecisionTreeClassifier` where `max_samples` is set to the average uniqueness (`avgU`) between samples.

   (a) `clf=DecisionTreeClassifier(criterion='entropy',max_features='auto',class_weight='balanced')`

   (b) `bc=BaggingClassifier(base_estimator=clf,n_estimators=1000,max_samples=avgU,max_features=1.)`

4. Use `BaggingClassifier` on `RandomForestClassifier` where `max_samples` is set to the average uniqueness (`avgU`) between samples.

---

[3] For an intuitive explanation of Random Forest, visit the following link: https://quantdare.com/random-forest-many-is-better-than-one/.

(a) `clf=RandomForestClassifier(n_estimators=1,criterion=`
`'entropy',bootstrap=False,class_weight='balanced_`
`subsample')`

(b) `bc=BaggingClassifier(base_estimator=clf,n_estimators=`
`1000,max_samples=avgU,max_features=1.)`

5. Modify the RF class to replace standard bootstrapping with sequential boot-strapping.

In summary, Snippet 6.2 demonstrates three alternative ways of setting up an RF, using different classes.

SNIPPET 6.2   THREE WAYS OF SETTING UP AN RF

```
clf0=RandomForestClassifier(n_estimators=1000,class_weight='balanced_subsample',
    criterion='entropy')
clf1=DecisionTreeClassifier(criterion='entropy',max_features='auto',
    class_weight='balanced')
clf1=BaggingClassifier(base_estimator=clf1,n_estimators=1000,max_samples=avgU)
clf2=RandomForestClassifier(n_estimators=1,criterion='entropy',bootstrap=False,
    class_weight='balanced_subsample')
clf2=BaggingClassifier(base_estimator=clf2,n_estimators=1000,max_samples=avgU,
    max_features=1.)
```

When fitting decision trees, a rotation of the features space in a direction that aligns with the axes typically reduces the number of levels needed by the tree. For this reason, I suggest you fit RF on a PCA of the features, as that may speed up calculations and reduce some overfitting (more on this in Chapter 8). Also, as discussed in Chapter 4, Section 4.8, `class_weight='balanced_subsample'` will help you prevent the trees from misclassifying minority classes.

6.5   BOOSTING

Kearns and Valiant [1989] were among the first to ask whether one could combine weak estimators in order to achieve one with high accuracy. Shortly after, Schapire [1990] demonstrated that the answer to that question was affirmative, using the procedure we today call boosting. In general terms, it works as follows: First, generate one training set by random sampling with replacement, according to some sample weights (initialized with uniform weights). Second, fit one estimator using that training set. Third, if the single estimator achieves an accuracy greater than the acceptance threshold (e.g., 50% in a binary classifier, so that it performs better than chance), the estimator is kept, otherwise it is discarded. Fourth, give more weight to misclassified observations, and less weight to correctly classified observations. Fifth, repeat the previous steps until N estimators are produced. Sixth, the ensemble forecast is the *weighted* average of the individual forecasts from the N models, where the weights

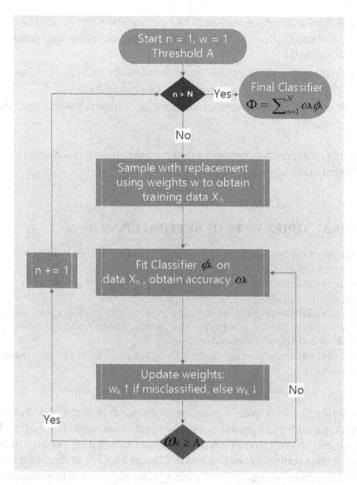

FIGURE 6.3   AdaBoost decision flow

are determined by the accuracy of the individual estimators. There are many boosting algorithms, of which AdaBoost is one of the most popular (Geron [2017]). Figure 6.3 summarizes the decision flow of a standard AdaBoost implementation.

6.6   BAGGING VS. BOOSTING IN FINANCE

From the above description, a few aspects make boosting quite different from bagging:[4]

- Individual classifiers are fit sequentially.
- Poor-performing classifiers are dismissed.

---

[4] For a visual explanation of the difference between bagging and boosting, visit: https://quantdare.com/what-is-the-difference-between-bagging-and-boosting/.

- Observations are weighted differently in each iteration.
- The ensemble forecast is a weighted average of the individual learners.

Boosting's main advantage is that it reduces both variance and bias in forecasts. However, correcting bias comes at the cost of greater risk of overfitting. It could be argued that in financial applications bagging is generally preferable to boosting. Bagging addresses overfitting, while boosting addresses underfitting. Overfitting is often a greater concern than underfitting, as it is not difficult to overfit an ML algorithm to financial data, because of the low signal-to-noise ratio. Furthermore, bagging can be parallelized, while generally boosting requires sequential running.

6.7   BAGGING FOR SCALABILITY

As you know, several popular ML algorithms do not scale well with the sample size. Support vector machines (SVMs) are a prime example. If you attempt to fit an SVM on a million observations, it may take a while until the algorithm converges. And even once it has converged, there is no guarantee that the solution is a global optimum, or that it is not overfit.

One practical approach is to build a bagging algorithm, where the base estimator belongs to a class that does not scale well with the sample size, like SVM. When defining that base estimator, we will impose a tight early stopping condition. For example, in sklearn's SVM implementation, you could set a low value for the `max_iter` parameter, say 1E5 iterations. The default value is `max_iter=-1`, which tells the estimator to continue performing iterations until errors fall below a tolerance level. Alternatively, you could raise the tolerance level through the parameter `tol`, which has a default value `tol=1E-3`. Either of these two parameters will force an early stop. You can stop other algorithms early with equivalent parameters, like the number of levels in an RF (`max_depth`), or the minimum weighted fraction of the sum total of weights (of all the input samples) required to be at a leaf node (`min_weight_fraction_leaf`).

Given that bagging algorithms can be parallelized, we are transforming a large sequential task into many smaller ones that are run simultaneously. Of course, the early stopping will increase the variance of the outputs from the individual base estimators; however, that increase can be more than offset by the variance reduction associated with the bagging algorithm. You can control that reduction by adding more independent base estimators. Used in this way, bagging will allow you to achieve fast and robust estimates on extremely large datasets.

EXERCISES

6.1 Why is bagging based on random sampling with replacement? Would bagging still reduce a forecast's variance if sampling were without replacement?

6.2 Suppose that your training set is based on highly overlap labels (i.e., with low uniqueness, as defined in Chapter 4).

    (a) Does this make bagging prone to overfitting, or just ineffective? Why?

    (b) Is out-of-bag accuracy generally reliable in financial applications? Why?

6.3 Build an ensemble of estimators, where the base estimator is a decision tree.

    (a) How is this ensemble different from an RF?

    (b) Using sklearn, produce a bagging classifier that behaves like an RF. What parameters did you have to set up, and how?

6.4 Consider the relation between an RF, the number of trees it is composed of, and the number of features utilized:

    (a) Could you envision a relation between the minimum number of trees needed in an RF and the number of features utilized?

    (b) Could the number of trees be too small for the number of features used?

    (c) Could the number of trees be too high for the number of observations available?

6.5 How is out-of-bag accuracy different from stratified k-fold (with shuffling) cross-validation accuracy?

REFERENCES

Geron, A. (2017): *Hands-on Machine Learning with Scikit-Learn and TensorFlow: Concepts, Tools, and Techniques to Build Intelligent Systems*, 1st edition. O'Reilly Media.

Kearns, M. and L. Valiant (1989): "Cryptographic limitations on learning Boolean formulae and finite automata." In Proceedings of the 21st Annual ACM Symposium on Theory of Computing, pp. 433–444, New York. Association for Computing Machinery.

Schapire, R. (1990): "The strength of weak learnability." *Machine Learning*. Kluwer Academic Publishers. Vol. 5 No. 2, pp. 197–227.

BIBLIOGRAPHY

Gareth, J., D. Witten, T. Hastie, and R. Tibshirani (2013): *An Introduction to Statistical Learning: With Applications in R*, 1st ed. Springer-Verlag.

Hackeling, G. (2014): *Mastering Machine Learning with Scikit-Learn*, 1st ed. Packt Publishing.

Hastie, T., R. Tibshirani and J. Friedman (2016): *The Elements of Statistical Learning*, 2nd ed. Springer-Verlag.

Hauck, T. (2014): *Scikit-Learn Cookbook*, 1st ed. Packt Publishing.

Raschka, S. (2015): *Python Machine Learning*, 1st ed. Packt Publishing.

CHAPTER 7

Cross-Validation in Finance

7.1 MOTIVATION

The purpose of cross-validation (CV) is to determine the generalization error of an ML algorithm, so as to prevent overfitting. CV is yet another instance where standard ML techniques fail when applied to financial problems. Overfitting will take place, and CV will not be able to detect it. In fact, CV will contribute to overfitting through hyper-parameter tuning. In this chapter we will learn why standard CV fails in finance, and what can be done about it.

7.2 THE GOAL OF CROSS-VALIDATION

One of the purposes of ML is to learn the general structure of the data, so that we can produce predictions on future, unseen features. When we test an ML algorithm on the same dataset as was used for training, not surprisingly, we achieve spectacular results. When ML algorithms are misused that way, they are no different from file lossy-compression algorithms: They can summarize the data with extreme fidelity, yet with zero forecasting power.

CV splits observations drawn from an IID process into two sets: the *training* set and the *testing* set. Each observation in the complete dataset belongs to one, and only one, set. This is done as to prevent leakage from one set into the other, since that would defeat the purpose of testing on unseen data. Further details can be found in the books and articles listed in the references section.

There are many alternative CV schemes, of which one of the most popular is k-fold CV. Figure 7.1 illustrates the k train/test splits carried out by a k-fold CV, where $k = 5$. In this scheme:

1. The dataset is partitioned into k subsets.
2. For $i = 1,...,k$

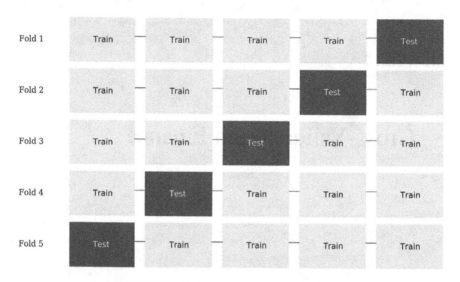

FIGURE 7.1   Train/test splits in a 5-fold CV scheme

(a) The ML algorithm is trained on all subsets excluding i.

(b) The fitted ML algorithm is tested on i.

The outcome from k-fold CV is a *kx1* array of cross-validated performance metrics. For example, in a binary classifier, the model is deemed to have learned something if the cross-validated accuracy is over 1/2, since that is the accuracy we would achieve by tossing a fair coin.

In finance, CV is typically used in two settings: model development (like hyperparameter tuning) and backtesting. Backtesting is a complex subject that we will discuss thoroughly in Chapters 10–16. In this chapter, we will focus on CV for model development.

7.3   WHY K-FOLD CV FAILS IN FINANCE

By now you may have read quite a few papers in finance that present k-fold CV evidence that an ML algorithm performs well. Unfortunately, it is almost certain that those results are wrong. One reason k-fold CV fails in finance is because observations cannot be assumed to be drawn from an IID process. A second reason for CV's failure is that the testing set is used multiple times in the process of developing a model, leading to multiple testing and selection bias. We will revisit this second cause of failure in Chapters 11–13. For the time being, let us concern ourselves exclusively with the first cause of failure.

Leakage takes place when the training set contains information that also appears in the testing set. Consider a serially correlated feature X that is associated with labels Y that are formed on overlapping data:

- Because of the serial correlation, $X_t \approx X_{t+1}$.
- Because labels are derived from overlapping datapoints, $Y_t \approx Y_{t+1}$.

By placing t and $t+1$ in different sets, information is leaked. When a classifier is first trained on (X_t, Y_t), and then it is asked to predict $E[Y_{t+1}|X_{t+1}]$ based on an observed X_{t+1}, this classifier is more likely to achieve $Y_{t+1} = E[Y_{t+1}|X_{t+1}]$ even if X is an irrelevant feature.

If X is a predictive feature, leakage will enhance the performance of an already valuable strategy. The problem is leakage in the presence of irrelevant features, as this leads to false discoveries. There are at least two ways to reduce the likelihood of leakage:

1. Drop from the training set any observation i where Y_i is a function of information used to determine Y_j, and j belongs to the testing set.
   (a) For example, Y_i and Y_j should not span overlapping periods (see Chapter 4 for a discussion of sample uniqueness).
2. Avoid overfitting the classifier. In this way, even if some leakage occurs, the classifier will not be able to profit from it. Use:
   (a) Early stopping of the base estimators (see Chapter 6).
   (b) Bagging of classifiers, while controlling for oversampling on redundant examples, so that the individual classifiers are as diverse as possible.
      i. Set max_samples to the average uniqueness.
      ii. Apply sequential bootstrap (Chapter 4).

Consider the case where X_i and X_j are formed on overlapping information, where i belongs to the training set and j belongs to the testing set. Is this a case of informational leakage? Not necessarily, as long as Y_i and Y_j are independent. For leakage to take place, it must occur that $(X_i, Y_i) \approx (X_j, Y_j)$, and it does not suffice that $X_i \approx X_j$ or even $Y_i \approx Y_j$.

7.4 A SOLUTION: PURGED K-FOLD CV

One way to reduce leakage is to purge from the training set all observations whose labels overlapped in time with those labels included in the testing set. I call this process "purging." In addition, since financial features often incorporate series that exhibit serial correlation (like ARMA processes), we should eliminate from the training set observations that immediately follow an observation in the testing set. I call this process "embargo."

7.4.1 Purging the Training Set

Suppose a testing observation whose label Y_j is decided based on the information set Φ_j. In order to prevent the type of leakage described in the previous section, we would like to purge from the training set any observation whose label Y_i is decided based on the information set Φ_i, such that $\Phi_i \cap \Phi_j = \emptyset$.

In particular, we will determine that there is informational overlap between two observations i and j whenever Y_i and Y_j are concurrent (see Chapter 4, Section 4.3), in the sense that both labels are contingent on at least one common random draw. For example, consider a label Y_j that is a function of observations in the closed range $t \in [t_{j,0}, t_{j,1}]$, $Y_j = f[[t_{j,0}, t_{j,1}]]$ (with some abuse of notation). For example, in the context of the triple-barrier labeling method (Chapter 3), it means that the label is the sign of the return spanning between price bars with indices $t_{j,0}$ and $t_{j,1}$, that is $\text{sgn}[r_{t_{j,0},t_{j,1}}]$. A label $Y_i = f[[t_{i,0}, t_{i,1}]]$ overlaps with Y_j if any of the three sufficient conditions is met:

1. $t_{j,0} \leq t_{i,0} \leq t_{j,1}$
2. $t_{j,0} \leq t_{i,1} \leq t_{j,1}$
3. $t_{i,0} \leq t_{j,0} \leq t_{j,1} \leq t_{i,1}$

Snippet 7.1 implements this purging of observations from the training set. If the testing set is contiguous, in the sense that no training observations occur between the first and last testing observation, then purging can be accelerated: The object testTimes can be a pandas series with a single item, spanning the entire testing set.

SNIPPET 7.1   PURGING OBSERVATION IN THE TRAINING SET

```
def getTrainTimes(t1,testTimes):
    '''
    Given testTimes, find the times of the training observations.
    -t1.index: Time when the observation started.
    -t1.value: Time when the observation ended.
    -testTimes: Times of testing observations.
    '''
    trn=t1.copy(deep=True)
    for i,j in testTimes.iteritems():
        df0=trn[(i<=trn.index)&(trn.index<=j)].index # train starts within test
        df1=trn[(i<=trn)&(trn<=j)].index # train ends within test
        df2=trn[(trn.index<=i)&(j<=trn)].index # train envelops test
        trn=trn.drop(df0.union(df1).union(df2))
    return trn
```

When leakage takes place, performance improves merely by increasing $k \rightarrow T$, where T is the number of bars. The reason is that the larger the number of testing splits, the greater the number of overlapping observations in the training set. In many cases, purging suffices to prevent leakage: Performance will improve as we increase k, because we allow the model to recalibrate more often. But beyond a certain value

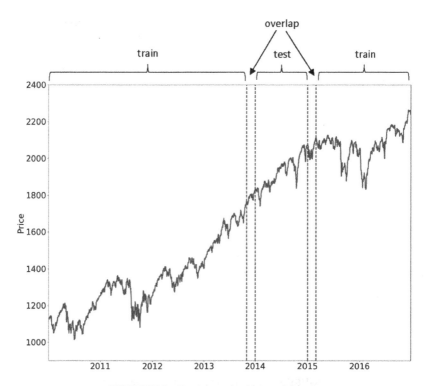

FIGURE 7.2   Purging overlap in the training set

k^*, performance will not improve, indicating that the backtest is not profiting from leaks. Figure 7.2 plots one partition of the k-fold CV. The test set is surrounded by two train sets, generating two overlaps that must be purged to prevent leakage.

7.4.2 Embargo

For those cases where purging is not able to prevent all leakage, we can impose an embargo on training observations *after* every test set. The embargo does not need to affect training observations prior to a test set, because training labels $Y_i = f[[t_{i,0}, t_{i,1}]]$, where $t_{i,1} < t_{j,0}$ (training ends before testing begins), contain information that was available at the testing time $t_{j,0}$. In other words, we are only concerned with training labels $Y_i = f[[t_{i,0}, t_{i,1}]]$ that take place immediately after the test, $t_{j,1} \leq t_{i,0} \leq t_{j,1} + h$. We can implement this embargo period h by setting $Y_j = f[[t_{j,0}, t_{j,1} + h]]$ before purging. A small value $h \approx .01T$ often suffices to prevent all leakage, as can be confirmed by testing that performance does not improve indefinitely by increasing $k \to T$. Figure 7.3 illustrates the embargoing of train observations immediately after the testing set. Snippet 7.2 implements the embargo logic.

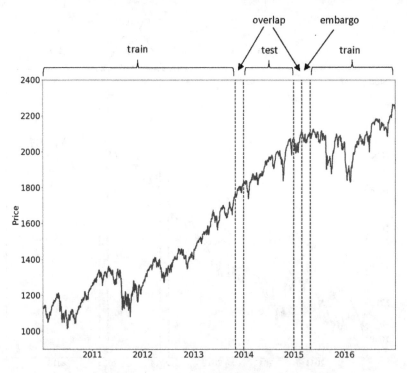

FIGURE 7.3 Embargo of post-test train observations

SNIPPET 7.2   EMBARGO ON TRAINING OBSERVATIONS

```
def getEmbargoTimes(times,pctEmbargo):
    # Get embargo time for each bar
    step=int(times.shape[0]*pctEmbargo)
    if step==0:
        mbrg=pd.Series(times,index=times)
    else:
        mbrg=pd.Series(times[step:],index=times[:-step])
        mbrg=mbrg.append(pd.Series(times[-1],index=times[-step:]))
    return mbrg
#————————————————————————————————————————————
testTimes=pd.Series(mbrg[dt1],index=[dt0]) # include embargo before purge
trainTimes=getTrainTimes(t1,testTimes)
testTimes=t1.loc[dt0:dt1].index
```

7.4.3   The Purged K-Fold Class

In the previous sections we have discussed how to produce training/testing splits when labels overlap. That introduced the notion of purging and embargoing, in the particular context of model development. In general, we need to purge and embargo overlapping training observations whenever we produce a train/test split, whether it is for hyper-parameter fitting, backtesting, or performance evaluation. Snippet 7.3 extends scikit-learn's KFold class to account for the possibility of leakages of testing information into the training set.

SNIPPET 7.3 CROSS-VALIDATION CLASS WHEN OBSERVATIONS OVERLAP

```
class PurgedKFold(_BaseKFold):
    '''
    Extend KFold to work with labels that span intervals
    The train is purged of observations overlapping test-label intervals
    Test set is assumed contiguous (shuffle=False), w/o training examples in between
    '''
    def __init__(self,n_splits=3,t1=None,pctEmbargo=0.):
        if not isinstance(t1,pd.Series):
            raise ValueError('Label Through Dates must be a pandas series')
        super(PurgedKFold,self).__init__(n_splits,shuffle=False,random_state=None)
        self.t1=t1
        self.pctEmbargo=pctEmbargo
    def split(self,X,y=None,groups=None):
        if (X.index==self.t1.index).sum()!=len(self.t1):
            raise ValueError('X and ThruDateValues must have the same index')
        indices=np.arange(X.shape[0])
        mbrg=int(X.shape[0]*self.pctEmbargo)
        test_starts=[(i[0],i[-1]+1) for i in \
            np.array_split(np.arange(X.shape[0]),self.n_splits)]
        for i,j in test_starts:
            t0=self.t1.index[i] # start of test set
            test_indices=indices[i:j]
            maxT1Idx=self.t1.index.searchsorted(self.t1[test_indices].max())
            train_indices=self.t1.index.searchsorted(self.t1[self.t1<=t0].index)
            train_indices=np.concatenate((train_indices,indices[maxT1Idx+mbrg:]))
            yield train_indices,test_indices
```

7.5 BUGS IN SKLEARN'S CROSS-VALIDATION

You would think that something as critical as cross-validation would be perfectly implemented in one of the most popular ML libraries. Unfortunately that is not the case, and this is one of the reasons you must always read all the code you run, and a strong point in favor of open source. One of the many upsides of open-source code is that you can verify everything and adjust it to your needs. Snippet 7.4 addresses two known sklearn bugs:

1. Scoring functions do not know `classes_`, as a consequence of sklearn's reliance on numpy arrays rather than pandas series: https://github.com/scikit-learn/scikit-learn/issues/6231
2. `cross_val_score` will give different results because it passes weights to the fit method, but not to the `log_loss` method: https://github.com/scikit-learn/scikit-learn/issues/9144

SNIPPET 7.4   USING THE `PurgedKFold` CLASS

```
def cvScore(clf,X,y,sample_weight,scoring='neg_log_loss',t1=None,cv=None,cvGen=None,
            pctEmbargo=None):
    if scoring not in ['neg_log_loss','accuracy']:
        raise Exception('wrong scoring method.')
    from sklearn.metrics import log_loss,accuracy_score
    from clfSequential import PurgedKFold
    if cvGen is None:
        cvGen=PurgedKFold(n_splits=cv,t1=t1,pctEmbargo=pctEmbargo) # purged
    score=[]
    for train,test in cvGen.split(X=X):
        fit=clf.fit(X=X.iloc[train,:],y=y.iloc[train],
                    sample_weight=sample_weight.iloc[train].values)
        if scoring=='neg_log_loss':
            prob=fit.predict_proba(X.iloc[test,:])
            score_=-log_loss(y.iloc[test],prob,
                sample_weight=sample_weight.iloc[test].values,labels=clf.classes_)
        else:
            pred=fit.predict(X.iloc[test,:])
            score_=accuracy_score(y.iloc[test],pred,sample_weight= \
                sample_weight.iloc[test].values)
        score.append(score_)
    return np.array(score)
```

Please understand that it may take a long time until a fix for these bugs is agreed upon, implemented, tested, and released. Until then, you should use `cvScore` in Snippet 7.4, and avoid running the function `cross_val_score`.

EXERCISES

7.1 Why is shuffling a dataset before conducting k-fold CV generally a bad idea in finance? What is the purpose of shuffling? Why does shuffling defeat the purpose of k-fold CV in financial datasets?

7.2 Take a pair of matrices (X, y), representing observed features and labels. These could be one of the datasets derived from the exercises in Chapter 3.

  (a) Derive the performance from a 10-fold CV of an RF classifier on (X, y), without shuffling.

  (b) Derive the performance from a 10-fold CV of an RF on (X, y), with shuffling.

  (c) Why are both results so different?

  (d) How does shuffling leak information?

7.3 Take the same pair of matrices (X, y) you used in exercise 2.

  (a) Derive the performance from a 10-fold purged CV of an RF on (X, y), with 1% embargo.

  (b) Why is the performance lower?

  (c) Why is this result more realistic?

7.4 In this chapter we have focused on one reason why k-fold CV fails in financial applications, namely the fact that some information from the testing set leaks into the training set. Can you think of a second reason for CV's failure?

7.5 Suppose you try one thousand configurations of the same investment strategy, and perform a CV on each of them. Some results are guaranteed to look good, just by sheer luck. If you only publish those positive results, and hide the rest, your audience will not be able to deduce that these results are false positives, a statistical fluke. This phenomenon is called "selection bias."

  (a) Can you imagine one procedure to prevent this?

  (b) What if we split the dataset in three sets: training, validation, and testing? The validation set is used to evaluate the trained parameters, and the testing is run only on the one configuration chosen in the validation phase. In what case does this procedure still fail?

  (c) What is the key to avoiding selection bias?

BIBLIOGRAPHY

Bharat Rao, R., G. Fung, and R. Rosales (2008): "On the dangers of cross-validation: An experimental evaluation." White paper, IKM CKS Siemens Medical Solutions USA. Available at http://people.csail.mit.edu/romer/papers/CrossVal_SDM08.pdf.

Bishop, C. (1995): *Neural Networks for Pattern Recognition*, 1st ed. Oxford University Press.

Breiman, L. and P. Spector (1992): "Submodel selection and evaluation in regression: The X-random case." White paper, Department of Statistics, University of California, Berkeley. Available at http://digitalassets.lib.berkeley.edu/sdtr/ucb/text/197.pdf.

Hastie, T., R. Tibshirani, and J. Friedman (2009): *The Elements of Statistical Learning*, 1st ed. Springer.

James, G., D. Witten, T. Hastie and R. Tibshirani (2013): *An Introduction to Statistical Learning*, 1st ed. Springer.

Kohavi, R. (1995): "A study of cross-validation and bootstrap for accuracy estimation and model selection." International Joint Conference on Artificial Intelligence. Available at http://web.cs.iastate.edu/~jtian/cs573/Papers/Kohavi-IJCAI-95.pdf.

Ripley, B. (1996): *Pattern Recognition and Neural Networks*, 1st ed. Cambridge University Press.

CHAPTER 8

Feature Importance

8.1 MOTIVATION

One of the most pervasive mistakes in financial research is to take some data, run it through an ML algorithm, backtest the predictions, and repeat the sequence until a nice-looking backtest shows up. Academic journals are filled with such pseudo-discoveries, and even large hedge funds constantly fall into this trap. It does not matter if the backtest is a walk-forward out-of-sample. The fact that we are repeating a test over and over on the same data will likely lead to a false discovery. This methodological error is so notorious among statisticians that they consider it scientific fraud, and the American Statistical Association warns against it in its ethical guidelines (American Statistical Association [2016], Discussion #4). It typically takes about 20 such iterations to discover a (false) investment strategy subject to the standard significance level (false positive rate) of 5%. In this chapter we will explore why such an approach is a waste of time and money, and how feature importance offers an alternative.

8.2 THE IMPORTANCE OF FEATURE IMPORTANCE

A striking facet of the financial industry is that so many very seasoned portfolio managers (including many with a quantitative background) do not realize how easy it is to overfit a backtest. How to backtest properly is not the subject of this chapter; we will address that extremely important topic in Chapters 11–15. The goal of this chapter is to explain one of the analyses that must be performed *before* any backtest is carried out.

Suppose that you are given a pair of matrices (X, y), that respectively contain features and labels for a particular financial instrument. We can fit a classifier on (X, y) and evaluate the generalization error through a purged k-fold cross-validation (CV), as we saw in Chapter 7. Suppose that we achieve good performance. The next

113

natural question is to try to understand what features contributed to that performance. Maybe we could add some features that strengthen the signal responsible for the classifier's predictive power. Maybe we could eliminate some of the features that are only adding noise to the system. Notably, understanding feature importance opens up the proverbial black box. We can gain insight into the patterns identified by the classifier if we understand what source of information is indispensable to it. This is one of the reasons why the black box mantra is somewhat overplayed by the ML skeptics. Yes, the algorithm has learned without us directing the process (that is the whole point of ML!) in a black box, but that does not mean that we cannot (or should not) take a look at what the algorithm has found. Hunters do not blindly eat everything their smart dogs retrieve for them, do they?

Once we have found what features are important, we can learn more by conducting a number of experiments. Are these features important all the time, or only in some specific environments? What triggers a change in importance over time? Can those regime switches be predicted? Are those important features also relevant to other related financial instruments? Are they relevant to other asset classes? What are the most relevant features across all financial instruments? What is the subset of features with the highest rank correlation across the entire investment universe? This is a much better way of researching strategies than the foolish backtest cycle. Let me state this maxim as one of the most critical lessons I hope you learn from this book:

SNIPPET 8.1   MARCOS' FIRST LAW OF BACKTESTING—IGNORE AT YOUR OWN PERIL

"Backtesting is not a research tool. Feature importance is."

—Marcos López de Prado
Advances in Financial Machine Learning (2018)

8.3   FEATURE IMPORTANCE WITH SUBSTITUTION EFFECTS

I find it useful to distinguish between feature importance methods based on whether they are impacted by substitution effects. In this context, a substitution effect takes place when the estimated importance of one feature is reduced by the presence of other related features. Substitution effects are the ML analogue of what the statistics and econometrics literature calls "multi-collinearity." One way to address linear substitution effects is to apply PCA on the raw features, and then perform the feature importance analysis on the orthogonal features. See Belsley et al. [1980], Goldberger [1991, pp. 245–253], and Hill et al. [2001] for further details.

8.3.1   Mean Decrease Impurity

Mean decrease impurity (MDI) is a fast, explanatory-importance (in-sample, IS) method specific to tree-based classifiers, like RF. At each node of each decision tree, the selected feature splits the subset it received in such a way that impurity is decreased. Therefore, we can derive for each decision tree how much of the overall impurity decrease can be assigned to each feature. And given that we have a forest of trees, we can average those values across all estimators and rank the features accordingly. See Louppe et al. [2013] for a detailed description. There are some important considerations you must keep in mind when working with MDI:

1. Masking effects take place when some features are systematically ignored by tree-based classifiers in favor of others. In order to avoid them, set `max_features=int(1)` when using sklearn's RF class. In this way, only one random feature is considered per level.

    (a) Every feature is given a chance (at some random levels of some random trees) to reduce impurity.

    (b) Make sure that features with zero importance are not averaged, since the only reason for a 0 is that the feature was not randomly chosen. Replace those values with `np.nan`.

2. The procedure is obviously IS. Every feature will have some importance, even if they have no predictive power whatsoever.

3. MDI cannot be generalized to other non-tree based classifiers.

4. By construction, MDI has the nice property that feature importances add up to 1, and every feature importance is bounded between 0 and 1.

5. The method does not address substitution effects in the presence of correlated features. MDI dilutes the importance of substitute features, because of their interchangeability: The importance of two identical features will be halved, as they are randomly chosen with equal probability.

6. Strobl et al. [2007] show experimentally that MDI is biased towards some predictor variables. White and Liu [1994] argue that, in case of single decision trees, this bias is due to an unfair advantage given by popular impurity functions toward predictors with a large number of categories.

Sklearn's `RandomForest` class implements MDI as the default feature importance score. This choice is likely motivated by the ability to compute MDI on the fly, with minimum computational cost.[1] Snippet 8.2 illustrates an implementation of MDI, incorporating the considerations listed earlier.

SNIPPET 8.2   MDI FEATURE IMPORTANCE

```
def featImpMDI(fit,featNames):
    # feat importance based on IS mean impurity reduction
    df0={i:tree.feature_importances_ for i,tree in enumerate(fit.estimators_)}
    df0=pd.DataFrame.from_dict(df0,orient='index')
    df0.columns=featNames
    df0=df0.replace(0,np.nan) # because max_features=1
```

[1] http://blog.datadive.net/selecting-good-features-part-iii-random-forests/.

```
imp=pd.concat({'mean':df0.mean(),'std':df0.std()*df0.shape[0]**-.5},axis=1)
imp/=imp['mean'].sum()
return imp
```

8.3.2   Mean Decrease Accuracy

Mean decrease accuracy (MDA) is a slow, predictive-importance (out-of-sample, OOS) method. First, it fits a classifier; second, it derives its performance OOS according to some performance score (accuracy, negative log-loss, etc.); third, it permutates each column of the features matrix (X), one column at a time, deriving the performance OOS after each column's permutation. The importance of a feature is a function of the loss in performance caused by its column's permutation. Some relevant considerations include:

1. This method can be applied to any classifier, not only tree-based classifiers.
2. MDA is not limited to accuracy as the sole performance score. For example, in the context of meta-labeling applications, we may prefer to score a classifier with F1 rather than accuracy (see Chapter 14, Section 14.8 for an explanation). That is one reason a better descriptive name would have been "permutation importance." When the scoring function does not correspond to a metric space, MDA results should be used as a ranking.
3. Like MDI, the procedure is also susceptible to substitution effects in the presence of correlated features. Given two identical features, MDA always considers one to be redundant to the other. Unfortunately, MDA will make both features appear to be outright irrelevant, even if they are critical.
4. Unlike MDI, it is possible that MDA concludes that all features are unimportant. That is because MDA is based on OOS performance.
5. The CV must be purged and embargoed, for the reasons explained in Chapter 7.

Snippet 8.3 implements MDA feature importance with sample weights, with purged k-fold CV, and with scoring by negative log-loss or accuracy. It measures MDA importance as a function of the improvement (from permutating to not permutating the feature), relative to the maximum possible score (negative log-loss of 0, or accuracy of 1). Note that, in some cases, the improvement may be negative, meaning that the feature is actually detrimental to the forecasting power of the ML algorithm.

SNIPPET 8.3   MDA FEATURE IMPORTANCE

```
def featImpMDA(clf,X,y,cv,sample_weight,t1,pctEmbargo,scoring='neg_log_loss'):
    # feat importance based on OOS score reduction
    if scoring not in ['neg_log_loss','accuracy']:
        raise Exception('wrong scoring method.')
    from sklearn.metrics import log_loss,accuracy_score
    cvGen=PurgedKFold(n_splits=cv,t1=t1,pctEmbargo=pctEmbargo) # purged cv
    scr0,scr1=pd.Series(),pd.DataFrame(columns=X.columns)
```

```
for i,(train,test) in enumerate(cvGen.split(X=X)):
    X0,y0,w0=X.iloc[train,:],y.iloc[train],sample_weight.iloc[train]
    X1,y1,w1=X.iloc[test,:],y.iloc[test],sample_weight.iloc[test]
    fit=clf.fit(X=X0,y=y0,sample_weight=w0.values)
    if scoring=='neg_log_loss':
        prob=fit.predict_proba(X1)
        scr0.loc[i]=-log_loss(y1,prob,sample_weight=w1.values,
                                  labels=clf.classes_)
    else:
        pred=fit.predict(X1)
        scr0.loc[i]=accuracy_score(y1,pred,sample_weight=w1.values)
    for j in X.columns:
        X1_=X1.copy(deep=True)
        np.random.shuffle(X1_[j].values) # permutation of a single column
        if scoring=='neg_log_loss':
            prob=fit.predict_proba(X1_)
            scr1.loc[i,j]=-log_loss(y1,prob,sample_weight=w1.values,
                                       labels=clf.classes_)
        else:
            pred=fit.predict(X1_)
            scr1.loc[i,j]=accuracy_score(y1,pred,sample_weight=w1.values)
imp=(-scr1).add(scr0,axis=0)
if scoring=='neg_log_loss':imp=imp/-scr1
else:imp=imp/(1.-scr1)
imp=pd.concat({'mean':imp.mean(),'std':imp.std()*imp.shape[0]**-.5},axis=1)
return imp,scr0.mean()
```

8.4 FEATURE IMPORTANCE WITHOUT SUBSTITUTION EFFECTS

Substitution effects can lead us to discard important features that happen to be redundant. This is not generally a problem in the context of prediction, but it could lead us to wrong conclusions when we are trying to understand, improve, or simplify a model. For this reason, the following single feature importance method can be a good complement to MDI and MDA.

8.4.1 Single Feature Importance

Single feature importance (SFI) is a cross-section predictive-importance (out-of-sample) method. It computes the OOS performance score of each feature in isolation. A few considerations:

1. This method can be applied to any classifier, not only tree-based classifiers.
2. SFI is not limited to accuracy as the sole performance score.
3. Unlike MDI and MDA, no substitution effects take place, since only one feature is taken into consideration at a time.
4. Like MDA, it can conclude that all features are unimportant, because performance is evaluated via OOS CV.

The main limitation of SFI is that a classifier with two features can perform better than the bagging of two single-feature classifiers. For example, (1) feature B may be useful only in combination with feature A; or (2) feature B may be useful in explaining the splits from feature A, even if feature B alone is inaccurate. In other words, joint effects and hierarchical importance are lost in SFI. One alternative would be to compute the OOS performance score from subsets of features, but that calculation will become intractable as more features are considered. Snippet 8.4 demonstrates one possible implementation of the SFI method. A discussion of the function `cvScore` can be found in Chapter 7.

SNIPPET 8.4   IMPLEMENTATION OF SFI

```
def auxFeatImpSFI(featNames,clf,trnsX,cont,scoring,cvGen):
    imp=pd.DataFrame(columns=['mean','std'])
    for featName in featNames:
        df0=cvScore(clf,X=trnsX[[featName]],y=cont['bin'],sample_weight=cont['w'],
                    scoring=scoring,cvGen=cvGen)
        imp.loc[featName,'mean']=df0.mean()
        imp.loc[featName,'std']=df0.std()*df0.shape[0]**-.5
    return imp
```

8.4.2   Orthogonal Features

As argued in Section 8.3, substitution effects dilute the importance of features measured by MDI, and significantly underestimate the importance of features measured by MDA. A partial solution is to orthogonalize the features before applying MDI and MDA. An orthogonalization procedure such as principal components analysis (PCA) does not prevent all substitution effects, but at least it should alleviate the impact of linear substitution effects.

Consider a matrix $\{X_{t,n}\}$ of stationary features, with observations $t = 1, \ldots, T$ and variables $n = 1, \ldots, N$. First, we compute the standardized features matrix Z, such that $Z_{t,n} = \sigma_n^{-1}(X_{t,n} - \mu_n)$, where μ_n is the mean of $\{X_{t,n}\}_{t=1,\ldots,T}$ and σ_n is the standard deviation of $\{X_{t,n}\}_{t=1,\ldots,T}$. Second, we compute the eigenvalues Λ and eigenvectors W such that $Z'ZW = W\Lambda$, where Λ is an NxN diagonal matrix with main entries sorted in descending order, and W is an NxN orthonormal matrix. Third, we derive the orthogonal features as $P = ZW$. We can verify the orthogonality of the features by noting that $P'P = W'Z'ZW = W'W\Lambda W'W = \Lambda$.

The diagonalization is done on Z rather than X, for two reasons: (1) centering the data ensures that the first principal component is correctly oriented in the main direction of the observations. It is equivalent to adding an intercept in a linear regression; (2) re-scaling the data makes PCA focus on explaining correlations rather than variances. Without re-scaling, the first principal components would be dominated by the columns of X with highest variance, and we would not learn much about the structure or relationship between the variables.

Snippet 8.5 computes the smallest number of orthogonal features that explain at least 95% of the variance of Z.

SNIPPET 8.5 COMPUTATION OF ORTHOGONAL FEATURES

```
def get_eVec(dot,varThres):
    # compute eVec from dot prod matrix, reduce dimension
    eVal,eVec=np.linalg.eigh(dot)
    idx=eVal.argsort()[::-1] # arguments for sorting eVal desc
    eVal,eVec=eVal[idx],eVec[:,idx]
    #2) only positive eVals
    eVal=pd.Series(eVal,index=['PC_'+str(i+1) for i in range(eVal.shape[0])])
    eVec=pd.DataFrame(eVec,index=dot.index,columns=eVal.index)
    eVec=eVec.loc[:,eVal.index]
    #3) reduce dimension, form PCs
    cumVar=eVal.cumsum()/eVal.sum()
    dim=cumVar.values.searchsorted(varThres)
    eVal,eVec=eVal.iloc[:dim+1],eVec.iloc[:,:dim+1]
    return eVal,eVec
#--------------------------------------------------------------------
def orthoFeats(dfX,varThres=.95):
    # Given a dataframe dfX of features, compute orthofeatures dfP
    dfZ=dfX.sub(dfX.mean(),axis=1).div(dfX.std(),axis=1) # standardize
    dot=pd.DataFrame(np.dot(dfZ.T,dfZ),index=dfX.columns,columns=dfX.columns)
    eVal,eVec=get_eVec(dot,varThres)
    dfP=np.dot(dfZ,eVec)
    return dfP
```

Besides addressing substitution effects, working with orthogonal features provides two additional benefits: (1) orthogonalization can also be used to reduce the dimensionality of the features matrix X, by dropping features associated with small eigenvalues. This usually speeds up the convergence of ML algorithms; (2) the analysis is conducted on features designed to explain the structure of the data.

Let me stress this latter point. An ubiquitous concern throughout the book is the risk of overfitting. ML algorithms will always find a pattern, even if that pattern is a statistical fluke. You should always be skeptical about the purportedly important features identified by any method, including MDI, MDA, and SFI. Now, suppose that you derive orthogonal features using PCA. Your PCA analysis has determined that some features are more "principal" than others, without any knowledge of the labels (unsupervised learning). That is, PCA has ranked features without any possible overfitting in a classification sense. When your MDI, MDA, or SFI analysis selects as most important (using label information) the same features that PCA chose as

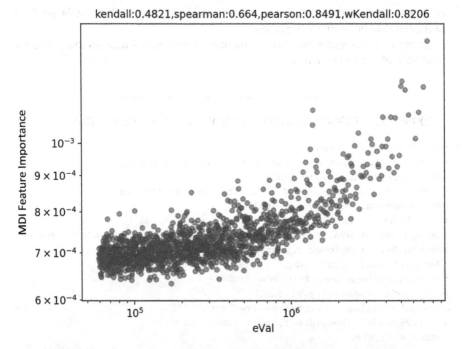

kendall:0.4821,spearman:0.664,pearson:0.8491,wKendall:0.8206

FIGURE 8.1   Scatter plot of eigenvalues (x-axis) and MDI levels (y-axis) in log-log scale

principal (ignoring label information), this constitutes confirmatory evidence that the pattern identified by the ML algorithm is not entirely overfit. If the features were entirely random, the PCA ranking would have no correspondance with the feature importance ranking. Figure 8.1 displays the scatter plot of eigenvalues associated with an eigenvector (x-axis) paired with MDI of the feature associated with an engenvector (y-axis). The Pearson correlation is 0.8491 (p-value below 1E-150), evidencing that PCA identified informative features and ranked them correctly without overfitting.

I find it useful to compute the weighted Kendall's tau between the feature importances and their associated eigenvalues (or equivalently, their inverse PCA rank). The closer this value is to 1, the stronger is the consistency between PCA ranking and feature importance ranking. One argument for preferring a weighted Kendall's tau over the standard Kendall is that we want to prioritize rank concordance among the most importance features. We do not care so much about rank concordance among irrelevant (likely noisy) features. The hyperbolic-weighted Kendall's tau for the sample in Figure 8.1 is 0.8206.

Snippet 8.6 shows how to compute this correlation using Scipy. In this example, sorting the features in descending importance gives us a PCA rank sequence very close to an ascending list. Because the `weightedtau` function gives higher weight to higher values, we compute the correlation on the inverse PCA ranking, `pcRank**-1`. The resulting weighted Kendall's tau is relatively high, at 0.8133.

SNIPPET 8.6   COMPUTATION OF WEIGHTED KENDALL'S TAU
BETWEEN FEATURE IMPORTANCE AND INVERSE PCA RANKING

```
>>> import numpy as np
>>> from scipy.stats import weightedtau
>>> featImp=np.array([.55,.33,.07,.05]) # feature importance
>>> pcRank=np.array([1,2,4,3]) # PCA rank
>>> weightedtau(featImp,pcRank**-1.)[0]
```

8.5   PARALLELIZED VS. STACKED FEATURE IMPORTANCE

There are at least two research approaches to feature importance. First, for each security i in an investment universe $i = 1, \dots, I$, we form a dataset (X_i, y_i), and derive the feature importance in parallel. For example, let us denote $\lambda_{i,j,k}$ the importance of feature j on instrument i according to criterion k. Then we can aggregate all results across the entire universe to derive a combined $\Lambda_{j,k}$ importance of feature j according to criterion k. Features that are important across a wide variety of instruments are more likely to be associated with an underlying phenomenon, particularly when these feature importances exhibit high rank correlation across the criteria. It may be worth studying in-depth the theoretical mechanism that makes these features predictive. The main advantage of this approach is that it is computationally fast, as it can be parallelized. A disadvantage is that, due to substitution effects, important features may swap their ranks across instruments, increasing the variance of the estimated $\lambda_{i,j,k}$. This disadvantage becomes relatively minor if we average $\lambda_{i,j,k}$ across instruments for a sufficiently large investment universe.

A second alternative is what I call "features stacking." It consists in stacking all datasets $\{(\tilde{X}_i, y_i)\}_{i=1,\dots,I}$ into a single combined dataset (X, y), where $\tilde{X}_i$ is a transformed instance of X_i (e.g., standardized on a rolling trailing window). The purpose of this transformation is to ensure some distributional homogeneity, $\tilde{X}_i \sim X$. Under this approach, the classifier must learn what features are more important across all instruments simultaneously, as if the entire investment universe were in fact a single instrument. Features stacking presents some advantages: (1) The classifier will be fit on a much larger dataset than the one used with the parallelized (first) approach; (2) the importance is derived directly, and no weighting scheme is required for combining the results; (3) conclusions are more general and less biased by outliers or overfitting; and (4) because importance scores are not averaged across instruments, substitution effects do not cause the dampening of those scores.

I usually prefer features stacking, not only for features importance but whenever a classifier can be fit on a set of instruments, including for the purpose of model prediction. That reduces the likelihood of overfitting an estimator to a particular instrument or small dataset. The main disadvantage of stacking is that it may consume a lot of

memory and resources, however that is where a sound knowledge of HPC techniques
will come in handy (Chapters 20–22).

8.6   EXPERIMENTS WITH SYNTHETIC DATA

In this section, we are going to test how these feature importance methods respond
to synthetic data. We are going to generate a dataset (X, y) composed on three kinds
of features:

1. Informative: These are features that are used to determine the label.
2. Redundant: These are random linear combinations of the informative features.
   They will cause substitution effects.
3. Noise: These are features that have no bearing on determining the observation's
   label.

Snippet 8.7 shows how we can generate a synthetic dataset of 40 features
where 10 are informative, 10 are redundant, and 20 are noise, on 10,000 observations. For details on how sklearn generates synthetic datasets, visit: http://scikit-
learn.org/stable/modules/generated/sklearn.datasets.make_classification.html.

SNIPPET 8.7   CREATING A SYNTHETIC DATASET

```
def getTestData(n_features=40,n_informative=10,n_redundant=10,n_samples=10000):
    # generate a random dataset for a classification problem
    from sklearn.datasets import make_classification
    trnsX,cont=make_classification(n_samples=n_samples,n_features=n_features,
        n_informative=n_informative,n_redundant=n_redundant,random_state=0,
        shuffle=False)
    df0=pd.DatetimeIndex(periods=n_samples,freq=pd.tseries.offsets.BDay(),
                        end=pd.datetime.today())
    trnsX,cont=pd.DataFrame(trnsX,index=df0),
                        pd.Series(cont,index=df0).to_frame('bin')
    df0=['I_'+str(i) for i in xrange(n_informative)]+
        ['R_'+str(i) for i in xrange(n_redundant)]
    df0+=['N_'+str(i) for i in xrange(n_features-len(df0))]
    trnsX.columns=df0
    cont['w']=1./cont.shape[0]
    cont['t1']=pd.Series(cont.index,index=cont.index)
    return trnsX,cont
```

Given that we know for certain what feature belongs to each class, we can evaluate
whether these three feature importance methods perform as designed. Now we need

a function that can carry out each analysis on the same dataset. Snippet 8.8 accomplishes that, using bagged decision trees as default classifier (Chapter 6).

SNIPPET 8.8 CALLING FEATURE IMPORTANCE FOR ANY METHOD

```
def featImportance(trnsX,cont,n_estimators=1000,cv=10,max_samples=1.,numThreads=24,
                pctEmbargo=0,scoring='accuracy',method='SFI',minWLeaf=0.,**kargs):
    # feature importance from a random forest
    from sklearn.tree import DecisionTreeClassifier
    from sklearn.ensemble import BaggingClassifier
    from mpEngine import mpPandasObj
    n_jobs=(-1 if numThreads>1 else 1) # run 1 thread with ht_helper in dirac1
    #1) prepare classifier,cv. max_features=1, to prevent masking
    clf=DecisionTreeClassifier(criterion='entropy',max_features=1,
        class_weight='balanced',min_weight_fraction_leaf=minWLeaf)
    clf=BaggingClassifier(base_estimator=clf,n_estimators=n_estimators,
        max_features=1.,max_samples=max_samples,oob_score=True,n_jobs=n_jobs)
    fit=clf.fit(X=trnsX,y=cont['bin'],sample_weight=cont['w'].values)
    oob=fit.oob_score_
    if method=='MDI':
        imp=featImpMDI(fit,featNames=trnsX.columns)
        oos=cvScore(clf,X=trnsX,y=cont['bin'],cv=cv,sample_weight=cont['w'],
                t1=cont['t1'],pctEmbargo=pctEmbargo,scoring=scoring).mean()
    elif method=='MDA':
        imp,oos=featImpMDA(clf,X=trnsX,y=cont['bin'],cv=cv,sample_weight=cont['w'],
                    t1=cont['t1'],pctEmbargo=pctEmbargo,scoring=scoring)
    elif method=='SFI':
        cvGen=PurgedKFold(n_splits=cv,t1=cont['t1'],pctEmbargo=pctEmbargo)
        oos=cvScore(clf,X=trnsX,y=cont['bin'],sample_weight=cont['w'],scoring=scoring,
            cvGen=cvGen).mean()
        clf.n_jobs=1 # paralellize auxFeatImpSFI rather than clf
        imp=mpPandasObj(auxFeatImpSFI,('featNames',trnsX.columns),numThreads,
            clf=clf,trnsX=trnsX,cont=cont,scoring=scoring,cvGen=cvGen)
    return imp,oob,oos
```

Finally, we need a main function to call all components, from data generation to feature importance analysis to collection and processing of output. These tasks are performed by Snippet 8.9.

SNIPPET 8.9 CALLING ALL COMPONENTS

```
def testFunc(n_features=40,n_informative=10,n_redundant=10,n_estimators=1000,
            n_samples=10000,cv=10):
    # test the performance of the feat importance functions on artificial data
    # Nr noise features = n_features-n_informative-n_redundant
    trnsX,cont=getTestData(n_features,n_informative,n_redundant,n_samples)
```

```
dict0={'minWLeaf':[0.],'scoring':['accuracy'],'method':['MDI','MDA','SFI'],
       'max_samples':[1.]}
jobs,out=(dict(izip(dict0,i)) for i in product(*dict0.values())),[]
kargs={'pathOut':'./testFunc/','n_estimators':n_estimators,
       'tag':'testFunc','cv':cv}
for job in jobs:
    job['simNum']=job['method']+'_'+job['scoring']+'_'+'%.2f'%job['minWLeaf']+ \
                  '_'+str(job['max_samples'])
    print job['simNum']
    kargs.update(job)
    imp,oob,oos=featImportance(trnsX=trnsX,cont=cont,**kargs)
    plotFeatImportance(imp=imp,oob=oob,oos=oos,**kargs)
    df0=imp[['mean']]/imp['mean'].abs().sum()
    df0['type']=[i[0] for i in df0.index]
    df0=df0.groupby('type')['mean'].sum().to_dict()
    df0.update({'oob':oob,'oos':oos});df0.update(job)
    out.append(df0)
out=pd.DataFrame(out).sort_values(['method','scoring','minWLeaf','max_samples'])
out=out['method','scoring','minWLeaf','max_samples','I','R','N','oob','oos']
out.to_csv(kargs['pathOut']+'stats.csv')
return
```

For the aesthetically inclined, Snippet 8.10 provides a nice layout for plotting feature importances.

SNIPPET 8.10   FEATURE IMPORTANCE PLOTTING FUNCTION

```
def plotFeatImportance(pathOut,imp,oob,oos,method,tag=0,simNum=0,**kargs):
    # plot mean imp bars with std
    mpl.figure(figsize=(10,imp.shape[0]/5.))
    imp=imp.sort_values('mean',ascending=True)
    ax=imp['mean'].plot(kind='barh',color='b',alpha=.25,xerr=imp['std'],
                        error_kw={'ecolor':'r'})
    if method=='MDI':
        mpl.xlim([0,imp.sum(axis=1).max()])
        mpl.axvline(1./imp.shape[0],linewidth=1,color='r',linestyle='dotted')
    ax.get_yaxis().set_visible(False)
    for i,j in zip(ax.patches,imp.index):ax.text(i.get_width()/2,
                   i.get_y()+i.get_height()/2,j,ha='center',va='center',
                   color='black')
    mpl.title('tag='+tag+' | simNum='+str(simNum)+' | oob='+str(round(oob,4))+
              ' | oos='+str(round(oos,4)))
    mpl.savefig(pathOut+'featImportance_'+str(simNum)+'.png',dpi=100)
    mpl.clf();mpl.close()
    return
```

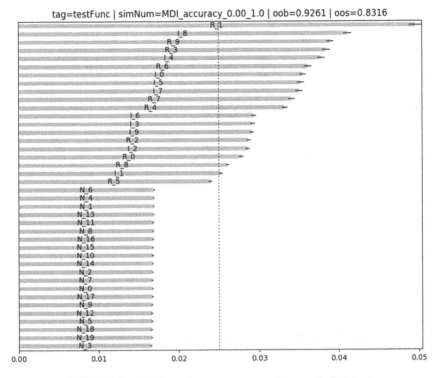

FIGURE 8.2   MDI feature importance computed on a synthetic dataset

Figure 8.2 shows results for MDI. For each feature, the horizontal bar indicates the mean MDI value across all the decision trees, and the horizontal line is the standard deviation of that mean. Since MDI importances add up to 1, if all features were equally important, each importance would have a value of 1/40. The vertical dotted line marks that 1/40 threshold, separating features whose importance exceeds what would be expected from undistinguishable features. As you can see, MDI does a very good job in terms of placing all informative and redundant features above the red dotted line, with the exception of R_5, which did not make the cut by a small margin. Substitution effects cause some informative or redundant features to rank better than others, which was expected.

Figure 8.3 shows that MDA also did a good job. Results are consistent with those from MDI's in the sense that all the informed and redundant features rank better than the noise feature, with the exception of R_6, likely due to a substitution effect. One not so positive aspect of MDA is that the standard deviation of the means are somewhat higher, although that could be addressed by increasing the number of partitions in the purged k-fold CV, from, say, 10 to 100 (at the cost of 10×the computation time without parallelization).

Figure 8.4 shows that SFI also does a decent job; however, a few important features rank worse than noise (I_6, I_2, I_9, I_1, I_3, R_5), likely due to joint effects.

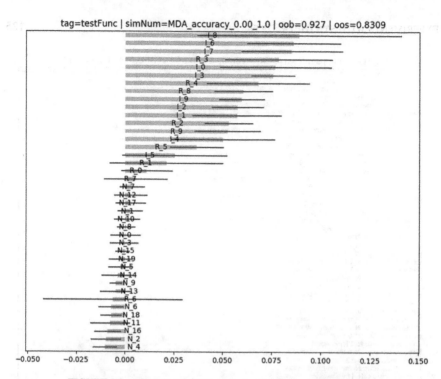

FIGURE 8.3 MDA feature importance computed on a synthetic dataset

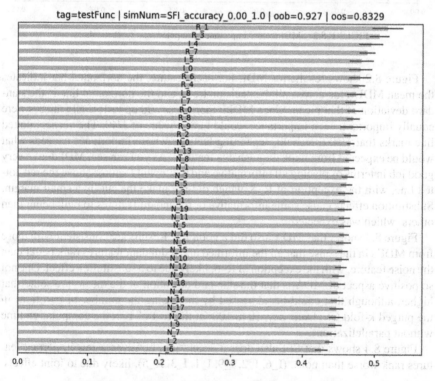

FIGURE 8.4 SFI feature importance computed on a synthetic dataset

The labels are a function of a combination of features, and trying to forecast them independently misses the joint effects. Still, SFI is useful as a complement to MDI and MDA, precisely because both types of analyses are affected by different kinds of problems.

EXERCISES

8.1 Using the code presented in Section 8.6:

    (a) Generate a dataset (X, y).

    (b) Apply a PCA transformation on X, which we denote $\dot{X}$.

    (c) Compute MDI, MDA, and SFI feature importance on $(\dot{X}, y)$, where the base estimator is RF.

    (d) Do the three methods agree on what features are important? Why?

8.2 From exercise 1, generate a new dataset $(\ddot{X}, y)$, where $\ddot{X}$ is a feature union of X and $\dot{X}$.

    (a) Compute MDI, MDA, and SFI feature importance on $(\ddot{X}, y)$, where the base estimator is RF.

    (b) Do the three methods agree on the important features? Why?

8.3 Take the results from exercise 2:

    (a) Drop the most important features according to each method, resulting in a features matrix $\dddot{X}$.

    (b) Compute MDI, MDA, and SFI feature importance on $(\dddot{X}, y)$, where the base estimator is RF.

    (c) Do you appreciate significant changes in the rankings of important features, relative to the results from exercise 2?

8.4 Using the code presented in Section 8.6:

    (a) Generate a dataset (X, y) of 1E6 observations, where 5 features are informative, 5 are redundant and 10 are noise.

    (b) Split (X, y) into 10 datasets $\{(X_i, y_i)\}_{i=1,...,10}$, each of 1E5 observations.

    (c) Compute the parallelized feature importance (Section 8.5), on each of the 10 datasets, $\{(X_i, y_i)\}_{i=1,...,10}$.

    (d) Compute the stacked feature importance on the combined dataset (X, y).

    (e) What causes the discrepancy between the two? Which one is more reliable?

8.5 Repeat all MDI calculations from exercises 1–4, but this time allow for masking effects. That means, do not set max_features=int(1) in Snippet 8.2. How do results differ as a consequence of this change? Why?

REFERENCES

American Statistical Association (2016): "Ethical guidelines for statistical practice." Committee on Professional Ethics of the American Statistical Association (April). Available at http://www.amstat.org/asa/files/pdfs/EthicalGuidelines.pdf.

Belsley, D., E. Kuh, and R. Welsch (1980): *Regression Diagnostics: Identifying Influential Data and Sources of Collinearity*, 1st ed. John Wiley & Sons.

Goldberger, A. (1991): *A Course in Econometrics*. Harvard University Press, 1st edition.

Hill, R. and L. Adkins (2001): "Collinearity." In Baltagi, Badi H. *A Companion to Theoretical Econometrics*, 1st ed. Blackwell, pp. 256–278.

Louppe, G., L. Wehenkel, A. Sutera, and P. Geurts (2013): "Understanding variable importances in forests of randomized trees." Proceedings of the 26th International Conference on Neural Information Processing Systems, pp. 431–439.

Strobl, C., A. Boulesteix, A. Zeileis, and T. Hothorn (2007): "Bias in random forest variable importance measures: Illustrations, sources and a solution." *BMC Bioinformatics*, Vol. 8, No. 25, pp. 1–11.

White, A. and W. Liu (1994): "Technical note: Bias in information-based measures in decision tree induction." *Machine Learning*, Vol. 15, No. 3, pp. 321–329.

CHAPTER 9

Hyper-Parameter Tuning with Cross-Validation

9.1 MOTIVATION

Hyper-parameter tuning is an essential step in fitting an ML algorithm. When this is not done properly, the algorithm is likely to overfit, and live performance will disappoint. The ML literature places special attention on cross-validating any tuned hyper-parameter. As we have seen in Chapter 7, cross-validation (CV) in finance is an especially difficult problem, where solutions from other fields are likely to fail. In this chapter we will discuss how to tune hyper-parameters using the purged k-fold CV method. The references section lists studies that propose alternative methods that may be useful in specific problems.

9.2 GRID SEARCH CROSS-VALIDATION

Grid search cross-validation conducts an exhaustive search for the combination of parameters that maximizes the CV performance, according to some user-defined score function. When we do not know much about the underlying structure of the data, this is a reasonable first approach. Scikit-learn has implemented this logic in the function `GridSearchCV`, which accepts a CV generator as an argument. For the reasons explained in Chapter 7, we need to pass our `PurgedKFold` class (Snippet 7.3) in order to prevent that `GridSearchCV` overfits the ML estimator to leaked information.

SNIPPET 9.1   GRID SEARCH WITH PURGED K-FOLD CROSS-VALIDATION

```
def clfHyperFit(feat,lbl,t1,pipe_clf,param_grid,cv=3,bagging=[0,None,1.],
                n_jobs=-1,pctEmbargo=0,**fit_params):
    if set(lbl.values)=={0,1}:scoring='f1' # f1 for meta-labeling
    else:scoring='neg_log_loss' # symmetric towards all cases
    #1) hyperparameter search, on train data
    inner_cv=PurgedKFold(n_splits=cv,t1=t1,pctEmbargo=pctEmbargo) # purged
    gs=GridSearchCV(estimator=pipe_clf,param_grid=param_grid,
        scoring=scoring,cv=inner_cv,n_jobs=n_jobs,iid=False)
    gs=gs.fit(feat,lbl,**fit_params).best_estimator_ # pipeline
    #2) fit validated model on the entirety of the data
    if bagging[1]>0:
        gs=BaggingClassifier(base_estimator=MyPipeline(gs.steps),
            n_estimators=int(bagging[0]),max_samples=float(bagging[1]),
            max_features=float(bagging[2]),n_jobs=n_jobs)
        gs=gs.fit(feat,lbl,sample_weight=fit_params \
            [gs.base_estimator.steps[-1][0]+'__sample_weight'])
        gs=Pipeline([('bag',gs)])
    return gs
```

Snippet 9.1 lists function `clfHyperFit`, which implements a purged `GridSearchCV`. The argument `fit_params` can be used to pass `sample_weight`, and `param_grid` contains the values that will be combined into a grid. In addition, this function allows for the bagging of the tuned estimator. Bagging an estimator is generally a good idea for the reasons explained in Chapter 6, and the above function incorporates logic to that purpose.

I advise you to use `scoring='f1'` in the context of meta-labeling applications, for the following reason. Suppose a sample with a very large number of negative (i.e., label '0') cases. A classifier that predicts all cases to be negative will achieve high `'accuracy'` or `'neg_log_loss'`, even though it has not learned from the features how to discriminate between cases. In fact, such a model achieves zero recall and undefined precision (see Chapter 3, Section 3.7). The `'f1'` score corrects for that performance inflation by scoring the classifier in terms of precision and recall (see Chapter 14, Section 14.8).

For other (non-meta-labeling) applications, it is fine to use `'accuracy'` or `'neg_log_loss'`, because we are equally interested in predicting all cases. Note that a relabeling of cases has no impact on `'accuracy'` or `'neg_log_loss'`, however it will have an impact on `'f1'`.

This example introduces nicely one limitation of sklearn's `Pipelines`: Their fit method does not expect a `sample_weight` argument. Instead, it expects a `fit_params` keyworded argument. That is a bug that has been reported in GitHub; however, it may take some time to fix it, as it involves rewriting and testing much functionality. Until then, feel free to use the workaround in Snippet 9.2. It creates a new class, called `MyPipeline`, which inherits all methods from sklearn's `Pipeline`. It overwrites the inherited fit method with a new one that handles the argument `sample_weight`, after which it redirects to the parent class.

SNIPPET 9.2   AN ENHANCED PIPELINE CLASS

```
class MyPipeline(Pipeline):
    def fit(self,X,y,sample_weight=None,**fit_params):
        if sample_weight is not None:
            fit_params[self.steps[-1][0]+'__sample_weight']=sample_weight
        return super(MyPipeline,self).fit(X,y,**fit_params)
```

If you are not familiar with this technique for expanding classes, you may want to read this introductory Stackoverflow post: http://stackoverflow.com/questions/576169/understanding-python-super-with-init-methods.

9.3   RANDOMIZED SEARCH CROSS-VALIDATION

For ML algorithms with a large number of parameters, a grid search cross-validation (CV) becomes computationally intractable. In this case, an alternative with good statistical properties is to sample each parameter from a distribution (Begstra et al. [2011, 2012]). This has two benefits: First, we can control for the number of combinations we will search for, regardless of the dimensionality of the problem (the equivalent to a computational budget). Second, having parameters that are relatively irrelevant performance-wise will not substantially increase our search time, as would be the case with grid search CV.

Rather than writing a new function to work with `RandomizedSearchCV`, let us expand Snippet 9.1 to incorporate an option to this purpose. A possible implementation is Snippet 9.3.

SNIPPET 9.3   RANDOMIZED SEARCH WITH PURGED K-FOLD CV

```
def clfHyperFit(feat,lbl,t1,pipe_clf,param_grid,cv=3,bagging=[0,None,1.],
                rndSearchIter=0,n_jobs=-1,pctEmbargo=0,**fit_params):
    if set(lbl.values)=={0,1}:scoring='f1' # f1 for meta-labeling
    else:scoring='neg_log_loss' # symmetric towards all cases
    #1) hyperparameter search, on train data
    inner_cv=PurgedKFold(n_splits=cv,t1=t1,pctEmbargo=pctEmbargo) # purged
    if rndSearchIter==0:
        gs=GridSearchCV(estimator=pipe_clf,param_grid=param_grid,
            scoring=scoring,cv=inner_cv,n_jobs=n_jobs,iid=False)
    else:
```

```
    gs=RandomizedSearchCV(estimator=pipe_clf,param_distributions= \
        param_grid,scoring=scoring,cv=inner_cv,n_jobs=n_jobs,
        iid=False,n_iter=rndSearchIter)
gs=gs.fit(feat,lbl,**fit_params).best_estimator_ # pipeline
#2) fit validated model on the entirety of the data
if bagging[1]>0:
    gs=BaggingClassifier(base_estimator=MyPipeline(gs.steps),
        n_estimators=int(bagging[0]),max_samples=float(bagging[1]),
        max_features=float(bagging[2]),n_jobs=n_jobs)
    gs=gs.fit(feat,lbl,sample_weight=fit_params \
        [gs.base_estimator.steps[-1][0]+'__sample_weight'])
    gs=Pipeline([('bag',gs)])
return gs
```

9.3.1 Log-Uniform Distribution

It is common for some ML algorithms to accept non-negative hyper-parameters only. That is the case of some very popular parameters, such as C in the SVC classifier and gamma in the RBF kernel.[1] We could draw random numbers from a uniform distribution bounded between 0 and some large value, say 100. That would mean that 99% of the values would be expected to be greater than 1. That is not necessarily the most effective way of exploring the feasibility region of parameters whose functions do not respond linearly. For example, an SVC can be as responsive to an increase in C from 0.01 to 1 as to an increase in C from 1 to 100.[2] So sampling C from a $U[0, 100]$ (uniform) distribution will be inefficient. In those instances, it seems more effective to draw values from a distribution where the logarithm of those draws will be distributed uniformly. I call that a "log-uniform distribution," and since I could not find it in the literature, I must define it properly.

A random variable x follows a log-uniform distribution between $a > 0$ and $b > a$ if and only if $\log[x] \sim U\left[\log[a], \log[b]\right]$. This distribution has a CDF:

$$F[x] = \begin{cases} \dfrac{\log[x] - \log[a]}{\log[b] - \log[a]} & \text{for } a \leq x \leq b \\ 0 & \text{for } x < a \\ 1 & \text{for } x > b \end{cases}$$

From this, we derive a PDF:

$$f[x] = \begin{cases} \dfrac{1}{x\log[b/a]} & \text{for } a \leq x \leq b \\ 0 & \text{for } x < a \\ 0 & \text{for } x > b \end{cases}$$

Note that the CDF is invariant to the base of the logarithm, since $\dfrac{\log\left[\frac{x}{a}\right]}{\log\left[\frac{b}{a}\right]} = \dfrac{\log_c\left[\frac{x}{a}\right]}{\log_c\left[\frac{b}{a}\right]}$ for any base c, thus the random variable is not a function of c. Snippet 9.4 implements

---

[1] http://scikit-learn.org/stable/modules/metrics.html.
[2] http://scikit-learn.org/stable/auto_examples/svm/plot_rbf_parameters.html.

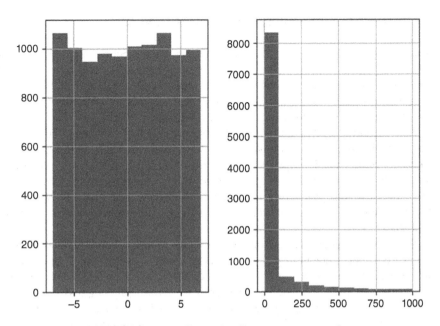

FIGURE 9.1 Result from testing the `logUniform_gen` class

(and tests) in `scipy.stats` a random variable where $[a, b] = [1E-3, 1E3]$, hence $\log[x] \sim U\left[\log[1E-3], \log[1E3]\right]$. Figure 9.1 illustrates the uniformity of the samples in log-scale.

SNIPPET 9.4 THE `logUniform_gen` CLASS

```
import numpy as np,pandas as pd,matplotlib.pyplot as mpl
from scipy.stats import rv_continuous,kstest
#————————————————————————————————
class logUniform_gen(rv_continuous):
    # random numbers log-uniformly distributed between 1 and e
    def _cdf(self,x):
        return np.log(x/self.a)/np.log(self.b/self.a)
def logUniform(a=1,b=np.exp(1)):return logUniform_gen(a=a,b=b,name='logUniform')
#————————————————————————————————
a,b,size=1E-3,1E3,10000
vals=logUniform(a=a,b=b).rvs(size=size)
print kstest(rvs=np.log(vals),cdf='uniform',args=(np.log(a),np.log(b/a)),N=size)
print pd.Series(vals).describe()
mpl.subplot(121)
pd.Series(np.log(vals)).hist()
mpl.subplot(122)
pd.Series(vals).hist()
mpl.show()
```

9.4   SCORING AND HYPER-PARAMETER TUNING

Snippets 9.1 and 9.3 set `scoring='f1'` for meta-labeling applications. For other applications, they set `scoring='neg_log_loss'` rather than the standard `scoring='accuracy'`. Although accuracy has a more intuitive interpretation, I suggest that you use `neg_log_loss` when you are tuning hyper-parameters for an investment strategy. Let me explain my reasoning.

Suppose that your ML investment strategy predicts that you should buy a security, with high probability. You will enter a large long position, as a function of the strategy's confidence. If the prediction was erroneous, and the market sells off instead, you will lose a lot of money. And yet, accuracy accounts equally for an erroneous buy prediction with high probability and for an erroneous buy prediction with low probability. Moreover, accuracy can offset a miss with high probability with a hit with low probability.

Investment strategies profit from predicting the right label with high confidence. Gains from good predictions with low confidence will not suffice to offset the losses from bad predictions with high confidence. For this reason, accuracy does not provide a realistic scoring of the classifier's performance. Conversely, log loss[3] (aka cross-entropy loss) computes the log-likelihood of the classifier given the true label, which takes predictions' probabilities into account. Log loss can be estimated as follows:

$$L[Y,P] = -\log\left[\text{Prob}\left[Y\,|P\right]\right] = -N^{-1}\sum_{n=0}^{N-1}\sum_{k=0}^{K-1} y_{n,k}\log\left[p_{n,k}\right]$$

where

- $p_{n,k}$ is the probability associated with prediction n of label k.
- Y is a 1-of-K binary indicator matrix, such that $y_{n,k} = 1$ when observation n was assigned label k out of K possible labels, and 0 otherwise.

Suppose that a classifier predicts two 1s, where the true labels are 1 and 0. The first prediction is a hit and the second prediction is a miss, thus accuracy is 50%. Figure 9.2 plots the cross-entropy loss when these predictions come from probabilities ranging [0.5, 0.9]. One can observe that on the right side of the figure, log loss is large due to misses with high probability, even though the accuracy is 50% in all cases.

There is a second reason to prefer cross-entropy loss over accuracy. CV scores a classifier by applying sample weights (see Chapter 7, Section 7.5). As you may recall from Chapter 4, observation weights were determined as a function of the observation's absolute return. The implication is that sample weighted cross-entropy loss estimates the classifier's performance in terms of variables involved in a PnL (mark-to-market profit and losses) calculation: It uses the correct label for the side, probability for the position size, and sample weight for the observation's return/outcome. That

---

[3] http://scikit-learn.org/stable/modules/model_evaluation.html#log-loss.

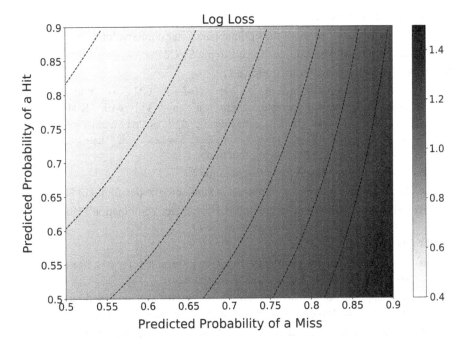

FIGURE 9.2 Log loss as a function of predicted probabilities of hit and miss

is the right ML performance metric for hyper-parameter tuning of financial applications, not accuracy.

When we use log loss as a scoring statistic, we often prefer to change its sign, hence referring to "neg log loss." The reason for this change is cosmetic, driven by intuition: A high neg log loss value is preferred to a low neg log loss value, just as with accuracy. Keep in mind this sklearn bug when you use `neg_log_loss`: https://github.com/scikit-learn/scikit-learn/issues/9144. To circumvent this bug, you should use the `cvScore` function presented in Chapter 7.

EXERCISES

9.1 Using the function `getTestData` from Chapter 8, form a synthetic dataset of 10,000 observations with 10 features, where 5 are informative and 5 are noise.
   (a) Use `GridSearchCV` on 10-fold CV to find the `C`, `gamma` optimal hyper-parameters on a SVC with RBF kernel, where `param_grid={'C':[1E-2,1E-1,1,10,100],'gamma':[1E-2,1E-1,1,10,100]}` and the scoring function is `neg_log_loss`.
   (b) How many nodes are there in the grid?
   (c) How many fits did it take to find the optimal solution?
   (d) How long did it take to find this solution?

(e) How can you access the optimal result?

(f) What is the CV score of the optimal parameter combination?

(g) How can you pass sample weights to the SVC?

9.2 Using the same dataset from exercise 1,

(a) Use `RandomizedSearchCV` on 10-fold CV to find the `C`, `gamma` optimal hyper-parameters on an SVC with RBF kernel, where `param_distributions = {'C':logUniform(a=1E-2,b=1E2),'gamma':logUniform(a=1E-2,b=1E2)},n_iter=25` and `neg_log_loss` is the scoring function.

(b) How long did it take to find this solution?

(c) Is the optimal parameter combination similar to the one found in exercise 1?

(d) What is the CV score of the optimal parameter combination? How does it compare to the CV score from exercise 1?

9.3 From exercise 1,

(a) Compute the Sharpe ratio of the resulting in-sample forecasts, from point 1.a (see Chapter 14 for a definition of Sharpe ratio).

(b) Repeat point 1.a, this time with `accuracy` as the scoring function. Compute the in-sample forecasts derived from the hyper-tuned parameters.

(c) What scoring method leads to higher (in-sample) Sharpe ratio?

9.4 From exercise 2,

(a) Compute the Sharpe ratio of the resulting in-sample forecasts, from point 2.a.

(b) Repeat point 2.a, this time with `accuracy` as the scoring function. Compute the in-sample forecasts derived from the hyper-tuned parameters.

(c) What scoring method leads to higher (in-sample) Sharpe ratio?

9.5 Read the definition of log loss, $L[Y,P]$.

(a) Why is the scoring function `neg_log_loss` defined as the negative log loss, $-L[Y,P]$?

(b) What would be the outcome of maximizing the log loss, rather than the negative log loss?

9.6 Consider an investment strategy that sizes its bets equally, regardless of the forecast's confidence. In this case, what is a more appropriate scoring function for hyper-parameter tuning, accuracy or cross-entropy loss?

REFERENCES

Bergstra, J., R. Bardenet, Y. Bengio, and B. Kegl (2011): "Algorithms for hyper-parameter optimization." *Advances in Neural Information Processing Systems*, pp. 2546–2554.

Bergstra, J. and Y. Bengio (2012): "Random search for hyper-parameter optimization." *Journal of Machine Learning Research*, Vol. 13, pp. 281–305.

BIBLIOGRAPHY

Chapelle, O., V. Vapnik, O. Bousquet, and S. Mukherjee (2002): "Choosing multiple parameters for support vector machines." *Machine Learning*, Vol. 46, pp. 131–159.

Chuong, B., C. Foo, and A. Ng (2008): "Efficient multiple hyperparameter learning for log-linear models." *Advances in Neural Information Processing Systems*, Vol. 20. Available at http://ai.stanford.edu/~chuongdo/papers/learn_reg.pdf.

Gorissen, D., K. Crombecq, I. Couckuyt, P. Demeester, and T. Dhaene (2010): "A surrogate modeling and adaptive sampling toolbox for computer based design." *Journal of Machine Learning Research*, Vol. 11, pp. 2051–2055.

Hsu, C., C. Chang, and C. Lin (2010): "A practical guide to support vector classification." Technical report, National Taiwan University.

Hutter, F., H. Hoos, and K. Leyton-Brown (2011): "Sequential model-based optimization for general algorithm configuration." Proceedings of the 5th international conference on Learning and Intelligent Optimization, pp. 507–523.

Larsen, J., L. Hansen, C. Svarer, and M. Ohlsson (1996): "Design and regularization of neural networks: The optimal use of a validation set." Proceedings of the 1996 IEEE Signal Processing Society Workshop.

Maclaurin, D., D. Duvenaud, and R. Adams (2015): "Gradient-based hyperparameter optimization through reversible learning." Working paper. Available at https://arxiv.org/abs/1502.03492.

Martinez-Cantin, R. (2014): "BayesOpt: A Bayesian optimization library for nonlinear optimization, experimental design and bandits." *Journal of Machine Learning Research*, Vol. 15, pp. 3915–3919.

PART 3

Backtesting

CHAPTER 10

Bet Sizing

10.1 MOTIVATION

There are fascinating parallels between strategy games and investing. Some of the best portfolio managers I have worked with are excellent poker players, perhaps more so than chess players. One reason is bet sizing, for which Texas Hold'em provides a great analogue and training ground. Your ML algorithm can achieve high accuracy, but if you do not size your bets properly, your investment strategy will inevitably lose money. In this chapter we will review a few approaches to size bets from ML predictions.

10.2 STRATEGY-INDEPENDENT BET SIZING APPROACHES

Consider two strategies on the same instrument. Let $m_{i,t} \in [-1, 1]$ be the bet size of strategy i at time t, where $m_{i,t} = -1$ indicates a full short position and $m_{i,t} = 1$ indicates a full long position. Suppose that one strategy produced a sequence of bet sizes $[m_{1,1}, m_{1,2}, m_{1,3}] = [.5, 1, 0]$, as the market price followed a sequence $[p_1, p_2, p_3] = [1, .5, 1.25]$, where p_t is the price at time t. The other strategy produced a sequence $[m_{2,1}, m_{2,2}, m_{2,3}] = [1, .5, 0]$, as it was forced to reduce its bet size once the market moved against the initial full position. Both strategies produced forecasts that turned out to be correct (the price increased by 25% between p_1 and p_3), however the first strategy made money (0.5) while the second strategy lost money (−.125).

We would prefer to size positions in such way that we reserve some cash for the possibility that the trading signal strengthens before it weakens. One option is to compute the series $c_t = c_{t,l} - c_{t,s}$, where $c_{t,l}$ is the number of concurrent long bets at time t, and $c_{t,s}$ is the number of concurrent short bets at time t. This bet concurrency is derived, for each side, similarly to how we computed label concurrency in Chapter 4 (recall the t1 object, with overlapping time spans). We fit a mixture of two Gaussians on $\{c_t\}$, applying a method like the one described in López de Prado and Foreman [2014]. Then, the bet size is derived as

$$
m_t = \begin{cases} \dfrac{F[c_t] - F[0]}{1 - F[0]} & \text{if } c_t \geq 0 \\[3mm] \dfrac{F[c_t] - F[0]}{F[0]} & \text{if } c_t < 0 \end{cases}
$$

where $F[x]$ is the CDF of the fitted mixture of two Gaussians for a value x. For example, we could size the bet as 0.9 when the probability of observing a signal of greater value is only 0.1. The stronger the signal, the smaller the probability that the signal becomes even stronger, hence the greater the bet size.

A second solution is to follow a budgeting approach. We compute the maximum number (or some other quantile) of concurrent long bets, $\max_i\{c_{i,l}\}$, and the maximum number of concurrent short bets, $\max_i\{c_{i,s}\}$. Then we derive the bet size as $m_t = c_{t,l}\dfrac{1}{\max_i\{c_{i,l}\}} - c_{t,s}\dfrac{1}{\max_i\{c_{i,s}\}}$, where $c_{t,l}$ is the number of concurrent long bets at time t, and $c_{t,s}$ is the number of concurrent short bets at time t. The goal is that the maximum position is not reached before the last concurrent signal is triggered.

A third approach is to apply meta-labeling, as we explained in Chapter 3. We fit a classifier, such as an SVC or RF, to determine the probability of misclassification, and use that probability to derive the bet size. [1] This approach has a couple of advantages: First, the ML algorithm that decides the bet sizes is independent of the primary model, allowing for the incorporation of features predictive of false positives (see Chapter 3). Second, the predicted probability can be directly translated into bet size. Let us see how.

10.3 BET SIZING FROM PREDICTED PROBABILITIES

Let us denote $p[x]$ the probability that label x takes place. For two possible outcomes, $x \in \{-1, 1\}$, we would like to test the null hypothesis $H_0 : p[x = 1] = \frac{1}{2}$. We compute the test statistic $z = \dfrac{p[x=1] - \frac{1}{2}}{\sqrt{p[x=1](1 - p[x=1])}} = \dfrac{2p[x=1] - 1}{2\sqrt{p[x=1](1 - p[x=1])}} \sim Z$, with $z \in (-\infty, +\infty)$ and where Z represents the standard Normal distribution. We derive the bet size as $m = 2Z[z] - 1$, where $m \in [-1, 1]$ and $Z[.]$ is the CDF of Z.

For more than two possible outcomes, we follow a one-versus-rest method. Let $X = \{-1, \ldots, 0, \ldots, 1\}$ be various labels associated with bet sizes, and $x \in X$ the predicted label. In other words, the label is identified by the bet size associated with it. For each label $i = 1, \ldots, \|X\|$, we estimate a probability p_i, with $\sum_{i=1}^{\|X\|} p_i = 1$. We define

---

[1] The references section lists a number of articles that explain how these probabilities are derived. Usually these probabilities incorporate information about the goodness of the fit, or confidence in the prediction. See Wu et al. [2004], and visit http://scikit-learn.org/stable/modules/svm.html#scores-and-probabilities.

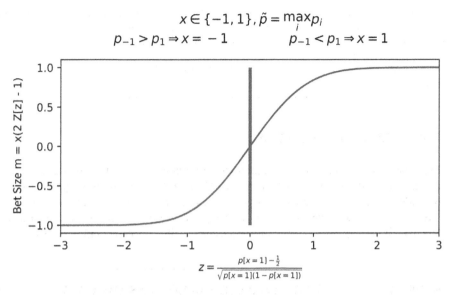

FIGURE 10.1   Bet size from predicted probabilities

$\tilde{p} = \max_i\{p_i\}$ as the probability of x, and we would like to test for $H_0 : \tilde{p} = \frac{1}{\|X\|}$.[2] We compute the test statistic $z = \frac{\tilde{p}-\frac{1}{\|X\|}}{\sqrt{\tilde{p}(1-\tilde{p})}} \sim Z$, with $z \in [0 , +\infty)$. We derive the bet size as $m = x\,\underbrace{(2Z\,[z] - 1)}_{\in[0,1]}$, where $m \in [-1, 1]$ and $Z\,[z]$ regulates the size for a prediction x (where the side is implied by x).

Figure 10.1 plots the bet size as a function of test statistic. Snippet 10.1 implements the translation from probabilities to bet size. It handles the possibility that the prediction comes from a meta-labeling estimator, as well from a standard labeling estimator. In step #2, it also averages active bets, and discretizes the final value, which we will explain in the following sections.

SNIPPET 10.1   FROM PROBABILITIES TO BET SIZE

```
def getSignal(events,stepSize,prob,pred,numClasses,numThreads,**kargs):
    # get signals from predictions
    if prob.shape[0]==0:return pd.Series()
    #1) generate signals from multinomial classification (one-vs-rest, OvR)
    signal0=(prob-1./numClasses)/(prob*(1.-prob))**.5 # t-value of OvR
    signal0=pred*(2*norm.cdf(signal0)-1) # signal=side*size
```

---

[2] Uncertainty is absolute when all outcomes are equally likely.

```
if 'side' in events:signal0*=events.loc[signal0.index,'side'] # meta-labeling
#2) compute average signal among those concurrently open
df0=signal0.to_frame('signal').join(events[['t1']],how='left')
df0=avgActiveSignals(df0,numThreads)
signal1=discreteSignal(signal0=df0,stepSize=stepSize)
return signal1
```

10.4 AVERAGING ACTIVE BETS

Every bet is associated with a holding period, spanning from the time it originated to the time the first barrier is touched, t1 (see Chapter 3). One possible approach is to override an old bet as a new bet arrives; however, that is likely to lead to excessive turnover. A more sensible approach is to average all sizes across all bets still active at a given point in time. Snippet 10.2 illustrates one possible implementation of this idea.

SNIPPET 10.2 BETS ARE AVERAGED AS LONG AS THEY ARE STILL ACTIVE

```
def avgActiveSignals(signals,numThreads):
    # compute the average signal among those active
    #1) time points where signals change (either one starts or one ends)
    tPnts=set(signals['t1'].dropna().values)
    tPnts=tPnts.union(signals.index.values)
    tPnts=list(tPnts);tPnts.sort()
    out=mpPandasObj(mpAvgActiveSignals,('molecule',tPnts),numThreads,signals=signals)
    return out
#————————————————————————————————————————
def mpAvgActiveSignals(signals,molecule):
    '''
    At time loc, average signal among those still active.
    Signal is active if:
        a) issued before or at loc AND
        b) loc before signal's endtime, or endtime is still unknown (NaT).
    '''
    out=pd.Series()
    for loc in molecule:
        df0=(signals.index.values<=loc)&((loc<signals['t1'])|pd.isnull(signals['t1']))
        act=signals[df0].index
        if len(act)>0:out[loc]=signals.loc[act,'signal'].mean()
        else:out[loc]=0 # no signals active at this time
    return out
```

10.5 SIZE DISCRETIZATION

Averaging reduces some of the excess turnover, but still it is likely that small trades will be triggered with every prediction. As this jitter would cause unnecessary

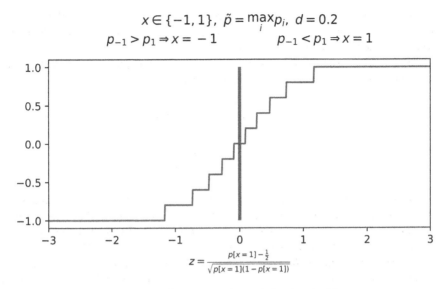

$$x \in \{-1, 1\}, \quad \tilde{p} = \max_i p_i, \quad d = 0.2$$
$$p_{-1} > p_1 \Rightarrow x = -1 \qquad\qquad p_{-1} < p_1 \Rightarrow x = 1$$

$$z = \frac{p[x=1] - \frac{1}{2}}{\sqrt{p[x=1](1 - p[x=1])}}$$

FIGURE 10.2   Discretization of the bet size, $d = 0.2$

overtrading, I suggest you discretize the bet size as $m^* = \text{round}\left[\frac{m}{d}\right] d$, where $d \in$ (0, 1] determines the degree of discretization. Figure 10.2 illustrates the discretization of the bet size. Snippet 10.3 implements this notion.

SNIPPET 10.3   SIZE DISCRETIZATION TO PREVENT OVERTRADING

```
def discreteSignal(signal0,stepSize):
    # discretize signal
    signal1=(signal0/stepSize).round()*stepSize # discretize
    signal1[signal1>1]=1 # cap
    signal1[signal1<-1]=-1 # floor
    return signal1
```

10.6   DYNAMIC BET SIZES AND LIMIT PRICES

Recall the triple-barrier labeling method presented in Chapter 3. Bar i is formed at time $t_{i,0}$, at which point we forecast the first barrier that will be touched. That prediction implies a forecasted price, $E_{t_{i,0}}[p_{t_{i,1}}]$, consistent with the barriers' settings. In the period elapsed until the outcome takes place, $t \in [t_{i,0}, t_{i,1}]$, the price p_t fluctuates and additional forecasts may be formed, $E_{t_{j,0}}[p_{t_{i,1}}]$, where $j \in [i+1, I]$ and $t_{j,0} \leq t_{i,1}$. In Sections 10.4 and 10.5 we discussed methods for averaging the active bets and discretizing the bet size as new forecasts are formed. In this section we will introduce an approach to adjust bet sizes as market price p_t and forecast price f_i fluctuate. In the process, we will derive the order's limit price.

Let q_t be the current position, Q the maximum absolute position size, and $\hat{q}_{i,t}$ the target position size associated with forecast f_i, such that

$$\hat{q}_{i,t} = \text{int}[m[\omega, f_i - p_t]Q]$$

$$m[\omega, x] = \frac{x}{\sqrt{\omega + x^2}}$$

where $m[\omega, x]$ is the bet size, $x = f_i - p_t$ is the divergence between the current market price and the forecast, ω is a coefficient that regulates the width of the sigmoid function, and $\text{Int}[x]$ is the integer value of x. Note that for a real-valued price divergence x, $-1 < m[\omega, x] < 1$, the integer value $\hat{q}_{i,t}$ is bounded $-Q < \hat{q}_{i,t} < Q$.

The target position size $\hat{q}_{i,t}$ can be dynamically adjusted as p_t changes. In particular, as $p_t \to f_i$ we get $\hat{q}_{i,t} \to 0$, because the algorithm wants to realize the gains. This implies a breakeven limit price $\bar{p}$ for the order size $\hat{q}_{i,t} - q_t$, to avoid realizing losses. In particular,

$$\bar{p} = \frac{1}{|\hat{q}_{i,t} - q_t|} \sum_{j=|q_t+\text{sgn}[\hat{q}_{i,t}-q_t]|}^{|\hat{q}_{i,t}|} L\left[f_i, \omega, \frac{j}{Q}\right]$$

where $L[f_i, \omega, m]$ is the inverse function of $m[\omega, f_i - p_t]$ with respect to p_t,

$$L[f_i, \omega, m] = f_i - m\sqrt{\frac{\omega}{1 - m^2}}$$

We do not need to worry about the case $m^2 = 1$, because $|\hat{q}_{i,t}| < 1$. Since this function is monotonic, the algorithm cannot realize losses as $p_t \to f_i$.

Let us calibrate ω. Given a user-defined pair (x, m^*), such that $x = f_i - p_t$ and $m^* = m[\omega, x]$, the inverse function of $m[\omega, x]$ with respect to ω is

$$\omega = x^2(m^{*-2} - 1)$$

Snippet 10.4 implements the algorithm that computes the dynamic position size and limit prices as a function of p_t and f_i. First, we calibrate the sigmoid function, so that it returns a bet size of $m^* = .95$ for a price divergence of $x = 10$. Second, we compute the target position $\hat{q}_{i,t}$ for a maximum position $Q = 100, f_i = 115$ and $p_t = 100$. If you try $f_i = 110$, you will get $\hat{q}_{i,t} = 95$, consistent with the calibration of ω. Third, the limit price for this order of size $\hat{q}_{i,t} - q_t = 97$ is $p_t < 112.3657 < f_i$, which is between the current price and the forecasted price.

SNIPPET 10.4 DYNAMIC POSITION SIZE AND LIMIT PRICE

```
def betSize(w,x):
    return x*(w+x**2)**-.5
#————————————————————————————————
def getTPos(w,f,mP,maxPos):
    return int(betSize(w,f-mP)*maxPos)
#————————————————————————————————
def invPrice(f,w,m):
    return f-m*(w/(1-m**2))**.5
#————————————————————————————————
def limitPrice(tPos,pos,f,w,maxPos):
    sgn=(1 if tPos>=pos else -1)
    lP=0
    for j in xrange(abs(pos+sgn),abs(tPos+1)):
        lP+=invPrice(f,w,j/float(maxPos))
    lP/=tPos-pos
    return lP
#————————————————————————————————
def getW(x,m):
  # 0<alpha<1
    return x**2*(m**-2-1)
#————————————————————————————————
def main():
    pos,maxPos,mP,f,wParams=0,100,100,115,{'divergence':10,'m':.95}
    w=getW(wParams['divergence'],wParams['m']) # calibrate w
    tPos=getTPos(w,f,mP,maxPos) # get tPos
    lP=limitPrice(tPos,pos,f,w,maxPos) # limit price for order
    return
#————————————————————————————————
if __name__=='__main__':main()
```

As an alternative to the sigmoid function, we could have used a power function $\tilde{m}[\omega,x] = \mathrm{sgn}[x]\,|x|^{\omega}$, where $\omega \geq 0$, $x \in [-1,1]$, which results in $\tilde{m}[\omega,x] \in [-1,1]$. This alternative presents the advantages that:

- $\tilde{m}[\omega,-1] = -1$, $\tilde{m}[\omega,1] = 1$.
- Curvature can be directly manipulated through ω.
- For $\omega > 1$, the function goes from concave to convex, rather than the other way around, hence the function is almost flat around the inflexion point.

We leave the derivation of the equations for a power function as an exercise. Figure 10.3 plots the bet sizes (y-axis) as a function of price divergence $f - p_t$ (x-axis) for both the sigmoid and power functions.

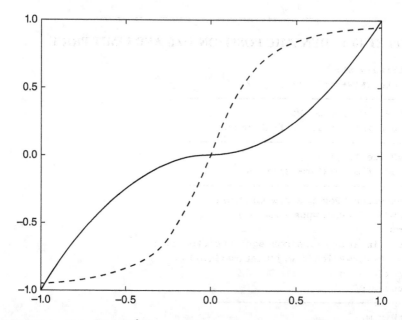

FIGURE 10.3 $f[x] = sgn[x]|x|^2$ (concave to convex) and $f[x] = x(.1 + x^2)^{-.5}$ (convex to concave)

EXERCISES

10.1 Using the formulation in Section 10.3, plot the bet size (m) as a function of the maximum predicted probability ($\tilde{p}$) when $\|X\| = 2, 3, \dots, 10$.

10.2 Draw 10,000 random numbers from a uniform distribution with bounds $U[.5, 1.]$.

    (a) Compute the bet sizes m for $\|X\| = 2$.

    (b) Assign 10,000 consecutive calendar days to the bet sizes.

    (c) Draw 10,000 random numbers from a uniform distribution with bounds $U[1, 25]$.

    (d) Form a pandas series indexed by the dates in 2.b, and with values equal to the index shifted forward the number of days in 2.c. This is a `t1` object similar to the ones we used in Chapter 3.

    (e) Compute the resulting average active bets, following Section 10.4.

10.3 Using the `t1` object from exercise 2.d:

    (a) Determine the maximum number of concurrent long bets, $\bar{c}_l$.

    (b) Determine the maximum number of concurrent short bets, $\bar{c}_s$.

    (c) Derive the bet size as $m_t = c_{t,l}\frac{1}{\bar{c}_l} - c_{t,s}\frac{1}{\bar{c}_s}$, where $c_{t,l}$ is the number of concurrent long bets at time t, and $c_{t,s}$ is the number of concurrent short bets at time t.

10.4 Using the `t1` object from exercise 2.d:

    (a) Compute the series $c_t = c_{t,l} - c_{t,s}$, where $c_{t,l}$ is the number of concurrent long bets at time t, and $c_{t,s}$ is the number of concurrent short bets at time t.

    (b) Fit a mixture of two Gaussians on $\{c_t\}$. You may want to use the method described in López de Prado and Foreman [2014].

    (c) Derive the bet size as $m_t = \begin{cases} \frac{F[c_t]-F[0]}{1-F[0]} & \text{if } c_t \geq 0 \\ \frac{F[c_t]-F[0]}{F[0]} & \text{if } c_t < 0 \end{cases}$, where $F[x]$ is the CDF of the fitted mixture of two Gaussians for a value x.

    (d) Explain how this series $\{m_t\}$ differ from the bet size series computed in exercise 3.

10.5 Repeat exercise 1, where you discretize m with a `stepSize=.01`, `stepSize=.05`, and `stepSize=.1`.

10.6 Rewrite the equations in Section 10.6, so that the bet size is determined by a power function rather than a sigmoid function.

10.7 Modify Snippet 10.4 so that it implements the equations you derived in exercise 6.

REFERENCES

López de Prado, M. and M. Foreman (2014): "A mixture of Gaussians approach to mathematical portfolio oversight: The EF3M algorithm." *Quantitative Finance*, Vol. 14, No. 5, pp. 913–930.

Wu, T., C. Lin and R. Weng (2004): "Probability estimates for multi-class classification by pairwise coupling." *Journal of Machine Learning Research*, Vol. 5, pp. 975–1005.

BIBLIOGRAPHY

Allwein, E., R. Schapire, and Y. Singer (2001): "Reducing multiclass to binary: A unifying approach for margin classifiers." *Journal of Machine Learning Research*, Vol. 1, pp. 113–141.

Hastie, T. and R. Tibshirani (1998): "Classification by pairwise coupling." *The Annals of Statistics*, Vol. 26, No. 1, pp. 451–471.

Refregier, P. and F. Vallet (1991): "Probabilistic approach for multiclass classification with neural networks." Proceedings of International Conference on Artificial Networks, pp. 1003–1007.

BIBLIOGRAPHY

18.4 Using the results from exercise 2.1

(a) Compute the ratio $c_i = \sigma_i / \sigma_{p,i}$, where $c_{p,i}$ is the number of concurrent long, below a time t, and σ_i is the number of concurrent short below a time t.

(b) The variance of predictions based on [a]. You may want to use the method described in López de Prado and Friedman [2014].

(c) Derive the value as $\sigma \to \infty$, where $A[x]$ is the CDF

$$
\begin{cases}
\dfrac{d \log[x]}{d x} & \text{if } x \geq 0 \\[2ex]
\dfrac{d \log[x]}{d x} & \text{if } x < 0
\end{cases}
$$

of the fitted mixture of two Gaussians for a given value x.

(d) Right, now this series for x defines both the pdf and zeros computed in exercise 1.

18.5 Repeat exercise 1, where you instantiate n with a series case $x_1, x_2, \ldots, x_{25}$, and outputs x_{26}, and outputs $x_{26}, \ldots, x_{50}$.

18.6 Rewrite the equations in Section 18.6, so that the bet size is determined by a power function rather than a logistic function.

18.7 Modify Snippet 18.4 so that it implements the equations you derived in exercise 1.

REFERENCES

López de Prado, M., and M. Foreman (2014). "A mixture of Gaussians approach to mathematical of portfolio oversight: The EF3M algorithm," *Quantitative Finance*, Vol. 14, No. 5, pp. 913–930.

Wu, T., C.-J. Lin and F. Weng (2006). "Probability estimation for multi-class classification by pairwise coupling," *Journal of Machine Learning Research*, Vol. 5, pp. 975–1005.

BIBLIOGRAPHY

Chang, C.-J., R. Scheiple, and R. Singer (2000). "Reducing misclassifies to binary: A unifying approach for margin classifiers," *Journal of Machine Learning Research*, Vol. 1, pp. 113–141.

Hastie, T., and R. Tibshirani (1998). "Classification by pairwise coupling," *Annals of Statistics*, Vol. 26, No. 1, pp. 451–471.

Refregier, P. and F. Vallet (1991). "Probabilistic approach for multiclass classification with neural networks," *Proceedings of International Conference on Artificial Networks*, pp. 1003–1007.

CHAPTER 11

The Dangers of Backtesting

11.1 MOTIVATION

Backtesting is one of the most essential, and yet least understood, techniques in the quant arsenal. A common misunderstanding is to think of backtesting as a research tool. Researching and backtesting is like drinking and driving. Do not research under the influence of a backtest. Most backtests published in journals are flawed, as the result of selection bias on multiple tests (Bailey, Borwein, López de Prado, and Zhu [2014]; Harvey et al. [2016]). A full book could be written listing all the different errors people make while backtesting. I may be the academic author with the largest number of journal articles on backtesting[1] and investment performance metrics, and still I do not feel I would have the stamina to compile all the different errors I have seen over the past 20 years. This chapter is not a crash course on backtesting, but a short list of some of the common errors that even seasoned professionals make.

11.2 MISSION IMPOSSIBLE: THE FLAWLESS BACKTEST

In its narrowest definition, a backtest is a historical simulation of how a strategy would have performed should it have been run over a past period of time. As such, it is a hypothetical, and by no means an experiment. At a physics laboratory, like Berkeley Lab, we can repeat an experiment while controlling for environmental variables, in order to deduce a precise cause-effect relationship. In contrast, a backtest is *not* an experiment, and it does not prove anything. A backtest guarantees nothing, not even achieving that Sharpe ratio if we could travel back in time in our retrofitted DeLorean DMC-12 (Bailey and López de Prado [2012]). Random draws would have been different. The past would not repeat itself.

---

[1] http://papers.ssrn.com/sol3/cf_dev/AbsByAuth.cfm?per_id=434076; http://www.QuantResearch.org/.

What is the point of a backtest then? It is a sanity check on a number of variables, including bet sizing, turnover, resilience to costs, and behavior under a given scenario. A good backtest can be extremely helpful, but backtesting well is extremely hard. In 2014 a team of quants at Deutsche Bank, led by Yin Luo, published a study under the title "Seven Sins of Quantitative Investing" (Luo et al. [2014]). It is a very graphic and accessible piece that I would advise everyone in this business to read carefully. In it, this team mentions the usual suspects:

1. **Survivorship bias:** Using as investment universe the current one, hence ignoring that some companies went bankrupt and securities were delisted along the way.

2. **Look-ahead bias:** Using information that was not public at the moment the simulated decision would have been made. Be certain about the timestamp for each data point. Take into account release dates, distribution delays, and backfill corrections.

3. **Storytelling:** Making up a story *ex-post* to justify some random pattern.

4. **Data mining and data snooping:** Training the model on the testing set.

5. **Transaction costs:** Simulating transaction costs is hard because the only way to be certain about that cost would have been to interact with the trading book (i.e., to do the actual trade).

6. **Outliers:** Basing a strategy on a few extreme outcomes that may never happen again as observed in the past.

7. **Shorting:** Taking a short position on cash products requires finding a lender. The cost of lending and the amount available is generally unknown, and depends on relations, inventory, relative demand, etc.

These are just a few basic errors that most papers published in journals make routinely. Other common errors include computing performance using a non-standard method (Chapter 14); ignoring hidden risks; focusing only on returns while ignoring other metrics; confusing correlation with causation; selecting an unrepresentative time period; failing to expect the unexpected; ignoring the existence of stop-out limits or margin calls; ignoring funding costs; and forgetting practical aspects (Sarfati [2015]). There are many more, but really, there is no point in listing them, because of the title of the next section.

11.3 EVEN IF YOUR BACKTEST IS FLAWLESS, IT IS PROBABLY WRONG

Congratulations! Your backtest is flawless in the sense that everyone can reproduce your results, and your assumptions are so conservative that not even your boss could object to them. You have paid for every trade more than double what anyone could possibly ask. You have executed hours after the information was known by half the globe, at a ridiculously low volume participation rate. Despite all these egregious costs, your backtest still makes a lot of money. Yet, this flawless backtest is probably wrong. Why? Because only an expert can produce a flawless backtest. Becoming an expert means that you have run tens of thousands of backtests over the years. In conclusion, this is not the first backtest you produce, so we need to account for the possibility that this is a false discovery, a statistical fluke that inevitably comes up after you run multiple tests on the same dataset.

The maddening thing about backtesting is that, the better you become at it, the more likely false discoveries will pop up. Beginners fall for the seven sins of Luo et al. [2014] (there are more, but who's counting?). Professionals may produce flawless backtests, and will still fall for multiple testing, selection bias, or backtest overfitting (Bailey and López de Prado [2014b]).

11.4   BACKTESTING IS NOT A RESEARCH TOOL

Chapter 8 discussed substitution effects, joint effects, masking, MDI, MDA, SFI, parallelized features, stacked features, etc. Even if some features are very important, it does not mean that they can be monetized through an investment strategy. Conversely, there are plenty of strategies that will appear to be profitable even though they are based on irrelevant features. Feature importance is a true research tool, because it helps us understand the nature of the patterns uncovered by the ML algorithm, regardless of their monetization. Critically, feature importance is derived *ex-ante*, before the historical performance is simulated.

In contrast, a backtest is not a research tool. It provides us with very little insight into the reason why a particular strategy would have made money. Just as a lottery winner may feel he has done something to deserve his luck, there is always some *ex-post* story (Luo's sin number three). Authors claim to have found hundreds of "alphas" and "factors," and there is always some convoluted explanation for them. Instead, what they have found are the lottery tickets that won the last game. The winner has cashed out, and those numbers are useless for the next round. If you would not pay extra for those lottery tickets, why would you care about those hundreds of alphas? Those authors never tell us about all the tickets that were sold, that is, the millions of simulations it took to find these "lucky" alphas.

The purpose of a backtest is to discard bad models, not to improve them. Adjusting your model based on the backtest results is a waste of time . . . and it's dangerous. Invest your time and effort in getting all the components right, as we've discussed elsewhere in the book: structured data, labeling, weighting, ensembles, cross-validation, feature importance, bet sizing, etc. By the time you are backtesting, it is too late. Never backtest until your model has been fully specified. If the backtest fails, start all over. If you do that, the chances of finding a false discovery will drop substantially, but still they will not be zero.

11.5   A FEW GENERAL RECOMMENDATIONS

Backtest overfitting can be defined as selection bias on multiple backtests. Backtest overfitting takes place when a strategy is developed to perform well on a backtest, by monetizing random historical patterns. Because those random patterns are unlikely to occur again in the future, the strategy so developed will fail. Every backtested strategy is overfit to some extent as a result of "selection bias": The only backtests that most people share are those that portray supposedly winning investment strategies.

How to address backtest overfitting is arguably the most fundamental question in quantitative finance. Why? Because if there was an easy answer to this question, investment firms would achieve high performance with certainty, as they would invest only in winning backtests. Journals would assess with confidence whether a strategy may be a false positive. Finance could become a true science in the Popperian and Lakatosian sense (López de Prado [2017]). What makes backtest overfitting so hard to assess is that the probability of false positives changes with every new test conducted on the same dataset, and that information is either unknown by the researcher or not shared with investors or referees. While there is no easy way to prevent overfitting, a number of steps can help reduce its presence.

1. Develop models for entire asset classes or investment universes, rather than for specific securities (Chapter 8). Investors diversify, hence they do not make mistake X only on security Y. If you find mistake X only on security Y, no matter how apparently profitable, it is likely a false discovery.

2. Apply bagging (Chapter 6) as a means to both prevent overfitting and reduce the variance of the forecasting error. If bagging deteriorates the performance of a strategy, it was likely overfit to a small number of observations or outliers.

3. Do not backtest until all your research is complete (Chapters 1–10).

4. Record every backtest conducted on a dataset so that the probability of backtest overfitting may be estimated on the final selected result (see Bailey, Borwein, López de Prado, and Zhu [2017a] and Chapter 14), and the Sharpe ratio may be properly deflated by the number of trials carried out (Bailey and López de Prado [2014b]).

5. Simulate scenarios rather than history (Chapter 12). A standard backtest is a historical simulation, which can be easily overfit. History is just the random path that was realized, and it could have been entirely different. Your strategy should be profitable under a wide range of scenarios, not just the anecdotal historical path. It is harder to overfit the outcome of thousands of "what if" scenarios.

6. If the backtest fails to identify a profitable strategy, start from scratch. Resist the temptation of reusing those results. Follow the Second Law of Backtesting.

SNIPPET 11.1   MARCOS' SECOND LAW OF BACKTESTING

"Backtesting while researching is like drinking and driving.
Do not research under the influence of a backtest."

—Marcos López de Prado
Advances in Financial Machine Learning (2018)

11.6   STRATEGY SELECTION

In Chapter 7 we discussed how the presence of serial conditionality in labels defeats standard k-fold cross-validation, because the random sampling will spatter redundant observations into both the training and testing sets. We must find a different (true out-of-sample) validation procedure: a procedure that evaluates our model on the observations least likely to be correlated/redundant to those used to train the model. See Arlot and Celisse [2010] for a survey.

Scikit-learn has implemented a walk-forward timefolds method.[2] Under this approach, testing moves forward (in the time direction) with the goal of preventing leakage. This is consistent with the way historical backtests (and trading) are done. However, in the presence of long-range serial dependence, testing one observation away from the end of the training set may not suffice to avoid informational leakage. We will retake this point in Chapter 12, Section 12.2.

One disadvantage of the walk-forward method is that it can be easily overfit. The reason is that without random sampling, there is a single path of testing that can be repeated over and over until a false positive appears. Like in standard CV, some randomization is needed to avoid this sort of performance targeting or backtest optimization, while avoiding the leakage of examples correlated to the training set into the testing set. Next, we will introduce a CV method for strategy selection, based on the estimation of the probability of backtest overfitting (PBO). We leave for Chapter 12 an explanation of CV methods for backtesting.

Bailey et al. [2017a] estimate the PBO through the combinatorially symmetric cross-validation (CSCV) method. Schematically, this procedure works as follows.

First, we form a matrix M by collecting the performance series from the N trials. In particular, each column $n = 1, \dots, N$ represents a vector of PnL (mark-to-market profits and losses) over $t = 1, \dots, T$ observations associated with a particular model configuration tried by the researcher. M is therefore a real-valued matrix of order (TxN). The only conditions we impose are that (1) M is a true matrix, that is, with the same number of rows for each column, where observations are synchronous for every row across the N trials, and (2) the performance evaluation metric used to choose the "optimal" strategy can be estimated on subsamples of each column. For example, if that metric is the Sharpe ratio, we assume that the IID Normal distribution assumption can be held on various slices of the reported performance. If different model configurations trade with different frequencies, observations are aggregated (downsampled) to match a common index $t = 1, \dots, T$.

Second, we partition M across rows, into an even number S of disjoint submatrices of equal dimensions. Each of these submatrices M_s, with $s = 1, \dots, S$, is of order $(\frac{T}{S}xN)$.

Third, we form all combinations C_S of M_s, taken in groups of size $\frac{S}{2}$. This gives a total number of combinations

$$\binom{S}{S/2} = \binom{S-1}{S/2-1} \frac{S}{S/2} = \dots = \prod_{i=0}^{S/2-1} \frac{S-i}{S/2-i}$$

For instance, if $S = 16$, we will form 12,780 combinations. Each combination $c \in C_S$ is composed of $S/2$ submatrices M_s.

Fourth, for each combination $c \in C_S$, we:

1. Form the *training set J*, by joining the $S/2$ submatrices M_s that constitute c. J is a matrix of order $\left(\frac{T}{S} \frac{S}{2} xN \right) = \left(\frac{T}{2} xN \right)$.

2. Form the *testing set $\bar{J}$*, as the complement of J in M. In other words, $\bar{J}$ is the $\left(\frac{T}{2} xN \right)$ matrix formed by all rows of M that are not part of J.

3. Form a vector R of performance statistics of order N, where the n-th item of R reports the performance associated with the n-th column of J (the training set).

4. Determine the element n^* such that $R_n \leq R_{n^*}, \forall n = 1, \ldots, N$. In other words, $n^* = \arg max_n \{R_n\}$.

5. Form a vector $\bar{R}$ of performance statistics of order N, where the n-th item of $\bar{R}$ reports the performance associated with the n-th column of $\bar{J}$ (the testing set).

6. Determine the relative rank of $\overline{R_{n^*}}$ within $\bar{R}$. We denote this relative rank as $\bar{\omega}_c$, where $\bar{\omega}_c \in (0, 1)$. This is the relative rank of the out-of-sample (OOS) performance associated with the trial chosen in-sample (IS). If the strategy optimization procedure does not overfit, we should observe that $\overline{R_{n^*}}$ systematically outperforms $\bar{R}$ (OOS), just as R_{n^*} outperformed R (IS).

7. Define the logit $\lambda_c = \log\left[\frac{\bar{\omega}_c}{1 - \bar{\omega}_c} \right]$. This presents the property that $\lambda_c = 0$ when $\overline{R_{n^*}}$ coincides with the median of $\bar{R}$. High logit values imply a consistency between IS and OOS performance, which indicates a low level of backtest overfitting.

Fifth, compute the distribution of ranks OOS by collecting all the λ_c, for $c \in C_S$. The probability distribution function $f(\lambda)$ is then estimated as the relative frequency at which λ occurred across all C_S, with $\int_{-\infty}^{\infty} f(\lambda) d\lambda = 1$. Finally, the PBO is estimated as $PBO = \int_{-\infty}^{0} f(\lambda) d\lambda$, as that is the probability associated with IS optimal strategies that underperform OOS.

The x-axis of Figure 11.1 shows the Sharpe ratio IS from the best strategy selected. The y-axis shows the Sharpe ratio OOS for that same best strategy selected. As it can be appreciated, there is a strong and persistent performance decay, caused by backtest overfitting. Applying the above algorithm, we can derive the PBO associated with this strategy selection process, as displayed in Figure 11.2.

The observations in each subset preserve the original time sequence. The random sampling is done on the relatively uncorrelated subsets, rather than on the observations. See Bailey et al. [2017a] for an experimental analysis of the accuracy of this methodology.

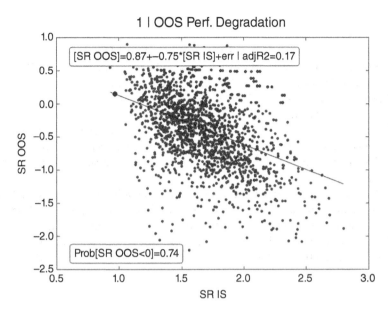

FIGURE 11.1 Best Sharpe ratio in-sample (SR IS) vs Sharpe ratio out-of-sample (SR OOS)

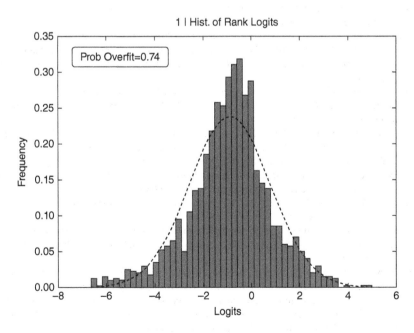

FIGURE 11.2 Probability of backtest overfitting derived from the distribution of logits

EXERCISES

11.1 An analyst fits an RF classifier where some of the features include seasonally adjusted employment data. He aligns with January data the seasonally adjusted value of January, etc. What "sin" has he committed?

11.2 An analyst develops an ML algorithm where he generates a signal using closing prices, and executed at close. What's the sin?

11.3 There is a 98.51% correlation between total revenue generated by arcades and computer science doctorates awarded in the United States. As the number of doctorates is expected to grow, should we invest in arcades companies? If not, what's the sin?

11.4 The *Wall Street Journal* has reported that September is the only month of the year that has negative average stock returns, looking back 20, 50, and 100 years. Should we sell stocks at the end of August? If not, what's the sin?

11.5 We download P/E ratios from Bloomberg, rank stocks every month, sell the top quartile, and buy the long quartile. Performance is amazing. What's the sin?

REFERENCES

Arlot, S. and A. Celisse (2010): "A survey of cross-validation procedures for model selection." *Statistics Surveys*, Vol. 4, pp. 40–79.

Bailey, D., J. Borwein, M. López de Prado, and J. Zhu (2014): "Pseudo-mathematics and financial charlatanism: The effects of backtest overfitting on out-of-sample performance." *Notices of the American Mathematical Society*, Vol. 61, No. 5 (May), pp. 458–471. Available at https://ssrn .com/abstract=2308659.

Bailey, D., J. Borwein, M. López de Prado, and J. Zhu (2017a): "The probability of backtest over-fitting." *Journal of Computational Finance*, Vol. 20, No. 4, pp. 39–70. Available at http://ssrn .com/abstract=2326253.

Bailey, D. and M. López de Prado (2012): "The Sharpe ratio efficient frontier." *Journal of Risk*, Vol. 15, No. 2 (Winter). Available at https://ssrn.com/abstract=1821643.

Bailey, D. and M. López de Prado (2014b): "The deflated Sharpe ratio: Correcting for selection bias, backtest overfitting and non-normality." *Journal of Portfolio Management*, Vol. 40, No. 5, pp. 94–107. Available at https://ssrn.com/abstract=2460551.

Harvey, C., Y. Liu, and H. Zhu (2016): ". . . and the cross-section of expected returns." *Review of Financial Studies*, Vol. 29, No. 1, pp. 5–68.

López de Prado, M. (2017): "Finance as an industrial science." *Journal of Portfolio Management*, Vol. 43, No. 4, pp. 5–9. Available at http://www.iijournals.com/doi/pdfplus/10.3905/jpm .2017.43.4.005.

Luo, Y., M. Alvarez, S. Wang, J. Jussa, A. Wang, and G. Rohal (2014): "Seven sins of quantitative investing." White paper, Deutsche Bank Markets Research, September 8.

Sarfati, O. (2015): "Backtesting: A practitioner's guide to assessing strategies and avoiding pitfalls." Citi Equity Derivatives. CBOE 2015 Risk Management Conference. Available at https://www.cboe.com/rmc/2015/olivier-pdf-Backtesting-Full.pdf.

BIBLIOGRAPHY

Bailey, D., J. Borwein, and M. López de Prado (2016): "Stock portfolio design and backtest overfitting." *Journal of Investment Management*, Vol. 15, No. 1, pp. 1–13. Available at https://ssrn.com/abstract=2739335.

Bailey, D., J. Borwein, M. López de Prado, A. Salehipour, and J. Zhu (2016): "Backtest overfitting in financial markets." *Automated Trader*, Vol. 39. Available at https://ssrn.com/abstract=2731886.

Bailey, D., J. Borwein, M. López de Prado, and J. Zhu (2017b): "Mathematical appendices to: 'The probability of backtest overfitting.'" *Journal of Computational Finance (Risk Journals)*, Vol. 20, No. 4. Available at https://ssrn.com/abstract=2568435.

Bailey, D., J. Borwein, A. Salehipour, and M. López de Prado (2017): "Evaluation and ranking of market forecasters." *Journal of Investment Management*, forthcoming. Available at https://ssrn.com/abstract=2944853.

Bailey, D., J. Borwein, A. Salehipour, M. López de Prado, and J. Zhu (2015): "Online tools for demonstration of backtest overfitting." Working paper. Available at https://ssrn.com/abstract=2597421.

Bailey, D., S. Ger, M. López de Prado, A. Sim and, K. Wu (2016): "Statistical overfitting and backtest performance." In *Risk-Based and Factor Investing*, Quantitative Finance Elsevier. Available at ttps://ssrn.com/abstract=2507040.

Bailey, D. and M. López de Prado (2014a): "Stop-outs under serial correlation and 'the triple penance rule.'" *Journal of Risk*, Vol. 18, No. 2, pp. 61–93. Available at https://ssrn.com/abstract=2201302.

Bailey, D. and M. López de Prado (2015): "Mathematical appendices to: 'Stop-outs under serial correlation.'" *Journal of Risk*, Vol. 18, No. 2. Available at https://ssrn.com/abstract=2511599.

Bailey, D., M. López de Prado, and E. del Pozo (2013): "The strategy approval decision: A Sharpe ratio indifference curve approach." *Algorithmic Finance*, Vol. 2, No. 1, pp. 99–109. Available at https://ssrn.com/abstract=2003638.

Carr, P. and M. López de Prado (2014): "Determining optimal trading rules without backtesting." Working paper. Available at https://ssrn.com/abstract=2658641.

López de Prado, M. (2012a): "Portfolio oversight: An evolutionary approach." Lecture at Cornell University. Available at https://ssrn.com/abstract=2172468.

López de Prado, M. (2012b): "The sharp razor: Performance evaluation with non-normal returns." Lecture at Cornell University. Available at https://ssrn.com/abstract=2150879.

López de Prado, M. (2013): "What to look for in a backtest." Lecture at Cornell University. Available at https://ssrn.com/abstract=2308682.

López de Prado, M. (2014a): "Optimal trading rules without backtesting." Lecture at Cornell University. Available at https://ssrn.com/abstract=2502613.

López de Prado, M. (2014b): "Deflating the Sharpe ratio." Lecture at Cornell University. Available at https://ssrn.com/abstract=2465675.

López de Prado, M. (2015a): "Quantitative meta-strategies." *Practical Applications, Institutional Investor Journals*, Vol. 2, No. 3, pp. 1–3. Available at https://ssrn.com/abstract=2547325.

López de Prado, M. (2015b): "The Future of empirical finance." *Journal of Portfolio Management*, Vol. 41, No. 4, pp. 140–144. Available at https://ssrn.com/abstract=2609734.

López de Prado, M. (2015c): "Backtesting." Lecture at Cornell University. Available at https://ssrn.com/abstract=2606462.

López de Prado, M. (2015d): "Recent trends in empirical finance." *Journal of Portfolio Management*, Vol. 41, No. 4, pp. 29–33. Available at https://ssrn.com/abstract=2638760.

López de Prado, M. (2015e): "Why most empirical discoveries in finance are likely wrong, and what can be done about it." Lecture at University of Pennsylvania. Available at https://ssrn.com/abstract=2599105.

López de Prado, M. (2015f): "Advances in quantitative meta-strategies." Lecture at Cornell University. Available at https://ssrn.com/abstract=2604812.

López de Prado, M. (2016): "Building diversified portfolios that outperform out-of-sample." *Journal of Portfolio Management*, Vol. 42, No. 4, pp. 59–69. Available at https://ssrn.com/abstract=2708678.

López de Prado, M. and M. Foreman (2014): "A mixture of Gaussians approach to mathematical portfolio oversight: The EF3M algorithm." *Quantitative Finance*, Vol. 14, No. 5, pp. 913–930. Available at https://ssrn.com/abstract=1931734.

López de Prado, M. and A. Peijan (2004): "Measuring loss potential of hedge fund strategies." *Journal of Alternative Investments*, Vol. 7, No. 1, pp. 7–31, Summer 2004. Available at https://ssrn.com/abstract=641702.

López de Prado, M., R. Vince, and J. Zhu (2015): "Risk adjusted growth portfolio in a finite investment horizon." Lecture at Cornell University. Available at https://ssrn.com/abstract=2624329.

CHAPTER 12

Backtesting through Cross-Validation

12.1 MOTIVATION

A backtest evaluates out-of-sample the performance of an investment strategy using past observations. These past observations can be used in two ways: (1) in a narrow sense, to simulate the historical performance of an investment strategy, as if it had been run in the past; and (2) in a broader sense, to simulate scenarios that did not happen in the past. The first (narrow) approach, also known as walk-forward, is so prevalent that, in fact, the term "backtest" has become a *de facto* synonym for "historical simulation." The second (broader) approach is far less known, and in this chapter we will introduce some novel ways to carry it out. Each approach has its pros and cons, and each should be given careful consideration.

12.2 THE WALK-FORWARD METHOD

The most common backtest method in the literature is the walk-forward (WF) approach. WF is a historical simulation of how the strategy would have performed in past. Each strategy decision is based on observations that predate that decision. As we saw in Chapter 11, carrying out a flawless WF simulation is a daunting task that requires extreme knowledge of the data sources, market microstructure, risk management, performance measurement standards (e.g., GIPS), multiple testing methods, experimental mathematics, etc. Unfortunately, there is no generic recipe to conduct a backtest. To be accurate and representative, each backtest must be customized to evaluate the assumptions of a particular strategy.

WF enjoys two key advantages: (1) WF has a clear historical interpretation. Its performance can be reconciled with paper trading. (2) History is a filtration; hence, using trailing data guarantees that the testing set is out-of-sample (no leakage), as long as purging has been properly implemented (see Chapter 7, Section 7.4.1). It is a common mistake to find leakage in WF backtests, where `t1.index` falls within the training set, but `t1.values` fall within the testing set (see Chapter 3). Embargoing is not needed in WF backtests, because the training set always predates the testing set.

12.2.1 Pitfalls of the Walk-Forward Method

WF suffers from three major disadvantages: First, a single scenario is tested (the historical path), which can be easily overfit (Bailey et al. [2014]). Second, WF is not necessarily representative of future performance, as results can be biased by the particular sequence of datapoints. Proponents of the WF method typically argue that predicting the past would lead to overly optimistic performance estimates. And yet, very often fitting an outperforming model on the reversed sequence of observations will lead to an underperforming WF backtest. The truth is, it is as easy to overfit a walk-forward backtest as to overfit a walk-backward backtest, and the fact that changing the sequence of observations yields inconsistent outcomes is evidence of that overfitting. If proponents of WF were right, we should observe that walk-backwards backtests systematically outperform their walk-forward counterparts. That is not the case, hence the main argument in favor of WF is rather weak.

To make this second disadvantage clearer, suppose an equity strategy that is backtested with a WF on S&P 500 data, starting January 1, 2007. Until March 15, 2009, the mix of rallies and sell-offs will train the strategy to be market neutral, with low confidence on every position. After that, the long rally will dominate the dataset, and by January 1, 2017, buy forecasts will prevail over sell forecasts. The performance would be very different had we played the information backwards, from January 1, 2017 to January 1, 2007 (a long rally followed by a sharp sell-off). By exploiting a particular sequence, a strategy selected by WF may set us up for a debacle.

The third disadvantage of WF is that the initial decisions are made on a smaller portion of the total sample. Even if a warm-up period is set, most of the information is used by only a small portion of the decisions. Consider a strategy with a warm-up period that uses t_0 observations out of T. This strategy makes half of its decisions $\left(\frac{T-t_0}{2}\right)$ on an average number of datapoints,

$$\left(\frac{T-t_0}{2}\right)^{-1}\left(t_0 + \frac{T+t_0}{2}\right)\frac{T-t_0}{4} = \frac{1}{4}T + \frac{3}{4}t_0$$

which is only a $\frac{3}{4}\frac{t_0}{T} + \frac{1}{4}$ fraction of the observations. Although this problem is attenuated by increasing the warm-up period, doing so also reduces the length of the backtest.

12.3 THE CROSS-VALIDATION METHOD

Investors often ask how a strategy would perform if subjected to a stress scenario as unforeseeable as the 2008 crisis, or the dot-com bubble, or the taper tantrum, or the China scare of 2015–2016, etc. One way to answer is to split the observations into two sets, one with the period we wish to test (testing set), and one with the rest (training set). For example, a classifier would be trained on the period January 1, 2009–January 1, 2017, then tested on the period January 1, 2008–December 31, 2008. The performance we will obtain for 2008 is not historically accurate, since the classifier was trained on data that was only available after 2008. But historical accuracy was not the goal of the test. The objective of the test was to subject a strategy *ignorant* of 2008 to a stress scenario such as 2008.

The goal of backtesting through cross-validation (CV) is not to derive historically accurate performance, but to infer future performance from a number of out-of-sample scenarios. For each period of the backtest, we simulate the performance of a classifier that knew everything except for that period.

Advantages

1. The test is not the result of a particular (historical) scenario. In fact, CV tests k alternative scenarios, of which only one corresponds with the historical sequence.
2. Every decision is made on sets of equal size. This makes outcomes comparable across periods, in terms of the amount of information used to make those decisions.
3. Every observation is part of one and only one testing set. There is no warm-up subset, thereby achieving the longest possible out-of-sample simulation.

Disadvantages

1. Like WF, a single backtest path is simulated (although not the historical one). There is one and only one forecast generated per observation.
2. CV has no clear historical interpretation. The output does not simulate how the strategy would have performed in the past, but how it may perform *in the future* under various stress scenarios (a useful result in its own right).
3. Because the training set does not trail the testing set, leakage is possible. Extreme care must be taken to avoid leaking testing information into the training set. See Chapter 7 for a discussion on how purging and embargoing can help prevent informational leakage in the context of CV.

12.4   THE COMBINATORIAL PURGED CROSS-VALIDATION METHOD

In this section I will present a new method, which addresses the main drawback of the WF and CV methods, namely that those schemes test a single path. I call it the "combinatorial purged cross-validation" (CPCV) method. Given a number φ of backtest paths targeted by the researcher, CPCV generates the precise number of combinations of training/testing sets needed to generate those paths, while purging training observations that contain leaked information.

	S1	S2	S3	S4	S5	S6	S7	S8	S9	S10	S11	S12	S13	S14	S15	Paths
G1	x	x	x	x	x											5
G2	x					x	x	x	x							5
G3		x				x				x	x	x				5
G4			x				x			x			x	x		5
G5				x				x			x		x		x	5
G6					x				x			x		x	x	5

FIGURE 12.1 Paths generated for $\varphi\,[6,2] = 5$

12.4.1 Combinatorial Splits

Consider T observations partitioned into N groups without shuffling, where groups $n = 1, \ldots, N-1$ are of size $\lfloor T/N \rfloor$, the Nth group is of size $T - \lfloor T/N \rfloor\,(N-1)$, and $\lfloor . \rfloor$ is the floor or integer function. For a testing set of size k groups, the number of possible training/testing splits is

$$\binom{N}{N-k} = \frac{\prod_{i=0}^{k-1}(N-i)}{k!}$$

Since each combination involves k tested groups, the total number of tested groups is $k\binom{N}{N-k}$. And since we have computed all possible combinations, these tested groups are uniformly distributed across all N (each group belongs to the same number of training and testing sets). The implication is that from k-sized testing sets on N groups we can backtest a total number of paths $\varphi\,[N,k]$,

$$\varphi\,[N,k] = \frac{k}{N}\binom{N}{N-k} = \frac{\prod_{i=1}^{k-1}(N-i)}{(k-1)!}$$

Figure 12.1 illustrates the composition of train/test splits for $N = 6$ and $k = 2$. There are $\binom{6}{4} = 15$ splits, indexed as $S1, \ldots, S15$. For each split, the figure marks with a cross (x) the groups included in the testing set, and leaves unmarked the groups that form the training set. Each group forms part of $\varphi\,[6,2] = 5$ testing sets, therefore this train/test split scheme allows us to compute 5 backtest paths.

Figure 12.2 shows the assignment of each tested group to one backtest path. For example, path 1 is the result of combining the forecasts from $(G1, S1)$, $(G2, S1)$,

	S1	S2	S3	S4	S5	S6	S7	S8	S9	S10	S11	S12	S13	S14	S15	Paths
G1	1	2	3	4	5											5
G2	1					2	3	4	5							5
G3		1				2				3	4	5				5
G4			1				2			3			4	5		5
G5				1				2			3		4		5	5
G6					1				2			3		4	5	5

FIGURE 12.2 Assignment of testing groups to each of the 5 paths

$(G3, S2)$, $(G4, S3)$, $(G5, S4)$ and $(G6, S5)$. Path 2 is the result of combining forecasts from $(G1, S2)$, $(G2, S6)$, $(G3, S6)$, $(G4, S7)$, $(G5, S8)$ and $(G6, S9)$, and so on.

These paths are generated by training the classifier on a portion $\theta = 1 - k/N$ of the data for each combination. Although it is theoretically possible to train on a portion $\theta < 1/2$, in practice we will assume that $k \leq N/2$. The portion of data in the training set θ increases with $N \rightarrow T$ but it decreases with $k \rightarrow N/2$. The number of paths $\varphi[N, k]$ increases with $N \rightarrow T$ and with $k \rightarrow N/2$. In the limit, the largest number of paths is achieved by setting $N = T$ and $k = N/2 = T/2$, at the expense of training the classifier on only half of the data for each combination ($\theta = 1/2$).

12.4.2 The Combinatorial Purged Cross-Validation Backtesting Algorithm

In Chapter 7 we introduced the concepts of purging and embargoing in the context of CV. We will now use these concepts for backtesting through CV. The CPCV backtesting algorithm proceeds as follows:

1. Partition T observations into N groups without shuffling, where groups $n = 1, \ldots, N - 1$ are of size $\lfloor T/N \rfloor$, and the Nth group is of size $T - \lfloor T/N \rfloor (N - 1)$.
2. Compute all possible training/testing splits, where for each split $N - k$ groups constitute the training set and k groups constitute the testing set.
3. For any pair of labels (y_i, y_j), where y_i belongs to the training set and y_j belongs to the testing set, apply the `PurgedKFold` class to purge y_i if y_i spans over a period used to determine label y_j. This class will also apply an embargo, should some testing samples predate some training samples.
4. Fit classifiers on the $\binom{N}{N-k}$ training sets, and produce forecasts on the respective $\binom{N}{N-k}$ testing sets.
5. Compute the $\varphi[N, k]$ backtest paths. You can calculate one Sharpe ratio from each path, and from that derive the empirical distribution of the strategy's Sharpe ratio (rather than a single Sharpe ratio, like WF or CV).

12.4.3 A Few Examples

For $k = 1$, we will obtain $\varphi[N, 1] = 1$ path, in which case CPCV reduces to CV. Thus, CPCV can be understood as a generalization of CV for $k > 1$.

For $k = 2$, we will obtain $\varphi[N, 2] = N - 1$ paths. This is a particularly interesting case, because while training the classifier on a large portion of the data, $\theta = 1 - 2/N$, we can generate almost as many backtest paths as the number of groups, $N - 1$. An easy rule of thumb is to partition the data into $N = \varphi + 1$ groups, where φ is the number of paths we target, and then form $\binom{N}{N-2}$ combinations. In the limit, we can assign one group per observation, $N = T$, and generate $\varphi[T, 2] = T - 1$ paths, while training the classifier on a portion $\theta = 1 - 2/T$ of the data per combination.

If even more paths are needed, we can increase $k \rightarrow N/2$, but as explained earlier that will come at the cost of using a smaller portion of the dataset for training. In practice, $k = 2$ is often enough to generate the needed φ paths, by setting $N = \varphi + 1 \leq T$.

12.5 HOW COMBINATORIAL PURGED CROSS-VALIDATION ADDRESSES BACKTEST OVERFITTING

Given a sample of IID random variables, $x_i \sim Z$, $i = 1, \ldots, I$, where Z is the standard normal distribution, the expected maximum of that sample can be approximated as

$$E[\max\{x_i\}_{i=1,\ldots,I}] \approx (1 - \gamma)Z^{-1}\left[1 - \frac{1}{I}\right] + \gamma Z^{-1}\left[1 - \frac{1}{I}e^{-1}\right] \leq \sqrt{2\log[I]}$$

where $Z^{-1}[.]$ is the inverse of the CDF of Z, $\gamma \approx 0.5772156649 \cdots$ is the Euler-Mascheroni constant, and $I \gg 1$ (see Bailey et al. [2014] for a proof). Now suppose that a researcher backtests I strategies on an instrument that behaves like a martingale, with Sharpe ratios $\{y_i\}_{i=1,\ldots,I}$, $E[y_i] = 0$, $\sigma^2[y_i] > 0$, and $\frac{y_i}{\sigma[y_i]} \sim Z$. Even though the true Sharpe ratio is zero, we expect to find one strategy with a Sharpe ratio of

$$E[\max\{y_i\}_{i=1,\ldots,I}] = E[\max\{x_i\}_{i=1,\ldots,I}]\sigma[y_i]$$

WF backtests exhibit high variance, $\sigma[y_i] \gg 0$, for at least one reason: A large portion of the decisions are based on a small portion of the dataset. A few observations will have a large weight on the Sharpe ratio. Using a warm-up period will reduce the backtest length, which may contribute to making the variance even higher. WF's high variance leads to false discoveries, because researchers will select the backtest with the maximum *estimated* Sharpe ratio, even if the *true* Sharpe ratio is zero. That is the reason it is imperative to control for the number of trials *(I)* in the context of WF backtesting. Without this information, it is not possible to determine the Family-Wise Error Rate (FWER), False Discovery Rate (FDR), Probability of Backtest Overfitting (PBO, see Chapter 11) or similar model assessment statistic.

CV backtests (Section 12.3) address that source of variance by training each classifier on equal and large portions of the dataset. Although CV leads to fewer false discoveries than WF, both approaches still estimate the Sharpe ratio from a single path for a strategy i, y_i, and that estimation may be highly volatile. In contrast, CPCV derives the distribution of Sharpe ratios from a large number of paths, $j = 1, \ldots, \varphi$, with mean $E[\{y_{i,j}\}_{j=1,\ldots,\varphi}] = \mu_i$ and variance $\sigma^2[\{y_{i,j}\}_{j=1,\ldots,\varphi}] = \sigma_i^2$. The variance of the sample mean of CPCV paths is

$$\sigma^2[\mu_i] = \varphi^{-2}\left(\varphi\sigma_i^2 + \varphi(\varphi - 1)\sigma_i^2\bar{\rho}_i\right) = \varphi^{-1}\sigma_i^2\left(1 + (\varphi - 1)\bar{\rho}_i\right)$$

where σ_i^2 is the variance of the Sharpe ratios across paths for strategy i, and $\bar{\rho}_i$ is the average off-diagonal correlation among $\{y_{i,j}\}_{j=1,\ldots,\varphi}$. CPCV leads to fewer false discoveries than CV and WF, because $\bar{\rho}_i < 1$ implies that the variance of the sample mean is lower than the variance of the sample,

$$\varphi^{-1}\sigma_i^2 \leq \sigma^2\left[\mu_i\right] < \sigma_i^2$$

The more uncorrelated the paths are, $\bar{\rho}_i \ll 1$, the lower CPCV's variance will be, and in the limit CPCV will report the true Sharpe ratio $E[y_i]$ with zero variance, $\lim_{\varphi \to \infty} \sigma^2[\mu_i] = 0$. There will not be selection bias, because the strategy selected out of $i = 1, \ldots, I$ will be the one with the highest *true* Sharpe ratio.

Of course, we know that zero variance is unachievable, since φ has an upper bound, $\varphi \leq \varphi\left[T, \frac{T}{2}\right]$. Still, for a large enough number of paths φ, CPCV could make the variance of the backtest so small as to make the probability of a false discovery negligible.

In Chapter 11, we argued that backtest overfitting may be the most important open problem in all of mathematical finance. Let us see how CPCV helps address this problem in practice. Suppose that a researcher submits a strategy to a journal, supported by an overfit WF backtest, selected from a large number of undisclosed trials. The journal could ask the researcher to repeat his experiments using a CPCV for a given N and k. Because the researcher did not know in advance the number and characteristics of the paths to be backtested, his overfitting efforts will be easily defeated. The paper will be rejected or withdrawn from consideration. Hopefully CPCV will be used to reduce the number of false discoveries published in journals and elsewhere.

EXERCISES

12.1 Suppose that you develop a momentum strategy on a futures contract, where the forecast is based on an AR(1) process. You backtest this strategy using the WF method, and the Sharpe ratio is 1.5. You then repeat the backtest on the reversed series and achieve a Sharpe ratio of −1.5. What would be the mathematical grounds for disregarding the second result, if any?

12.2 You develop a mean-reverting strategy on a futures contract. Your WF backtest achieves a Sharpe ratio of 1.5. You increase the length of the warm-up period, and the Sharpe ratio drops to 0.7. You go ahead and present only the result with the higher Sharpe ratio, arguing that a strategy with a shorter warm-up is more realistic. Is this selection bias?

12.3 Your strategy achieves a Sharpe ratio of 1.5 on a WF backtest, but a Sharpe ratio of 0.7 on a CV backtest. You go ahead and present only the result with the higher Sharpe ratio, arguing that the WF backtest is historically accurate, while the CV backtest is a scenario simulation, or an inferential exercise. Is this selection bias?

12.4 Your strategy produces 100,000 forecasts over time. You would like to derive the CPCV distribution of Sharpe ratios by generating 1,000 paths. What are the possible combinations of parameters (N, k) that will allow you to achieve that?

12.5 You discover a strategy that achieves a Sharpe ratio of 1.5 in a WF backtest. You write a paper explaining the theory that would justify such result, and submit it to an academic journal. The editor replies that one referee has requested you repeat your backtest using a CPCV method with $N = 100$ and $k = 2$, including your code and full datasets. You follow these instructions, and the mean Sharpe ratio is -1 with a standard deviation of 0.5. Furious, you do not reply, but instead withdraw your submission, and resubmit in a different journal of higher impact factor. After 6 months, your paper is accepted. You appease your conscience thinking that, if the discovery is false, it is the journal's fault for not having requested a CPCV test. You think, "It cannot be unethical, since it is permitted, and everybody does it." What are the arguments, scientific or ethical, to justify your actions?

REFERENCES

Bailey, D. and M. López de Prado (2012): "The Sharpe ratio efficient frontier." *Journal of Risk*, Vol. 15, No. 2 (Winter). Available at https://ssrn.com/abstract=1821643.

Bailey, D. and M. López de Prado (2014): "The deflated Sharpe ratio: Correcting for selection bias, backtest overfitting and non-normality." *Journal of Portfolio Management*, Vol. 40, No. 5, pp. 94–107. Available at https://ssrn.com/abstract=2460551.

Bailey, D., J. Borwein, M. López de Prado, and J. Zhu (2014): "Pseudo-mathematics and financial charlatanism: The effects of backtest overfitting on out-of-sample performance." *Notices of the American Mathematical Society*, Vol. 61, No. 5, pp. 458–471. Available at http://ssrn .com/abstract=2308659.

Bailey, D., J. Borwein, M. López de Prado, and J. Zhu (2017): "The probability of backtest overfitting." *Journal of Computational Finance*, Vol. 20, No. 4, pp. 39–70. Available at https://ssrn .com/abstract=2326253.

CHAPTER 13

Backtesting on Synthetic Data

13.1 MOTIVATION

In this chapter we will study an alternative backtesting method, which uses history to generate a synthetic dataset with statistical characteristics estimated from the observed data. This will allow us to backtest a strategy on a large number of unseen, synthetic testing sets, hence reducing the likelihood that the strategy has been fit to a particular set of datapoints.[1] This is a very extensive subject, and in order to reach some depth we will focus on the backtesting of trading rules.

13.2 TRADING RULES

Investment strategies can be defined as algorithms that postulate the existence of a market inefficiency. Some strategies rely on econometric models to predict prices, using macroeconomic variables such as GDP or inflation; other strategies use fundamental and accounting information to price securities, or search for arbitrage-like opportunities in the pricing of derivatives products, etc. For instance, suppose that financial intermediaries tend to sell off-the-run bonds two days before U.S. Treasury auctions, in order to raise the cash needed for buying the new "paper." One could monetize on that knowledge by selling off-the-run bonds three days before auctions. But how? Each investment strategy requires an implementation tactic, often referred to as "trading rules."

There are dozens of hedge fund styles, each running dozens of unique investment strategies. While strategies can be very heterogeneous in nature, tactics are relatively homogeneous. Trading rules provide the algorithm that must be followed to enter and exit a position. For example, a position will be entered when the strategy's signal

---

[1] I would like to thank Professor Peter Carr (New York University) for his contributions to this chapter.

reaches a certain value. Conditions for exiting a position are often defined through
thresholds for profit-taking and stop-losses. These entry and exit rules rely on parameters that are usually calibrated via historical simulations. This practice leads to the
problem of *backtest overfitting*, because these parameters target specific observations
in-sample, to the point that the investment strategy is so attached to the past that it
becomes unfit for the future.

An important clarification is that we are interested in the exit corridor conditions
that maximize performance. In other words, the position already exists, and the question is how to exit it optimally. This is the dilemma often faced by execution traders,
and it should not be mistaken with the determination of entry and exit thresholds
for investing in a security. For a study of that alternative question, see, for example,
Bertram [2009].

Bailey et al. [2014, 2017] discuss the problem of backtest overfitting, and provide
methods to determine to what extent a simulated performance may be inflated due
to overfitting. While assessing the probability of backtest overfitting is a useful tool
to discard superfluous investment strategies, it would be better to avoid the risk of
overfitting, at least in the context of calibrating a trading rule. In theory this could be
accomplished by deriving the optimal parameters for the trading rule directly from
the stochastic process that generates the data, rather than engaging in historical simulations. This is the approach we take in this chapter. Using the entire historical sample, we will characterize the stochastic process that generates the observed stream
of returns, and derive the optimal values for the trading rule's parameters without
requiring a historical simulation.

13.3   THE PROBLEM

Suppose an investment strategy S invests in $i = 1, \dots I$ opportunities or bets. At each
opportunity i, S takes a position of m_i units of security X, where $m_i \in (-\infty, \infty)$. The
transaction that entered such opportunity was priced at a value $m_i P_{i,0}$, where $P_{i,0}$
is the average price per unit at which the m_i securities were transacted. As other
market participants transact security X, we can mark-to-market (MtM) the value of
that opportunity i after t observed transactions as $m_i P_{i,t}$. This represents the value of
opportunity i if it were liquidated at the price observed in the market after t transactions. Accordingly, we can compute the MtM profit/loss of opportunity i after t
transactions as $\pi_{i,t} = m_i(P_{i,t} - P_{i,0})$.

A standard trading rule provides the logic for exiting opportunity i at $t = T_i$. This
occurs as soon as one of two conditions is verified:

- $\pi_{i,T_i} \geq \bar{\pi}$, where $\bar{\pi} > 0$ is the profit-taking threshold.
- $\pi_{i,T_i} \leq \underline{\pi}$, where $\underline{\pi} < 0$ is the stop-loss threshold.

These thresholds are equivalent to the horizontal barriers we discussed in the context of meta-labelling (Chapter 3). Because $\underline{\pi} < \bar{\pi}$, one and only one of the two exit
conditions can trigger the exit from opportunity i. Assuming that opportunity i can

be exited at T_i, its final profit/loss is π_{i,T_i}. At the onset of each opportunity, the goal is to realize an expected profit $E_0[\pi_{i,T_i}] = m_i(E_0[P_{i,T_i}] - P_{i,0})$, where $E_0[P_{i,T_i}]$ is the forecasted price and $P_{i,0}$ is the entry level of opportunity i.

Definition 1: Trading Rule: A trading rule for strategy S is defined by the set of parameters $R := \{\underline{\pi}, \bar{\pi}\}$.

One way to calibrate (by brute force) the trading rule is to:

1. Define a set of alternative values of R, $\Omega := \{R\}$.
2. Simulate historically (backtest) the performance of S under alternative values of $R \in \Omega$.
3. Select the optimal R^*.

More formally:

$$R^* = \arg\max_{R \in \Omega}\{SR_R\}$$

$$SR_R = \frac{E[\pi_{i,T_i}|R]}{\sigma[\pi_{i,T_i}|R]} \tag{13.1}$$

where $E[.]$ and $\sigma[.]$ are respectively the expected value and standard deviation of π_{i,T_i}, conditional on trading rule R, over $i = 1, \ldots I$. In other words, equation (13.1) maximizes the Sharpe ratio of S on I opportunities over the space of alternative trading rules R (see Bailey and López de Prado [2012] for a definition and analysis of the Sharpe ratio). Because we count with two variables to maximize SR_R over a sample of size I, it is easy to overfit R. A trivial overfit occurs when a pair $(\underline{\pi}, \bar{\pi})$ targets a few outliers. Bailey et al. [2017] provide a rigorous definition of backtest overfitting, which can be applied to our study of trading rules as follows.

Definition 2: Overfit Trading Rule: R^* is overfit if $E\left[\dfrac{E\left[\pi_{j,T_j}|R^*\right]}{\sigma\left[\pi_{j,T_j}|R^*\right]}\right] <$

$Me_\Omega\left[E\left[\dfrac{E\left[\pi_{j,T_j}|R\right]}{\sigma\left[\pi_{j,T_j}|R\right]}\right]\right]$, where $j = I + 1, \ldots J$ and $Me_\Omega[.]$ is the median.

Intuitively, an optimal in-sample (IS, $i \in [1, I]$) trading rule R^* is overfit when it is expected to underperform the median of alternative trading rules $R \in \Omega$ out-of-sample (OOS, $j \in [I + 1, J]$). This is essentially the same definition we used in chapter 11 to derive PBO. Bailey et al. [2014] argue that it is hard not to overfit a backtest, particularly when there are free variables able to target specific observations IS, or the number of elements in Ω is large. A trading rule introduces such free variables, because R^* can be determined independently from S. The outcome is that the backtest profits from random noise IS, making R^* unfit for OOS opportunities. Those same authors show that overfitting leads to negative performance OOS when $\Delta\pi_{i,t}$ exhibits serial dependence. While PBO provides a useful method to evaluate to what extent a backtest has been overfit, it would be convenient to avoid this problem in the first place.[2] To that aim we dedicate the following section.

13.4 OUR FRAMEWORK

Until now we have not characterized the stochastic process from which observations $\pi_{i,t}$ are drawn. We are interested in finding an optimal trading rule (OTR) for those scenarios where overfitting would be most damaging, such as when $\pi_{i,t}$ exhibits serial correlation. In particular, suppose a discrete Ornstein-Uhlenbeck (O-U) process on prices

$$P_{i,t} = (1 - \varphi)\,\mathrm{E}_0[P_{i,T_i}] + \varphi P_{i,t-1} + \sigma\varepsilon_{i,t} \tag{13.2}$$

such that the random shocks are IID distributed $\varepsilon_{i,t} \sim N(0, 1)$. The seed value for this process is $P_{i,0}$, the level targeted by opportunity i is $\mathrm{E}_0[P_{i,T_i}]$, and φ determines the speed at which $P_{i,0}$ converges towards $\mathrm{E}_0[P_{i,T_i}]$. Because $\pi_{i,t} = m_i(P_{i,t} - P_{i,0})$, equation (13.2) implies that the performance of opportunity i is characterized by the process

$$\frac{1}{m_i}\pi_{i,t} = (1 - \varphi)\mathrm{E}_0[P_{i,T_i}] - P_{i,0} + \varphi P_{i,t-1} + \sigma\varepsilon_{i,t} \tag{13.3}$$

From the proof to Proposition 4 in Bailey and López de Prado [2013], it can be shown that the distribution of the process specified in equation (13.2) is Gaussian with parameters

$$\pi_{i,t} \sim N\left[m_i\left((1 - \varphi)\,\mathrm{E}_0[P_{i,T_i}]\sum_{j=0}^{t-1}\varphi^j - P_{i,0}\right), m_i^2\sigma^2\sum_{j=0}^{t-1}\varphi^{2j}\right] \tag{13.4}$$

and a necessary and sufficient condition for its stationarity is that $\varphi \in (-1, 1)$. Given a set of input parameters $\{\sigma, \varphi\}$ and initial conditions $\{P_{i,0}, \mathrm{E}_0[P_{i,T_i}]\}$ associated with opportunity i, is there an OTR $R^* := (\underline{\pi}, \bar{\pi})$? Similarly, should strategy S predict a profit target $\bar{\pi}$, can we compute the optimal stop-loss $\underline{\pi}$ given the input values $\{\sigma, \varphi\}$? If the answer to these questions is affirmative, no backtest would be needed in order to determine R^*, thus avoiding the problem of overfitting the trading rule. In the next section we will show how to answer these questions experimentally.

---

[2] The strategy may still be the result of backtest overfitting, but at least the trading rule would not have contributed to that problem.

13.5   NUMERICAL DETERMINATION OF OPTIMAL TRADING RULES

In the previous section we used an O-U specification to characterize the stochastic process generating the returns of strategy S. In this section we will present a procedure to numerically derive the OTR for any specification in general, and the O-U specification in particular.

13.5.1   The Algorithm

The algorithm consists of five sequential steps.

> **Step 1**: We estimate the input parameters $\{\sigma, \varphi\}$, by linearizing equation (13.2) as:

$$P_{i,t} = \mathrm{E}_0[P_{i,T_i}] + \varphi(P_{i,t-1} - \mathrm{E}_0[P_{i,T_i}]) + \xi_t \qquad (13.5)$$

We can then form vectors X and Y by sequencing opportunities:

$$X = \begin{bmatrix} P_{0,0} - \mathrm{E}_0[P_{0,T_0}] \\ P_{0,1} - \mathrm{E}_0[P_{0,T_0}] \\ \cdots \\ P_{0,T-1} - \mathrm{E}_0[P_{0,T_0}] \\ \cdots \\ P_{I,0} - \mathrm{E}_0[P_{I,T_I}] \\ \cdots \\ P_{I,T-1} - \mathrm{E}_0[P_{I,T_I}] \end{bmatrix}; \ Y = \begin{bmatrix} P_{0,1} \\ P_{0,2} \\ \cdots \\ P_{0,T} \\ \cdots \\ P_{I,1} \\ \cdots \\ P_{I,T} \end{bmatrix}; \ Z = \begin{bmatrix} \mathrm{E}_0[P_{0,T_0}] \\ \mathrm{E}_0[P_{0,T_0}] \\ \cdots \\ \mathrm{E}_0[P_{0,T_0}] \\ \cdots \\ \mathrm{E}_0[P_{I,T_I}] \\ \cdots \\ \mathrm{E}_0[P_{I,T_I}] \end{bmatrix} \qquad (13.6)$$

Applying OLS on equation (13.5), we can estimate the original O-U parameters as,

$$\begin{aligned} \hat{\varphi} &= \frac{\mathrm{cov}\,[Y, X]}{\mathrm{cov}\,[X, X]} \\ \hat{\xi}_t &= Y - Z - \hat{\varphi}X \\ \hat{\sigma} &= \sqrt{\mathrm{cov}[\hat{\xi}_t, \hat{\xi}_t]} \end{aligned} \qquad (13.7)$$

where $\mathrm{cov}\,[\cdot, \cdot]$ is the covariance operator.

> **Step 2**: We construct a mesh of stop-loss and profit-taking pairs, $(\underline{\pi}, \bar{\pi})$. For example, a Cartesian product of $\underline{\pi} = \{-\frac{1}{2}\sigma, -\sigma, \dots, -10\sigma\}$ and $\bar{\pi} = \{\frac{1}{2}\sigma, \sigma, \dots, 10\sigma\}$ give us 20×20 nodes, each constituting an alternative trading rule $R \in \Omega$.

Step 3: We generate a large number of paths (e.g., 100,000) for $\pi_{i,t}$ applying our estimates $\{\hat{\sigma}, \hat{\varphi}\}$. As seed values, we use the observed initial conditions $\{P_{i,0}, E_0[P_{i,T_i}]\}$ associated with an opportunity i. Because a position cannot be held for an unlimited period of time, we can impose a maximum holding period (e.g., 100 observations) at which point the position is exited even though $\underline{\pi} \leq \pi_{i,100} \leq \bar{\pi}$. This maximum holding period is equivalent to the vertical bar of the triple-barrier method (Chapter 3).[3]

Step 4: We apply the 100,000 paths generated in Step 3 on each node of the 20 × 20 mesh $(\underline{\pi}, \bar{\pi})$ generated in Step 2. For each node, we apply the stop-loss and profit-taking logic, giving us 100,000 values of π_{i,T_i}. Likewise, for each node we compute the Sharpe ratio associated with that trading rule as described in equation (13.1). See Bailey and López de Prado [2012] for a study of the confidence interval of the Sharpe ratio estimator. This result can be used in three different ways: Step 5a, Step 5b and Step 5c).

Step 5a: We determine the pair $(\underline{\pi}, \bar{\pi})$ within the mesh of trading rules that is optimal, given the input parameters $\{\hat{\sigma}, \hat{\varphi}\}$ and the observed initial conditions $\{P_{i,0}, E_0[P_{i,T_i}]\}$.

Step 5b: If strategy S provides a profit target $\bar{\pi}_i$ for a particular opportunity i, we can use that information in conjunction with the results in Step 4 to determine the optimal stop-loss, $\underline{\pi}_i$.

Step 5c: If the trader has a maximum stop-loss $\underline{\pi}_i$ imposed by the fund's management for opportunity i, we can use that information in conjunction with the results in Step 4 to determine the optimal profit-taking $\bar{\pi}_i$ within the range of stop-losses $[0, \underline{\pi}_i]$.

Bailey and López de Prado [2013] prove that the half-life of the process in equation (13.2) is $\tau = -\frac{\log[2]}{\log[\varphi]}$, with the requirement that $\varphi \in (0, 1)$. From that result, we can determine the value of φ associated with a certain half-life τ as $\varphi = 2^{-1/\tau}$.

13.5.2 Implementation

Snippet 13.1 provides an implementation in Python of the experiments conducted in this chapter. Function `main` produces a Cartesian product of parameters $(E_0[P_{i,T_i}], \tau)$, which characterize the stochastic process from equation (13.5). Without loss of generality, in all simulations we have used $\sigma = 1$. Then, for each pair $(E_0[P_{i,T_i}], \tau)$, function `batch` computes the Sharpe ratios associated with various trading rules.

---

[3] The trading rule R could be characterized as a function of the three barriers, instead of the horizontal ones. That change would have no impact on the procedure. It would merely add one more dimension to the mesh (20 × 20 × 20). In this chapter we do not consider that setting, because it would make the visualization of the method less intuitive.

SNIPPET 13.1 PYTHON CODE FOR THE DETERMINATION OF OPTIMAL TRADING RULES

```
import numpy as np
from random import gauss
from itertools import product
#——————————————————————————
def main():
    rPT=rSLm=np.linspace(0,10,21)
    count=0
    for prod_ in product([10,5,0,-5,-10],[5,10,25,50,100]):
        count+=1
        coeffs={'forecast':prod_[0],'hl':prod_[1],'sigma':1}
        output=batch(coeffs,nIter=1e5,maxHP=100,rPT=rPT,rSLm=rSLm)
    return output
```

Snippet 13.2 computes a 20×20 mesh of Sharpe ratios, one for each trading rule $(\underline{\pi}, \bar{\pi})$, given a pair of parameters $(E_0[P_{i,T_i}], \tau)$. There is a vertical barrier, as the maximum holding period is set at 100 ($\texttt{maxHP} = 100$). We have fixed $P_{i,0} = 0$, since it is the distance $(P_{i,t-1} - E_0[P_{i,T_i}])$ in equation (13.5) that drives the convergence, not particular absolute price levels. Once the first out of three barriers is touched, the exit price is stored, and the next iteration starts. After all iterations are completed (1E5), the Sharpe ratio can be computed for that pair $(\underline{\pi}, \bar{\pi})$, and the algorithm moves to the next pair. When all pairs of trading rules have been processed, results are reported back to $\texttt{main}$. This algorithm can be parallelized, similar to what we did for the triple-barrier method in Chapter 3. We leave that task as an exercise.

SNIPPET 13.2 PYTHON CODE FOR THE DETERMINATION OF OPTIMAL TRADING RULES

```
def batch(coeffs,nIter=1e5,maxHP=100,rPT=np.linspace(.5,10,20),
    rSLm=np.linspace(.5,10,20),seed=0):
    phi,output1=2**(-1./coeffs['hl']),[]
    for comb_ in product(rPT,rSLm):
        output2=[]
        for iter_ in range(int(nIter)):
            p,hp,count=seed,0,0
            while True:
                p=(1-phi)*coeffs['forecast']+phi*p+coeffs['sigma']*gauss(0,1)
                cP=p-seed;hp+=1
                if cP>comb_[0] or cP<-comb_[1] or hp>maxHP:
                    output2.append(cP)
                    break
```

```
    mean,std=np.mean(output2),np.std(output2)
    print comb_[0],comb_[1],mean,std,mean/std
    output1.append((comb_[0],comb_[1],mean,std,mean/std))
return output1
```

13.6 EXPERIMENTAL RESULTS

Table 13.1 lists the combinations analyzed in this study. Although different values
for these input parameters would render different numerical results, the combinations applied allow us to analyze the most general cases. Column "Forecast" refers
to $E_0[P_{i,T_i}]$; column "Half-Life" refers to τ; column "Sigma" refers to σ; column
"maxHP" stands for maximum holding period.

In the following figures, we have plotted the non-annualized Sharpe ratios that
result from various combinations of profit-taking and stop-loss exit conditions. We
have omitted the negative sign in the y-axis (stop-losses) for simplicity. Sharpe ratios

TABLE 13.1 Input Parameter Combinations Used in the Simulations

Figure	Forecast	Half-Life	Sigma	maxHP
16.1	0	5	1	100
16.2	0	10	1	100
16.3	0	25	1	100
16.4	0	50	1	100
16.5	0	100	1	100
16.6	5	5	1	100
16.7	5	10	1	100
16.8	5	25	1	100
16.9	5	50	1	100
16.10	5	100	1	100
16.11	10	5	1	100
16.12	10	10	1	100
16.13	10	25	1	100
16.14	10	50	1	100
16.15	10	100	1	100
16.16	−5	5	1	100
16.17	−5	10	1	100
16.18	−5	25	1	100
16.19	−5	50	1	100
16.20	−5	100	1	100
16.21	−10	5	1	100
16.22	−10	10	1	100
16.23	−10	25	1	100
16.24	−10	50	1	100
16.25	−10	100	1	100

are represented in grayscale (lighter indicating better performance; darker indicating worse performance), in a format known as a heat-map. Performance (π_{i,T_i}) is computed per unit held $(m_i = 1)$, since other values of m_i would simply re-scale performance, with no impact on the Sharpe ratio. Transaction costs can be easily added, but for educational purposes it is better to plot results without them, so that you can appreciate the symmetry of the functions.

13.6.1 Cases with Zero Long-Run Equilibrium

Cases with zero long-run equilibrium are consistent with the business of market-makers, who provide liquidity under the assumption that price deviations from current levels will correct themselves over time. The smaller τ, the smaller is the autoregressive coefficient $(\varphi = 2^{-1/\tau})$. A small autoregressive coefficient in conjunction with a zero expected profit has the effect that most of the pairs $(\underline{\pi}_i, \overline{\pi}_i)$ deliver a zero performance.

Figure 13.1 shows the heat-map for the parameter combination $\{E_0[P_{i,T_i}], \tau, \sigma\} = \{0, 5, 1\}$. The half-life is so small that performance is maximized in a narrow range of combinations of small profit-taking with large stop-losses. In other words, the optimal trading rule is to hold an inventory long enough until a small profit arises, even at the expense of experiencing some 5-fold or 7-fold unrealized losses. Sharpe ratios are

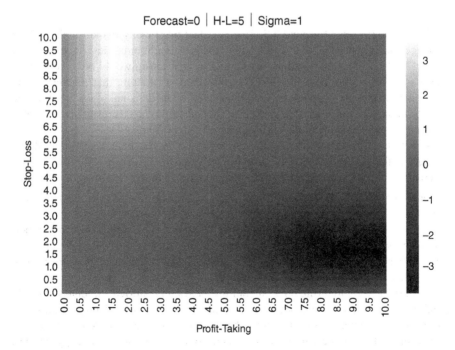

FIGURE 13.1   Heat-map for $\{E_0[P_{i,T_i}], \tau, \sigma\} = \{0, 5, 1\}$

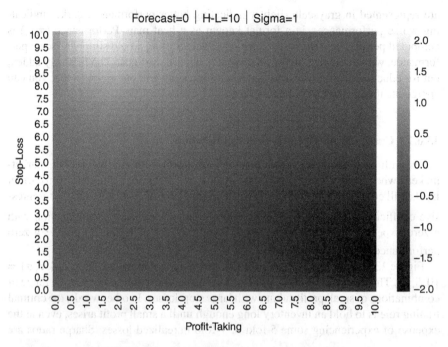

FIGURE 13.2   Heat-map for $\{E_0[P_{i,T_i}], \tau, \sigma\} = \{0, 10, 1\}$

high, reaching levels of around 3.2. This is in fact what many market-makers do in practice, and is consistent with the "asymmetric payoff dilemma" described in Easley et al. [2011]. The worst possible trading rule in this setting would be to combine a short stop-loss with a large profit-taking threshold, a situation that market-makers avoid in practice. Performance is closest to neutral in the diagonal of the mesh, where profit-taking and stop-losses are symmetric. You should keep this result in mind when labeling observations using the triple-barrier method (Chapter 3).

Figure 13.2 shows that, if we increase τ from 5 to 10, the areas of highest and lowest performance spread over the mesh of pairs $(\underline{\pi}, \bar{\pi})$, while the Sharpe ratios decrease. This is because, as the half-life increases, so does the magnitude of the autoregressive coefficient (recall that $\varphi = 2^{-1/\tau}$), thus bringing the process closer to a random walk.

In Figure 13.3, $\tau = 25$, which again spreads the areas of highest and lowest performance while reducing the Sharpe ratio. Figure 13.4 ($\tau = 50$) and Figure 13.5 ($\tau = 100$) continue that progression. Eventually, as $\varphi \to 1$, there are no recognizable areas where performance can be maximized.

Calibrating a trading rule on a random walk through historical simulations would lead to backtest overfitting, because one random combination of profit-taking and stop-loss that happened to maximize Sharpe ratio would be selected. This is why backtesting of synthetic data is so important: to avoid choosing a strategy because some statistical fluke took place in the past (a single random path). Our procedure

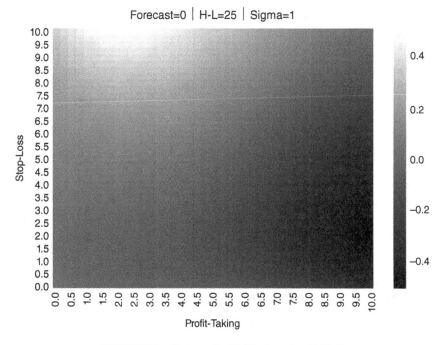

FIGURE 13.3   Heat-map for $\{E_0[P_{i,T_i}], \tau, \sigma\} = \{0, 25, 1\}$

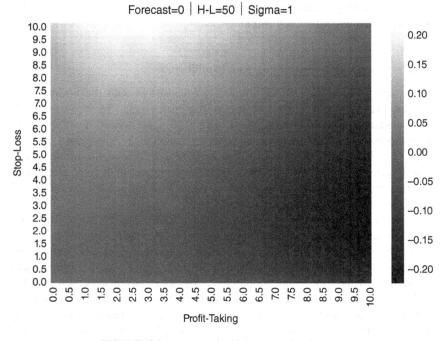

FIGURE 13.4   Heat-map for $\{E_0[P_{i,T_i}], \tau, \sigma\} = \{0, 50, 1\}$

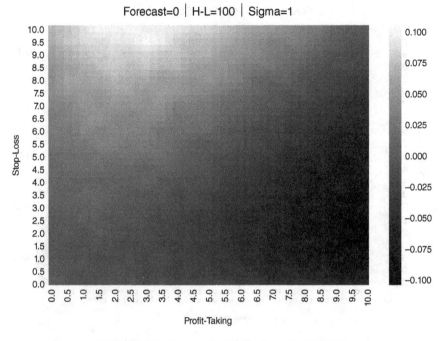

FIGURE 13.5 Heat-map for $\{E_0[P_{i,T_i}], \tau, \sigma\} = \{0, 100, 1\}$

prevents overfitting by recognizing that performance exhibits no consistent pattern, indicating that there is no optimal trading rule.

13.6.2 Cases with Positive Long-Run Equilibrium

Cases with positive long-run equilibrium are consistent with the business of a position-taker, such as a hedge-fund or asset manager. Figure 13.6 shows the results for the parameter combination $\{E_0[P_{i,T_i}], \tau, \sigma\} = \{5, 5, 1\}$. Because positions tend to make money, the optimal profit-taking is higher than in the previous cases, centered around 6, with stop-losses that range between 4 and 10. The region of the optimal trading rule takes a characteristic rectangular shape, as a result of combining a wide stop-loss range with a narrower profit-taking range. Performance is highest across all experiments, with Sharpe ratios of around 12.

In Figure 13.7, we have increased the half-life from $\tau = 5$ to $\tau = 10$. Now the optimal performance is achieved at a profit-taking centered around 5, with stop-losses that range between 7 and 10. The range of optimal profit-taking is wider, while the range of optimal stop-losses narrows, shaping the former rectangular area closer to a square. Again, a larger half-life brings the process closer to a random walk, and therefore performance is now relatively lower than before, with Sharpe ratios of around 9.

In Figure 13.8, we have made $\tau = 25$. The optimal profit-taking is now centered around 3, while the optimal stop-losses range between 9 and 10. The previous squared

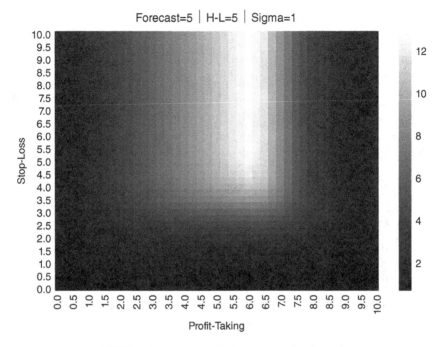

FIGURE 13.6   Heat-map for $\{E_0[P_{i,T_i}], \tau, \sigma\} = \{5, 5, 1\}$

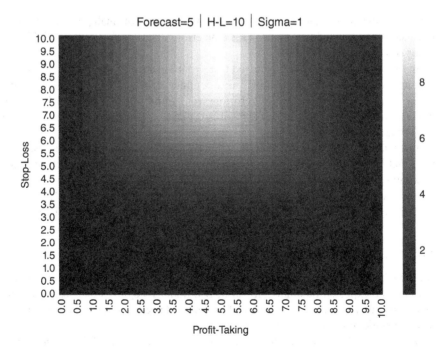

FIGURE 13.7   Heat-map for $\{E_0[P_{i,T_i}], \tau, \sigma\} = \{5, 10, 1\}$

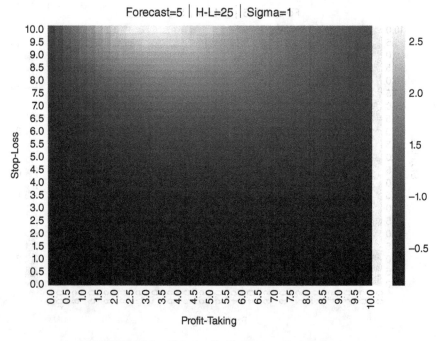

FIGURE 13.8 Heat-map for $\{E_0[P_{i,T_i}], \tau, \sigma\} = \{5, 25, 1\}$

area of optimal performance has given way to a semi-circle of small profit-taking with large stop-loss thresholds. Again we see a deterioration of performance, with Sharpe ratios of 2.7.

In Figure 13.9, the half-life is raised to $\tau = 50$. As a result, the region of optimal performance spreads, while Sharpe ratios continue to fall to 0.8. This is the same effect we observed in the case of zero long-run equilibrium (Section 13.6.1), with the difference that because now $E_0[P_{i,T_i}] > 0$, there is no symmetric area of worst performance.

In Figure 13.10, we appreciate that $\tau = 100$ leads to the natural conclusion of the trend described above. The process is now so close to a random walk that the maximum Sharpe ratio is a mere 0.32.

We can observe a similar pattern in Figures 13.11 through 13.15, where $E_0[P_{i,T_i}] = 10$ and τ is progressively increased from 5 to 10, 25, 50, and 100, respectively.

13.6.3 Cases with Negative Long-Run Equilibrium

A rational market participant would not initiate a position under the assumption that a loss is the expected outcome. However, if a trader recognizes that losses are the expected outcome of a pre-existing position, she still needs a strategy to stop-out that position while minimizing such losses.

We have obtained Figure 13.16 as a result of applying parameters $\{E_0[P_{i,T_i}], \tau, \sigma\} = \{-5, 5, 1\}$. If we compare Figure 13.16 with Figure 13.6, it

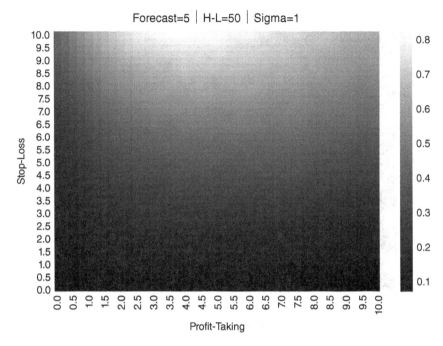

FIGURE 13.9 Heat-map for $\{E_0[P_{i,T_i}], \tau, \sigma\} = \{5, 50, 1\}$

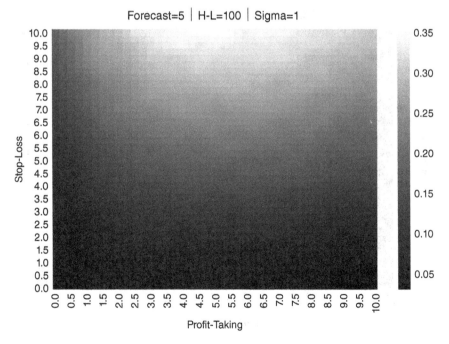

FIGURE 13.10 Heat-map for $\{E_0[P_{i,T_i}], \tau, \sigma\} = \{5, 100, 1\}$

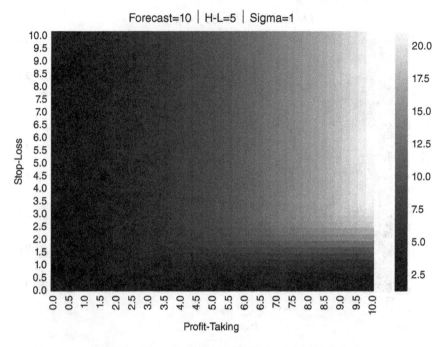

FIGURE 13.11   Heat-map for $\{E_0[P_{i,T_i}], \tau, \sigma\} = \{10, 5, 1\}$

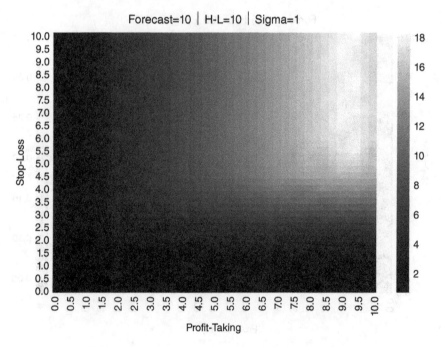

FIGURE 13.12   Heat-map for $\{E_0[P_{i,T_i}], \tau, \sigma\} = \{10, 10, 1\}$

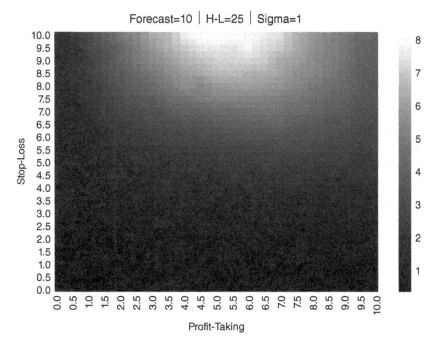

FIGURE 13.13   Heat-map for $\{E_0[P_{i,T_i}], \tau, \sigma\} = \{10, 25, 1\}$

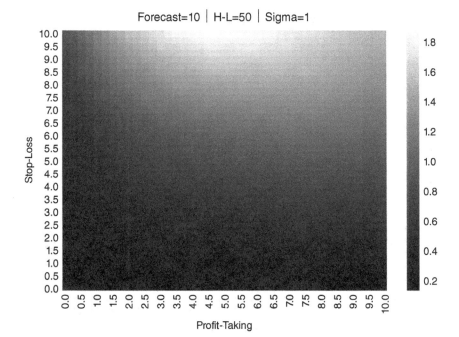

FIGURE 13.14   Heat-map for $\{E_0[P_{i,T_i}], \tau, \sigma\} = \{10, 50, 1\}$

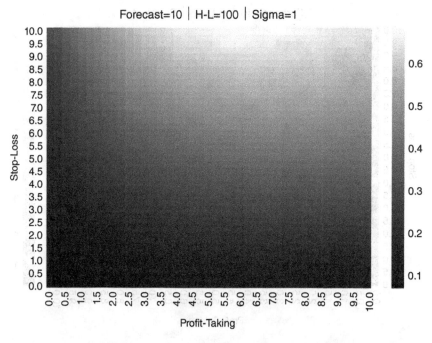

FIGURE 13.15   Heat-map for $\{E_0[P_{i,T_i}], \tau, \sigma\} = \{10, 100, 1\}$

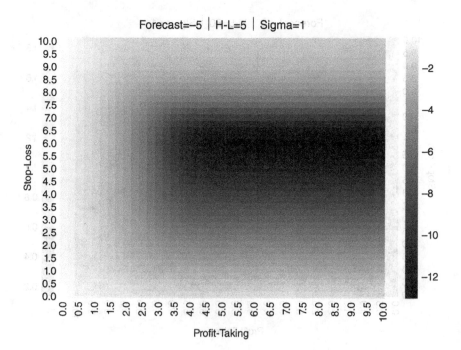

FIGURE 13.16   Heat-map for $\{E_0[P_{i,T_i}], \tau, \sigma\} = \{-5, 5, 1\}$

appears as if one is a rotated complementary of the other. Figure 13.6 resembles a rotated photographic negative of Figure 13.16. The reason is that the profit in Figure 13.6 is translated into a loss in Figure 13.16, and the loss in Figure 13.6 is translated into a profit in Figure 13.16. One case is a reverse image of the other, just as a gambler's loss is the house's gain.

As expected, Sharpe ratios are negative, with a worst performance region centered around the stop-loss of 6, and profit-taking thresholds that range between 4 and 10. Now the rectangular shape does not correspond to a region of best performance, but to a region of worst performance, with Sharpe ratios of around −12.

In Figure 13.17, $\tau = 10$, and now the proximity to a random walk plays in our favor. The region of worst performance spreads out, and the rectangular area becomes a square. Performance becomes less negative, with Sharpe ratios of about −9.

This familiar progression can be appreciated in Figures 13.18, 13.19, and 13.20, as τ is raised to 25, 50, and 100. Again, as the process approaches a random walk, performance flattens and optimizing the trading rule becomes a backtest-overfitting exercise.

Figures 13.21 through 13.25 repeat the same process for $E_0[P_{i,T_i}] = -10$ and τ that is progressively increased from 5 to 10, 25, 50, and 100. The same pattern, a rotated complementary to the case of positive long-run equilibrium, arises.

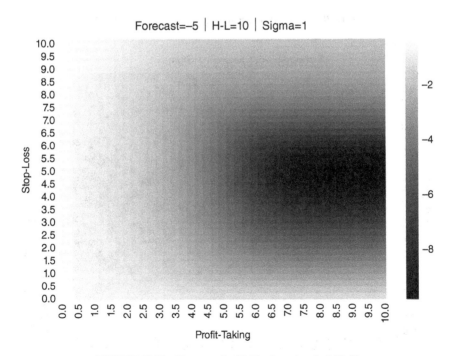

FIGURE 13.17   Heat-map for $\{E_0[P_{i,T_i}], \tau, \sigma\} = \{-5, 10, 1\}$

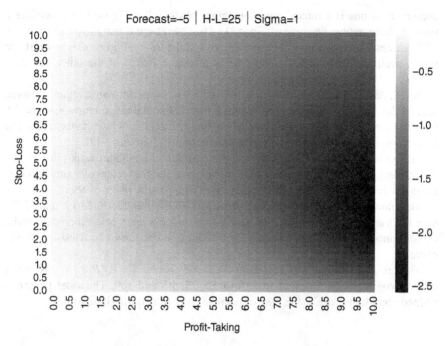

FIGURE 13.18 Heat-map for $\{E_0[P_{i,T_i}], \tau, \sigma\} = \{-5, 25, 1\}$

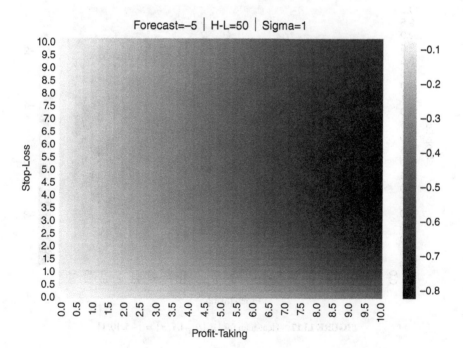

FIGURE 13.19 Heat-map for $\{E_0[P_{i,T_i}], \tau, \sigma\} = \{-5, 50, 1\}$

Forecast=–5 │ H-L=100 │ Sigma=1

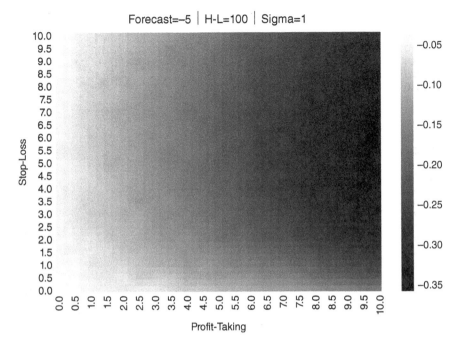

FIGURE 13.20 Heat-map for $\{E_0[P_{i,T_i}], \tau, \sigma\} = \{-5, 100, 1\}$

Forecast=–10 │ H-L=5 │ Sigma=1

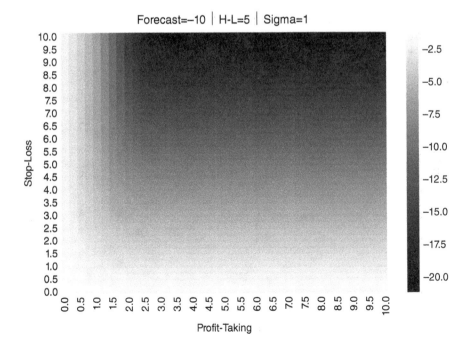

FIGURE 13.21 Heat-map for $\{E_0[P_{i,T_i}], \tau, \sigma\} = \{-10, 5, 1\}$

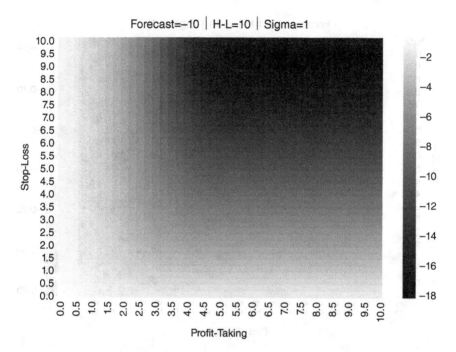

FIGURE 13.22   Heat-map for $\{E_0[P_{i,T_i}], \tau, \sigma\} = \{-10, 10, 1\}$

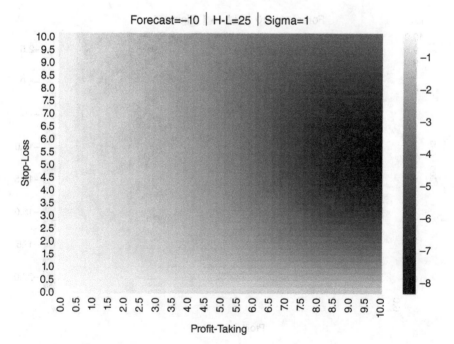

FIGURE 13.23   Heat-map for $\{E_0[P_{i,T_i}], \tau, \sigma\} = \{-10, 25, 1\}$

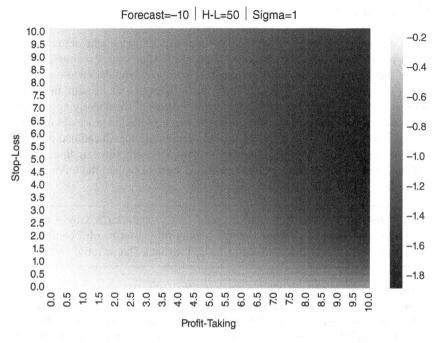

FIGURE 13.24   Heat-map for $\{E_0[P_{i,T_i}], \tau, \sigma\} = \{-10, 50, 1\}$

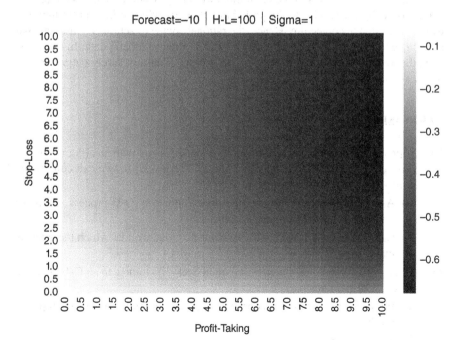

FIGURE 13.25   Heat-map for $\{E_0[P_{i,T_i}], \tau, \sigma\} = \{-10, 100, 1\}$

13.7 CONCLUSION

In this chapter we have shown how to determine experimentally the optimal trading strategy associated with prices following a discrete O-U process. Because the derivation of such trading strategy is not the result of a historical simulation, our procedure avoids the risks associated with overfitting the backtest to a single path. Instead, the optimal trading rule is derived from the characteristics of the underlying stochastic process that drives prices. The same approach can be applied to processes other than O-U, and we have focused on this particular process only for educational purposes.

While we do not derive the closed-form solution to the optimal trading strategies problem in this chapter, our experimental results seem to support the following OTR conjecture:

> **Conjecture:** Given a financial instrument's price characterized by a discrete O-U process, there is a unique optimal trading rule in terms of a combination of profit-taking and stop-loss that maximizes the rule's Sharpe ratio.

Given that these optimal trading rules can be derived numerically within a few seconds, there is little practical incentive to obtain a closed-form solution. As it is becoming more common in mathematical research, the experimental analysis of a conjecture can help us achieve a goal even in the absence of a proof. It could take years if not decades to prove the above conjecture, and yet all experiments conducted so far confirm it empirically. Let me put it this way: The probability that this conjecture is false is negligible relative to the probability that you will overfit your trading rule by disregarding the conjecture. Hence, the rational course of action is to assume that the conjecture is right, and determine the OTR through synthetic data. In the worst case, the trading rule will be suboptimal, but still it will almost surely outperform an overfit trading rule.

EXERCISES

13.1 Suppose you are an execution trader. A client calls you with an order to cover a short position she entered at a price of 100. She gives you two exit conditions: profit-taking at 90 and stop-loss at 105.

    (a) Assuming the client believes the price follows an O-U process, are these levels reasonable? For what parameters?

    (b) Can you think of an alternative stochastic process under which these levels make sense?

13.2 Fit the time series of dollar bars of E-mini S&P 500 futures to an O-U process. Given those parameters:

    (a) Produce a heat-map of Sharpe ratios for various profit-taking and stop-loss levels.

    (b) What is the OTR?

13.3 Repeat exercise 2, this time on a time series of dollar bars of

(a) 10-year U.S. Treasure Notes futures

(b) WTI Crude Oil futures

(c) Are the results significantly different? Does this justify having execution traders specialized by product?

13.4 Repeat exercise 2 after splitting the time series into two parts:

(a) The first time series ends on 3/15/2009.

(b) The second time series starts on 3/16/2009.

(c) Are the OTRs significantly different?

13.5 How long do you estimate it would take to derive OTRs on the 100 most liquid futures contracts worldwide? Considering the results from exercise 4, how often do you think you may have to re-calibrate the OTRs? Does it make sense to pre-compute this data?

13.6 Parallelize Snippets 13.1 and 13.2 using the `mpEngine` module described in Chapter 20.

REFERENCES

Bailey, D. and M. López de Prado (2012): "The Sharpe ratio efficient frontier." *Journal of Risk*, Vol. 15, No. 2, pp. 3–44. Available at http://ssrn.com/abstract=1821643.

Bailey, D. and M. López de Prado (2013): "Drawdown-based stop-outs and the triple penance rule." *Journal of Risk*, Vol. 18, No. 2, pp. 61–93. Available at http://ssrn.com/abstract=2201302.

Bailey, D., J. Borwein, M. López de Prado, and J. Zhu (2014): "Pseudo-mathematics and financial charlatanism: The effects of backtest overfitting on out-of-sample performance." *Notices of the American Mathematical Society*, 61(5), pp. 458–471. Available at http://ssrn.com/abstract=2308659.

Bailey, D., J. Borwein, M. López de Prado, and J. Zhu (2017): "The probability of backtest overfitting." *Journal of Computational Finance*, Vol. 20, No. 4, pp. 39–70. Available at http://ssrn.com/abstract=2326253.

Bertram, W. (2009): "Analytic solutions for optimal statistical arbitrage trading." Working paper. Available at http://ssrn.com/abstract=1505073.

Easley, D., M. Lopez de Prado, and M. O'Hara (2011): "The exchange of flow-toxicity." *Journal of Trading*, Vol. 6, No. 2, pp. 8–13. Available at http://ssrn.com/abstract=1748633.

CHAPTER 14

Backtest Statistics

14.1 MOTIVATION

In the previous chapters, we have studied three backtesting paradigms: First, historical simulations (the walk-forward method, Chapters 11 and 12). Second, scenario simulations (CV and CPCV methods, Chapter 12). Third, simulations on synthetic data (Chapter 13). Regardless of the backtesting paradigm you choose, you need to report the results according to a series of statistics that investors will use to compare and judge your strategy against competitors. In this chapter we will discuss some of the most commonly used performance evaluation statistics. Some of these statistics are included in the Global Investment Performance Standards (GIPS),[1] however a comprehensive analysis of performance requires metrics specific to the ML strategies under scrutiny.

14.2 TYPES OF BACKTEST STATISTICS

Backtest statistics comprise metrics used by investors to assess and compare various investment strategies. They should help us uncover potentially problematic aspects of the strategy, such as substantial asymmetric risks or low capacity. Overall, they can be categorized into general characteristics, performance, runs/drawdowns, implementation shortfall, return/risk efficiency, classification scores, and attribution.

---

[1] For further details, visit https://www.gipsstandards.org.

14.3   GENERAL CHARACTERISTICS

The following statistics inform us about the general characteristics of the backtest:

- **Time range:** Time range specifies the start and end dates. The period used to test the strategy should be sufficiently long to include a comprehensive number of regimes (Bailey and López de Prado [2012]).
- **Average AUM:** This is the average dollar value of the assets under management. For the purpose of computing this average, the dollar value of long and short positions is considered to be a positive real number.
- **Capacity:** A strategy's capacity can be measured as the highest AUM that delivers a target risk-adjusted performance. A minimum AUM is needed to ensure proper bet sizing (Chapter 10) and risk diversification (Chapter 16). Beyond that minimum AUM, performance will decay as AUM increases, due to higher transaction costs and lower turnover.
- **Leverage:** Leverage measures the amount of borrowing needed to achieve the reported performance. If leverage takes place, costs must be assigned to it. One way to measure leverage is as the ratio of average dollar position size to average AUM.
- **Maximum dollar position size:** Maximum dollar position size informs us whether the strategy at times took dollar positions that greatly exceeded the average AUM. In general we will prefer strategies that take maximum dollar positions close to the average AUM, indicating that they do not rely on the occurrence of extreme events (possibly outliers).
- **Ratio of longs:** The ratio of longs show what proportion of the bets involved long positions. In long-short, market neutral strategies, ideally this value is close to 0.5. If not, the strategy may have a position bias, or the backtested period may be too short and unrepresentative of future market conditions.
- **Frequency of bets:** The frequency of bets is the number of bets per year in the backtest. A sequence of positions on the same side is considered part of the same bet. A bet ends when the position is flattened or flipped to the opposite side. The number of bets is always smaller than the number of trades. A trade count would overestimate the number of independent opportunities discovered by the strategy.
- **Average holding period:** The average holding period is the average number of days a bet is held. High-frequency strategies may hold a position for a fraction of seconds, whereas low frequency strategies may hold a position for months or even years. Short holding periods may limit the capacity of the strategy. The holding period is related but different to the frequency of bets. For example, a strategy may place bets on a monthly basis, around the release of nonfarm payrolls data, where each bet is held for only a few minutes.
- **Annualized turnover:** Annualized turnover measures the ratio of the average dollar amount traded per year to the average annual AUM. High turnover may occur even with a low number of bets, as the strategy may require constant tuning of the position. High turnover may also occur with a low number of

trades, if every trade involves flipping the position between maximum long and maximum short.

- **Correlation to underlying:** This is the correlation between strategy returns and the returns of the underlying investment universe. When the correlation is significantly positive or negative, the strategy is essentially holding or short-selling the investment universe, without adding much value.

Snippet 14.1 lists an algorithm that derives the timestamps of flattening or flipping trades from a pandas series of target positions (tPos). This gives us the number of bets that have taken place.

SNIPPET 14.1   DERIVING THE TIMING OF BETS FROM A SERIES OF TARGET POSITIONS

```
# A bet takes place between flat positions or position flips
df0=tPos[tPos==0].index
df1=tPos.shift(1);df1=df1[df1!=0].index
bets=df0.intersection(df1) # flattening
df0=tPos.iloc[1:]*tPos.iloc[:-1].values
bets=bets.union(df0[df0<0].index).sort_values() # tPos flips
if tPos.index[-1] not in bets:bets=bets.append(tPos.index[-1:]) # last bet
```

Snippet 14.2 illustrates the implementation of an algorithm that estimates the average holding period of a strategy, given a pandas series of target positions (tPos).

SNIPPET 14.2   IMPLEMENTATION OF A HOLDING PERIOD ESTIMATOR

```
def getHoldingPeriod(tPos):
    # Derive avg holding period (in days) using avg entry time pairing algo
    hp,tEntry=pd.DataFrame(columns=['dT','w']),0.
    pDiff,tDiff=tPos.diff(),(tPos.index-tPos.index[0])/np.timedelta64(1,'D')
    for i in xrange(1,tPos.shape[0]):
        if pDiff.iloc[i]*tPos.iloc[i-1]>=0: # increased or unchanged
            if tPos.iloc[i]!=0:
                tEntry=(tEntry*tPos.iloc[i-1]+tDiff[i]*pDiff.iloc[i])/tPos.iloc[i]
        else: # decreased
            if tPos.iloc[i]*tPos.iloc[i-1]<0: # flip
                hp.loc[tPos.index[i],['dT','w']]=(tDiff[i]-tEntry,abs(tPos.iloc[i-1]))
                tEntry=tDiff[i] # reset entry time
            else:
                hp.loc[tPos.index[i],['dT','w']]=(tDiff[i]-tEntry,abs(pDiff.iloc[i]))
    if hp['w'].sum()>0:hp=(hp['dT']*hp['w']).sum()/hp['w'].sum()
    else:hp=np.nan
    return hp
```

14.4 PERFORMANCE

Performance statistics are dollar and returns numbers without risk adjustments. Some useful performance measurements include:

- **PnL:** The total amount of dollars (or the equivalent in the currency of denomination) generated over the entirety of the backtest, including liquidation costs from the terminal position.
- **PnL from long positions:** The portion of the PnL dollars that was generated exclusively by long positions. This is an interesting value for assessing the bias of long-short, market neutral strategies.
- **Annualized rate of return:** The time-weighted average annual rate of total return, including dividends, coupons, costs, etc.
- **Hit ratio:** The fraction of bets that resulted in a positive PnL.
- **Average return from hits:** The average return from bets that generated a profit.
- **Average return from misses:** The average return from bets that generated a loss.

14.4.1 Time-Weighted Rate of Return

Total return is the rate of return from realized and unrealized gains and losses, including accrued interest, paid coupons, and dividends for the measurement period. GIPS rules calculate time-weighted rate of returns (TWRR), adjusted for external cash flows (CFA Institute [2010]). Periodic and sub-periodic returns are geometrically linked. For periods beginning on or after January 1, 2005, GIPS rules mandate calculating portfolio returns that adjust for daily-weighted external cash flows.

We can compute the TWRR by determining the value of the portfolio at the time of each external cash flow.[2] The TWRR for portfolio i between subperiods $[t-1, t]$ is denoted $r_{i,t}$, with equations

$$r_{i,t} = \frac{\pi_{i,t}}{K_{i,t}}$$

$$\pi_{i,t} = \sum_{j=1}^{J}[(\Delta P_{j,t} + A_{j,t})\theta_{i,j,t-1} + \Delta\theta_{i,j,t}(P_{j,t} - \overline{P}_{j,t-1})]$$

$$K_{i,t} = \sum_{j=1}^{J}\tilde{P}_{j,t-1}\theta_{i,j,t-1} + \max\left\{0, \sum_{j=1}^{J}\tilde{\overline{P}}_{j,t}\Delta\theta_{i,j,t}\right\}$$

---

[2] External cash flows are assets (cash or investments) that enter or exit a portfolio. Dividend and interest income payments, for example, are not considered external cash flows.

where

- $\pi_{i,t}$ is the mark-to-market (MtM) profit or loss for portfolio i at time t.
- $K_{i,t}$ is the market value of the assets under management by portfolio i through subperiod t. The purpose of including the max $\{.\}$ term is to fund additional purchases (ramp-up).
- $A_{j,t}$ is the interest accrued or dividend paid by one unit of instrument j at time t.
- $P_{j,t}$ is the clean price of security j at time t.
- $\theta_{i,j,t}$ are the holdings of portfolio i on security j at time t.
- $\tilde{P}_{j,t}$ is the dirty price of security j at time t.
- $\overline{P}_{j,t}$ is the average transacted clean price of portfolio i on security j over subperiod t.
- $\overline{\tilde{P}}_{j,t}$ is the average transacted dirty price of portfolio i on security j over subperiod t.

Cash inflows are assumed to occur at the beginning of the day, and cash outflows are assumed to occur at the end of the day. These sub-period returns are then linked geometrically as

$$\varphi_{i,T} = \prod_{t=1}^{T}(1 + r_{i,t})$$

The variable $\varphi_{i,T}$ can be understood as the performance of one dollar invested in portfolio i over its entire life, $t = 1, \ldots, T$. Finally, the annualized rate of return of portfolio i is

$$R_i = (\varphi_{i,T})^{-y_i} - 1$$

where y_i is the number of years elapsed between $r_{i,1}$ and $r_{i,T}$.

14.5   RUNS

Investment strategies rarely generate returns drawn from an IID process. In the absence of this property, strategy returns series exhibit frequent runs. Runs are uninterrupted sequences of returns of the same sign. Consequently, runs increase downside risk, which needs to be evaluated with proper metrics.

14.5.1   Returns Concentration

Given a time series of returns from bets, $\{r_t\}_{t=1,\ldots,T}$, we compute two weight series, w^- and w^+:

$$r^+ = \{r_t | r_t \geq 0\}_{t=1,\ldots,T}$$
$$r^- = \{r_t | r_t < 0\}_{t=1,\ldots,T}$$

$$w^+ = \left\{ r_t^+ \left(\sum_t r_t^+ \right)^{-1} \right\}_{t=1,\ldots,T}$$

$$w^- = \left\{ r_t^- \left(\sum_t r_t^- \right)^{-1} \right\}_{t=1,\ldots,T}$$

Inspired by the Herfindahl-Hirschman Index (HHI), for $||w^+|| > 1$, where $||.||$ is the size of the vector, we define the concentration of positive returns as

$$h^+ \equiv \frac{\sum_t \left(w_t^+\right)^2 - ||w^+||^{-1}}{1 - ||w^+||^{-1}} = \left(\frac{E\left[\left(r_t^+\right)^2\right]}{E\left[r_t^+\right]^2} - 1 \right) \left(||r^+|| - 1\right)^{-1}$$

and the equivalent for concentration of negative returns, for $||w^-|| > 1$, as

$$h^- \equiv \frac{\sum_t \left(w_t^-\right)^2 - ||w^-||^{-1}}{1 - ||w^-||^{-1}} = \left(\frac{E\left[\left(r_t^-\right)^2\right]}{E\left[r_t^-\right]^2} - 1 \right) \left(||r^-|| - 1\right)^{-1}$$

From Jensen's inequality, we know that $E[r_t^+]^2 \leq E[(r_t^+)^2]$. And because $\frac{E[(r_t^+)^2]}{E[r_t^+]^2} \leq$ $||r^+||$, we deduce that $E[r_t^+]^2 \leq E[(r_t^+)^2] \leq E[r_t^+]^2||r^+||$, with an equivalent boundary on negative bet returns. These definitions have a few interesting properties:

1. $0 \leq h^+ \leq 1$
2. $h^+ = 0 \Leftrightarrow w_t^+ = ||w^+||^{-1}, \forall t$ (uniform returns)
3. $h^+ = 1 \Leftrightarrow \exists i | w_i^+ = \sum_t w_t^+$ (only one non-zero return)

It is easy to derive a similar expression for the concentration of bets across months, $h[t]$. Snippet 14.3 implements these concepts. Ideally, we are interested in strategies where *bets'* returns exhibit:

- high Sharpe ratio
- high number of bets per year, $||r^+|| + ||r^-|| = T$
- high hit ratio (relatively low $||r^-||$)
- low h^+ (no right fat-tail)
- low h^- (no left fat-tail)
- low $h[t]$ (bets are not concentrated in time)

SNIPPET 14.3   ALGORITHM FOR DERIVING HHI CONCENTRATION

```
rHHIPos=getHHI(ret[ret>=0]) # concentration of positive returns per bet
rHHINeg=getHHI(ret[ret<0]) # concentration of negative returns per bet
tHHI=getHHI(ret.groupby(pd.TimeGrouper(freq='M')).count()) # concentr. bets/month
#——————————————————————————————————
def getHHI(betRet):
    if betRet.shape[0]<=2:return np.nan
    wght=betRet/betRet.sum()
    hhi=(wght**2).sum()
    hhi=(hhi-betRet.shape[0]**-1)/(1.-betRet.shape[0]**-1)
    return hhi
```

14.5.2   Drawdown and Time under Water

Intuitively, a drawdown (DD) is the maximum loss suffered by an investment between two consecutive high-watermarks (HWMs). The time under water (TuW) is the time elapsed between an HWM and the moment the PnL exceeds the previous maximum PnL. These concepts are best understood by reading Snippet 14.4. This code derives both DD and TuW series from either (1) the series of returns (dollars = False) or; (2) the series of dollar performance (dollar = True). Figure 14.1 provides an example of DD and TuW.

SNIPPET 14.4   DERIVING THE SEQUENCE OF DD AND TuW

```
def computeDD_TuW(series,dollars=False):
    # compute series of drawdowns and the time under water associated with them
    df0=series.to_frame('pnl')
    df0['hwm']=series.expanding().max()
    df1=df0.groupby('hwm').min().reset_index()
    df1.columns=['hwm','min']
    df1.index=df0['hwm'].drop_duplicates(keep='first').index # time of hwm
    df1=df1[df1['hwm']>df1['min']] # hwm followed by a drawdown
    if dollars:dd=df1['hwm']-df1['min']
    else:dd=1-df1['min']/df1['hwm']
    tuw=((df1.index[1:]-df1.index[:-1])/np.timedelta64(1,'Y')).values# in years
    tuw=pd.Series(tuw,index=df1.index[:-1])
    return dd,tuw
```

14.5.3   Runs Statistics for Performance Evaluation

Some useful measurements of runs statistics include:

- **HHI index on positive returns:** This is getHHI(ret[ret >= 0]) in Snippet 14.3.

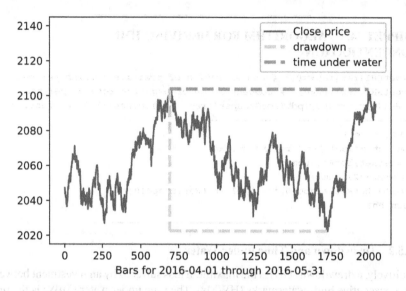

FIGURE 14.1   Examples of drawdown (DD) and time under water + (TuW)

- **HHI index on negative returns:** This is getHHI(ret[ret<0]) in Snippet 14.3.
- **HHI index on time between bets:** This is getHHI(ret.groupby (pd.TimeGrouper (freq='M')).count()) in Snippet 14.3.
- **95-percentile DD:** This is the 95th percentile of the DD series derived by Snippet 14.4.
- **95-percentile TuW:** This is the 95th percentile of the TuW series derived by Snippet 14.4.

14.6   IMPLEMENTATION SHORTFALL

Investment strategies often fail due to wrong assumptions regarding execution costs. Some important measurements of this include:

- **Broker fees per turnover:** These are the fees paid to the broker for turning the portfolio over, including exchange fees.
- **Average slippage per turnover:** These are execution costs, excluding broker fees, involved in one portfolio turnover. For example, it includes the loss caused by buying a security at a fill-price higher than the mid-price at the moment the order was sent to the execution broker.
- **Dollar performance per turnover:** This is the ratio between dollar performance (including brokerage fees and slippage costs) and total portfolio turnovers. It signifies how much costlier the execution could become before the strategy breaks even.

- **Return on execution costs:** This is the ratio between dollar performance (including brokerage fees and slippage costs) and total execution costs. It should be a large multiple, to ensure that the strategy will survive worse-than-expected execution.

14.7 EFFICIENCY

Until now, all performance statistics considered profits, losses, and costs. In this section, we account for the risks involved in achieving those results.

14.7.1 The Sharpe Ratio

Suppose that a strategy's excess returns (in excess of the risk-free rate), $\{r_t\}_{t=1,\ldots,T}$, are IID Gaussian with mean μ and variance σ^2. The Sharpe ratio (SR) is defined as

$$SR = \frac{\mu}{\sigma}$$

The purpose of SR is to evaluate the skills of a particular strategy or investor. Since μ, σ are usually unknown, the true SR value cannot be known for certain. The inevitable consequence is that Sharpe ratio calculations may be the subject of substantial estimation errors.

14.7.2 The Probabilistic Sharpe Ratio

The probabilistic Sharpe ratio (PSR) provides an adjusted estimate of SR, by removing the inflationary effect caused by short series with skewed and/or fat-tailed returns. Given a user-defined benchmark[3] Sharpe ratio (SR^*) and an observed Sharpe ratio $\widehat{SR}$, PSR estimates the probability that $\widehat{SR}$ is greater than a hypothetical SR^*. Following Bailey and López de Prado [2012], PSR can be estimated as

$$\widehat{PSR}\left[SR^*\right] = Z\left[\frac{\left(\widehat{SR} - SR^*\right)\sqrt{T-1}}{\sqrt{1 - \hat{\gamma}_3\widehat{SR} + \frac{\hat{\gamma}_4 - 1}{4}\widehat{SR}^2}}\right]$$

where $Z[.]$ is the cumulative distribution function (CDF) of the standard Normal distribution, T is the number of observed returns, $\hat{\gamma}_3$ is the skewness of the returns, and $\hat{\gamma}_4$ is the kurtosis of the returns ($\hat{\gamma}_4 = 3$ for Gaussian returns). For a given SR^*, $\widehat{PSR}$ increases with greater $\widehat{SR}$ (in the original sampling frequency, i.e. non-annualized), or longer track records (T), or positively skewed returns ($\hat{\gamma}_3$), but it decreases with fatter

---

[3] This could be set to a default value of zero (i.e., comparing against no investment skill).

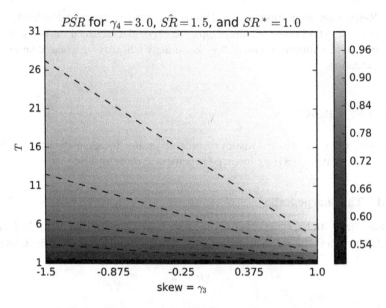

FIGURE 14.2   PSR as a function of skewness and sample length

tails ($\hat{\gamma}_4$). Figure 14.2 plots $\widehat{PSR}$ for $\hat{\gamma}_4 = 3$, $\widehat{SR} = 1.5$ and $SR^* = 1.0$ as a function of $\hat{\gamma}_3$ and T.

14.7.3   The Deflated Sharpe Ratio

The deflated Sharpe ratio (DSR) is a PSR where the rejection threshold is adjusted to reflect the multiplicity of trials. Following Bailey and López de Prado [2014], DSR can be estimated as $\widehat{PSR}\,[SR^*]$, where the benchmark Sharpe ratio, SR^*, is no longer user-defined. Instead, SR^* is estimated as

$$SR^* = \sqrt{V\left[\left\{\widehat{SR}_n\right\}\right]}\left((1-\gamma)Z^{-1}\left[1-\frac{1}{N}\right] + \gamma Z^{-1}\left[1-\frac{1}{N}e^{-1}\right]\right)$$

where $V[\{\widehat{SR}_n\}]$ is the variance across the trials' estimated SR, N is the number of independent trials, $Z\,[.]$ is the CDF of the standard Normal distribution, γ is the Euler-Mascheroni constant, and $n = 1,...,N$. See López de Prado [2018] for a detailed explanation of how to estimate N and $V[\{\widehat{SR}_n\}]$. Figure 14.3 plots SR^* as a function of $V[\{\widehat{SR}_n\}]$ and N.

   The rationale behind DSR is the following: Given a set of SR estimates, $\{\widehat{SR}_n\}$, its expected maximum is greater than zero, even if the true SR is zero. Under the null hypothesis that the actual Sharpe ratio is zero, $H_0 : SR = 0$, we know that the expected maximum $\widehat{SR}$ can be estimated as the SR^*. Indeed, SR^* increases quickly as more independent trials are attempted (N), or the trials involve a greater variance ($V[\{\widehat{SR}_n\}]$). From this knowledge we derive the third law of backtesting.

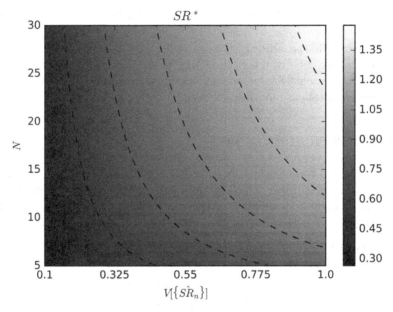

FIGURE 14.3 SR^* as a function of $V[\{\widehat{SR}_n\}]$ and N

SNIPPET 14.5   MARCOS' THIRD LAW OF BACKTESTING. MOST DISCOVERIES IN FINANCE ARE FALSE BECAUSE OF ITS VIOLATION

"Every backtest result must be reported in conjunction with all the trials involved in its production. Absent that information, it is impossible to assess the backtest's 'false discovery' probability."

—Marcos López de Prado
Advances in Financial Machine Learning (2018)

14.7.4   Efficiency Statistics

Useful efficiency statistics include:

- **Annualized Sharpe ratio:** This is the SR value, annualized by a factor $\sqrt{a}$, where a is the average number of returns observed per year. This common annualization method relies on the assumption that returns are IID.
- **Information ratio:** This is the SR equivalent of a portfolio that measures its performance relative to a benchmark. It is the annualized ratio between the average excess return and the tracking error. The excess return is measured as the portfolio's return in excess of the benchmark's return. The tracking error is estimated as the standard deviation of the excess returns.
- **Probabilistic Sharpe ratio:** PSR corrects SR for inflationary effects caused by non-Normal returns or track record length. It should exceed 0.95, for the

standard significance level of 5%. It can be computed on absolute or relative
returns.

- **Deflated Sharpe ratio:** DSR corrects SR for inflationary effects caused by
  non-Normal returns, track record length, and multiple testing/selection bias.
  It should exceed 0.95, for the standard significance level of 5%. It can be computed on absolute or relative returns.

14.8   CLASSIFICATION SCORES

In the context of meta-labeling strategies (Chapter 3, Section 3.6), it is useful to
understand the performance of the ML overlay algorithm in isolation. Remember that
the primary algorithm identifies opportunities, and the secondary (overlay) algorithm
decides whether to pursue them or pass. A few useful statistics include:

- **Accuracy:** Accuracy is the fraction of opportunities correctly labeled by the
  overlay algorithm,

$$accuracy = \frac{TP + TN}{TP + TN + FP + FN}$$

  where TP is the number of true positives, TN is the number of true negatives,
  FP is the number of false positives, and FN is the number of false negatives.

- **Precision:** Precision is the fraction of true positives among the predicted
  positives,

$$precision = \frac{TP}{TP + FP}$$

- **Recall:** Recall is the fraction of true positives among the positives,

$$recall = \frac{TP}{TP + FN}$$

- **F1**: Accuracy may not be an adequate classification score for meta-labeling
  applications. Suppose that, after you apply meta-labeling, there are many more
  negative cases (label '0') than positive cases (label '1'). Under that scenario, a
  classifier that predicts every case to be negative will achieve high accuracy, even
  though recall=0 and precision is undefined. The F1 score corrects for that flaw,
  by assessing the classifier in terms of the (equally weighted) harmonic mean of
  precision and recall,

$$F_1 = 2\frac{precision \cdot recall}{precision + recall}$$

As a side note, consider the unusual scenario where, after applying meta-
labeling, there are many more positive cases than negative cases. A classifier that predicts all cases to be positive will achieve TN=0 and FN=0, hence
accuracy=precision and recall=1. Accuracy will be high, and F1 will not be
smaller than accuracy, even though the classifier is not able to discriminate
between the observed samples. One solution would be to switch the definitions

of positive and negative cases, so that negative cases are predominant, and then score with F1.

- **Negative log-loss:** Negative log-loss was introduced in Chapter 9, Section 9.4, in the context of hyper-parameter tuning. Please refer to that section for details. The key conceptual difference between accuracy and negative log-loss is that negative log-loss takes into account not only whether our predictions were correct or not, but the probability of those predictions as well.

See Chapter 3, Section 3.7 for a visual representation of precision, recall, and accuracy. Table 14.1 characterizes the four degenerate cases of binary classification. As you can see, the F1 score is not defined in two of those cases. For this reason, when Scikit-learn is asked to compute F1 on a sample with no observed 1s or with no predicted 1s, it will print a warning (UndefinedMetricWarning), and set the F1 value to 0.

TABLE 14.1   The Four Degenerate Cases of Binary Classification

Condition	Collapse	Accuracy	Precision	Recall	F1
Observed all 1s	TN=FP=0	=recall	1	[0,1]	[0,1]
Observed all 0s	TP=FN=0	[0,1]	0	NaN	NaN
Predicted all 1s	TN=FN=0	=precision	[0,1]	1	[0,1]
Predicted all 0s	TP=FP=0	[0,1]	NaN	0	NaN

When all observed values are positive (label '1'), there are no true negatives or false positives, thus precision is 1, recall is a positive real number between 0 and 1 (inclusive), and accuracy equals recall. Then, $F_1 = 2\frac{recall}{1+recall} \geq recall$.

When all predicted values are positive (label '1'), there are no true negatives or false negatives, thus precision is a positive real number between 0 and 1 (inclusive), recall is 1, and accuracy equals precision. Then, $F_1 = 2\frac{precision}{1+precision} \geq precision$.

14.9   ATTRIBUTION

The purpose of performance attribution is to decompose the PnL in terms of risk classes. For example, a corporate bond portfolio manager typically wants to understand how much of its performance comes from his exposure to the following risks classes: duration, credit, liquidity, economic sector, currency, sovereign, issuer, etc. Did his duration bets pay off? What credit segments does he excel at? Or should he focus on his issuer selection skills?

These risks are not orthogonal, so there is always an overlap between them. For example, highly liquid bonds tend to have short durations and high credit rating, and are normally issued by large entities with large amounts outstanding, in U.S. dollars. As a result, the sum of the attributed PnLs will not match the total PnL, but at least we will be able to compute the Sharpe ratio (or information ratio) per risk class. Perhaps the most popular example of this approach is Barra's multi-factor method. See Barra [1998, 2013] and Zhang and Rachev [2004] for details.

Of equal interest is to attribute PnL across categories within each class. For example, the duration class could be split between short duration (less than 5 years), medium duration (between 5 and 10 years), and long duration (in excess of 10 years). This PnL attribution can be accomplished as follows: First, to avoid the overlapping problem we referred to earlier, we need to make sure that each member of the investment universe belongs to one and only one category of each risk class at any point in time. In other words, for each risk class, we split the entire investment universe into disjoint partitions. Second, for each risk class, we form one index per risk category. For example, we will compute the performance of an index of short duration bonds, another index of medium duration bonds, and another index of long duration bonds. The weightings for each index are the re-scaled weights of our investment portfolio, so that each index's weightings add up to one. Third, we repeat the second step, but this time we form those risk category indices using the weights from the investment universe (e.g., Markit iBoxx Investment Grade), again re-scaled so that each index's weightings add up to one. Fourth, we compute the performance metrics we discussed earlier in the chapter on each of these indices' returns and excess returns. For the sake of clarity, in this context the excess return of a short duration index is the return using (re-scaled) portfolio weightings (step 2) minus the return using (re-scaled) universe weightings (step 3).

EXERCISES

14.1 A strategy exhibits a high turnover, high leverage, and high number of bets, with a short holding period, low return on execution costs, and a high Sharpe ratio. Is it likely to have large capacity? What kind of strategy do you think it is?

14.2 On the dollar bars dataset for E-mini S&P 500 futures, compute

    (a) HHI index on positive returns.

    (b) HHI index on negative returns.

    (c) HHI index on time between bars.

    (d) The 95-percentile DD.

    (e) The 95-percentile TuW.

    (f) Annualized average return.

    (g) Average returns from hits (positive returns).

    (h) Average return from misses (negative returns).

    (i) Annualized SR.

    (j) Information ratio, where the benchmark is the risk-free rate.

    (k) PSR.

    (l) DSR, where we assume there were 100 trials, and the variance of the trials' SR was 0.5.

14.3 Consider a strategy that is long one futures contract on even years, and is short one futures contract on odd years.

    (a) Repeat the calculations from exercise 2.

    (b) What is the correlation to the underlying?

14.4 The results from a 2-year backtest are that monthly returns have a mean of 3.6%, and a standard deviation of 0.079%.

    (a) What is the SR?

    (b) What is the annualized SR?

14.5 Following on exercise 1:

    (a) The returns have a skewness of 0 and a kurtosis of 3. What is the PSR?

    (b) The returns have a skewness of -2.448 and a kurtosis of 10.164. What is the PSR?

14.6 What would be the PSR from 2.b, if the backtest had been for a length of 3 years?

14.7 A 5-year backtest has an annualized SR of 2.5, computed on daily returns. The skewness is -3 and the kurtosis is 10.

    (a) What is the PSR?

    (b) In order to find that best result, 100 trials were conducted. The variance of the Sharpe ratios on those trials is 0.5. What is the DSR?

REFERENCES

Bailey, D. and M. López de Prado (2012): "The Sharpe ratio efficient frontier." *Journal of Risk*, Vol. 15, No. 2, pp. 3–44.

Bailey, D. and M. López de Prado (2014): "The deflated Sharpe ratio: Correcting for selection bias, backtest overfitting and non-normality." *Journal of Portfolio Management*, Vol. 40, No. 5. Available at https://ssrn.com/abstract=2460551.

Barra (1998): *Risk Model Handbook: U.S. Equities*, 1st ed. Barra. Available at http://www.alacra.com/alacra/help/barra_handbook_US.pdf.

Barra (2013): *MSCI BARRA Factor Indexes Methodology*, 1st ed. MSCI Barra. Available at https://www.msci.com/eqb/methodology/meth_docs/MSCI_Barra_Factor%20Indices_Methodology_Nov13.pdf.

CFA Institute (2010): "Global investment performance standards." CFA Institute, Vol. 2010, No. 4, February. Available at https://www.gipsstandards.org/.

López de Prado, M. (2018): "Detection of False Investment Strategies Using Unsupervised Learning Methods." Working paper. Available at https://ssrn.com/abstract=3167017

Zhang, Y. and S. Rachev (2004): "Risk attribution and portfolio performance measurement— An overview." Working paper, University of California, Santa Barbara. Available at http://citeseerx.ist.psu.edu/viewdoc/summary?doi=10.1.1.318.7169.

BIBLIOGRAPHY

American Statistical Society (1999): "Ethical guidelines for statistical practice." Available at http://www.amstat.org/committees/ethics/index.html.

Bailey, D., J. Borwein, M. López de Prado, and J. Zhu (2014): "Pseudo-mathematics and financial charlatanism: The effects of backtest overfitting on out-of-sample performance." *Notices of the American Mathematical Society*, Vol. 61, No. 5. Available at http://ssrn.com/abstract=2308659.

Bailey, D., J. Borwein, M. López de Prado, and J. Zhu (2017): "The probability of backtest overfitting." *Journal of Computational Finance*, Vol. 20, No. 4, pp. 39–70. Available at http://ssrn.com/abstract=2326253.

Bailey, D. and M. López de Prado (2012): "Balanced baskets: A new approach to trading and hedging risks." *Journal of Investment Strategies (Risk Journals)*, Vol. 1, No. 4, pp. 21–62.

Beddall, M. and K. Land (2013): "The hypothetical performance of CTAs." Working paper, Winton Capital Management.

Benjamini, Y. and Y. Hochberg (1995): "Controlling the false discovery rate: A practical and powerful approach to multiple testing." *Journal of the Royal Statistical Society, Series B (Methodological)*, Vol. 57, No. 1, pp. 289–300.

Bennet, C., A. Baird, M. Miller, and G. Wolford (2010): "Neural correlates of interspecies perspective taking in the post-mortem Atlantic salmon: An argument for proper multiple comparisons correction." *Journal of Serendipitous and Unexpected Results*, Vol. 1, No. 1, pp. 1–5.

Bruss, F. (1984): "A unified approach to a class of best choice problems with an unknown number of options." *Annals of Probability*, Vol. 12, No. 3, pp. 882–891.

Dmitrienko, A., A.C. Tamhane, and F. Bretz (2010): *Multiple Testing Problems in Pharmaceutical Statistics*, 1st ed. CRC Press.

Dudoit, S. and M.J. van der Laan (2008): *Multiple Testing Procedures with Applications to Genomics*, 1st ed. Springer.

Fisher, R.A. (1915): "Frequency distribution of the values of the correlation coefficient in samples of an indefinitely large population." *Biometrika (Biometrika Trust)*, Vol. 10, No. 4, pp. 507–521.

Hand, D. J. (2014): *The Improbability Principle*, 1st ed. Scientific American/Farrar, Straus and Giroux.

Harvey, C., Y. Liu, and H. Zhu (2013): ". . . And the cross-section of expected returns." Working paper, Duke University. Available at http://ssrn.com/abstract=2249314.

Harvey, C. and Y. Liu (2014): "Backtesting." Working paper, Duke University. Available at http://ssrn.com/abstract=2345489.

Hochberg Y. and A. Tamhane (1987): *Multiple Comparison Procedures*, 1st ed. John Wiley and Sons.

Holm, S. (1979): "A simple sequentially rejective multiple test procedure." *Scandinavian Journal of Statistics*, Vol. 6, pp. 65–70.

Ioannidis, J.P.A. (2005): "Why most published research findings are false." *PloS Medicine*, Vol. 2, No. 8, pp. 696–701.

Ingersoll, J., M. Spiegel, W. Goetzmann, and I. Welch (2007): "Portfolio performance manipulation and manipulation-proof performance measures." *Review of Financial Studies*, Vol. 20, No. 5, pp. 1504–1546.

Lo, A. (2002): "The statistics of Sharpe ratios." *Financial Analysts Journal*, Vol. 58, No. 4 (July/August), pp. 36–52.

López de Prado M., and A. Peijan (2004): "Measuring loss potential of hedge fund strategies." *Journal of Alternative Investments*, Vol. 7, No. 1 (Summer), pp. 7–31. Available at http://ssrn.com/abstract=641702.

Mertens, E. (2002): "Variance of the IID estimator in Lo (2002)." Working paper, University of Basel.

Roulston, M. and D. Hand (2013): "Blinded by optimism." Working paper, Winton Capital Management.

Schorfheide, F. and K. Wolpin (2012): "On the use of holdout samples for model selection." *American Economic Review*, Vol. 102, No. 3, pp. 477–481.

Sharpe, W. (1966): "Mutual fund performance." *Journal of Business*, Vol. 39, No. 1, pp. 119–138.

Sharpe, W. (1975): "Adjusting for risk in portfolio performance measurement." *Journal of Portfolio Management*, Vol. 1, No. 2 (Winter), pp. 29–34.

Sharpe, W. (1994): "The Sharpe ratio." *Journal of Portfolio Management*, Vol. 21, No. 1 (Fall), pp. 49–58.

Studený M. and Vejnarová J. (1999): "The multiinformation function as a tool for measuring stochastic dependence," in M. I. Jordan, ed., *Learning in Graphical Models*. MIT Press, pp. 261–296.

Wasserstein R., and Lazar N. (2016) "The ASA's statement on p-values: Context, process, and purpose." *American Statistician*, Vol. 70, No. 2, pp. 129–133. DOI: 10.1080/00031305.2016.1154108.

Watanabe S. (1960): "Information theoretical analysis of multivariate correlation." *IBM Journal of Research and Development*, Vol. 4, pp. 66–82.

CHAPTER 15

Understanding Strategy Risk

15.1 MOTIVATION

As we saw in Chapters 3 and 13, investment strategies are often implemented in terms of positions held until one of two conditions are met: (1) a condition to exit the position with profits (profit-taking), or (2) a condition to exit the position with losses (stop-loss). Even when a strategy does not explicitly declare a stop-loss, there is always an implicit stop-loss limit, at which the investor can no longer finance her position (margin call) or bear the pain caused by an increasing unrealized loss. Because most strategies have (implicitly or explicitly) these two exit conditions, it makes sense to model the distribution of outcomes through a binomial process. This in turn will help us understand what combinations of betting frequency, odds, and payouts are uneconomic. The goal of this chapter is to help you evaluate when a strategy is vulnerable to small changes in any of these variables.

15.2 SYMMETRIC PAYOUTS

Consider a strategy that produces n IID bets per year, where the outcome X_i of a bet $i \in [1, n]$ is a profit $\pi > 0$ with probability $P[X_i = \pi] = p$, and a loss $-\pi$ with probability $P[X_i = -\pi] = 1 - p$. You can think of p as the precision of a binary classifier where a positive means betting on an opportunity, and a negative means passing on an opportunity: True positives are rewarded, false positives are punished, and negatives (whether true or false) have no payout. Since the betting outcomes $\{X_i\}_{i=1,\ldots,n}$ are independent, we will compute the expected moments per bet. The expected profit from one bet is $E[X_i] = \pi p + (-\pi)(1 - p) = \pi(2p - 1)$. The variance is $V[X_i] = E[X_i^2] - E[X_i]^2$, where $E[X_i^2] = \pi^2 p + (-\pi)^2(1 - p) = \pi^2$, thus

$V[X_i] = \pi^2 - \pi^2(2p-1)^2 = \pi^2[1-(2p-1)^2] = 4\pi^2p(1-p)$. For n IID bets per year, the annualized Sharpe ratio (θ) is

$$\theta[p,n] = \frac{nE[X_i]}{\sqrt{nV[X_i]}} = \underbrace{\frac{2p-1}{2\sqrt{p(1-p)}}}_{\substack{\text{t-value of } p \\ \text{under } H_0 : p = \frac{1}{2}}}\sqrt{n}$$

Note how π cancels out of the above equation, because the payouts are symmetric. Just as in the Gaussian case, $\theta[p,n]$ can be understood as a re-scaled t-value. This illustrates the point that, even for a small $p > \frac{1}{2}$, the Sharpe ratio can be made high for a sufficiently large n. This is the economic basis for high-frequency trading, where p can be barely above .5, and the key to a successful business is to increase n. The Sharpe ratio is a function of precision rather than accuracy, because passing on an opportunity (a negative) is not rewarded or punished directly (although too many negatives may lead to a small n, which will depress the Sharpe ratio toward zero).

For example, for $p = .55$, $\frac{2p-1}{2\sqrt{p(1-p)}} = 0.1005$, and achieving an annualized Sharpe ratio of 2 requires 396 bets per year. Snippet 15.1 verifies this result experimentally. Figure 15.1 plots the Sharpe ratio as a function of precision, for various betting frequencies.

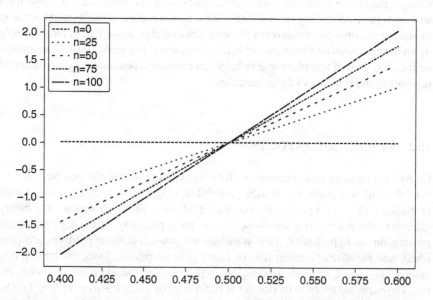

FIGURE 15.1   The relation between precision (x-axis) and sharpe ratio (y-axis) for various bet frequencies (n)

SNIPPET 15.1 TARGETING A SHARPE RATIO AS A FUNCTION OF THE NUMBER OF BETS

```
out,p=[],.55
for i in xrange(1000000):
    rnd=np.random.binomial(n=1,p=p)
    x=(1 if rnd==1 else -1)
    out.append(x)
print np.mean(out),np.std(out),np.mean(out)/np.std(out)
```

Solving for $0 \le p \le 1$, we obtain $-4p^2 + 4p - \frac{n}{\theta^2 + n} = 0$, with solution

$$p = \frac{1}{2}\left(1 + \sqrt{1 - \frac{n}{\theta^2 + n}}\right)$$

This equation makes explicit the trade-off between precision (p) and frequency (n) for a given Sharpe ratio (θ). For example, a strategy that only produces weekly bets ($n = 52$) will need a fairly high precision of $p = 0.6336$ to deliver an annualized Sharpe of 2.

15.3 ASYMMETRIC PAYOUTS

Consider a strategy that produces n IID bets per year, where the outcome X_i of a bet $i \in [1, n]$ is π_+ with probability $P[X_i = \pi_+] = p$, and an outcome π_-, $\pi_- < \pi_+$ occurs with probability $P[X_i = \pi_-] = 1 - p$. The expected profit from one bet is $E[X_i] = p\pi_+ + (1 - p)\pi_- = (\pi_+ - \pi_-)p + \pi_-$. The variance is $V[X_i] = E[X_i^2] - E[X_i]^2$, where $E[X_i^2] = p\pi_+^2 + (1 - p)\pi_-^2 = (\pi_+^2 - \pi_-^2)p + \pi_-^2$, thus $V[X_i] = (\pi_+ - \pi_-)^2 p(1 - p)$. For n IID bets per year, the annualized Sharpe ratio (θ) is

$$\theta[p, n, \pi_-, \pi_+] = \frac{nE[X_i]}{\sqrt{nV[X_i]}} = \frac{(\pi_+ - \pi_-)p + \pi_-}{(\pi_+ - \pi_-)\sqrt{p(1 - p)}}\sqrt{n}$$

And for $\pi_- = -\pi_+$ we can see that this equation reduces to the symmetric case: $\theta[p, n, -\pi_+, \pi_+] = \frac{2\pi_+ p + \pi_+}{2\pi_+ \sqrt{p(1-p)}}\sqrt{n} = \frac{2p-1}{2\sqrt{p(1-p)}}\sqrt{n} = \theta[p, n]$. For example, for $n = 260, \pi_- = -.01, \pi_+ = .005, p = .7$, we get $\theta = 1.173$.

Finally, we can solve the previous equation for $0 \le p \le 1$, to obtain

$$p = \frac{-b + \sqrt{b^2 - 4ac}}{2a}$$

where:

- $a = (n + \theta^2)(\pi_+ - \pi_-)^2$
- $b = [2n\pi_- - \theta^2(\pi_+ - \pi_-)]\,(\pi_+ - \pi_-)$
- $c = n\pi_-^2$

As a side note, Snippet 15.2 verifies these symbolic operations using SymPy Live: http://live.sympy.org/.

SNIPPET 15.2 USING THE SymPy LIBRARY FOR SYMBOLIC OPERATIONS

```
>>> from sympy import *
>>> init_printing(use_unicode=False,wrap_line=False,no_global=True)
>>> p,u,d=symbols('p u d')
>>> m2=p*u**2+(1-p)*d**2
>>> m1=p*u+(1-p)*d
>>> v=m2-m1**2
>>> factor(v)
```

The above equation answers the following question: Given a trading rule characterized by parameters $\{\pi_-, \pi_+, n\}$, what is the precision rate p required to achieve a Sharpe ratio of θ^*? For example, for $n = 260, \pi_- = -.01, \pi_+ = .005$, in order to get $\theta = 2$ we require a $p = .72$. Thanks to the large number of bets, a very small change in p (from $p = .7$ to $p = .72$) has propelled the Sharpe ratio from $\theta = 1.173$ to $\theta = 2$. On the other hand, this also tells us that the strategy is vulnerable to small changes in p. Snippet 15.3 implements the derivation of the implied precision. Figure 15.2 displays the implied precision as a function of n and π_-, where $\pi_+ = 0.1$ and $\theta^* = 1.5$. As π_- becomes more negative for a given n, a higher p is required to achieve θ^* for a given π_+. As n becomes smaller for a given π_-, a higher p is required to achieve θ^* for a given π_+.

SNIPPET 15.3 COMPUTING THE IMPLIED PRECISION

```
def binHR(sl,pt,freq,tSR):
    '''
    Given a trading rule characterized by the parameters {sl,pt,freq},
    what's the min precision p required to achieve a Sharpe ratio tSR?
    1) Inputs
    sl: stop loss threshold
    pt: profit taking threshold
    freq: number of bets per year
```

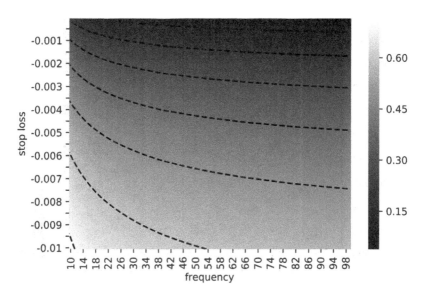

FIGURE 15.2   Heat-map of the implied precision as a function of n and π_-, with $\pi_+ = 0.1$ and $\theta^* = 1.5$

```
tSR: target annual Sharpe ratio
2) Output
p: the min precision rate p required to achieve tSR
'''
a=(freq+tSR**2)*(pt-sl)**2
b=(2*freq*sl-tSR**2*(pt-sl))*(pt-sl)
c=freq*sl**2
p=(-b+(b**2-4*a*c)**.5)/(2.*a)
return p
```

Snippet 15.4 solves $\theta[p, n, \pi_-, \pi_+]$ for the implied betting frequency, n. Figure 15.3 plots the implied frequency as a function of p and π_-, where $\pi_+ = 0.1$ and $\theta^* = 1.5$. As π_- becomes more negative for a given p, a higher n is required to achieve θ^* for a given π_+. As p becomes smaller for a given π_-, a higher n is required to achieve θ^* for a given π_+.

SNIPPET 15.4   COMPUTING THE IMPLIED BETTING FREQUENCY

```
def binFreq(sl,pt,p,tSR):
    '''
    Given a trading rule characterized by the parameters {sl,pt,freq},
    what's the number of bets/year needed to achieve a Sharpe ratio
    tSR with precision rate p?
    Note: Equation with radicals, check for extraneous solution.
```

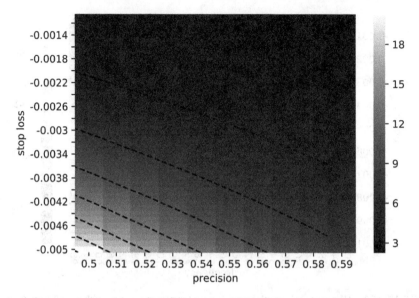

FIGURE 15.3   Implied frequency as a function of p and, with $= 0.1$ and $= 1.5$

```
1) Inputs
sl: stop loss threshold
pt: profit taking threshold
p: precision rate p
tSR: target annual Sharpe ratio
2) Output
freq: number of bets per year needed
'''
freq=(tSR*(pt-sl))**2*p*(1-p)/((pt-sl)*p+sl)**2 # possible extraneous
if not np.isclose(binSR(sl,pt,freq,p),tSR):return
return freq
```

15.4   THE PROBABILITY OF STRATEGY FAILURE

In the example above, parameters $\pi_- = -.01$, $\pi_+ = .005$ are set by the portfolio manager, and passed to the traders with the execution orders. Parameter $n = 260$ is also set by the portfolio manager, as she decides what constitutes an opportunity worth betting on. The two parameters that are not under the control of the portfolio manager are p (determined by the market) and θ^* (the objective set by the investor). Because p is unknown, we can model it as a random variable, with expected value $E[p]$. Let us define p_{θ^*} as the value of p below which the strategy will underperform a target Sharpe ratio θ^*, that is, $p_{\theta^*} = \max\{p | \theta \le \theta^*\}$. We can use the equations above (or the binHR function) to conclude that for $p_{\theta^*=0} = \frac{2}{3}$, $p < p_{\theta^*=0} \Rightarrow \theta \le 0$. This highlights the risks involved in this strategy, because a relatively small drop in p (from $p = .7$ to $p = .67$) will wipe out all the profits. The strategy is intrinsically risky, even if the holdings are not. That is the critical difference we wish to establish with this chapter: *Strategy risk* should not be confused with *portfolio risk.*

Most firms and investors compute, monitor, and report portfolio risk without realizing that this tells us nothing about the risk of the strategy itself. Strategy risk is not the risk of the underlying portfolio, as computed by the chief risk officer. Strategy risk is the risk that the investment strategy will fail to succeed over time, a question of far greater relevance to the chief investment officer. The answer to the question "What is the probability that this strategy will fail?" is equivalent to computing $P[p < p_{\theta*}]$. The following algorithm will help us compute the strategy risk.

15.4.1 Algorithm

In this section we will describe a procedure to compute $P[p < p_{\theta*}]$. Given a time series of bet outcomes $\{\pi_t\}_{t=1,\ldots,T}$, first we estimate $\pi_- = E[\{\pi_t | \pi_t \leq 0\}_{t=1,\ldots,T}]$, and $\pi_+ = E[\{\pi_t | \pi_t > 0\}_{t=1,\ldots,T}]$. Alternatively, $\{\pi_-, \pi_+\}$ could be derived from fitting a mixture of two Gaussians, using the EF3M algorithm (López de Prado and Foreman [2014]). Second, the annual frequency n is given by $n = \frac{T}{y}$, where y is the number of years elapsed between $t = 1$ and $t = T$. Third, we bootstrap the distribution of p as follows:

1. For iterations $i = 1, \ldots, I$:
   (a) Draw $\lfloor nk \rfloor$ samples from $\{\pi_t\}_{t=1,\ldots,T}$ with replacement, where k is the number of years used by investors to assess a strategy (e.g., 2 years). We denote the set of these drawn samples as $\{\pi_j^{(i)}\}_{j=1,\ldots,\lfloor nk \rfloor}$.
   (b) Derive the observed precision from iteration i as $p_i = \frac{1}{\lfloor nk \rfloor} \| \{\pi_j^{(i)} | \pi_j^{(i)} > 0\}_{j=1,\ldots,\lfloor nk \rfloor} \|$.
2. Fit the PDF of p, denoted $f[p]$, by applying a Kernel Density Estimator (KDE) on $\{p_i\}_{i=1,\ldots,I}$.

For a sufficiently large k, we can approximate this third step as $f[p] \sim N[\bar{p}, \bar{p}(1-\bar{p})]$, where $\bar{p} = E[p] = \frac{1}{T} \| \{\pi_t^{(i)} | \pi_t^{(i)} > 0\}_{t=1,\ldots,T} \|$. Fourth, given a threshold θ^* (the Sharpe ratio that separates failure from success), derive $p_{\theta*}$ (see Section 15.4). Fifth, the strategy risk is computed as $P[p < p_{\theta*}] = \int_{-\infty}^{p_{\theta*}} f[p]dp$.

15.4.2 Implementation

Snippet 15.5 lists one possible implementation of this algorithm. Typically we would disregard strategies where $P[p < p_{\theta*}] > .05$ as too risky, even if they invest in low volatility instruments. The reason is that even if they do not lose much money, the probability that they will fail to achieve their target is too high. In order to be deployed, the strategy developer must find a way to reduce $p_{\theta*}$.

SNIPPET 15.5 CALCULATING THE STRATEGY RISK IN PRACTICE

```python
import numpy as np,scipy.stats as ss
#----------------------------------------------------------
def mixGaussians(mu1,mu2,sigma1,sigma2,prob1,nObs):
    # Random draws from a mixture of gaussians
    ret1=np.random.normal(mu1,sigma1,size=int(nObs*prob1))
    ret2=np.random.normal(mu2,sigma2,size=int(nObs)-ret1.shape[0])
    ret=np.append(ret1,ret2,axis=0)
    np.random.shuffle(ret)
    return ret
#----------------------------------------------------------
def probFailure(ret,freq,tSR):
    # Derive probability that strategy may fail
    rPos,rNeg=ret[ret>0].mean(),ret[ret<=0].mean()
    p=ret[ret>0].shape[0]/float(ret.shape[0])
    thresP=binHR(rNeg,rPos,freq,tSR)
    risk=ss.norm.cdf(thresP,p,p*(1-p)) # approximation to bootstrap
    return risk
#----------------------------------------------------------
def main():
    #1) Parameters
    mu1,mu2,sigma1,sigma2,prob1,nObs=.05,-.1,.05,.1,.75,2600
    tSR,freq=2.,260
    #2) Generate sample from mixture
    ret=mixGaussians(mu1,mu2,sigma1,sigma2,prob1,nObs)
    #3) Compute prob failure
    probF=probFailure(ret,freq,tSR)
    print 'Prob strategy will fail',probF
    return
#----------------------------------------------------------
if __name__=='__main__':main()
```

This approach shares some similarities with PSR (see Chapter 14, and Bailey and López de Prado [2012, 2014]). PSR derives the probability that the true Sharpe ratio exceeds a given threshold under non-Gaussian returns. Similarly, the method introduced in this chapter derives the strategy's probability of failure based on asymmetric binary outcomes. The key difference is that, while PSR does not distinguish between parameters under or outside the portfolio manager's control, the method discussed here allows the portfolio manager to study the viability of the strategy subject to the parameters under her control: $\{\pi_-, \pi_+, n\}$. This is useful when designing or assessing the viability of a trading strategy.

EXERCISES

15.1 A portfolio manager intends to launch a strategy that targets an annualized SR of 2. Bets have a precision rate of 60%, with weekly frequency. The exit conditions are 2% for profit-taking, and –2% for stop-loss.

    (a) Is this strategy viable?

    (b) *Ceteris paribus*, what is the required precision rate that would make the strategy profitable?

    (c) For what betting frequency is the target achievable?

    (d) For what profit-taking threshold is the target achievable?

    (e) What would be an alternative stop-loss?

15.2 Following up on the strategy from exercise 1.

    (a) What is the sensitivity of SR to a 1% change in each parameter?

    (b) Given these sensitivities, and assuming that all parameters are equally hard to improve, which one offers the lowest hanging fruit?

    (c) Does changing any of the parameters in exercise 1 impact the others? For example, does changing the betting frequency modify the precision rate, etc.?

15.3 Suppose a strategy that generates monthly bets over two years, with returns following a mixture of two Gaussian distributions. The first distribution has a mean of –0.1 and a standard deviation of 0.12. The second distribution has a mean of 0.06 and a standard deviation of 0.03. The probability that a draw comes from the first distribution is 0.15.

    (a) Following López de Prado and Peijan [2004] and López de Prado and Foreman [2014], derive the first four moments for the mixture's returns.

    (b) What is the annualized SR?

    (c) Using those moments, compute PSR[1] (see Chapter 14). At a 95% confidence level, would you discard this strategy?

15.4 Using Snippet 15.5, compute $P[p < p_{\theta^*=1}]$ for the strategy described in exercise 3. At a significance level of 0.05, would you discard this strategy? Is this result consistent with $PSR[\theta^*]$?

15.5 In general, what result do you expect to be more accurate, $PSR[\theta^*]$ or $P[p < p_{\theta^*=1}]$? How are these two methods complementary?

15.6 Re-examine the results from Chapter 13, in light of what you have learned in this chapter.

    (a) Does the asymmetry between profit taking and stop-loss thresholds in OTRs make sense?

    (b) What is the range of p implied by Figure 13.1, for a daily betting frequency?

    (c) What is the range of p implied by Figure 13.5, for a weekly betting frequency?

REFERENCES

Bailey, D. and M. López de Prado (2014): "The deflated Sharpe ratio: Correcting for selection bias, backtest overfitting and non-normality." *Journal of Portfolio Management*, Vol. 40, No. 5. Available at https://ssrn.com/abstract=2460551.

Bailey, D. and M. López de Prado (2012): "The Sharpe ratio efficient frontier." *Journal of Risk*, Vol. 15, No. 2, pp. 3–44. Available at https://ssrn.com/abstract=1821643.

López de Prado, M. and M. Foreman (2014): "A mixture of Gaussians approach to mathematical portfolio oversight: The EF3M algorithm." *Quantitative Finance*, Vol. 14, No. 5, pp. 913–930. Available at https://ssrn.com/abstract=1931734.

López de Prado, M. and A. Peijan (2004): "Measuring loss potential of hedge fund strategies." *Journal of Alternative Investments*, Vol. 7, No. 1 (Summer), pp. 7–31. Available at http://ssrn.com/abstract=641702.

CHAPTER 16

Machine Learning Asset Allocation

16.1 MOTIVATION

This chapter introduces the Hierarchical Risk Parity (HRP) approach.[1] HRP portfolios address three major concerns of quadratic optimizers in general and Markowitz's Critical Line Algorithm (CLA) in particular: instability, concentration, and underperformance. HRP applies modern mathematics (graph theory and machine learning techniques) to build a diversified portfolio based on the information contained in the covariance matrix. However, unlike quadratic optimizers, HRP does not require the invertibility of the covariance matrix. In fact, HRP can compute a portfolio on an ill-degenerated or even a singular covariance matrix, an impossible feat for quadratic optimizers. Monte Carlo experiments show that HRP delivers lower out-of-sample variance than CLA, even though minimum-variance is CLA's optimization objective. HRP produces less risky portfolios out-of-sample compared to traditional risk parity methods. Historical analyses have also shown that HRP would have performed better than standard approaches (Kolanovic et al. [2017], Raffinot [2017]). A practical application of HRP is to determine allocations across multiple machine learning (ML) strategies.

16.2 THE PROBLEM WITH CONVEX PORTFOLIO OPTIMIZATION

Portfolio construction is perhaps the most recurrent financial problem. On a daily basis, investment managers must build portfolios that incorporate their views and forecasts on risks and returns. This is the primordial question that 24-year-old Harry Markowitz attempted to answer more than six decades ago. His monumental insight

---

[1] A short version of this chapter appeared in the *Journal of Portfolio Management,* Vol. 42, No. 4, pp. 59–69, Summer of 2016.

221

was to recognize that various levels of risk are associated with different optimal portfolios in terms of risk-adjusted returns, hence the notion of "efficient frontier" (Markowitz [1952]). One implication is that it is rarely optimal to allocate all assets to the investments with highest expected returns. Instead, we should take into account the correlations across alternative investments in order to build a diversified portfolio.

Before earning his PhD in 1954, Markowitz left academia to work for the RAND Corporation, where he developed the Critical Line Algorithm. CLA is a quadratic optimization procedure specifically designed for inequality-constrained portfolio optimization problems. This algorithm is notable in that it guarantees that the exact solution is found after a known number of iterations, and that it ingeniously circumvents the Karush-Kuhn-Tucker conditions (Kuhn and Tucker [1951]). A description and open-source implementation of this algorithm can be found in Bailey and López de Prado [2013]. Surprisingly, most financial practitioners still seem unaware of CLA, as they often rely on generic-purpose quadratic programming methods that do not guarantee the correct solution or a stopping time.

Despite of the brilliance of Markowitz's theory, a number of practical problems make CLA solutions somewhat unreliable. A major caveat is that small deviations in the forecasted returns will cause CLA to produce very different portfolios (Michaud [1998]). Given that returns can rarely be forecasted with sufficient accuracy, many authors have opted for dropping them altogether and focusing on the covariance matrix. This has led to risk-based asset allocation approaches, of which "risk parity" is a prominent example (Jurczenko [2015]). Dropping the forecasts on returns improves but does not prevent the instability issues. The reason is that quadratic programming methods require the inversion of a positive-definite covariance matrix (all eigenvalues must be positive). This inversion is prone to large errors when the covariance matrix is numerically ill-conditioned, that is, when it has a high condition number (Bailey and López de Prado [2012]).

16.3 MARKOWITZ'S CURSE

The condition number of a covariance, correlation (or normal, thus diagonalizable) matrix is the absolute value of the ratio between its maximal and minimal (by moduli) eigenvalues. Figure 16.1 plots the sorted eigenvalues of several correlation matrices, where the condition number is the ratio between the first and last values of each line. This number is lowest for a diagonal correlation matrix, which is its own inverse. As we add correlated (multicollinear) investments, the condition number grows. At some point, the condition number is so high that numerical errors make the inverse matrix too unstable: A small change on any entry will lead to a very different inverse. This is Markowitz's curse: The more correlated the investments, the greater the need for diversification, and yet the more likely we will receive unstable solutions. The benefits of diversification often are more than offset by estimation errors.

Increasing the size of the covariance matrix will only make matters worse, as each covariance coefficient is estimated with fewer degrees of freedom. In general, we need at least $\frac{1}{2}N(N + 1)$ independent and identically distributed (IID) observations in order

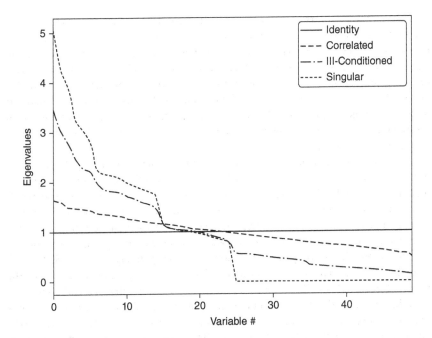

FIGURE 16.1 Visualization of Markowitz's curse
A diagonal correlation matrix has the lowest condition number. As we add correlated investments, the maximum eigenvalue is greater and the minimum eigenvalue is lower. The condition number rises quickly, leading to unstable inverse correlation matrices. At some point, the benefits of diversification are more than offset by estimation errors.

to estimate a covariance matrix of size N that is not singular. For example, estimating an invertible covariance matrix of size 50 requires, at the very least, 5 years of daily IID data. As most investors know, correlation structures do not remain invariant over such long periods by any reasonable confidence level. The severity of these challenges is epitomized by the fact that even naïve (equally-weighted) portfolios have been shown to beat mean-variance and risk-based optimization out-of-sample (De Miguel et al. [2009]).

16.4 FROM GEOMETRIC TO HIERARCHICAL RELATIONSHIPS

These instability concerns have received substantial attention in recent years, as Kolm et al. [2014] have carefully documented. Most alternatives attempt to achieve robustness by incorporating additional constraints (Clarke et al. [2002]), introducing Bayesian priors (Black and Litterman [1992]), or improving the numerical stability of the covariance matrix's inverse (Ledoit and Wolf [2003]).

All the methods discussed so far, although published in recent years, are derived from (very) classical areas of mathematics: geometry, linear algebra, and calculus. A correlation matrix is a linear algebra object that measures the cosines of the angles between any two vectors in the vector space formed by the returns series (see Calkin and López de Prado [2014a, 2015b]). One reason for the instability of quadratic optimizers is that the vector space is modelled as a complete (fully connected) graph, where every node is a potential candidate to substitute another. In algorithmic terms, inverting the matrix means evaluating the partial correlations across the complete graph. Figure 16.2(a) visualizes the relationships implied by a covariance matrix of 50×50, that is 50 nodes and 1225 edges. This complex structure magnifies small estimation errors, leading to incorrect solutions. Intuitively, it would be desirable to drop unnecessary edges.

Let us consider for a moment the practical implications of such a topological structure. Suppose that an investor wishes to build a diversified portfolio of securities, including hundreds of stocks, bonds, hedge funds, real estate, private placements, etc. Some investments seem closer substitutes of one another, and other investments seem complementary to one another. For example, stocks could be grouped in terms of liquidity, size, industry, and region, where stocks within a given group compete for allocations. In deciding the allocation to a large publicly traded U.S. financial stock like J. P. Morgan, we will consider adding or reducing the allocation to another large publicly traded U.S. bank like Goldman Sachs, rather than a small community bank in Switzerland, or a real estate holding in the Caribbean. Yet, to a correlation matrix, all investments are potential substitutes to one another. In other words, correlation matrices lack the notion of *hierarchy*. This lack of hierarchical structure allows weights to vary freely in unintended ways, which is a root cause of CLA's instability. Figure 16.2(b) visualizes a hierarchical structure known as a tree. A tree structure introduces two desirable features: (1) It has only $N - 1$ edges to connect N nodes, so the weights only rebalance among peers at various hierarchical levels; and (2) the weights are distributed top-down, consistent with how many asset managers build their portfolios (e.g., from asset class to sectors to individual securities). For these reasons, hierarchical structures are better designed to give not only stable but also intuitive results.

In this chapter we will study a new portfolio construction method that addresses CLA's pitfalls using modern mathematics: graph theory and machine learning. This Hierarchical Risk Parity method uses the information contained in the covariance matrix without requiring its inversion or positive-definitiveness. HRP can even compute a portfolio based on a singular covariance matrix. The algorithm operates in three stages: tree clustering, quasi-diagonalization, and recursive bisection.

16.4.1 Tree Clustering

Consider a *TxN* matrix of observations *X*, such as returns series of *N* variables over *T* periods. We would like to combine these *N* column-vectors into a hierarchical structure of clusters, so that allocations can flow downstream through a tree graph.

First, we compute an *NxN* correlation matrix with entries $\rho = \{\rho_{i,j}\}_{i,j=1,...,N}$, where $\rho_{i,j} = \rho[X_i, X_j]$. We define the distance measure $d : (X_i, X_j) \subset B \to \mathbb{R} \in [0, 1]$, $d_{i,j} = d[X_i, X_j] = \sqrt{\frac{1}{2}(1 - \rho_{i,j})}$, where B is the Cartesian product of items

(a)

(b)

FIGURE 16.2 The complete-graph (top) and the tree-graph (bottom) structures
Correlation matrices can be represented as complete graphs, which lack the notion of hierarchy: Each
investment is substitutable with another. In contrast, tree structures incorporate hierarchical relationships.

in $\{1, \ldots, i, \ldots, N\}$. This allows us to compute an NxN distance matrix $D = \{d_{i,j}\}_{i,j=1,\ldots,N}$. Matrix D is a proper metric space (see Appendix 16.A.1 for a proof), in the sense that $d[x, y] \geq 0$ (non-negativity), $d[x, y] = 0 \Leftrightarrow X = Y$ (coincidence), $d[x, y] = d[Y, X]$ (symmetry), and $d[X, Z] \leq d[x, y] + d[Y, Z]$ (sub-additivity). See Example 16.1.

$$\{\rho_{i,j}\} = \begin{bmatrix} 1 & .7 & .2 \\ .7 & 1 & -.2 \\ .2 & -.2 & 1 \end{bmatrix} \rightarrow \{d_{i,j}\} = \begin{bmatrix} 0 & .3873 & .6325 \\ .3873 & 0 & .7746 \\ .6325 & .7746 & 0 \end{bmatrix}$$

Example 16.1 Encoding a correlation matrix ρ as a distance matrix D

Second, we compute the Euclidean distance between any two column-vectors of D, $\tilde{d} : (D_i, D_j) \subset B \rightarrow \mathbb{R} \in [0, \sqrt{N}]$, $\tilde{d}_{i,j} = \tilde{d}[D_i, D_j] = \sqrt{\sum_{n=1}^{N} (d_{n,i} - d_{n,j})^2}$. Note the difference between distance metrics $d_{i,j}$ and $\tilde{d}_{i,j}$. Whereas $d_{i,j}$ is defined on column-vectors of X, $\tilde{d}_{i,j}$ is defined on column-vectors of D (a distance of distances). There-fore, $\tilde{d}$ is a distance defined over the entire metric space D, as each $\tilde{d}_{i,j}$ is a function of the entire correlation matrix (rather than a particular cross-correlation pair). See Example 16.2.

$$\{d_{i,j}\} = \begin{bmatrix} 0 & .3873 & .6325 \\ .3873 & 0 & .7746 \\ .6325 & .7746 & 0 \end{bmatrix} \rightarrow \{\tilde{d}_{i,j}\}_{i,j=\{1,2,3\}} = \begin{bmatrix} 0 & .5659 & .9747 \\ .5659 & 0 & 1.1225 \\ .9747 & 1.1225 & 0 \end{bmatrix}$$

Example 16.2 Euclidean distance of correlation distances

Third, we cluster together the pair of columns (i^*, j^*) such that $(i^*, j^*) = \operatorname{argmin}(i, j)_{i \neq j} \{\tilde{d}_{i,j}\}$, and denote this cluster as $u[1]$. See Example 16.3.

$$\{\tilde{d}_{i,j}\}_{i,j=\{1,2,3\}} = \begin{bmatrix} 0 & .5659 & .9747 \\ .5659 & 0 & 1.1225 \\ .9747 & 1.1225 & 0 \end{bmatrix} \rightarrow u[1] = (1, 2)$$

Example 16.3 Clustering items

Fourth, we need to define the distance between a newly formed cluster $u[1]$ and the single (unclustered) items, so that $\{\tilde{d}_{i,j}\}$ may be updated. In hierarchical clustering analysis, this is known as the "linkage criterion." For example, we can define the distance between an item i of $\tilde{d}$ and the new cluster $u[1]$ as $\dot{d}_{i,u[1]} = \min[\{\tilde{d}_{i,j}\}_{j \in u[1]}]$ (the nearest point algorithm). See Example 16.4.

$$u[1] = (1, 2) \rightarrow \{\dot{d}_{i,u[1]}\} = \begin{bmatrix} \min[0, .5659] \\ \min[.5659, 0] \\ \min[.9747, 1.1225] \end{bmatrix} = \begin{bmatrix} 0 \\ 0 \\ .9747 \end{bmatrix}$$

Example 16.4 Updating matrix $\{\tilde{d}_{i,j}\}$ with the new cluster u

Fifth, matrix $\{\tilde{d}_{i,j}\}$ is updated by appending $\dot{d}_{i,u[1]}$ and dropping the clustered columns and rows $j \in u[1]$. See Example 16.5.

$$\{\tilde{d}_{i,j}\}_{i,j=\{1,2,3,4\}} = \begin{bmatrix} 0 & .5659 & .9747 & 0 \\ .5659 & 0 & 1.1225 & 0 \\ .9747 & 1.1225 & 0 & .9747 \\ 0 & 0 & .9747 & 0 \end{bmatrix}$$

$$\{\tilde{d}_{i,j}\}_{i,j=\{3,4\}} = \begin{bmatrix} 0 & .9747 \\ .9747 & 0 \end{bmatrix}$$

Example 16.5 Updating matrix $\{\tilde{d}_{i,j}\}$ with the new cluster u

Sixth, applied recursively, steps 3, 4, and 5 allow us to append $N - 1$ such clusters to matrix D, at which point the final cluster contains all of the original items, and the clustering algorithm stops. See Example 16.6.

$$\{\tilde{d}_{i,j}\}_{i,j=\{3,4\}} = \begin{bmatrix} 0 & .9747 \\ .9747 & 0 \end{bmatrix} \rightarrow u[2] = (3, 4) \rightarrow \text{Stop}$$

Example 16.6 Recursion in search of remaining clusters

Figure 16.3 displays the clusters formed at each iteration for this example, as well as the distances $\tilde{d}_{i^* j^*}$ that triggered every cluster (third step). This procedure can be applied to a wide array of distance metrics $d_{i,j}$, $\tilde{d}_{i,j}$ and $\dot{d}_{i,u}$, beyond those illustrated in this chapter. See Rokach and Maimon [2005] for alternative metrics, the discussion on Fiedler's vector and Stewart's spectral clustering method in Brualdi [2010], as

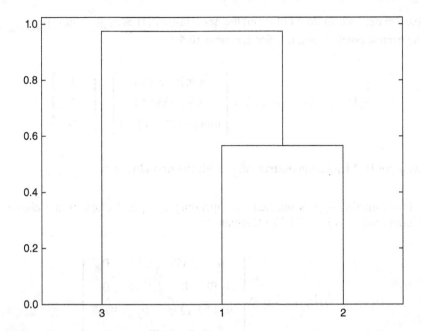

FIGURE 16.3   Sequence of cluster formation
A tree structure derived from our numerical example, here plotted as a dendogram. The y-axis measures
the distance between the two merging leaves.

well as algorithms in the scipy library.[2] Snippet 16.1 provides an example of tree
clustering using scipy functionality.

SNIPPET 16.1   TREE CLUSTERING USING SCIPY FUNCTIONALITY

```
import scipy.cluster.hierarchy as sch
import numpy as np
import pandas as pd
cov,corr=x.cov(),x.corr()
dist=((1-corr)/2.)**.5 # distance matrix
link=sch.linkage(dist,'single') # linkage matrix
```

This stage allows us to define a linkage matrix as an $(N-1)x4$ matrix with struc-
ture $Y = \{(y_{m,1}, y_{m,2}, y_{m,3}, y_{m,4})\}_{m=1,\dots,N-1}$ (i.e., with one 4-tuple per cluster). Items
$(y_{m,1}, y_{m,2})$ report the constituents. Item $y_{m,3}$ reports the distance between $y_{m,1}$ and

---

[2] For additional metrics see:

    http://docs.scipy.org/doc/scipy/reference/generated/scipy.spatial.distance.pdist.html
    http://docs.scipy.org/doc/scipy-0.16.0/reference/generated/scipy.cluster.hierarchy.linkage.html

$y_{m,2}$, that is $y_{m,3} = \tilde{d}_{y_{m,1},y_{m,2}}$. Item $y_{m,4} \leq N$ reports the number of original items included in cluster m.

16.4.2 Quasi-Diagonalization

This stage reorganizes the rows and columns of the covariance matrix, so that the largest values lie along the diagonal. This quasi-diagonalization of the covariance matrix (without requiring a change of basis) renders a useful property: Similar investments are placed together, and dissimilar investments are placed far apart (see Figures 16.5 and 16.6 for an example). The algorithm works as follows: We know that each row of the linkage matrix merges two branches into one. We replace clusters in $(y_{N-1,1}, y_{N-1,2})$ with their constituents recursively, until no clusters remain. These replacements preserve the order of the clustering. The output is a sorted list of original (unclustered) items. This logic is implemented in Snippet 16.2.

SNIPPET 16.2   QUASI-DIAGONALIZATION

```
def getQuasiDiag(link):
    # Sort clustered items by distance
    link=link.astype(int)
    sortIx=pd.Series([link[-1,0],link[-1,1]])
    numItems=link[-1,3] # number of original items
    while sortIx.max()>=numItems:
        sortIx.index=range(0,sortIx.shape[0]*2,2) # make space
        df0=sortIx[sortIx>=numItems] # find clusters
        i=df0.index;j=df0.values-numItems
        sortIx[i]=link[j,0] # item 1
        df0=pd.Series(link[j,1],index=i+1)
        sortIx=sortIx.append(df0) # item 2
        sortIx=sortIx.sort_index() # re-sort
        sortIx.index=range(sortIx.shape[0]) # re-index
    return sortIx.tolist()
```

16.4.3 Recursive Bisection

Stage 2 has delivered a quasi-diagonal matrix. The inverse-variance allocation is optimal for a diagonal covariance matrix (see Appendix 16.A.2 for a proof). We can take advantage of these facts in two different ways: (1) bottom-up, to define the variance of a contiguous subset as the variance of an inverse-variance allocation; or (2) top-down, to split allocations between adjacent subsets in inverse proportion to their aggregated variances. The following algorithm formalizes this idea:

1. The algorithm is initialized by:
   (a) setting the list of items: $L = \{L_0\}$, with $L_0 = \{n\}_{n=1,\dots,N}$
   (b) assigning a unit weight to all items: $w_n = 1$, $\forall n = 1, \dots, N$

2. If $|L_i| = 1$, $\forall L_i \in L$, then stop.
3. For each $L_i \in L$ such that $|L_i| > 1$:
   (a) bisect L_i into two subsets, $L_i^{(1)} \cup L_i^{(2)} = L_i$, where $|L_i^{(1)}| = \text{int}[\frac{1}{2}|L_i|]$, and the order is preserved
   (b) define the variance of $L_i^{(j)}$, $j = 1, 2$, as the quadratic form $\tilde{V}_i^{(j)} \equiv \tilde{w}_i^{(j)'} V_i^{(j)} \tilde{w}_i^{(j)}$, where $V_i^{(j)}$ is the covariance matrix between the constituents of the $L_i^{(j)}$ bisection, and $\tilde{w}_i^{(j)} = \text{diag}[V_i^{(j)}]^{-1} \frac{1}{\text{tr}[\text{diag}[V_i^{(j)}]^{-1}]}$, where diag[.] and tr[.] are the diagonal and trace operators
   (c) compute the split factor: $\alpha_i = 1 - \frac{\tilde{V}_i^{(1)}}{\tilde{V}_i^{(1)} + \tilde{V}_i^{(2)}}$, so that $0 \leq \alpha_i \leq 1$
   (d) re-scale allocations w_n by a factor of α_i, $\forall n \in L_i^{(1)}$
   (e) re-scale allocations w_n by a factor of $(1 - \alpha_i)$, $\forall n \in L_i^{(2)}$
4. Loop to step 2

Step 3b takes advantage of the quasi-diagonalization bottom-up, because it defines the variance of the partition $L_i^{(j)}$ using inverse-variance weightings $\tilde{w}_i^{(j)}$. Step 3c takes advantage of the quasi-diagonalization top-down, because it splits the weight in inverse proportion to the cluster's variance. This algorithm guarantees that $0 \leq w_i \leq 1$, $\forall i = 1, \dots, N$, and $\sum_{i=1}^{N} w_i = 1$, because at each iteration we are splitting the weights received from higher hierarchical levels. Constraints can be easily introduced in this stage, by replacing the equations in steps 3c, 3d, and 3e according to the user's preferences. Stage 3 is implemented in Snippet 16.3.

SNIPPET 16.3   RECURSIVE BISECTION

```
def getRecBipart(cov,sortIx):
    # Compute HRP alloc
    w=pd.Series(1,index=sortIx)
    cItems=[sortIx] # initialize all items in one cluster
    while len(cItems)>0:
        cItems=[i[j:k] for i in cItems for j,k in ((0,len(i)/2),\
            (len(i)/2,len(i))) if len(i)>1] # bi-section
        for i in xrange(0,len(cItems),2): # parse in pairs
            cItems0=cItems[i] # cluster 1
            cItems1=cItems[i+1] # cluster 2
            cVar0=getClusterVar(cov,cItems0)
            cVar1=getClusterVar(cov,cItems1)
            alpha=1-cVar0/(cVar0+cVar1)
            w[cItems0]*=alpha # weight 1
            w[cItems1]*=1-alpha # weight 2
    return w
```

This concludes a first description of the HRP algorithm, which solves the allocation problem in best-case deterministic logarithmic time, $T(n) = \mathcal{O}\left(\log_2[n]\right)$, and worst-case deterministic linear time, $T(n) = \mathcal{O}(n)$. Next, we will put to practice what we have learned, and evaluate the method's accuracy out-of-sample.

16.5   A NUMERICAL EXAMPLE

We begin by simulating a matrix of observations X, of order $(10000x10)$. The correlation matrix is visualized in Figure 16.4 as a heatmap. Figure 16.5 displays the dendogram of the resulting clusters (stage 1). Figure 16.6 shows the same correlation matrix, reorganized in blocks according to the identified clusters (stage 2). Appendix 16.A.3 provides the code used to generate this numerical example.

On this random data, we compute HRP's allocations (stage 3), and compare them to the allocations from two competing methodologies: (1) Quadratic optimization, as represented by CLA's minimum-variance portfolio (the only portfolio of the efficient frontier that does not depend on returns' means); and (2) traditional risk parity, exemplified by the Inverse-Variance Portfolio (IVP). See Bailey and López de Prado [2013] for a comprehensive implementation of CLA, and Appendix 16.A.2 for a

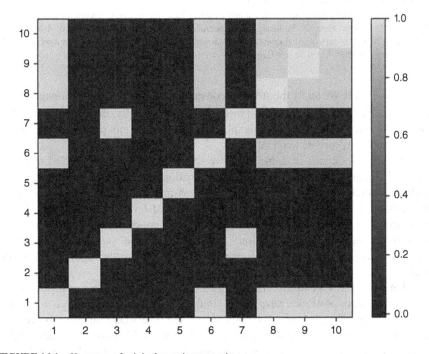

FIGURE 16.4   Heat-map of original covariance matrix
This correlation matrix has been computed using function `generateData` from snippet 16.4 (see Section 16.A.3). The last five columns are partially correlated to some of the first five series.

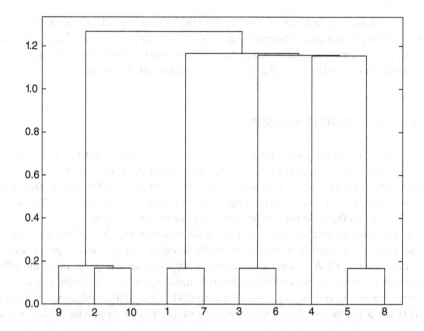

FIGURE 16.5   Dendogram of cluster formation
The clustering procedure has correctly identified that series 9 and 10 were perturbations of series 2, hence
(9, 2, 10) are clustered together. Similarly, 7 is a perturbation of 1, 6 is a perturbation of 3, and 8 is a
perturbation of 5. The only original item that was not perturbated is 4, and that is the one item for which
the clustering algorithm found no similarity.

derivation of IVP. We apply the standard constraints that $0 \leq w_i \leq 1$ (non-negativity),
$\forall i = 1, \ldots, N$, and $\sum_{i=1}^{N} w_i = 1$ (full investment). Incidentally, the condition number
for the covariance matrix in this example is only 150.9324, not particularly high and
therefore not unfavorable to CLA.

From the allocations in Table 16.1, we can appreciate a few stylized features:
First, CLA concentrates 92.66% of the allocation on the top-5 holdings, while
HRP concentrates only 62.57%. Second, CLA assigns zero weight to 3 investments
(without the $0 \leq w_i$ constraint, the allocation would have been negative). Third,
HRP seems to find a compromise between CLA's concentrated solution and traditional risk parity's IVP allocation. The reader can use the code in Appendix
16.A.3 to verify that these findings generally hold for alternative random covariance
matrices.

What drives CLA's extreme concentration is its goal of minimizing the portfolio's
risk. And yet both portfolios have a very similar standard deviation ($\sigma_{HRP} = 0.4640$,
$\sigma_{CLA} = 0.4486$). So CLA has discarded half of the investment universe in favor of
a minor risk reduction. The reality of course is that CLA's portfolio is deceitfully
diversified, because any distress situation affecting the top-5 allocations will have a
much greater negative impact on CLA's than on HRP's portfolio.

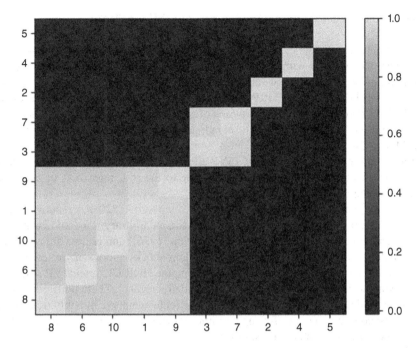

FIGURE 16.6   Clustered covariance matrix
Stage 2 quasi-diagonalizes the correlation matrix, in the sense that the largest values lie along the diagonal. However, unlike PCA or similar procedures, HRP does not require a change of basis. HRP solves the allocation problem robustly, while working with the original investments.

TABLE 16.1   A Comparison of Three Allocations

Weight #	CLA	HRP	IVP
1	14.44%	7.00%	10.36%
2	19.93%	7.59%	10.28%
3	19.73%	10.84%	10.36%
4	19.87%	19.03%	10.25%
5	18.68%	9.72%	10.31%
6	0.00%	10.19%	9.74%
7	5.86%	6.62%	9.80%
8	1.49%	9.10%	9.65%
9	0.00%	7.12%	9.64%
10	0.00%	12.79%	9.61%

A characteristic outcome of the three methods studied: CLA concentrates weights on a few investments, hence becoming exposed to idiosyncratic shocks. IVP evenly spreads weights through all investments, ignoring the correlation structure. This makes it vulnerable to systemic shocks. HRP finds a compromise between diversifying across all investments and diversifying across cluster, which makes it more resilient against both types of shocks.

16.6   OUT-OF-SAMPLE MONTE CARLO SIMULATIONS

In our numerical example, CLA's portfolio has lower risk than HRP's in-sample. However, the portfolio with minimum variance in-sample is not necessarily the one with minimum variance out-of-sample. It would be all too easy for us to pick a particular historical dataset where HRP outperforms CLA and IVP (see Bailey and López de Prado [2014], and recall our discussion of selection bias in Chapter 11). Instead, in this section we follow the backtesting paradigm explained in Chapter 13, and evaluate via Monte Carlo the performance out-of-sample of HRP against CLA's minimum-variance and traditional risk parity's IVP allocations. This will also help us understand what features make a method preferable to the rest, regardless of anecdotal counter-examples.

First, we generate 10 series of random Gaussian returns (520 observations, equivalent to 2 years of daily history), with 0 mean and an arbitrary standard deviation of 10%. Real prices exhibit frequent jumps (Merton [1976]) and returns are not cross-sectionally independent, so we must add random shocks and a random correlation structure to our generated data. Second, we compute HRP, CLA, and IVP portfolios by looking back at 260 observations (a year of daily history). These portfolios are re-estimated and rebalanced every 22 observations (equivalent to a monthly frequency). Third, we compute the out-of-sample returns associated with those three portfolios. This procedure is repeated 10,000 times.

All mean portfolio returns out-of-sample are essentially 0, as expected. The critical difference comes from the variance of the out-of-sample portfolio returns: $\sigma^2_{CLA} = 0.1157$, $\sigma^2_{IVP} = 0.0928$, and $\sigma^2_{HRP} = 0.0671$. Although CLA's goal is to deliver the lowest variance (that is the objective of its optimization program), its performance happens to exhibit the highest variance out-of-sample, and 72.47% greater variance than HRP's. This experimental finding is consistent with the historical evidence in De Miguel et al. [2009]. In other words, HRP would improve the out-of-sample Sharpe ratio of a CLA strategy by about 31.3%, a rather significant boost. Assuming that the covariance matrix is diagonal brings some stability to the IVP; however, its variance is still 38.24% greater than HRP's. This variance reduction out-of-sample is critically important to risk parity investors, given their use of substantial leverage. See Bailey et al. [2014] for a broader discussion of in-sample vs. out-of-sample performance.

The mathematical proof for HRP's outperformance over Markowitz's CLA and traditional risk parity's IVP is somewhat involved and beyond the scope of this chapter. In intuitive terms, we can understand the above empirical results as follows: Shocks affecting a specific investment penalize CLA's concentration. Shocks involving several correlated investments penalize IVP's ignorance of the correlation structure. HRP provides better protection against both common and idiosyncratic shocks by finding a compromise between diversification across all investments and diversification across clusters of investments at multiple hierarchical levels. Figure 16.7 plots the time series of allocations for the first of the 10,000 runs.

Appendix 16.A.4 provides the Python code that implements the above study. The reader can experiment with different parameter configurations and reach similar conclusions. In particular, HRP's out-of-sample outperformance becomes even

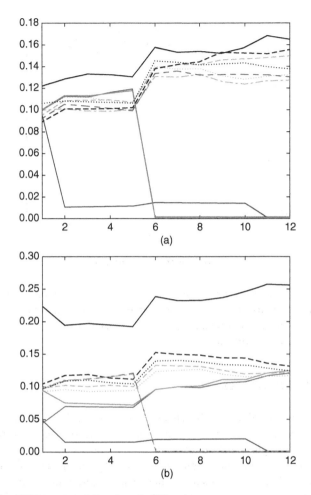

FIGURE 16.7   (a) Time series of allocations for IVP.

Between the first and second rebalance, one investment receives an idiosyncratic shock, which increases its variance. IVP's response is to reduce the allocation to that investment, and spread that former exposure across all other investments. Between the fifth and sixth rebalance, two investments are affected by a common shock. IVP's response is the same. As a result, allocations among the seven unaffected investments grow over time, regardless of their correlation.

(b) Time series of allocations for HRP

HRP's response to the idiosyncratic shock is to reduce the allocation to the affected investment, and use that reduced amount to increase the allocation to a correlated investment that was unaffected. As a response to the common shock, HRP reduces allocation to the affected investments and increases allocation to uncorrelated ones (with lower variance).

(c) Time series of allocations for CLA

CLA allocations respond erratically to idiosyncratic and common shocks. If we had taken into account rebalancing costs, CLA's performance would have been very negative.

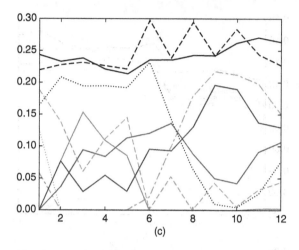

FIGURE 16.7   (*Continued*)

more substantial for larger investment universes, or when more shocks are added, or a stronger correlation structure is considered, or rebalancing costs are taken into account. Each of these CLA rebalances incurs transaction costs that can accumulate into prohibitive losses over time.

16.7   FURTHER RESEARCH

The methodology introduced in this chapter is flexible, scalable and admits multiple variations of the same ideas. Using the code provided, readers can research and evaluate what HRP configurations work best for their particular problem. For example, at stage 1 they can apply alternative definitions of $d_{i,j}$, $\tilde{d}_{i,j}$ and $\dot{d}_{i,u}$, or different clustering algorithms, like biclustering; at stage 3, they can use different functions for $\tilde{w}_m$ and α, or alternative allocation constraints. Instead of carrying out a recursive bisection, stage 3 could also split allocations top-down using the clusters from stage 1.

It is relatively straightforward to incorporate forecasted returns, Ledoit-Wolf shrinkage, and Black-Litterman–style views to this hierarchical approach. In fact, the inquisitive reader may have realized that, at its core, HRP is essentially a robust procedure to avoid matrix inversions, and the same ideas underlying HRP can be used to replace many econometric regression methods, notorious for their unstable outputs (like VAR or VECM). Figure 16.8 displays (a) a large correlation matrix of fixed income securities before and (b) after clustering, with over 2.1 million entries. Traditional optimization or econometric methods fail to recognize the hierarchical structure of financial Big Data, where the numerical instabilities defeat the benefits of the analysis, resulting in unreliable and detrimental outcomes.

Kolanovic et al. [2017] conducted a lengthy study of HRP, concluding that "HRP delivers superior risk-adjusted returns. Whilst both the HRP and the MV portfolios deliver the highest returns, the HRP portfolios match with volatility targets much better than MV portfolios. We also run simulation studies to confirm the robustness

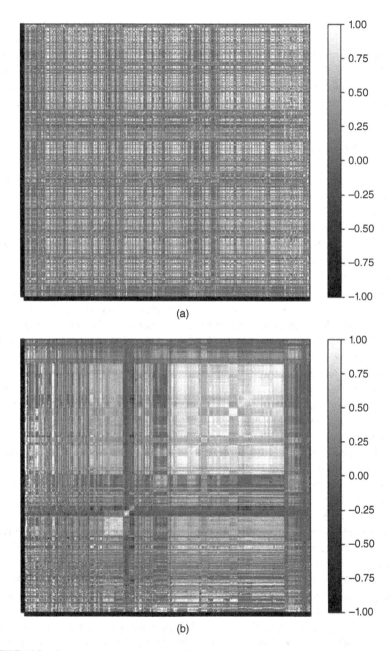

FIGURE 16.8 Correlation matrix before and after clustering
The methodology described in this chapter can be applied to problems beyond optimization. For example, a PCA analysis of a large fixed income universe suffers the same drawbacks we described for CLA. Small-data techniques developed decades and centuries ago (factor models, regression analysis, econometrics) fail to recognize the hierarchical nature of financial big data.

of our findings, in which HRP consistently deliver a superior performance over MV and other risk-based strategies [...] HRP portfolios are truly diversified with a higher number of uncorrelated exposures, and less extreme weights and risk allocations."

Raffinot [2017] concludes that "empirical results indicate that hierarchical clustering based portfolios are robust, truly diversified and achieve statistically better risk-adjusted performances than commonly used portfolio optimization techniques."

16.8 CONCLUSION

Exact analytical solutions can perform much worse than approximate ML solutions. Although mathematically correct, quadratic optimizers in general, and Markowitz's CLA in particular, are known to deliver generally unreliable solutions due to their instability, concentration, and underperformance. The root cause for these issues is that quadratic optimizers require the inversion of a covariance matrix. Markowitz's curse is that the more correlated investments are, the greater is the need for a diversified portfolio, and yet the greater are that portfolio's estimation errors.

In this chapter, we have exposed a major source of quadratic optimizers' instability: A matrix of size N is associated with a complete graph with $\frac{1}{2}N(N-1)$ edges. With so many edges connecting the nodes of the graph, weights are allowed to rebalance with complete freedom. This lack of hierarchical structure means that small estimation errors will lead to entirely different solutions. HRP replaces the covariance structure with a tree structure, accomplishing three goals: (1) Unlike traditional risk parity methods, it fully utilizes the information contained in the covariance matrix, (2) weights' stability is recovered and (3) the solution is intuitive by construction. The algorithm converges in deterministic logarithmic (best case) or linear (worst case) time.

HRP is robust, visual, and flexible, allowing the user to introduce constraints or manipulate the tree structure without compromising the algorithm's search. These properties are derived from the fact that HRP does not require covariance invertibility. Indeed, HRP can compute a portfolio on an ill-degenerated or even a singular covariance matrix.

This chapter focuses on a portfolio construction application; however, the reader will find other practical uses for making decisions under uncertainty, particularly in the presence of a nearly singular covariance matrix: capital allocation to portfolio managers, allocations across algorithmic strategies, bagging and boosting of machine learning signals, forecasts from random forests, replacement to unstable econometric models (VAR, VECM), etc.

Of course, quadratic optimizers like CLA produce the minimum-variance portfolio in-sample (that is its objective function). Monte Carlo experiments show that HRP delivers lower out-of-sample variance than CLA or traditional risk parity methods (IVP). Since Bridgewater pioneered risk parity in the 1990s, some of the largest asset managers have launched funds that follow this approach, for combined assets in excess of $500 billion. Given their extensive use of leverage, these funds should benefit from adopting a more stable risk parity allocation method, thus achieving superior risk-adjusted returns and lower rebalance costs.

APPENDICES

16.A.1   CORRELATION-BASED METRIC

Consider two real-valued vectors X, Y of size T, and a correlation variable $\rho[x, y]$, with the only requirement that $\sigma[x, y] = \rho[x, y]\sigma[X]\sigma[Y]$, where $\sigma[x, y]$ is the covariance between the two vectors, and $\sigma[.]$ is the standard deviation. Note that Pearson's is not the only correlation to satisfy these requirements.

Let us prove that $d[x, y] = \sqrt{\frac{1}{2}(1 - \rho[x, y])}$ is a true metric. First, the Euclidean distance between the two vectors is $d[x, y] = \sqrt{\sum_{t=1}^{T} (X_t - Y_t)^2}$. Second, we z-standardize those vectors as $x = \frac{X - \bar{X}}{\sigma[X]}$, $y = \frac{Y - \bar{Y}}{\sigma[Y]}$. Consequently, $0 \le \rho[x, y] = \rho[x, y]$. Third, we derive the Euclidean distance $d[x, y]$ as,

$$d[x, y] = \sqrt{\sum_{t=1}^{T} (x_t - y_t)^2} = \sqrt{\sum_{t=1}^{T} x_t^2 + \sum_{t=1}^{T} y_t^2 - 2\sum_{t=1}^{T} x_t y_t}$$

$$= \sqrt{T + T - 2T\sigma[x, y]} = \sqrt{2T\left(1 - \underbrace{\rho[x, y]}_{=\rho[x,y]}\right)} = \sqrt{4T}d[x, y]$$

In other words, the distance $d[x, y]$ is a linear multiple of the Euclidean distance between the vectors $\{X, Y\}$ after z-standardization, hence it inherits the true-metric properties of the Euclidean distance.

Similarly, we can prove that $d[x, y] = \sqrt{1 - |\rho[x, y]|}$ descends to a true metric on the $\mathbb{Z}/2\mathbb{Z}$ quotient. In order to do that, we redefine $y = \frac{Y - \bar{Y}}{\sigma[Y]}\text{sgn}\,[\rho[x, y]]$, where sgn $[.]$ is the sign operator, so that $0 \le \rho[x, y] = |\rho[x, y]|$. Then,

$$d[x, y] = \sqrt{2T\left(1 - \underbrace{\rho[x, y]}_{=|\rho[x,y]|}\right)} = \sqrt{2T}d[x, y]$$

16.A.2   INVERSE VARIANCE ALLOCATION

Stage 3 (see Section 16.4.3) splits a weight in inverse proportion to the subset's variance. We now prove that such allocation is optimal when the covariance matrix is diagonal. Consider the standard quadratic optimization problem of size N,

$$\min_{\omega} \omega' V \omega$$

$$\text{s.t. :}\;\; \omega' a = 1_I$$

with solution $\omega = \frac{V^{-1}a}{a'V^{-1}a}$. For the characteristic vector $a = 1_N$, the solution is the minimum variance portfolio. If V is diagonal, $\omega_n = \frac{V_{n,n}^{-1}}{\sum_{i=1}^{N} V_{i,i}^{-1}}$. In the particular case of $N = 2$, $\omega_1 = \frac{\frac{1}{V_{1,1}}}{\frac{1}{V_{1,1}} + \frac{1}{V_{2,2}}} = 1 - \frac{V_{1,1}}{V_{1,1} + V_{2,2}}$, which is how stage 3 splits a weight between two bisections of a subset.

16.A.3 REPRODUCING THE NUMERICAL EXAMPLE

Snippet 16.4 can be used to reproduce our results and simulate additional numerical examples. Function `generateData` produces a matrix of time series where a number `size0` of vectors are uncorrelated, and a number `size1` of vectors are correlated. The reader can change the `np.random.seed` in `generateData` to run alternative examples and gain an intuition of how HRP works. Scipy's function `linkage` can be used to perform stage 1 (Section 16.4.1), function `getQuasiDiag` performs stage 2 (Section 16.4.2), and function `getRecBipart` carries out stage 3 (Section 16.4.3).

SNIPPET 16.4   FULL IMPLEMENTATION OF THE HRP ALGORITHM

```
import matplotlib.pyplot as mpl
import scipy.cluster.hierarchy as sch,random,numpy as np,pandas as pd
#————————————————————————————————
def getIVP(cov,**kargs):
    # Compute the inverse-variance portfolio
    ivp=1./np.diag(cov)
    ivp/=ivp.sum()
    return ivp
#————————————————————————————————
def getClusterVar(cov,cItems):
    # Compute variance per cluster
    cov_=cov.loc[cItems,cItems] # matrix slice
    w_=getIVP(cov_).reshape(-1,1)
    cVar=np.dot(np.dot(w_.T,cov_),w_)[0,0]
    return cVar
#————————————————————————————————
def getQuasiDiag(link):
    # Sort clustered items by distance
    link=link.astype(int)
    sortIx=pd.Series([link[-1,0],link[-1,1]])
    numItems=link[-1,3] # number of original items
    while sortIx.max()>=numItems:
        sortIx.index=range(0,sortIx.shape[0]*2,2) # make space
        df0=sortIx[sortIx>=numItems] # find clusters
        i=df0.index;j=df0.values-numItems
        sortIx[i]=link[j,0] # item 1
```

```
            df0=pd.Series(link[j,1],index=i+1)
            sortIx=sortIx.append(df0) # item 2
            sortIx=sortIx.sort_index() # re-sort
            sortIx.index=range(sortIx.shape[0]) # re-index
    return sortIx.tolist()
#————————————————————————————————————
def getRecBipart(cov,sortIx):
    # Compute HRP alloc
    w=pd.Series(1,index=sortIx)
    cItems=[sortIx] # initialize all items in one cluster
    while len(cItems)>0:
        cItems=[i[j:k] for i in cItems for j,k in ((0,len(i)/2), \
            (len(i)/2,len(i))) if len(i)>1] # bi-section
        for i in xrange(0,len(cItems),2): # parse in pairs
            cItems0=cItems[i] # cluster 1
            cItems1=cItems[i+1] # cluster 2
            cVar0=getClusterVar(cov,cItems0)
            cVar1=getClusterVar(cov,cItems1)
            alpha=1-cVar0/(cVar0+cVar1)
            w[cItems0]*=alpha # weight 1
            w[cItems1]*=1-alpha # weight 2
    return w
#————————————————————————————————————
def correlDist(corr):
    # A distance matrix based on correlation, where 0<=d[i,j]<=1
    # This is a proper distance metric
    dist=((1-corr)/2.)**.5 # distance matrix
    return dist
#————————————————————————————————————
def plotCorrMatrix(path,corr,labels=None):
    # Heatmap of the correlation matrix
    if labels is None:labels=[]
    mpl.pcolor(corr)
    mpl.colorbar()
    mpl.yticks(np.arange(.5,corr.shape[0]+.5),labels)
    mpl.xticks(np.arange(.5,corr.shape[0]+.5),labels)
    mpl.savefig(path)
    mpl.clf();mpl.close() # reset pylab
    return
#————————————————————————————————————
def generateData(nObs,size0,size1,sigma1):
    # Time series of correlated variables
    #1) generating some uncorrelated data
    np.random.seed(seed=12345);random.seed(12345)
    x=np.random.normal(0,1,size=(nObs,size0)) # each row is a variable
    #2) creating correlation between the variables
    cols=[random.randint(0,size0-1) for i in xrange(size1)]
    y=x[:,cols]+np.random.normal(0,sigma1,size=(nObs,len(cols)))
    x=np.append(x,y,axis=1)
```

```
      x=pd.DataFrame(x,columns=range(1,x.shape[1]+1))
      return x,cols
#————————————————————————————————————
def main():
    #1) Generate correlated data
    nObs,size0,size1,sigma1=10000,5,5,.25
    x,cols=generateData(nObs,size0,size1,sigma1)
    print [(j+1,size0+i) for i,j in enumerate(cols,1)]
    cov,corr=x.cov(),x.corr()
    #2) compute and plot correl matrix
    plotCorrMatrix('HRP3_corr0.png',corr,labels=corr.columns)
    #3) cluster
    dist=correlDist(corr)
    link=sch.linkage(dist,'single')
    sortIx=getQuasiDiag(link)
    sortIx=corr.index[sortIx].tolist() # recover labels
    df0=corr.loc[sortIx,sortIx] # reorder
    plotCorrMatrix('HRP3_corr1.png',df0,labels=df0.columns)
    #4) Capital allocation
    hrp=getRecBipart(cov,sortIx)
    print hrp
    return
#————————————————————————————————————
if __name__=='__main__':main()
```

16.A.4   REPRODUCING THE MONTE CARLO EXPERIMENT

Snippet 16.5 implements Monte Carlo experiments on three allocation methods: HRP, CLA, and IVP. All libraries are standard except for HRP, which is provided in Appendix 16.A.3, and CLA, which can be found in Bailey and López de Prado [2013]. The subroutine generateData simulates the correlated data, with two types of random shocks: common to various investments and specific to a single investment. There are two shocks of each type, one positive and one negative. The variables for the experiments are set as arguments of hrpMC. They were chosen arbitrarily, and the user can experiment with alternative combinations.

SNIPPET 16.5   MONTE CARLO EXPERIMENT ON HRP OUT-OF-SAMPLE PERFORMANCE

```
import scipy.cluster.hierarchy as sch,random,numpy as np,pandas as pd,CLA
from HRP import correlDist,getIVP,getQuasiDiag,getRecBipart
#————————————————————————————————————
def generateData(nObs,sLength,size0,size1,mu0,sigma0,sigma1F):
    # Time series of correlated variables
    #1) generate random uncorrelated data
```

```
    x=np.random.normal(mu0,sigma0,size=(nObs,size0))
    #2) create correlation between the variables
    cols=[random.randint(0,size0-1) for i in xrange(size1)]
    y=x[:,cols]+np.random.normal(0,sigma0*sigma1F,size=(nObs,len(cols)))
    x=np.append(x,y,axis=1)
    #3) add common random shock
    point=np.random.randint(sLength,nObs-1,size=2)
    x[np.ix_(point,[cols[0],size0])]=np.array([[-.5,-.5],[2,2]])
    #4) add specific random shock
    point=np.random.randint(sLength,nObs-1,size=2)
    x[point,cols[-1]]=np.array([-.5,2])
    return x,cols
    #---------------------------------------------
def getHRP(cov,corr):
    # Construct a hierarchical portfolio
    corr,cov=pd.DataFrame(corr),pd.DataFrame(cov)
    dist=correlDist(corr)
    link=sch.linkage(dist,'single')
    sortIx=getQuasiDiag(link)
    sortIx=corr.index[sortIx].tolist() # recover labels
    hrp=getRecBipart(cov,sortIx)
    return hrp.sort_index()
    #---------------------------------------------
def getCLA(cov,**kargs):
    # Compute CLA's minimum variance portfolio
    mean=np.arange(cov.shape[0]).reshape(-1,1) # Not used by C portf
    lB=np.zeros(mean.shape)
    uB=np.ones(mean.shape)
    cla=CLA.CLA(mean,cov,lB,uB)
    cla.solve()
    return cla.w[-1].flatten()
#---------------------------------------------
def hrpMC(numIters=1e4,nObs=520,size0=5,size1=5,mu0=0,sigma0=1e-2, \
    sigma1F=.25,sLength=260,rebal=22):
    # Monte Carlo experiment on HRP
    methods=[getIVP,getHRP,getCLA]
    stats,numIter={i.__name__:pd.Series() for i in methods},0
    pointers=range(sLength,nObs,rebal)
    while numIter<numIters:
        print numIter
        #1) Prepare data for one experiment
        x,cols=generateData(nObs,sLength,size0,size1,mu0,sigma0,sigma1F)
        r={i.__name__:pd.Series() for i in methods}
        #2) Compute portfolios in-sample
        for pointer in pointers:
            x_=x[pointer-sLength:pointer]
            cov_,corr_=np.cov(x_,rowvar=0),np.corrcoef(x_,rowvar=0)
            #3) Compute performance out-of-sample
            x_=x[pointer:pointer+rebal]
```

```
        for func in methods:
            w_=func(cov=cov_,corr=corr_) # callback
            r_=pd.Series(np.dot(x_,w_))
            r[func.__name__]=r[func.__name__].append(r_)
    #4) Evaluate and store results
    for func in methods:
        r_=r[func.__name__].reset_index(drop=True)
        p_=(1+r_).cumprod()
        stats[func.__name__].loc[numIter]=p_.iloc[-1]-1
    numIter+=1
#5) Report results
stats=pd.DataFrame.from_dict(stats,orient='columns')
stats.to_csv('stats.csv')
df0,df1=stats.std(),stats.var()
print pd.concat([df0,df1,df1/df1['getHRP']-1],axis=1)
return
#————————————————————————————————————
if __name__=='__main__':hrpMC()
```

EXERCISES

16.1 Given the PnL series on N investment strategies:

  (a) Align them to the average frequency of their bets (e.g., weekly observations for strategies that trade on a weekly basis). Hint: This kind of data alignment is sometimes called "downsampling."

  (b) Compute the covariance of their returns, V.

  (c) Identify the hierarchical clusters among the N strategies.

  (d) Plot the clustered correlation matrix of the N strategies.

16.2 Using the clustered covariance matrix V from exercise 1:

  (a) Compute the HRP allocations.

  (b) Compute the CLA allocations.

  (c) Compute the IVP allocations.

16.3 Using the covariance matrix V from exercise 1:

  (a) Perform a spectral decomposition: $VW = W\Lambda$.

  (b) Form an array ε by drawing N random numbers from a $U[0, 1]$ distribution.

  (c) Form an NxN matrix $\tilde{\Lambda}$, where $\tilde{\Lambda}_{n,n} = N\varepsilon_n\Lambda_{n,n}(\sum_{n=1}^{N} \varepsilon_n)^{-1}, n = 1, \ldots, N$.

  (d) Compute $\tilde{V} = W\tilde{\Lambda}W^{-1}$.

  (e) Repeat exercise 2, this time using $\tilde{V}$ as covariance matrix. What allocation method has been most impacted by the re-scaling of spectral variances?

16.4 How would you modify the HRP algorithm to produce allocations that add up to 0, where $|w_n| \leq 1$, $\forall n = 1, \ldots, N$?

16.5 Can you think of an easy way to incorporate expected returns in the HRP allocations?

REFERENCES

Bailey, D. and M. López de Prado (2012): "Balanced baskets: A new approach to trading and hedging risks." *Journal of Investment Strategies*, Vol. 1, No. 4, pp. 21–62. Available at http://ssrn.com/abstract=2066170.

Bailey, D. and M. López de Prado (2013): "An open-source implementation of the critical-line algorithm for portfolio optimization." *Algorithms*, Vol. 6, No. 1, pp. 169–196. Available at http://ssrn.com/abstract=2197616.

Bailey, D., J. Borwein, M. López de Prado, and J. Zhu (2014) "Pseudo-mathematics and financial charlatanism: The effects of backtest overfitting on out-of-sample performance." *Notices of the American Mathematical Society*, Vol. 61, No. 5, pp. 458–471. Available at http://ssrn.com/abstract=2308659.

Bailey, D. and M. López de Prado (2014): "The deflated Sharpe ratio: Correcting for selection bias, backtest overfitting and non-normality." *Journal of Portfolio Management*, Vol. 40, No. 5, pp. 94–107.

Black, F. and R. Litterman (1992): "Global portfolio optimization." *Financial Analysts Journal*, Vol. 48, pp. 28–43.

Brualdi, R. (2010): "The mutually beneficial relationship of graphs and matrices." Conference Board of the Mathematical Sciences, Regional Conference Series in Mathematics, Nr. 115.

Calkin, N. and M. López de Prado (2014): "Stochastic flow diagrams." *Algorithmic Finance*, Vol. 3, No. 1, pp. 21–42. Availble at http://ssrn.com/abstract=2379314.

Calkin, N. and M. López de Prado (2014): "The topology of macro financial flows: An application of stochastic flow diagrams." *Algorithmic Finance*, Vol. 3, No. 1, pp. 43–85. Available at http://ssrn.com/abstract=2379319.

Clarke, R., H. De Silva, and S. Thorley (2002): "Portfolio constraints and the fundamental law of active management." *Financial Analysts Journal*, Vol. 58, pp. 48–66.

De Miguel, V., L. Garlappi, and R. Uppal (2009): "Optimal versus naive diversification: How inefficient is the 1/N portfolio strategy?" *Review of Financial Studies*, Vol. 22, pp. 1915–1953.

Jurczenko, E. (2015): *Risk-Based and Factor Investing*, 1st ed. Elsevier Science.

Kolanovic, M., A. Lau, T. Lee, and R. Krishnamachari (2017): "Cross asset portfolios of tradable risk premia indices. Hierarchical risk parity: Enhancing returns at target volatility." White paper, Global Quantitative & Derivatives Strategy. J.P. Morgan, April 26.

Kolm, P., R. Tutuncu and F. Fabozzi (2014): "60 years of portfolio optimization." *European Journal of Operational Research*, Vol. 234, No. 2, pp. 356–371.

Kuhn, H. W. and A. W. Tucker (1951): "Nonlinear programming." Proceedings of 2nd Berkeley Symposium. Berkeley, University of California Press, pp. 481–492.

Markowitz, H. (1952): "Portfolio selection." *Journal of Finance*, Vol. 7, pp. 77–91.

Merton, R. (1976): "Option pricing when underlying stock returns are discontinuous." *Journal of Financial Economics*, Vol. 3, pp. 125–144.

Michaud, R. (1998): *Efficient Asset Allocation: A Practical Guide to Stock Portfolio Optimization and Asset Allocation*, 1st ed. Harvard Business School Press.

Ledoit, O. and M. Wolf (2003): "Improved estimation of the covariance matrix of stock returns with an application to portfolio selection." *Journal of Empirical Finance*, Vol. 10, No. 5, pp. 603–621.

Raffinot, T. (2017): "Hierarchical clustering based asset allocation." *Journal of Portfolio Management*, forthcoming.

Rokach, L. and O. Maimon (2005): "Clustering methods," in Rokach, L. and O. Maimon, eds., *Data Mining and Knowledge Discovery Handbook*. Springer, pp. 321–352.

PART 4

Useful Financial Features

CHAPTER 17

Structural Breaks

17.1 MOTIVATION

In developing an ML-based investment strategy, we typically wish to bet when there is a confluence of factors whose predicted outcome offers a favorable risk-adjusted return. Structural breaks, like the transition from one market regime to another, is one example of such a confluence that is of particular interest. For instance, a mean-reverting pattern may give way to a momentum pattern. As this transition takes place, most market participants are caught off guard, and they will make costly mistakes. This sort of errors is the basis for many profitable strategies, because the actors on the losing side will typically become aware of their mistake once it is too late. Before they accept their losses, they will act irrationally, try to hold the position, and hope for a comeback. Sometimes they will even increase a losing position, in desperation. Eventually they will be forced to stop loss or stop out. Structural breaks offer some of the best risk/rewards. In this chapter, we will review some methods that measure the likelihood of structural breaks, so that informative features can be built upon them.

17.2 TYPES OF STRUCTURAL BREAK TESTS

We can classify structural break tests in two general categories:

- **CUSUM tests:** These test whether the cumulative forecasting errors significantly deviate from white noise.
- **Explosiveness tests:** Beyond deviation from white noise, these test whether the process exhibits exponential growth or collapse, as this is inconsistent with a random walk or stationary process, and it is unsustainable in the long run.

249

○ **Right-tail unit-root tests:** These tests evaluate the presence of exponential growth or collapse, while assuming an autoregressive specification.

○ **Sub/super-martingale tests:** These tests evaluate the presence of exponential growth or collapse under a variety of functional forms.

17.3   CUSUM TESTS

In Chapter 2 we introduced the CUSUM filter, which we applied in the context of event-based sampling of bars. The idea was to sample a bar whenever some variable, like cumulative prediction errors, exceeded a predefined threshold. This concept can be further extended to test for structural breaks.

17.3.1   Brown-Durbin-Evans CUSUM Test on Recursive Residuals

This test was proposed by Brown, Durbin and Evans [1975]. Let us assume that at every observation $t = 1, \ldots, T$, we count with an array of features x_t predictive of a value y_t. Matrix X_t is composed of the time series of features $t \leq T$, $\{x_i\}_{i=1,\ldots,t}$. These authors propose that we compute recursive least squares (RLS) estimates of β, based on the specification

$$y_t = \beta_t' x_t + \varepsilon_t$$

which is fit on subsamples ($[1, k+1], [1, k+2], \ldots, [1, T]$), giving $T - k$ least squares estimates $(\hat{\beta}_{k+1}, \ldots, \hat{\beta}_T)$. We can compute the standardized 1-step ahead recursive residuals as

$$\hat{\omega}_t = \frac{y_t - \hat{\beta}_{t-1}' x_t}{\sqrt{f_t}}$$

$$f_t = \hat{\sigma}_\varepsilon^2 \left[1 + x_t' \left(X_t' X_t \right)^{-1} x_t \right]$$

The CUSUM statistic is defined as

$$S_t = \sum_{j=k+1}^{t} \frac{\hat{\omega}_j}{\hat{\sigma}_\omega}$$

$$\hat{\sigma}_\omega^2 = \frac{1}{T-k} \sum_{t=k}^{T} (\hat{\omega}_t - \mathrm{E}[\hat{\omega}_t])^2$$

Under the null hypothesis that β is some constant value, $H_0 : \beta_t = \beta$, then $S_t \sim N[0, t - k - 1]$. One caveat of this procedure is that the starting point is chosen arbitrarily, and results may be inconsistent due to that.

17.3.2   Chu-Stinchcombe-White CUSUM Test on Levels

This test follows Homm and Breitung [2012]. It simplifies the previous method by dropping $\{x_t\}_{t=1,...,T}$, and assuming that $H_0 : \beta_t = 0$, that is, we forecast no change ($E_{t-1}[\Delta y_t] = 0$). This will allow us to work directly with y_t levels, hence reducing the computational burden. We compute the standardized departure of log-price y_t relative to the log-price at y_n, $t > n$, as

$$S_{n,t} = (y_t - y_n)\left(\hat{\sigma}_t \sqrt{t - n}\right)^{-1}$$

$$\hat{\sigma}_t^2 = (t - 1)^{-1} \sum_{i=2}^{t} (\Delta y_i)^2$$

Under the null hypothesis $H_0 : \beta_t = 0$, then $S_{n,t} \sim N[0, 1]$. The time-dependent critical value for the *one-sided test* is

$$c_\alpha[n, t] = \sqrt{b_\alpha + \log[t - n]}$$

These authors derived via Monte Carlo that $b_{0.05} = 4.6$. One disadvantage of this method is that the reference level y_n is set somewhat arbitrarily. To overcome this pitfall, we could estimate $S_{n,t}$ on a series of backward-shifting windows $n \in [1, t]$, and pick $S_t = \sup_{n \in [1,t]} \{S_{n,t}\}$.

17.4   EXPLOSIVENESS TESTS

Explosiveness tests can be generally divided between those that test for one bubble and those that test for multiple bubbles. In this context, bubbles are not limited to price rallies, but they also include sell-offs. Tests that allow for multiple bubbles are more robust in the sense that a cycle of bubble-burst-bubble will make the series appear to be stationary to single-bubble tests. Maddala and Kim [1998], and Breitung [2014] offer good overviews of the literature.

17.4.1   Chow-Type Dickey-Fuller Test

A family of explosiveness tests was inspired by the work of Gregory Chow, starting with Chow [1960]. Consider the first order autoregressive process

$$y_t = \rho y_{t-1} + \varepsilon_t$$

where ε_t is white noise. The null hypothesis is that y_t follows a random walk, H_0: $\rho = 1$, and the alternative hypothesis is that y_t starts as a random walk but changes at time $\tau^* T$, where $\tau^* \in (0, 1)$, into an explosive process:

$$H_1 : y_t = \begin{cases} y_{t-1} + \varepsilon_t & \text{for } t = 1, \ldots, \tau^* T \\ \rho y_{t-1} + \varepsilon_t & \text{for } t = \tau^* T + 1, \ldots, T, \text{ with } \rho > 1 \end{cases}$$

At time T we can test for a switch (from random walk to explosive process) having taken place at time τ^*T (break date). In order to test this hypothesis, we fit the following specification,

$$\Delta y_t = \delta y_{t-1} D_t[\tau^*] + \varepsilon_t$$

where $D_t[\tau^*]$ is a dummy variable that takes zero value if $t < \tau^*T$, and takes the value one if $t \geq \tau^*T$. Then, the null hypothesis $H_0 : \delta = 0$ is tested against the (one-sided) alternative $H_1 : \delta > 1$:

$$DFC_{\tau^*} = \frac{\hat{\delta}}{\hat{\sigma}_\delta}$$

The main drawback of this method is that τ^* is unknown. To address this issue, Andrews [1993] proposed a new test where all possible τ^* are tried, within some interval $\tau^* \in [\tau_0, 1 - \tau_0]$. As Breitung [2014] explains, we should leave out some of the possible τ^* at the beginning and end of the sample, to ensure that either regime is fitted with enough observations (there must be enough zeros and enough ones in $D_t[\tau^*]$). The test statistic for an unknown τ^* is the maximum of all $T(1 - 2\tau_0)$ values of DFC_{τ^*}.

$$SDFC = \sup_{\tau^* \in [\tau_0, 1-\tau_0]} \{DFC_{\tau^*}\}$$

Another drawback of Chow's approach is that it assumes that there is only one break date τ^*T, and that the bubble runs up to the end of the sample (there is no switch back to a random walk). For situations where three or more regimes (random walk $\rightarrow$ bubble $\rightarrow$ random walk ...) exist, we need to discuss the Supremum Augmented Dickey-Fuler (SADF) test.

17.4.2 Supremum Augmented Dickey-Fuller

In the words of Phillips, Wu and Yu [2011], "standard unit root and cointegration tests are inappropriate tools for detecting bubble behavior because they cannot effectively distinguish between a stationary process and a periodically collapsing bubble model. Patterns of periodically collapsing bubbles in the data look more like data generated from a unit root or stationary autoregression than a potentially explosive process." To address this flaw, these authors propose fitting the regression specification

$$\Delta y_t = \alpha + \beta y_{t-1} + \sum_{l=1}^{L} \gamma_l \Delta y_{t-l} + \varepsilon_t$$

where we test for $H_0 : \beta \leq 0$, $H_1 : \beta > 0$. Inspired by Andrews [1993], Phillips and Yu [2011] and Phillips, Wu and Yu [2011] proposed the Supremum Augmented

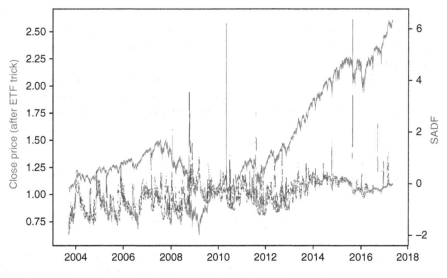

FIGURE 17.1   Prices (left y-axis) and SADF (right y-axis) over time

Dickey-Fuller test (SADF). SADF fits the above regression at each end point t with backwards expanding start points, then computes

$$SADF_t = \sup_{t_0 \in [1,t-\tau]} \{ADF_{t_0,t}\} = \sup_{t_0 \in [1,t-\tau]} \left\{ \frac{\hat{\beta}_{t_0,t}}{\hat{\sigma}_{\beta_{t_0,t}}} \right\}$$

where $\hat{\beta}_{t_0,t}$ is estimated on a sample that starts at t_0 and ends at t, τ is the minimum sample length used in the analysis, t_0 is the left bound of the backwards expanding window, and $t = \tau, \dots, T$. For the estimation of $SADF_t$, the right side of the window is fixed at t. The standard ADF test is a special case of $SADF_t$, where $\tau = t - 1$.

There are two critical differences between $SADF_t$ and SDFC: First, $SADF_t$ is computed at each $t \in [\tau, T]$, whereas SDFC is computed only at T. Second, instead of introducing a dummy variable, SADF recursively expands the beginning of the sample $(t_0 \in [1, t - \tau])$. By trying all combinations of a nested double loop on (t_0, t), SADF does not assume a known number of regime switches or break dates. Figure 17.1 displays the series of E-mini S&P 500 futures prices after applying the ETF trick (Chapter 2, Section 2.4.1), as well as the SADF derived from that price series. The SADF line spikes when prices exhibit a bubble-like behavior, and returns to low levels when the bubble bursts. In the following sections, we will discuss some enhancements to Phillips' original SADF method.

17.4.2.1   Raw vs. Log Prices
It is common to find in the literature studies that carry out structural break tests on raw prices. In this section we will explore why log prices should be preferred, particularly when working with long time series involving bubbles and bursts.

For raw prices $\{y_t\}$, if ADF's null hypotesis is rejected, it means that prices are stationary, with finite variance. The implication is that returns $\frac{y_t}{y_{t-1}} - 1$ are not time invariant, for returns' volatility must decrease as prices rise and increase as prices fall in order to keep the price variance constant. When we run ADF on raw prices, we assume that returns' variance is not invariant to price levels. If returns variance happens to be invariant to price levels, the model will be structurally heteroscedastic.

In contrast, if we work with log prices, the ADF specification will state that

$$\Delta\log[y_t] \propto \log[y_{t-1}]$$

Let us make a change of variable, $x_t = ky_t$. Now, $\log[x_t] = \log[k] + \log[y_t]$, and the ADF specification will state that

$$\Delta\log[x_t] \propto \log[x_{t-1}] \propto \log[y_{t-1}]$$

Under this alternative specification based on log prices, price levels condition returns' mean, not returns' volatility. The difference may not matter in practice for small samples, where $k \approx 1$, but SADF runs regressions across decades and bubbles produce levels that are significantly different between regimes ($k \neq 1$).

17.4.2.2 Computational Complexity

The algorithm runs in $\mathcal{O}(n^2)$, as the number of ADF tests that SADF requires for a total sample length T is

$$\sum_{t=\tau}^{T} t - \tau + 1 = \frac{1}{2}(T - \tau + 2)(T - \tau + 1) = \binom{T - \tau + 2}{2}$$

Consider a matrix representation of the ADF specification, where $X \in \mathbb{R}^{T \times N}$ and $y \in \mathbb{R}^{T \times 1}$. Solving a single ADF regression involves the floating point operations (FLOPs) listed in Table 17.1.

This gives a total of $f(N, T) = N^3 + N^2(2T + 3) + N(4T - 1) + 2T + 2$ FLOPs per ADF estimate. A single SADF update requires $g(N, T, \tau) = \sum_{t=\tau}^{T} f(N, t) + T - \tau$ FLOPs ($T - \tau$ operations to find the maximum ADF stat), and the estimation of a full SADF series requires $\sum_{t=\tau}^{T} g(N, T, \tau)$.

Consider a dollar bar series on E-mini S&P 500 futures. For $(T, N) = (356631, 3)$, an ADF estimate requires 11,412,245 FLOPs, and a SADF update requires 2,034,979,648,799 operations (roughly 2.035 TFLOPs). A full SADF time series requires 241,910,974,617,448,672 operations (roughly 242 PFLOPs). This number will increase quickly, as the T continues to grow. And this estimate excludes notoriously expensive operations like alignment, pre-processing of data, I/O jobs, etc. Needless to say, this algorithm's double loop requires a large number of operations. An HPC cluster running an efficiently parallelized implementation of the algorithm may be needed to estimate the SADF series within a reasonable amount of time. Chapter 20 will present some parallelization strategies useful in these situations.

TABLE 17.1   FLOPs per ADF Estimate

Matrix Operation	FLOPs
$o_1 = X'y$	$(2T-1)N$
$o_2 = X'X$	$(2T-1)N^2$
$o_3 = o_2^{-1}$	$N^3 + N^2 + N$
$o_4 = o_3 o_1$	$2N^2 - N$
$o_5 = y - Xo_4$	$T + (2N-1)T$
$o_6 = o_5' o_5$	$2T - 1$
$o_7 = o_3 o_6 \dfrac{1}{T-N}$	$2 + N^2$
$o_8 = \dfrac{o_4[0,0]}{\sqrt{o_7[0,0]}}$	1

17.4.2.3   Conditions for Exponential Behavior

Consider the zero-lag specification on log prices, $\Delta\log[y_t] = \alpha + \beta\log[y_{t-1}] + \varepsilon_t$. This can be rewritten as $\log[\tilde{y}_t] = (1+\beta)\log[\tilde{y}_{t-1}] + \varepsilon_t$, where $\log[\tilde{y}_t] = \log[y_t] + \frac{\alpha}{\beta}$. Rolling back t discrete steps, we obtain $E[\log[\tilde{y}_t]] = (1+\beta)^t\log[\tilde{y}_0]$, or $E[\log[y_t]] = -\frac{\alpha}{\beta} + (1+\beta)^t(\log[y_0] + \frac{\alpha}{\beta})$. The index t can be reset at a given time, to project the future trajectory of $y_0 \to y_t$ after the next t steps. This reveals the conditions that characterize the three states for this dynamic system:

- Steady: $\beta < 0 \Rightarrow \lim_{t\to\infty} E[\log[y_t]] = -\frac{\alpha}{\beta}$.
  - The disequilibrium is $\log[y_t] - (-\frac{\alpha}{\beta}) = \log[\tilde{y}_t]$.
  - Then $\frac{E[\log[\tilde{y}_t]]}{\log[\tilde{y}_0]} = (1+\beta)^t = \frac{1}{2}$ at $t = -\frac{\log[2]}{\log[1+\beta]}$ (half-life).
- Unit-root: $\beta = 0$, where the system is non-stationary, and behaves as a martingale.
- Explosive: $\beta > 0$, where $\lim_{t\to\infty} E[\log[y_t]] = \begin{cases} -\infty, & \text{if } \log[y_0] < \frac{\alpha}{\beta} \\ +\infty, & \text{if } \log[y_0] > \frac{\alpha}{\beta} \end{cases}$.

17.4.2.4   Quantile ADF

SADF takes the supremum of a series on t-values, $SADF_t = \sup_{t_0 \in [1,t-\tau]}\{ADF_{t_0,t}\}$. Selecting the extreme value introduces some robustness problems, where SADF estimates could vary significantly depending on the sampling frequency and the specific timestamps of the samples. A more robust estimator of ADF extrema would be the following: First, let $s_t = \{ADF_{t_0,t}\}_{t_0 \in [0, t_1-\tau]}$. Second, we define $Q_{t,q} = Q[s_t, q]$ the q quantile of s_t, as a measure of centrality of high ADF values, where $q \in [0,1]$. Third, we define $\dot{Q}_{t,q,v} = Q_{t,q+v} - Q_{t,q-v}$, with $0 < v \le \min\{q, 1-q\}$, as a measure of dispersion of high ADF values. For example, we could set $q = 0.95$ and $v = 0.025$. Note that SADF is merely a particular case of QADF, where $SADF_t = Q_{t,1}$ and $\dot{Q}_{t,q,v}$ is not defined because $q = 1$.

17.4.2.5 Conditional ADF

Alternatively, we can address concerns on SADF robustness by computing conditional moments. Let $f[x]$ be the probability distribution function of $s_t = \{ADF_{t_0,t}\}_{t_0 \in [1,t_1-\tau]}$, with $x \in s_t$. Then, we define $C_{t,q} = K^{-1} \int_{Q_{t,q}}^{\infty} xf[x]dx$ as a measure of centrality of high ADF values, and $\dot{C}_{t,q} = \sqrt{K^{-1} \int_{Q_{t,q}}^{\infty} (x - C_{t,q})^2 f[x]dx}$ as a measure of dispersion of high ADF values, with regularization constant $K = \int_{Q_{t,q}}^{\infty} f[x]dx$. For example, we could use $q = 0.95$.

By construction, $C_{t,q} \leq SADF_t$. A scatter plot of $SADF_t$ against $C_{t,q}$ shows that lower boundary, as an ascending line with approximately unit gradient (see Figure 17.2). When SADF grows beyond -1.5, we can appreciate some horizontal trajectories, consistent with a sudden widening of the right fat tail in s_t. In other words, $(SADF_t - C_{t,q})/\dot{C}_{t,q}$ can reach significantly large values even if $C_{t,q}$ is relatively small, because $SADF_t$ is sensitive to outliers.

Figure 17.3(a) plots $(SADF_t - C_{t,q})/\dot{C}_{t,q}$ for the E-mini S&P 500 futures prices over time. Figure 17.3(b) is the scatter-plot of $(SADF_t - C_{t,q})/\dot{C}_{t,q}$ against $SADF_t$, computed on the E-mini S&P 500 futures prices. It shows evidence that outliers in s_t bias $SADF_t$ upwards.

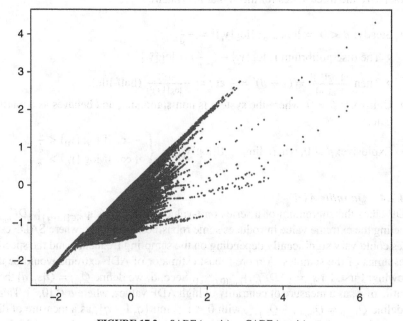

FIGURE 17.2   SADF (x-axis) vs CADF (y-axis)

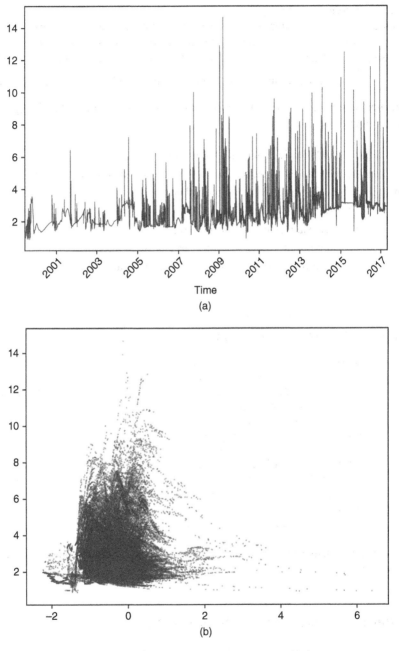

FIGURE 17.3 (a) $(SADF_t - C_{t,q})/\dot{C}_{t,q}$ over time (b) $(SADF_t - C_{t,q})/\dot{C}_{t,q}$ (y-axis) as a function of $SADF_t$ (x-axis)

17.4.2.6 *Implementation of SADF*

This section presents an implementation of the SADF algorithm. The purpose of this code is not to estimate SADF quickly, but to clarify the steps involved in its estimation. Snippet 17.1 lists SADF's inner loop. That is the part that estimates $SADF_t = \sup_{t_0 \in [1, t-\tau]} \{\frac{\hat{\beta}_{t_0,t}}{\hat{\sigma}_{\beta_{t_0,t}}}\}$, which is the backshifting component of the algorithm. The outer loop (not shown here) repeats this calculation for an advancing t, $\{SADF_t\}_{t=1,\dots,T}$. The arguments are:

- logP: a pandas series containing log-prices
- minSL: the minimum sample length (τ), used by the final regression
- constant: the regression's time trend component
  - 'nc': no time trend, only a constant
  - 'ct': a constant plus a linear time trend
  - 'ctt': a constant plus a second-degree polynomial time trend
- lags: the number of lags used in the ADF specification

SNIPPET 17.1 SADF'S INNER LOOP

```
def get_bsadf(logP,minSL,constant,lags):
    y,x=getYX(logP,constant=constant,lags=lags)
    startPoints,bsadf,allADF=range(0,y.shape[0]+lags-minSL+1),None,[]
    for start in startPoints:
        y_,x_=y[start:],x[start:]
        bMean_,bStd_=getBetas(y_,x_)
        bMean_,bStd_=bMean_[0,0],bStd_[0,0]**.5
        allADF.append(bMean_/bStd_)
        if allADF[-1]>bsadf:bsadf=allADF[-1]
    out={'Time':logP.index[-1],'gsadf':bsadf}
    return out
```

Snippet 17.2 lists function getYX, which prepares the numpy objects needed to conduct the recursive tests.

SNIPPET 17.2 PREPARING THE DATASETS

```
def getYX(series,constant,lags):
    series_=series.diff().dropna()
    x=lagDF(series_,lags).dropna()
    x.iloc[:,0]=series.values[-x.shape[0]-1:-1,0] # lagged level
    y=series_.iloc[-x.shape[0]:].values
```

```
if constant!='nc':
    x=np.append(x,np.ones((x.shape[0],1)),axis=1)
    if constant[:2]=='ct':
        trend=np.arange(x.shape[0]).reshape(-1,1)
        x=np.append(x,trend,axis=1)
    if constant=='ctt':
        x=np.append(x,trend**2,axis=1)
return y,x
```

Snippet 17.3 lists function `lagDF`, which applies to a dataframe the lags specified in its argument `lags`.

SNIPPET 17.3   APPLY LAGS TO DATAFRAME

```
def lagDF(df0,lags):
    df1=pd.DataFrame()
    if isinstance(lags,int):lags=range(lags+1)
    else:lags=[int(lag) for lag in lags]
    for lag in lags:
        df_=df0.shift(lag).copy(deep=True)
        df_.columns=[str(i)+'_'+str(lag) for i in df_.columns]
        df1=df1.join(df_,how='outer')
    return df1
```

Finally, Snippet 17.4 lists function `getBetas`, which carries out the actual regressions.

SNIPPET 17.4   FITTING THE ADF SPECIFICATION

```
def getBetas(y,x):
    xy=np.dot(x.T,y)
    xx=np.dot(x.T,x)
    xxinv=np.linalg.inv(xx)
    bMean=np.dot(xxinv,xy)
    err=y-np.dot(x,bMean)
    bVar=np.dot(err.T,err)/(x.shape[0]-x.shape[1])*xxinv
    return bMean,bVar
```

17.4.3   Sub- and Super-Martingale Tests

In this section we will introduce explosiveness tests that do not rely on the standard ADF specification. Consider a process that is either a sub- or super-martingale. Given some observations $\{y_t\}$, we would like to test for the existence of an explosive time trend, $H_0 : \beta = 0, H_1 : \beta \neq 0$, under alternative specifications:

- Polynomial trend (SM-Poly1):

$$y_t = \alpha + \gamma t + \beta t^2 + \varepsilon_t$$

- Polynomial trend (SM-Poly2):

$$\log[y_t] = \alpha + \gamma t + \beta t^2 + \varepsilon_t$$

- Exponential trend (SM-Exp):

$$y_t = \alpha e^{\beta t} + \varepsilon_t \Rightarrow \log[y_t] = \log[\alpha] + \beta t + \xi_t$$

- Power trend (SM-Power):

$$y_t = \alpha t^\beta + \varepsilon_t \Rightarrow \log[y_t] = \log[\alpha] + \beta \log[t] + \xi_t$$

Similar to SADF, we fit any of these specifications to each end point $t = \tau, \dots, T$, with backwards expanding start points, then compute

$$SMT_t = \sup_{t_0 \in [1, t-\tau]} \left\{ \frac{|\hat{\beta}_{t_0,t}|}{\hat{\sigma}_{\beta_{t_0,t}}} \right\}$$

The reason for the absolute value is that we are equally interested in explosive growth and collapse. In the simple regression case (Greene [2008], p. 48), the variance of β is $\hat{\sigma}_\beta^2 = \frac{\hat{\sigma}_\varepsilon^2}{\hat{\sigma}_{xx}^2(t-t_0)}$, hence $\lim_{t\to\infty} \hat{\sigma}_{\beta_{t_0,t}} = 0$. The same result is generalizable to the multivariate linear regression case (Greene [2008], pp. 51–52). The $\hat{\sigma}_\beta^2$ of a weak long-run bubble may be smaller than the $\hat{\sigma}_\beta^2$ of a strong short-run bubble, hence biasing the method towards long-run bubbles. To correct for this bias, we can penalize large sample lengths by determining the coefficient $\varphi \in [0, 1]$ that yields best explosiveness signals.

$$SMT_t = \sup_{t_0 \in [1, t-\tau]} \left\{ \frac{|\hat{\beta}_{t_0,t}|}{\hat{\sigma}_{\beta_{t_0,t}}(t-t_0)^\varphi} \right\}$$

For instance, when $\varphi = 0.5$, we compensate for the lower $\hat{\sigma}_{\beta_{t_0,t}}$ associated with longer sample lengths, in the simple regression case. For $\varphi \to 0$, SMT_t will exhibit longer trends, as that compensation wanes and long-run bubbles mask short-run bubbles. For $\varphi \to 1$, SMT_t becomes noisier, because more short-run bubbles are selected over long-run bubbles. Consequently, this is a natural way to adjust the explosiveness signal, so that it filters opportunities targeting a particular holding period. The features used by the ML algorithm may include SMT_t estimated from a wide range of φ values.

EXERCISES

17.1 On a dollar bar series on E-mini S&P 500 futures,
  (a) Apply the Brown-Durbin-Evans method. Does it recognize the dot-com bubble?
  (b) Apply the Chu-Stinchcombe-White method. Does it find a bubble in 2007–2008?

17.2 On a dollar bar series on E-mini S&P 500 futures,
  (a) Compute the $SDFC$ (Chow-type) explosiveness test. What break date does this method select? Is this what you expected?
  (b) Compute and plot the SADF values for this series. Do you observe extreme spikes around the dot-com bubble and before the Great Recession? Did the bursts also cause spikes?

17.3 Following on exercise 2,
  (a) Determine the periods where the series exhibited
    (i) Steady conditions
    (ii) Unit-Root conditions
    (iii) Explosive conditions
  (b) Compute QADF.
  (c) Compute CADF.

17.4 On a dollar bar series on E-mini S&P 500 futures,
  (a) Compute SMT for SM-Poly1 and SM-Poly 2, where $\varphi = 1$. What is their correlation?
  (b) Compute SMT for SM-Exp, where $\varphi = 1$ and $\varphi = 0.5$. What is their correlation?
  (c) Compute SMT for SM-Power, where $\varphi = 1$ and $\varphi = 0.5$. What is their correlation?

17.5 If you compute the reciprocal of each price, the series $\{y_t^{-1}\}$ turns bubbles into bursts and bursts into bubbles.
  (a) Is this transformation needed, to identify bursts?
  (b) What methods in this chapter can identify bursts without requiring this transformation?

REFERENCES

Andrews, D. (1993): "Tests for parameter instability and structural change with unknown change point." *Econometrics*, Vol. 61, No. 4 (July), pp. 821–856.

Breitung, J. and R. Kruse (2013): "When Bubbles Burst: Econometric Tests Based on Structural Breaks." *Statistical Papers*, Vol. 54, pp. 911–930.

Breitung, J. (2014): "Econometric tests for speculative bubbles." *Bonn Journal of Economics*, Vol. 3, No. 1, pp. 113–127.

Brown, R.L., J. Durbin, and J.M. Evans (1975): "Techniques for Testing the Constancy of Regression Relationships over Time." *Journal of the Royal Statistical Society, Series B*, Vol. 35, pp. 149–192.

Chow, G. (1960). "Tests of equality between sets of coefficients in two linear regressions." *Econometrica*, Vol. 28, No. 3, pp. 591–605.

Greene, W. (2008): *Econometric Analysis*, 6th ed. Pearson Prentice Hall.

Homm, U. and J. Breitung (2012): "Testing for speculative bubbles in stock markets: A comparison of alternative methods." *Journal of Financial Econometrics*, Vol. 10, No. 1, 198–231.

Maddala, G. and I. Kim (1998): *Unit Roots, Cointegration and Structural Change*, 1st ed. Cambridge University Press.

Phillips, P., Y. Wu, and J. Yu (2011): "Explosive behavior in the 1990s Nasdaq: When did exuberance escalate asset values?" *International Economic Review*, Vol. 52, pp. 201–226.

Phillips, P. and J. Yu (2011): "Dating the timeline of financial bubbles during the subprime crisis." *Quantitative Economics*, Vol. 2, pp. 455–491.

Phillips, P., S. Shi, and J. Yu (2013): "Testing for multiple bubbles 1: Historical episodes of exuberance and collapse in the S&P 500." Working paper 8–2013, Singapore Management University.

CHAPTER 18

Entropy Features

18.1 MOTIVATION

Price series convey information about demand and supply forces. In perfect markets, prices are unpredictable, because each observation transmits everything that is known about a product or service. When markets are not perfect, prices are formed with partial information, and as some agents know more than others, they can exploit that informational asymmetry. It would be helpful to estimate the informational content of price series, and form features on which ML algorithms can learn the likely outcomes. For example, the ML algorithm may find that momentum bets are more profitable when prices carry little information, and that mean-reversion bets are more profitable when prices carry a lot of information. In this chapter, we will explore ways to determine the amount of information contained in a price series.

18.2 SHANNON'S ENTROPY

In this section we will review a few concepts from information theory that will be useful in the remainder of the chapter. The reader can find a complete exposition in MacKay [2003]. The father of information theory, Claude Shannon, defined entropy as the average amount of information (over long messages) produced by a stationary source of data. It is the smallest number of bits per character required to describe the message in a uniquely decodable way. Mathematically, Shannon [1948] defined the entropy of a discrete random variable X with possible values $x \in A$ as

$$H[X] \equiv - \sum_{x \in A} p[x] \log_2 p[x]$$

with $0 \leq H[X] \leq \log_2[\|A\|]$ where: $p[x]$ is the probability of x; $H[X] = 0 \Leftrightarrow$ $\exists x | p[x] = 1$; $H[X] = \log_2[\|A\|] \Leftrightarrow p[x] = \frac{1}{\|A\|}$ for all x; and $\|A\|$ is the size of the set A. This can be interpreted as the probability weighted average of informational content in X, where the bits of information are measured as $\log_2 \frac{1}{p[x]}$. The rationale for measuring information as $\log_2 \frac{1}{p[x]}$ comes from the observation that low-probability outcomes reveal more information than high-probability outcomes. In other words, we learn when something unexpected happens. Similarly, redundancy is defined as

$$R[X] \equiv 1 - \frac{H[X]}{\log_2[\|A\|]}$$

with $0 \leq R[X] \leq 1$. Kolmogorov [1965] formalized the connection between redundancy and complexity of a Markov information source. The mutual information between two variables is defined as the Kullback-Leibler divergence from the joint probability density to the product of the marginal probability densities.

$$MI[X, Y] = E_{f[x,y]} \left[\log \frac{f[x, y]}{f[x]f[y]} \right] = H[X] + H[Y] - H[X, Y]$$

The mutual information (MI) is always non-negative, symmetric, and equals zero if and only if X and Y are independent. For normally distributed variables, the mutual information is closely related to the familiar Pearson correlation, ρ.

$$MI[X, Y] = -\frac{1}{2} \log[1 - \rho^2]$$

Therefore, mutual information is a natural measure of the association between variables, regardless of whether they are linear or nonlinear in nature (Hausser and Strimmer [2009]). The normalized variation of information is a metric derived from mutual information. For several entropy estimators, see:

- In R: http://cran.r-project.org/web/packages/entropy/entropy.pdf
- In Python: https://code.google.com/archive/p/pyentropy/

18.3   THE PLUG-IN (OR MAXIMUM LIKELIHOOD) ESTIMATOR

In this section we will follow the exposition of entropy's maximum likelihood estimator in Gao et al. [2008]. The nomenclature may seem a bit peculiar at first (no pun intended), but once you become familiar with it you will find it convenient. Given a data sequence x_1^n, comprising the string of values starting in position 1 and ending in position n, we can form a dictionary of all words of length $w < n$ in that sequence, A^w. Consider an arbitrary word $y_1^w \in A^w$ of length w. We denote $\hat{p}_w[y_1^w]$ the empirical probability of the word y_1^w in x_1^n, which means that $\hat{p}_w[y_1^w]$ is the frequency with which

y_1^w appears in x_1^n. Assuming that the data is generated by a stationary and ergodic process, then the law of large numbers guarantees that, for a fixed w and large n, the empirical distribution $\hat{p}_w$ will be close to the true distribution p_w. Under these circumstances, a natural estimator for the entropy rate (i.e., average entropy per bit) is

$$\hat{H}_{n,w} = -\frac{1}{w} \sum_{y_1^w \in A^w} \hat{p}_w \left[y_1^w \right] \log_2 \hat{p}_w \left[y_1^w \right]$$

Since the empirical distribution is also the maximum likelihood estimate of the true distribution, this is also often referred to as the maximum likelihood entropy estimator. The value w should be large enough for $\hat{H}_{n,w}$ to be acceptably close to the true entropy H. The value of n needs to be much larger than w, so that the empirical distribution of order w is close to the true distribution. Snippet 18.1 implements the plug-in entropy estimator.

SNIPPET 18.1 PLUG-IN ENTROPY ESTIMATOR

```
import time,numpy as np
#——————————————————————————
def plugIn(msg,w):
    # Compute plug-in (ML) entropy rate
    pmf=pmf1(msg,w)
    out=-sum([pmf[i]*np.log2(pmf[i]) for i in pmf])/w
    return out,pmf
#——————————————————————————
def pmf1(msg,w):
    # Compute the prob mass function for a one-dim discrete rv
    # len(msg)-w occurrences
    lib={}
    if not isinstance(msg,str):msg=''.join(map(str,msg))
    for i in xrange(w,len(msg)):
        msg_=msg[i-w:i]
        if msg_ not in lib:lib[msg_]=[i-w]
        else:lib[msg_]=lib[msg_]+[i-w]
    pmf=float(len(msg)-w)
    pmf={i:len(lib[i])/pmf for i in lib}
    return pmf
```

18.4 LEMPEL-ZIV ESTIMATORS

Entropy can be interpreted as a measure of complexity. A complex sequence contains more information than a regular (predictable) sequence. The Lempel-Ziv (LZ) algorithm efficiently decomposes a message into non-redundant substrings (Ziv and Lempel [1978]). We can estimate the compression rate of a message as a function of the number of items in a Lempel-Ziv dictionary relative to the length of the message. The intuition here is that complex messages have high entropy, which will require large dictionaries relative to the length of the string to be transmitted. Snippet 18.2 shows an implementation of the LZ compression algorithm.

SNIPPET 18.2   A LIBRARY BUILT USING THE LZ ALGORITHM

```
def lempelZiv_lib(msg):
    i,lib=1,[msg[0]]
    while i<len(msg):
        for j in xrange(i,len(msg)):
            msg_=msg[i:j+1]
            if msg_ not in lib:
                lib.append(msg_)
                break
        i=j+1
    return lib
```

Kontoyiannis [1998] attempts to make a more efficient use of the information available in a message. What follows is a faithful summary of the exposition in Gao et al. [2008]. We will reproduce the steps in that paper, while complementing them with code snippets that implement their ideas. Let us define L_i^n as 1 plus the length of the longest match found in the n bits prior to i,

$$L_i^n = 1 + \max\left\{l \,\middle|\, x_i^{i+l} = x_j^{j+l} \text{ for some } i - n \leq j \leq i - 1, l \in [0, n]\right\}$$

Snippet 18.3 implements the algorithm that determines the length of the longest match. A few notes worth mentioning:

- The value n is constant for a sliding window, and $n = i$ for an expanding window.
- Computing L_i^n requires data x_{i-n}^{i+n-1}. In other words, index i must be at the center of the window. This is important in order to guarantee that both matching strings are of the same length. If they are not of the same length, l will have a limited range and its maximum will be underestimated.
- Some overlap between the two substrings is allowed, although obviously both cannot start at i.

SNIPPET 18.3 FUNCTION THAT COMPUTES THE LENGTH OF THE LONGEST MATCH

```
def matchLength(msg,i,n):
    # Maximum matched length+1, with overlap.
    # i>=n & len(msg)>=i+n
    subS=''
    for l in xrange(n):
        msg1=msg[i:i+l+1]
        for j in xrange(i-n,i):
            msg0=msg[j:j+l+1]
            if msg1==msg0:
                subS=msg1
                break # search for higher l.
    return len(subS)+1,subS # matched length + 1
```

Ornstein and Weiss [1993] formally established that

$$\lim_{n \to \infty} \frac{L_i^n}{\log_2[n]} = \frac{1}{H}$$

Kontoyiannis uses this result to estimate Shannon's entropy rate. He estimates the average $\frac{L_i^n}{\log_2[n]}$, and uses the reciprocal of that average to estimate H. The general intuition is, as we increase the available history, we expect that messages with high entropy will produce relatively shorter non-redundant substrings. In contrast, messages with low entropy will produce relatively longer non-redundant substrings as we parse through the message. Given a data realization $x_{-\infty}^{\infty}$, a window length $n \geq 1$, and a number of matches $k \geq 1$, the sliding-window LZ estimator $\hat{H}_{n,k} = \hat{H}_{n,k}[x_{-n+1}^{n+k-1}]$ is defined by

$$\hat{H}_{n,k} = \left[\frac{1}{k} \sum_{i=1}^{k} \frac{L_i^n}{\log_2[n]} \right]^{-1}$$

Similarly, the increasing window LZ estimator $\hat{H}_n = \hat{H}_n \left[x_0^{2n-1} \right]$, is defined by

$$\hat{H}_n = \left[\frac{1}{n} \sum_{i=2}^{n} \frac{L_i^i}{\log_2[i]} \right]^{-1}$$

The window size n is constant when computing $\hat{H}_{n,k}$, thus L_i^n. However, when computing $\hat{H}_n$, the window size increases with i, thus L_i^i, with $n = \frac{N}{2}$. In this

expanding window case the length of the message N should be an even number to
ensure that all bits are parsed (recall that x_i is at the center, so for an odd-length message the last bit would not be read).

The above expressions have been derived under the assumptions of: stationarity,
ergodicity, that the process takes finitely many values, and that the process satisfies
the Doeblin condition. Intuitively, this condition requires that, after a finite number
of steps r, no matter what has occurred before, anything can happen with positive
probability. It turns out that this Doeblin condition can be avoided altogether if we
consider a modified version of the above estimators:

$$\tilde{H}_{n,k} = \frac{1}{k} \sum_{i=1}^{k} \frac{\log_2[n]}{L_i^n}$$

$$\tilde{H}_n = \frac{1}{n} \sum_{i=2}^{n} \frac{\log_2[i]}{L_i^i}$$

One practical question when estimating $\tilde{H}_{n,k}$ is how to determine the window
size n. Gao et al. [2008] argue that $k + n = N$ should be approximately equal to
the message length. Considering that the bias of L_i^n is of order $\mathcal{O}[^1/_{\log_2[n]}]$ and
the variance of L_j^n is order $\mathcal{O}[^1/_k]$, the bias/variance trade-off is balanced at around
$k \approx \mathcal{O}[(\log_2[n])^2]$. That is, n could be chosen such that $N \approx n + (\log_2[n])^2$. For
example, for $N = 2^8$, a balanced bias/variance window size would be $n \approx 198$, in
which case $k \approx 58$.

Kontoyiannis [1998] proved that $\hat{H}[X]$ converges to Shannon's entropy rate with
probability 1 as n approaches infinity. Snippet 18.4 implements the ideas discussed
in Gao et al. [2008], which improve on Kontoyiannis [1997] by looking for the maximum redundancy between two substrings of the same size.

**SNIPPET 18.4   IMPLEMENTATION OF ALGORITHMS DISCUSSED
IN GAO ET AL. [2008]**

```
def konto(msg,window=None):
    '''
    * Kontoyiannis' LZ entropy estimate, 2013 version (centered window).
    * Inverse of the avg length of the shortest non-redundant substring.
    * If non-redundant substrings are short, the text is highly entropic.
    * window==None for expanding window, in which case len(msg)%2==0
    * If the end of msg is more relevant, try konto(msg[::-1])
    '''
    out={'num':0,'sum':0,'subS':[]}
    if not isinstance(msg,str):msg=''.join(map(str,msg))
    if window is None:
        points=xrange(1,len(msg)/2+1)
```

```
    else:
        window=min(window,len(msg)/2)
        points=xrange(window,len(msg)-window+1)
    for i in points:
        if window is None:
            l,msg_=matchLength(msg,i,i)
            out['sum']+=np.log2(i+1)/l # to avoid Doeblin condition
        else:
            l,msg_=matchLength(msg,i,window)
            out['sum']+=np.log2(window+1)/l # to avoid Doeblin condition
        out['subS'].append(msg_)
        out['num']+=1
    out['h']=out['sum']/out['num']
    out['r']=1-out['h']/np.log2(len(msg)) # redundancy, 0<=r<=1
    return out
#————————————————————————————————————————————
if __name__=='__main__':
    msg='101010'
    print konto(msg*2)
    print konto(msg+msg[::-1])
```

One caveat of this method is that entropy rate is defined in the limit. In the words of Kontoyiannis, "we fix a large integer N as the size of our database." The theorems used by Kontoyiannis' paper prove asymptotic convergence; however, nowhere is a monotonicity property claimed. When a message is short, a solution may be to repeat the same message multiple times.

A second caveat is that, because the window for matching must be symmetric (same length for the dictionary as for the substring being matched), the last bit is only considered for matching if the message's length corresponds to an even number. One solution is to remove the first bit of a message with odd length.

A third caveat is that some final bits will be dismissed when preceded by irregular sequences. This is also a consequence of the symmetric matching window. For example, the entropy rate for "10000111" equals the entropy rate for "10000110," meaning that the final bit is irrelevant due to the unmatchable "11" in the sixth and seventh bit. When the end of the message is particularly relevant, a good solution may be to analyze the entropy of the reversed message. This not only ensures that the final bits (i.e., the initial ones after the reversing) are used, but actually they will be used to potentially match every bit. Following the previous example, the entropy rate of "11100001" is 0.96, while the entropy rate for "01100001' is 0.84.

18.5 ENCODING SCHEMES

Estimating entropy requires the encoding of a message. In this section we will review a few encoding schemes used in the literature, which are based on returns. Although not discussed in what follows, it is advisable to encode information from fractionally (rather than integer) differentiated series (Chapter 4), as they still contain some memory.

18.5.1 Binary Encoding

Entropy rate estimation requires the discretization of a continuous variable, so that each value can be assigned a code from a finite alphabet. For example, a stream of returns r_t can be encoded according to the sign, 1 for $r_t > 0$, 0 for $r_t < 0$, removing cases where $r_t = 0$. Binary encoding arises naturally in the case of returns series sampled from price bars (i.e., bars that contain prices fluctuating between two symmetric horizontal barriers, centered around the start price), because $|r_t|$ is approximately constant.

When $|r_t|$ can adopt a wide range of outcomes, binary encoding discards potentially useful information. That is particularly the case when working with intraday time bars, which are affected by the heteroscedasticity that results from the inhomogeneous nature of tick data. One way to partially address this heteroscedasticity is to sample prices according to a subordinated stochastic process. Examples of that are trade bars and volume bars, which contain a fixed number of trades or trades for a fixed amount of volume (see Chapter 2). By operating in this non-chronological, market-driven clock, we sample more frequently during highly active periods, and less frequently during periods of less activity, hence regularizing the distribution of $|r_t|$ and reducing the need for a large alphabet.

18.5.2 Quantile Encoding

Unless price bars are used, it is likely that more than two codes will be needed. One approach consists in assigning a code to each r_t according to the quantile it belongs to. The quantile boundaries are determined using an in-sample period (training set). There will be the same number of observations assigned to each letter for the overall in-sample, and close to the same number of observations per letter out-of-sample. When using the method, some codes span a greater fraction of r_t's range than others. This uniform (in-sample) or close to uniform (out-of-sample) distribution of codes tends to increase entropy readings on average.

18.5.3 Sigma Encoding

As an alternative approach, rather than fixing the number of codes, we could let the price stream determine the actual dictionary. Suppose we fix a discretization step, σ. Then, we assign the value 0 to $r_t \in [\min\{r\}, \min\{r\} + \sigma)$, 1 to $r_t \in [\min\{r\} + \sigma, \min\{r\} + 2\sigma)$ and so on until every observation has been encoded with a total of ceil $\left\lceil \frac{\max\{r\} - \min\{r\}}{\sigma} \right\rceil$ codes, where ceil [.] is the ceiling function. Unlike quantile encoding, now each code covers the same fraction of r_t's range. Because codes are not uniformly distributed, entropy readings will tend to be smaller than in quantile encoding on average; however, the appearance of a "rare" code will cause spikes in entropy readings.

18.6 ENTROPY OF A GAUSSIAN PROCESS

The entropy of an IID Normal random process (see Norwich [2003]) can be derived as

$$H = \frac{1}{2}\log[2\pi e \sigma^2]$$

For the standard Normal, $H \approx 1.42$. There are at least two uses of this result. First, it allows us to benchmark the performance of an entropy estimator. We can draw samples from a standard normal distribution, and find what combination of estimator, message length, and encoding gives us an entropy estimate $\hat{H}$ sufficiently close to the theoretically derived value H. For example, Figure 18.1 plots the bootstrapped distributions of entropy estimates under 10, 7, 5, and 2 letter encodings, on messages of length 100, using Kontoyiannis' method. For alphabets of at least 10 letters, the algorithm in Snippet 18.4 delivers the correct answer. When alphabets are too small, information is discarded and entropy is underestimated.

Second, we can use the above equation to connect entropy with volatility, by noting that $\sigma_H = \frac{e^{H-1/2}}{\sqrt{2\pi}}$. This gives us an entropy-implied volatility estimate, provided that returns are indeed drawn from a Normal distribution.

18.7 ENTROPY AND THE GENERALIZED MEAN

Here is a practical way of thinking about entropy. Consider a set of real numbers $x = \{x_i\}_{i=1,\dots,n}$ and weights $p = \{p_i\}_{i=1,\dots,n}$, such that $0 \leq p_i \leq 1$, $\forall i$ and $\sum_{i=1}^n p_i = 1$. The generalized weighted mean of x with weights p on a power $q \neq 0$ is defined as

$$M_q[x,p] = \left(\sum_{i=1}^n p_i x_i^q\right)^{1/q}$$

For $q < 0$, we must require that $x_i > 0$, $\forall i$. The reason this is a generalized mean is that other means can be obtained as special cases:

- Minimum: $\lim_{q \to -\infty} M_q[x,p] = \min_i\{x_i\}$
- Harmonic mean: $M_{-1}[x,p] = \left(\sum_{i=1}^n p_i x_i^{-1}\right)^{-1}$
- Geometric mean: $\lim_{q \to 0} M_q[x,p] = e^{\sum_{i=1}^n p_i \log[x_i]} = \prod_{i=1}^n x_i^{p_i}$
- Arithmetic mean: $M_1[x, \{n^{-1}\}_{i=1,\dots,n}] = n^{-1} \sum_{i=1}^n x_i$

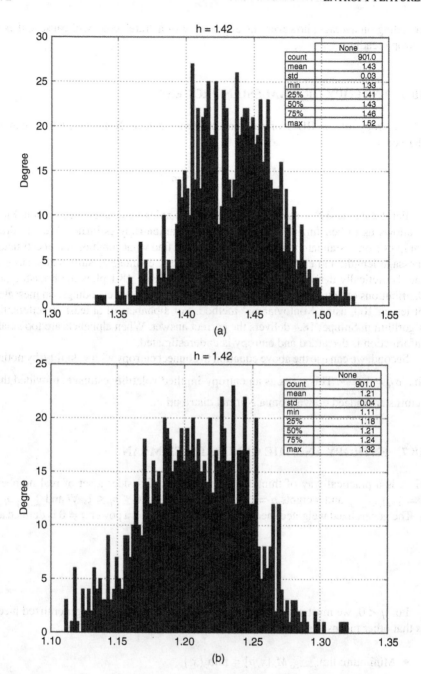

FIGURE 18.1   Distribution of entropy estimates under 10 (top), 7 (bottom), letter encodings, on messages of length 100

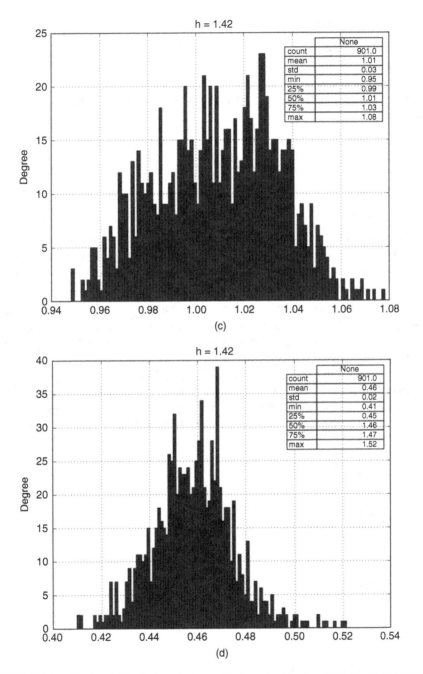

FIGURE 18.1 (*Continued*) Distribution of entropy estimates under 5 (top), and 2 (bottom) letter encodings, on messages of length 100

- Weighted mean: $M_1[x, p] = \sum_{i=1}^{n} p_i x_i$
- Quadratic mean: $M_2[x, p] = \left(\sum_{i=1}^{n} p_i x_i^2\right)^{1/2}$
- Maximum: $\lim_{q \to +\infty} M_q[x, p] = \max_i \{x_i\}$

In the context of information theory, an interesting special case is $x = \{p_i\}_{i=1,\ldots,n}$, hence

$$M_q[p, p] = \left(\sum_{i=1}^{n} p_i p_i^q\right)^{1/q}$$

Let us define the quantity $N_q[p] = \frac{1}{M_{q-1}[p,p]}$, for some $q \neq 1$. Again, for $q < 1$ in $N_q[p]$, we must have $p_i > 0, \forall i$. If $p_i = \frac{1}{k}$ for $k \in [1, n]$ different indices and $p_i = 0$ elsewhere, then the weight is spread evenly across k different items, and $N_q[p] = k$ for $q > 1$. In other words, $N_q[p]$ gives us the *effective number* or *diversity* of items in p, according to some weighting scheme set by q.

Using Jensen's inequality, we can prove that $\frac{\partial M_q[p,p]}{\partial q} \geq 0$, hence $\frac{\partial N_q[p]}{\partial q} \leq 0$. Smaller values of q assign a more uniform weight to elements of the partition, giving relatively more weight to less common elements, and $\lim_{q \to 0} N_q[p]$ is simply the total number of nonzero p_i.

Shannon's entropy is $H[p] = \sum_{i=1}^{n} -p_i \log[p_i] = -\log[\lim_{q \to 0} M_q[p]] = \log[\lim_{q \to 1} N_q[p]]$. This shows that entropy can be interpreted as the logarithm of the *effective number* of items in a list p, where $q \to 1$. Figure 18.2 illustrates how the log effective numbers for a family of randomly generated p arrays converge to

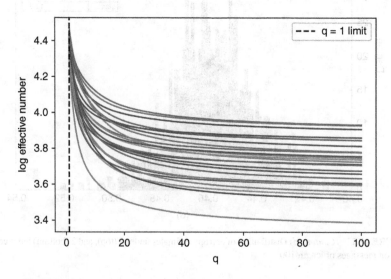

FIGURE 18.2   Log effective numbers for a family of randomly generated p arrays

Shannon's entropy as q approaches 1. Notice, as well, how their behavior stabilizes as q grows large.

Intuitively, entropy measures information as the level of *diversity* contained in a random variable. This intuition is formalized through the notion of generalized mean. The implication is that Shannon's entropy is a special case of a diversity measure (hence its connection with volatility). We can now define and compute alternative measures of diversity, other than entropy, where $q \neq 1$.

18.8   A FEW FINANCIAL APPLICATIONS OF ENTROPY

In this section we will introduce a few applications of entropy to the modelling of financial markets.

18.8.1   Market Efficiency

When arbitrage mechanisms exploit the complete set of opportunities, prices instantaneously reflect the full amount of available information, becoming unpredictable (i.e., a martingale), with no discernable patterns. Conversely, when arbitrage is not perfect, prices contain incomplete amounts of information, which gives rise to predictable patterns. Patterns occur when a string contains redundant information, which enables its compression. The entropy rate of a string determines its optimal compression rate. The higher the entropy, the lower the redundancy and the greater the informational content. Consequently, the entropy of a price string tells us the degree of market efficiency at a given point in time. A "decompressed" market is an efficient market, because price information is non-redundant. A "compressed" market is an inefficient market, because price information is redundant. Bubbles are formed in compressed (low entropy) markets.

18.8.2   Maximum Entropy Generation

In a series of papers, Fiedor [2014a, 2014b, 2014c] proposes to use Kontoyiannis [1997] to estimate the amount of entropy present in a price series. He argues that, out of the possible future outcomes, the one that maximizes entropy may be the most profitable, because it is the one that is least predictable by frequentist statistical models. It is the black swan scenario most likely to trigger stop losses, thus generating a feedback mechanism that will reinforce and exacerbate the move, resulting in runs in the signs of the returns time series.

18.8.3   Portfolio Concentration

Consider an NxN covariance matrix V, computed on returns. First, we compute an eigenvalue decomposition of the matrix, $VW = W\Lambda$. Second, we obtain the factor loadings vector as $f_\omega = W'\omega$, where ω is the vector of allocations, $\sum_{n=1}^{N} \omega_n = 1$.[1]

---

[1] Alternatively, we could have worked with a vector of holdings, should the covariance matrix had been computed on price changes.

Third, we derive the portion of risk contributed by each principal component (Bailey and López de Prado [2012]) as

$$\theta_i = \frac{[f_\omega]_i^2 \Lambda_{i,i}}{\sum_{n=1}^N [f_\omega]_n^2 \Lambda_{n,n}}$$

where $\sum_{i=1}^N \theta_i = 1$, and $\theta_i \in [0,1]$, $\forall i = 1, \dots, N$. Fourth, Meucci [2009] proposed the following entropy-inspired definition of portfolio concentration,

$$H = 1 - \frac{1}{N} e^{-\sum_{n=1}^N \theta_i \log[\theta_i]}$$

At first, this definition of portfolio concentration may sound striking, because θ_i is not a probability. The connection between this notion of concentration and entropy is due to the generalized mean, which we discussed in Chapter 18, Section 18.7.

18.8.4 Market Microstructure

Easley et al. [1996, 1997] showed that, when the odds of good news / bad news are even, the probability of informed trading (PIN) can be derived as

$$PIN = \frac{\alpha \mu}{\alpha \mu + 2\varepsilon}$$

where μ is the rate of arrival of informed traders, ε is the rate of arrival of uninformed traders, and α is the probability of an informational event. PIN can be interpreted as the fraction of orders that arise from informed traders relative to the overall order flow.

Within a volume bar of size V, we can classify ticks as buy or sell according to some algorithm, such as the tick rule or the Lee-Ready algorithm. Let V_τ^B be the sum of the volumes from buy ticks included in volume bar τ, and V_τ^S the sum of the volumes from sell ticks within volume bar τ. Easley et al. [2012a, 2012b] note that $E[|V_\tau^B - V_\tau^S|] \approx \alpha \mu$ and that the expected total volume is $E[V_\tau^B + V_\tau^S] = \alpha \mu + 2\varepsilon$. By using a volume clock (Easley et al. [2012c]), we can set the value of $E[V_\tau^B + V_\tau^S] = \alpha \mu + 2\varepsilon = V$ exogenously. This means that, under a volume clock, PIN reduces to

$$VPIN = \frac{\alpha \mu}{\alpha \mu + 2\varepsilon} = \frac{\alpha \mu}{V} \approx \frac{1}{V} E[|2V_\tau^B - V|] = E[|2v_\tau^B - 1|]$$

where $v_\tau^B = \frac{V_\tau^B}{V}$. Note that $2v_\tau^B - 1$ represents the order flow imbalance, OI_τ, which is a bounded real-valued variable, where $OI_\tau \in [-1, 1]$. The VPIN theory thus provides a formal link between the probability of informed trading (PIN) and the persistency of order flow imbalances under a volume clock. See Chapter 19 for further details on this microstructural theory.

Persistent order flow imbalance is a necessary, non-sufficient condition for adverse selection. For market makers to provide liquidity to informed traders, that order flow imbalance $|OI_\tau|$ must also have been relatively unpredictable. In other words, market makers are not adversely selected when their prediction of order flow imbalance is accurate, even if $|OI_\tau| \gg 0$. In order to determine the probability of adverse selection, we must determine how unpredictable the order flow imbalance is. We can determine this by applying information theory.

Consider a long sequence of symbols. When that sequence contains few redundant patterns, it encompasses a level of complexity that makes it hard to describe and predict. Kolmogorov [1965] formulated this connection between redundancy and complexity. In information theory, lossless compression is the task of perfectly describing a sequence with as few bits as possible. The more redundancies a sequence contains, the greater compression rates can be achieved. Entropy characterizes the redundancy of a source, hence its Kolmogorov complexity and its predictability. We can use this connection between the redundancy of a sequence and its unpredictability (by market makers) to derive the probability of adverse selection.

Here we will discuss one particular procedure that derives the probability of adverse selection as a function of the complexity ingrained in the order flow imbalance. First, given a sequence of volume bars indexed by $\tau = 1, \ldots, N$, each bar of size V, we determine the portion of volume classified as buy, $v_\tau^B \in [0, 1]$. Second, we compute the q-quantiles on $\{v_\tau^B\}$ that define a set K of q disjoint subsets, $K = \{K_1, \ldots, K_q\}$. Third, we produce a mapping from each v_τ^B to one of the disjoint subsets, $f : v_\tau^B \to \{1, \ldots, q\}$, where $f[v_\tau^B] = i \Leftrightarrow v_\tau^B \in K_i, \forall i \in [1, q]$. Fourth, we quantize $\{v_\tau^B\}$ by assigning to each value v_τ^B the index of the subset K it belongs to, $f[v_\tau^B]$. This results in a translation of the set of order imbalances $\{v_\tau^B\}$ into a quantized message $X = [f[v_1^B], f[v_2^B], \ldots, f[v_N^B]]$. Fifth, we estimate the entropy $H[X]$ using Kontoyiannis' Lempel-Ziv algorithm. Sixth, we derive the cumulative distribution function, $F[H[X]]$, and use the time series of $\{F[H[X_\tau]]\}_{\tau=1,\ldots,N}$ as a feature to predict adverse selection.

EXERCISES

18.1 Form dollar bars on E-mini S&P 500 futures:
- **(a)** Quantize the returns series using the binary method.
- **(b)** Quantize the returns series using the quantile encoding, using 10 letters.
- **(c)** Quantize the returns series using the sigma encoding, where σ is the standard deviation of all bar returns.
- **(d)** Compute the entropy of the three encoded series, using the plug-in method.
- **(e)** Compute the entropy of the three encoded series, using Kontoyiannis' method, with a window size of 100.

18.2 Using the bars from exercise 1:
- **(a)** Compute the returns series, $\{r_t\}$.
- **(b)** Encode the series as follows: 0 if $r_t r_{t-1} < 0$, and 1 if $r_t r_{t-1} \geq 0$.

(c) Partition the series into 1000 non-overlapping subsets of equal size (you may have to drop some observations at the beginning).

(d) Compute the entropy of each of the 1000 encoded subsets, using the plug-in method.

(e) Compute the entropy of each of the 1000 encoded subsets, using the Kontoyiannis method, with a window size of 100.

(f) Compute the correlation between results 2.d and 2.e.

18.3 Draw 1000 observations from a standard Normal distribution:

(a) What is the true entropy of this process?

(b) Label the observations according to 8 quantiles.

(c) Estimate the entropy using the plug-in method.

(d) Estimate the entropy using the Kontoyiannis method:
    (i) using a window size of 10.
    (ii) using a window size of 100.

18.4 Using the draws from exercise 3, $\{x_t\}_{t=1,\ldots,1000}$:

(a) Compute $y_t = \rho y_{t-1} + x_t$, where $\rho = .5$, $y_0 = 0$.

(b) Label $\{y_t\}$ the observations according to 8 quantiles.

(c) Estimate the entropy using the plug-in method.

(d) Estimate the entropy using the Kontoyiannis method
    (i) using a window size of 10.
    (ii) using a window size of 100.

18.5 Suppose a portfolio of 10 holdings with equal dollar allocations.

(a) The portion of the total risk contributed by the ith principal component is $\frac{1}{10}$, $i = 1, \ldots, 10$. What is the portfolio's entropy?

(b) The portion of the total risk contributed by the ith principal component is $1 - \frac{i}{55}$, $i = 1, \ldots, 10$. What is the portfolio's entropy?

(c) The portion of the total risk contributed by the ith principal component is $\alpha\frac{1}{10} + (1 - \alpha)(1 - \frac{i}{55})$, $i = 1, \ldots, 10$, $\alpha \in [0, 1]$. Plot the portolio's entropy as a function of α.

REFERENCES

Bailey, D. and M. López de Prado (2012): "Balanced baskets: A new approach to trading and hedging risks." *Journal of Investment Strategies*, Vol. 1, No. 4, pp. 21–62. Available at https://ssrn.com/abstract=2066170.

Easley D., M. Kiefer, M. O'Hara, and J. Paperman (1996): "Liquidity,information, and infrequently traded stocks." *Journal of Finance*, Vol. 51, No. 4, pp. 1405–1436.

Easley D., M. Kiefer and, M. O'Hara (1997): "The information content of the trading process." *Journal of Empirical Finance*, Vol. 4, No. 2, pp. 159–185.

Easley, D., M. López de Prado, and M. O'Hara (2012a): "Flow toxicity and liquidity in a high frequency world." *Review of Financial Studies*, Vol. 25, No. 5, pp. 1547–1493.

Easley, D., M. López de Prado, and M. O'Hara (2012b): "The volume clock: Insights into the high frequency paradigm." *Journal of Portfolio Management*, Vol. 39, No. 1, pp. 19–29.

Gao, Y., I. Kontoyiannis and E. Bienestock (2008): "Estimating the entropy of binary time series: Methodology, some theory and a simulation study." Working paper, arXiv. Available at https://arxiv.org/abs/0802.4363v1.

Fiedor, Pawel (2014a): "Mutual information rate-based networks in financial markets." Working paper, arXiv. Available at https://arxiv.org/abs/1401.2548.

Fiedor, Pawel (2014b): "Information-theoretic approach to lead-lag effect on financial markets." Working paper, arXiv. Available at https://arxiv.org/abs/1402.3820.

Fiedor, Pawel (2014c): "Causal non-linear financial networks." Working paper, arXiv. Available at https://arxiv.org/abs/1407.5020.

Hausser, J. and K. Strimmer (2009): "Entropy inference and the James-Stein estimator, with application to nonlinear gene association networks," *Journal of Machine Learning Research*, Vol. 10, pp. 1469–1484. http://www.jmlr.org/papers/volume10/hausser09a/hausser09a.pdf.

Kolmogorov, A. (1965): "Three approaches to the quantitative definition of information." *Problems in Information Transmission*, Vol. 1, No. 1, pp. 1–7.

Kontoyiannis, I. (1997): "The complexity and entropy of literary styles", *NSF Technical Report #97*.

Kontoyiannis (1998): "Asymptotically optimal lossy Lempel-Ziv coding," *ISIT*, Cambridge, MA, August 16–August 21.

MacKay, D. (2003): *Information Theory, Inference, and Learning Algorithms, 1st ed.* Cambridge University Press.

Meucci, A. (2009): "Managing diversification." *Risk Magazine*, Vol. 22, pp. 74–79.

Norwich, K. (2003): *Information, Sensation and Perception, 1st ed.* Academic Press.

Ornstein, D.S. and B. Weiss (1993): "Entropy and data compression schemes." *IEEE Transactions on Information Theory*, Vol. 39, pp. 78–83.

Shannon, C. (1948): "A mathematical theory of communication." *Bell System Technical Journal*, Vol. 27, No. 3, pp. 379–423.

Ziv, J. and A. Lempel (1978): "Compression of individual sequences via variable-rate coding." *IEEE Transactions on Information Theory*, Vol. 24, No. 5, pp. 530–536.

BIBLIOGRAPHY

Easley, D., R. Engle, M. O'Hara, and L. Wu (2008): "Time-varying arrival rates of informed and uninformed traders." *Journal of Financial Econometrics*, Vol. 6, No. 2, pp. 171–207.

Easley, D., M. López de Prado, and M. O'Hara (2011): "The microstructure of the flash crash." *Journal of Portfolio Management*, Vol. 37, No. 2, pp. 118–128.

Easley, D., M. López de Prado, and M. O'Hara (2012c): "Optimal execution horizon." *Mathematical Finance*, Vol. 25, No. 3, pp. 640–672.

Gnedenko, B. and I. Yelnik (2016): "Minimum entropy as a measure of effective dimensionality." Working paper. Available at https://ssrn.com/abstract=2767549.

CHAPTER 19

Microstructural Features

19.1 MOTIVATION

Market microstructure studies "the process and outcomes of exchanging assets under explicit trading rules" (O'Hara [1995]). Microstructural datasets include primary information about the auctioning process, like order cancellations, double auction book, queues, partial fills, aggressor side, corrections, replacements, etc. The main source is Financial Information eXchange (FIX) messages, which can be purchased from exchanges. The level of detail contained in FIX messages provides researchers with the ability to understand how market participants conceal and reveal their intentions. That makes microstructural data one of the most important ingredients for building predictive ML features.

19.2 REVIEW OF THE LITERATURE

The depth and complexity of market microstructure theories has evolved over time, as a function of the amount and variety of the data available. The first generation of models used solely price information. The two foundational results from those early days are trade classification models (like the tick rule) and the Roll [1984] model. The second generation of models came after volume datasets started to become available, and researchers shifted their attention to study the impact that volume has on prices. Two examples for this generation of models are Kyle [1985] and Amihud [2002].

The third generation of models came after 1996, when Maureen O'Hara, David Easley, and others published their "probability of informed trading" (PIN) theory (Easley et al. [1996]). This constituted a major breakthrough, because PIN explained the bid-ask spread as the consequence of a sequential strategic decision between liquidity providers (market makers) and position takers (informed traders). Essentially, it illustrated that market makers were sellers of the option to be adversely selected by informed traders, and the bid-ask spread is the premium they charge for that option. Easley et al. [2012a, 2012b] explain how to estimate VPIN, a high-frequency estimate of PIN under volume-based sampling.

These are the main theoretical frameworks used by the microstructural literature. O'Hara [1995] and Hasbrouck [2007] offer a good compendium of low-frequency microstructural models. Easley et al. [2013] present a modern treatment of high-frequency microstructural models.

19.3   FIRST GENERATION: PRICE SEQUENCES

The first generation of microstructural models concerned themselves with estimating the bid-ask spread and volatility as proxies for illiquidity. They did so with limited data and without imposing a strategic or sequential structure to the trading process.

19.3.1   The Tick Rule

In a double auction book, quotes are placed for selling a security at various price levels (offers) or for buying a security at various price levels (bids). Offer prices always exceed bid prices, because otherwise there would be an instant match. A trade occurs whenever a buyer matches an offer, or a seller matches a bid. Every trade has a buyer and a seller, but only one side initiates the trade.

The tick rule is an algorithm used to determine a trade's aggressor side. A buy-initiated trade is labeled "1", and a sell-initiated trade is labeled "-1", according to this logic:

$$b_t = \begin{cases} 1 & \text{if } \Delta p_t > 0 \\ -1 & \text{if } \Delta p_t < 0 \\ b_{t-1} & \text{if } \Delta p_t = 0 \end{cases}$$

where p_t is the price of the trade indexed by $t = 1, ..., T$, and b_0 is arbitrarily set to 1. A number of studies have determined that the tick rule achieves high classification accuracy, despite its relative simplicity (Aitken and Frino [1996]). Competing classification methods include Lee and Ready [1991] and Easley et al. [2016].

Transformations of the $\{b_t\}$ series can result in informative features. Such transformations include: (1) Kalman Filters on its future expected value, $E_t[b_{t+1}]$; (2) structural breaks on such predictions (Chapter 17); (3) entropy of the $\{b_t\}$ sequence (Chapter 18); (4) t-values from Wald-Wolfowitz's tests of runs on $\{b_t\}$; (5) fractional differentiation of the cumulative $\{b_t\}$ series, $\sum_{i=1}^{t} b_i$ (Chapter 5); etc.

19.3.2   The Roll Model

Roll [1984] was one of the first models to propose an explanation for the effective bid-ask spread at which a security trades. This is useful in that bid-ask spreads are a function of liquidity, hence Roll's model can be seen as an early attempt to measure the liquidity of a security. Consider a mid-price series $\{m_t\}$, where prices follow a Random Walk with no drift,

$$m_t = m_{t-1} + u_t$$

hence price changes $\Delta m_t = m_t - m_{t-1}$ are independently and identically drawn from a Normal distribution

$$\Delta m_t \sim N\left[0, \sigma_u^2\right]$$

These assumptions are, of course, against all empirical observations, which suggest that financial time series have a drift, they are heteroscedastic, exhibit serial dependency, and their returns distribution is non-Normal. But with a proper sampling procedure, as we saw in Chapter 2, these assumptions may not be too unrealistic. The observed prices, $\{p_t\}$, are the result of sequential trading against the bid-ask spread:

$$p_t = m_t + b_t c$$

where c is half the bid-ask spread, and $b_t \in \{-1, 1\}$ is the aggressor side. The Roll model assumes that buys and sells are equally likely, $P[b_t = 1] = P[b_t = -1] = \frac{1}{2}$, serially independent, $E[b_t b_{t-1}] = 0$, and independent from the noise, $E[b_t u_t] = 0$. Given these assumptions, Roll derives the values of c and σ_u^2 as follows:

$$\sigma^2\left[\Delta p_t\right] = E\left[\left(\Delta p_t\right)^2\right] - \left(E\left[\left(\Delta p_t\right)\right]\right)^2 = 2c^2 + \sigma_u^2$$

$$\sigma\left[\Delta p_t, \Delta p_{t-1}\right] = -c^2$$

resulting in $c = \sqrt{\max\{0, -\sigma[\Delta p_t, \Delta p_{t-1}]\}}$ and $\sigma_u^2 = \sigma^2[\Delta p_t] + 2\sigma[\Delta p_t, \Delta p_{t-1}]$. In conclusion, the bid-ask spread is a function of the serial covariance of price changes, and the true (unobserved) price's noise, excluding microstructural noise, is a function of the observed noise and the serial covariance of price changes.

The reader may question the need for Roll's model nowadays, when datasets include bid-ask prices at multiple book levels. One reason the Roll model is still in use, despite its limitations, is that it offers a relatively direct way to determine the *effective* bid-ask spread of securities that are either rarely traded, or where the published quotes are not representative of the levels at which market makers' are willing to provide liquidity (e.g., corporate, municipal, and agency bonds). Using Roll's estimates, we can derive informative features regarding the market's liquidity conditions.

19.3.3 High-Low Volatility Estimator

Beckers [1983] shows that volatility estimators based on high-low prices are more accurate than the standard estimators of volatility based on closing prices. Parkinson

[1980] derives that, for continuously observed prices following a geometric Brownian motion,

$$E\left[\frac{1}{T}\sum_{t=1}^{T}\left(\log\left[\frac{H_t}{L_t}\right]\right)^2\right] = k_1\sigma_{HL}^2$$

$$E\left[\frac{1}{T}\sum_{t=1}^{T}\left(\log\left[\frac{H_t}{L_t}\right]\right)\right] = k_2\sigma_{HL}$$

where $k_1 = 4\log[2]$, $k_2 = \sqrt{\frac{8}{\pi}}$, H_t is the high price for bar t, and L_t is the low price for bar t. Then the volatility feature σ_{HL} can be robustly estimated based on observed high-low prices.

19.3.4 Corwin and Schultz

Building on the work of Beckers [1983], Corwin and Schultz [2012] introduce a bid-ask spread estimator from high and low prices. The estimator is based on two principles: First, high prices are almost always matched against the offer, and low prices are almost always matched against the bid. The ratio of high-to-low prices reflects fundamental volatility as well as the bid-ask spread. Second, the component of the high-to-low price ratio that is due to volatility increases proportionately with the time elapsed between two observations.

Corwin and Schultz show that the spread, as a percentage of price, can be estimated as

$$S_t = \frac{2(e^{\alpha_t} - 1)}{1 + e^{\alpha_t}}$$

where

$$\alpha_t = \frac{\sqrt{2\beta_t} - \sqrt{\beta_t}}{3 - 2\sqrt{2}} - \sqrt{\frac{\gamma_t}{3 - 2\sqrt{2}}}$$

$$\beta_t = E\left[\sum_{j=0}^{1}\left[\log\left(\frac{H_{t-j}}{L_{t-j}}\right)\right]^2\right]$$

$$\gamma_t = \left[\log\left(\frac{H_{t-1,t}}{L_{t-1,t}}\right)\right]^2$$

and $H_{t-1,t}$ is the high price over 2 bars ($t-1$ and t), whereas $L_{t-1,t}$ is the low price over 2 bars ($t-1$ and t). Because $\alpha_t < 0 \Rightarrow S_t < 0$, the authors recommend setting negative alphas to 0 (see Corwin and Schultz [2012], p. 727). Snippet 19.1 implements this algorithm. The `corwinSchultz` function receives two arguments, a series dataframe with columns (`High,Low`), and an integer value `sl` that defines the sample length used to estimate β_t.

SNIPPET 19.1   IMPLEMENTATION OF THE CORWIN-SCHULTZ ALGORITHM

```
def getBeta(series,sl):
    hl=series[['High','Low']].values
    hl=np.log(hl[:,0]/hl[:,1])**2
    hl=pd.Series(hl,index=series.index)
    beta=pd.stats.moments.rolling_sum(hl,window=2)
    beta=pd.stats.moments.rolling_mean(beta,window=sl)
    return beta.dropna()
#------------------------------------------------
def getGamma(series):
    h2=pd.stats.moments.rolling_max(series['High'],window=2)
    l2=pd.stats.moments.rolling_min(series['Low'],window=2)
    gamma=np.log(h2.values/l2.values)**2
    gamma=pd.Series(gamma,index=h2.index)
    return gamma.dropna()
#------------------------------------------------
def getAlpha(beta,gamma):
    den=3-2*2**.5
    alpha=(2**.5-1)*(beta**.5)/den
    alpha-=(gamma/den)**.5
    alpha[alpha<0]=0 # set negative alphas to 0 (see p.727 of paper)
    return alpha.dropna()
#------------------------------------------------
def corwinSchultz(series,sl=1):
    # Note: S<0 iif alpha<0
    beta=getBeta(series,sl)
    gamma=getGamma(series)
    alpha=getAlpha(beta,gamma)
    spread=2*(np.exp(alpha)-1)/(1+np.exp(alpha))
    startTime=pd.Series(series.index[0:spread.shape[0]],index=spread.index)
    spread=pd.concat([spread,startTime],axis=1)
    spread.columns=['Spread','Start_Time'] # 1st loc used to compute beta
    return spread
```

Note that volatility does not appear in the final Corwin-Schultz equations. The reason is that volatility has been replaced by its high/low estimator. As a byproduct of this model, we can derive the Becker-Parkinson volatility as shown in Snippet 19.2.

SNIPPET 19.2   ESTIMATING VOLATILITY FOR HIGH-LOW PRICES

```
def getSigma(beta,gamma):
    k2=(8/np.pi)**.5
    den=3-2*2**.5
    sigma=(2**-.5-1)*beta**.5/(k2*den)
    sigma+=(gamma/(k2**2*den))**.5
    sigma[sigma<0]=0
    return sigma
```

This procedure is particularly helpful in the corporate bond market, where there is no centralized order book, and trades occur through bids wanted in competition (BWIC). The resulting feature, bid-ask spread S, can be estimated recursively over a rolling window, and values can be smoothed using a Kalman filter.

19.4   SECOND GENERATION: STRATEGIC TRADE MODELS

Second generation microstructural models focus on understanding and measuring illiquidity. Illiquidity is an important informative feature in financial ML models, because it is a risk that has an associated premium. These models have a stronger theoretical foundation than first-generation models, in that they explain trading as the strategic interaction between informed and uninformed traders. In doing so, they pay attention to signed volume and order flow imbalance.

Most of these features are estimated through regressions. In practice, I have observed that the t-values associated with these microstructural estimates are more informative than the (mean) estimates themselves. Although the literature does not mention this observation, there is a good argument for preferring features based on t-values over features based on mean values: t-values are re-scaled by the standard deviation of the estimation error, which incorporates another dimension of information absent in mean estimates.

19.4.1   Kyle's Lambda

Kyle [1985] introduced the following strategic trade model. Consider a risky asset with terminal value $v \sim N[p_0, \Sigma_0]$, as well as two traders:

- A noise trader who trades a quantity $u = N[0, \sigma_u^2]$, independent of v.
- An informed trader who knows v and demands a quantity x, through a market order.

The market maker observes the total order flow $y = x + u$, and sets a price p accordingly. In this model, market makers cannot distinguish between orders from noise traders and informed traders. They adjust prices as a function of the order flow imbalance, as that may indicate the presence of an informed trader. Hence, there is a positive relationship between price change and order flow imbalance, which is called market impact.

The informed trader conjectures that the market maker has a linear price adjustment function, $p = \lambda y + \mu$, where λ is an inverse measure of liquidity. The informed trader's profits are $\pi = (v - p)x$, which are maximized at $x = \frac{v-\mu}{2\lambda}$, with second order condition $\lambda > 0$.

Conversely, the market maker conjectures that the informed trader's demand is a linear function of v: $x = \alpha + \beta v$, which implies $\alpha = -\frac{\mu}{2\lambda}$ and $\beta = \frac{1}{2\lambda}$. Note that lower liquidity means higher λ, which means lower demand from the informed trader.

Kyle argues that the market maker must find an equilibrium between profit maximization and market efficiency, and that under the above linear functions, the only possible solution occurs when

$$\mu = p_0$$

$$\alpha = p_0 \sqrt{\frac{\sigma_u^2}{\Sigma_0}}$$

$$\lambda = \frac{1}{2}\sqrt{\frac{\Sigma_0}{\sigma_u^2}}$$

$$\beta = \sqrt{\frac{\sigma_u^2}{\Sigma_0}}$$

Finally, the informed trader's expected profit can be rewritten as

$$E[\pi] = \frac{(v - p_0)^2}{2}\sqrt{\frac{\sigma_u^2}{\Sigma_0}} = \frac{1}{4\lambda}(v - p_0)^2$$

The implication is that the informed trader has three sources of profit:

- The security's mispricing.
- The variance of the noise trader's net order flow. The higher the noise, the easier the informed trader can conceal his intentions.
- The reciprocal of the terminal security's variance. The lower the volatility, the easier to monetize the mispricing.

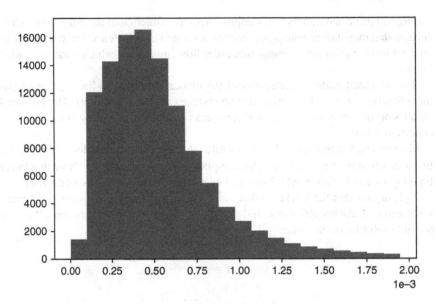

FIGURE 19.1   Kyle's Lambdas Computed on E-mini S&P 500 Futures

In Kyle's model, the variable λ captures price impact. Illiquidity increases with uncertainty about v and decreases with the amount of noise. As a feature, it can be estimated by fitting the regression

$$\Delta p_t = \lambda \left(b_t V_t \right) + \varepsilon_t$$

where $\{p_t\}$ is the time series of prices, $\{b_t\}$ is the time series of aggressor flags, $\{V_t\}$ is the time series of traded volumes, and hence $\{b_t V_t\}$ is the time series of signed volume or net order flow. Figure 19.1 plots the histogram of Kyle's lambdas estimated on the E-mini S&P 500 futures series.

19.4.2   Amihud's Lambda

Amihud [2002] studies the positive relationship between absolute returns and illiquidity. In particular, he computes the daily price response associated with one dollar of trading volume, and argues its value is a proxy of price impact. One possible implementation of this idea is

$$\left| \Delta \log \left[\tilde{p}_\tau \right] \right| = \lambda \sum_{t \in B_\tau} \left(p_t V_t \right) + \varepsilon_\tau$$

where B_τ is the set of trades included in bar τ, $\tilde{p}_\tau$ is the closing price of bar τ, and $p_t V_t$ is the dollar volume involved in trade $t \in B_\tau$. Despite its apparent simplicity, Hasbrouck [2009] found that daily Amihud's lambda estimates exhibit a high rank

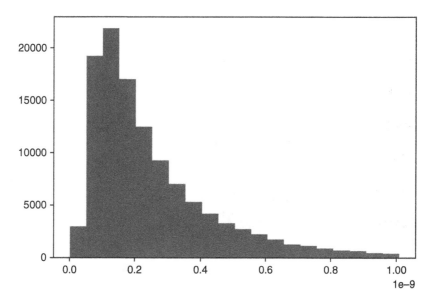

FIGURE 19.2   Amihud's lambdas estimated on E-mini S&P 500 futures

correlation to intraday estimates of effective spread. Figure 19.2 plots the histogram of Amihud's lambdas estimated on the E-mini S&P 500 futures series.

19.4.3   Hasbrouck's Lambda

Hasbrouck [2009] follows up on Kyle's and Amihud's ideas, and applies them to estimating the price impact coefficient based on trade-and-quote (TAQ) data. He uses a Gibbs sampler to produce a Bayesian estimation of the regression specification

$$\log\left[\tilde{p}_{i,\tau}\right] - \log\left[\tilde{p}_{i,\tau-1}\right] = \lambda_i \sum_{t \in B_{i,\tau}} \left(b_{i,t}\sqrt{p_{i,t}V_{i,t}}\right) + \varepsilon_{i,\tau}$$

where $B_{i,\tau}$ is the set of trades included in bar τ for security i, with $i = 1, \dots, I$, $\tilde{p}_{i,\tau}$ is the closing price of bar τ for security i, $b_{i,t} \in \{-1, 1\}$ indicates whether trade $t \in B_{i,\tau}$ was buy-initiated or sell-initiated; and $p_{i,t}V_{i,t}$ is the dollar volume involved in trade $t \in B_{i,\tau}$. We can then estimate λ_i for every security i, and use it as a feature that approximates the effective cost of trading (market impact).

Consistent with most of the literature, Hasbrouck recommends 5-minute time-bars for sampling ticks. However, for the reasons discussed in Chapter 2, better results can be achieved through stochastic sampling methods that are synchronized with market activity. Figure 19.3 plots the histogram of Hasbrouck's lambdas estimated on the E-mini S&P 500 futures series.

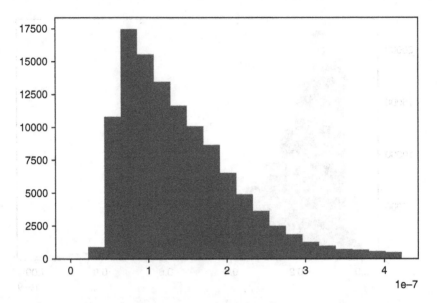

FIGURE 19.3   Hasbrouck's lambdas estimated on E-mini S&P 500 futures

19.5   THIRD GENERATION: SEQUENTIAL TRADE MODELS

As we have seen in the previous section, strategic trade models feature a single informed trader who can trade at multiple times. In this section we will discuss an alternative kind of model, where randomly selected traders arrive at the market sequentially and independently.

Since their appearance, sequential trade models have become very popular among market makers. One reason is, they incorporate the sources of uncertainty faced by liquidity providers, namely the probability that an informational event has taken place, the probability that such event is negative, the arrival rate of noise traders, and the arrival rate of informed traders. With those variables, market makers must update quotes dynamically, and manage their inventories.

19.5.1   Probability of Information-based Trading

Easley et al. [1996] use trade data to determine the probability of information-based trading (PIN) of individual securities. This microstructure model views trading as a game between market makers and position takers that is repeated over multiple trading periods.

Denote a security's price as S, with present value S_0. However, once a certain amount of new information has been incorporated into the price, S will be either S_B (bad news) or S_G (good news). There is a probability α that new information will arrive within the timeframe of the analysis, a probability δ that the news will be bad, and a probability $(1 - \delta)$ that the news will be good. These authors prove that the expected value of the security's price can then be computed at time t as

$$E\left[S_t\right] = \left(1 - \alpha_t\right) S_0 + \alpha_t \left[\delta_t S_B + \left(1 - \delta_t\right) S_G\right]$$

Following a Poisson distribution, informed traders arrive at a rate μ, and uninformed traders arrive at a rate ε. Then, in order to avoid losses from informed traders, market makers reach breakeven at a bid level B_t,

$$E\left[B_t\right] = E\left[S_t\right] - \frac{\mu\alpha_t\delta_t}{\varepsilon + \mu\alpha_t\delta_t} \left(E\left[S_t\right] - S_B\right)$$

and the breakeven ask level A_t at time t must be,

$$E\left[A_t\right] = E\left[S_t\right] + \frac{\mu\alpha_t\left(1 - \delta_t\right)}{\varepsilon + \mu\alpha_t\left(1 - \delta_t\right)} \left(S_G - E\left[S_t\right]\right)$$

It follows that the breakeven bid-ask spread is determined as

$$E\left[A_t - B_t\right] = \frac{\mu\alpha_t\left(1 - \delta_t\right)}{\varepsilon + \mu\alpha_t\left(1 - \delta_t\right)} \left(S_G - E\left[S_t\right]\right) + \frac{\mu\alpha_t\delta_t}{\varepsilon + \mu\alpha_t\delta_t} \left(E\left[S_t\right] - S_B\right)$$

For the standard case when $\delta_t = \frac{1}{2}$, we obtain

$$\delta_t = \frac{1}{2} \Rightarrow E\left[A_t - B_t\right] = \frac{\alpha_t\mu}{\alpha_t\mu + 2\varepsilon} \left(S_G - S_B\right)$$

This equation tells us that the critical factor that determines the price range at which market makers provide liquidity is

$$PIN_t = \frac{\alpha_t\mu}{\alpha_t\mu + 2\varepsilon}$$

The subscript t indicates that the probabilities α and δ are estimated at that point in time. The authors apply a Bayesian updating process to incorporate information after each trade arrives to the market.

In order to determine the value PIN_t, we must estimate four non-observable parameters, namely $\{\alpha, \delta, \mu, \varepsilon\}$. A maximum-likelihood approach is to fit a mixture of three Poisson distributions,

$$P[V^B, V^S] = (1 - \alpha)P[V^B, \varepsilon]P[V^S, \varepsilon]$$
$$+ \alpha(\delta P[V^B, \varepsilon]P[V^S, \mu + \varepsilon] + (1 - \delta)P[V^B, \mu + \varepsilon]P[V^S, \varepsilon])$$

where V^B is the volume traded against the ask (buy-initiated trades), and V^S is the volume traded against the bid (sell-initiated trades).

19.5.2   Volume-Synchronized Probability of Informed Trading

Easley et al. [2008] proved that

$$E\left[V^B - V^S\right] = (1 - \alpha)(\varepsilon - \varepsilon) + \alpha(1 - \delta)(\varepsilon - (\mu + \varepsilon)) + \alpha\delta(\mu + \varepsilon - \varepsilon)$$
$$= \alpha\mu(1 - 2\delta)$$

and in particular, for a sufficiently large μ,

$$E[|V^B - V^S|] \approx \alpha\mu$$

Easley et al. [2011] proposed a high-frequency estimate of PIN, which they named volume-synchronized probability of informed trading (VPIN). This procedure adopts a *volume clock*, which synchronizes the data sampling with market activity, as captured by volume (see Chapter 2). We can then estimate

$$\frac{1}{n}\sum_{\tau=1}^{n}\left|V_\tau^B - V_\tau^S\right| \approx \alpha\mu$$

where V_τ^B is the sum of volumes from buy-initiated trades within volume bar τ, V_τ^S is the sum of volumes from sell-initiated trades within volume bar τ, and n is the number of bars used to produce this estimate. Because all volume bars are of the same size, V, we know that by construction

$$\frac{1}{n}\sum_{\tau=1}^{n}\left(V_\tau^B + V_\tau^S\right) = V = \alpha\mu + 2\varepsilon$$

Hence, PIN can be estimated in high-frequency as

$$VPIN_\tau = \frac{\sum_{\tau=1}^{n}\left|V_\tau^B - V_\tau^S\right|}{\sum_{\tau=1}^{n}\left(V_\tau^B + V_\tau^S\right)} = \frac{\sum_{\tau=1}^{n}\left|V_\tau^B - V_\tau^S\right|}{nV}$$

For additional details and case studies of VPIN, see Easley et al. [2013]. Using linear regressions, Andersen and Bondarenko [2013] concluded that VPIN is not a good predictor of volatility. However, a number of studies have found that VPIN indeed has predictive power: Abad and Yague [2012], Bethel et al. [2012], Cheung et al. [2015], Kim et al. [2014], Song et al. [2014], Van Ness et al. [2017], and Wei et al. [2013], to cite a few. In any case, linear regression is a technique that was already known to 18th-century mathematicians (Stigler [1981]), and economists should not be surprised when it fails to recognize complex non-linear patterns in 21st-century financial markets.

19.6 ADDITIONAL FEATURES FROM MICROSTRUCTURAL DATASETS

The features we have studied in Sections 19.3 to 19.5 were suggested by market microstructure theory. In addition, we should consider alternative features that, although not suggested by the theory, we suspect carry important information about the way market participants operate, and their future intentions. In doing so, we will harness the power of ML algorithms, which can learn how to use these features without being specifically directed by theory.

19.6.1 Distibution of Order Sizes

Easley et al. [2016] study the frequency of trades per trade size, and find that trades with round sizes are abnormally frequent. For example, the frequency rates quickly decay as a function of trade size, with the exception of round trade sizes $\{5, 10, 20, 25, 50, 100, 200, \dots\}$. These authors attribute this phenomenon to so-called "mouse" or "GUI" traders, that is, human traders who send orders by clicking buttons on a GUI (Graphical User Interface). In the case of the E-mini S&P 500, for example, size 10 is 2.9 times more frequent than size 9; size 50 is 10.9 times more likely than size 49; size 100 is 16.8 times more frequent than size 99; size 200 is 27.2 times more likely than size 199; size 250 is 32.5 times more frequent than size 249; size 500 is 57.1 times more frequent than size 499. Such patterns are not typical of "silicon traders," who usually are programmed to randomize trades to disguise their footprint in markets.

A useful feature may be to determine the normal frequency of round-sized trades, and monitor deviations from that expected value. The ML algorithm could, for example, determine if a larger-than-usual proportion of round-sized trades is associated with trends, as human traders tend to bet with a fundamental view, belief, or conviction. Conversely, a lower-than-usual proportion of round-sized trades may increase the likelihood that prices will move sideways, as silicon traders do not typically hold long-term views.

19.6.2 Cancellation Rates, Limit Orders, Market Orders

Eisler et al. [2012] study the impact of market orders, limit orders, and quote cancellations. These authors find that small stocks respond differently than large stocks to these events. They conclude that measuring these magnitudes is relevant to model the dynamics of the bid-ask spread.

Easley et al. [2012] also argue that large quote cancellation rates may be indicative of low liquidity, as participants are publishing quotes that do not intend to get filled. They discuss four categories of predatory algorithms:

- **Quote stuffers:** They engage in "latency arbitrage." Their strategy involves overwhelming an exchange with messages, with the sole intention of slowing down competing algorithms, which are forced to parse messages that only the originators know can be ignored.

- **Quote danglers:** This strategy sends quotes that force a squeezed trader to chase a price against her interests. O'Hara [2011] presents evidence of their disruptive activities.

- **Liquidity squeezers:** When a distressed large investor is forced to unwind her position, predatory algorithms trade in the same direction, draining as much liquidity as possible. As a result, prices overshoot and they make a profit (Carlin et al. [2007]).

- **Pack hunters:** Predators hunting independently become aware of one another's activities, and form a pack in order to maximize the chances of triggering a cascading effect (Donefer [2010], Fabozzi et al. [2011], Jarrow and Protter [2011]). NANEX [2011] shows what appears to be pack hunters forcing a stop loss. Although their individual actions are too small to raise the regulator's suspicion, their collective action may be market-manipulative. When that is the case, it is very hard to prove their collusion, since they coordinate in a decentralized, spontaneous manner.

These predatory algorithms utilize quote cancellations and various order types in an attempt to adversely select market makers. They leave different signatures in the trading record, and measuring the rates of quote cancellation, limit orders, and market orders can be the basis for useful features, informative of their intentions.

19.6.3 Time-Weighted Average Price Execution Algorithms

Easley et al. [2012] demonstrate how to recognize the presence of execution algorithms that target a particular time-weighted average price (TWAP). A TWAP algorithm is an algorithm that slices a large order into small ones, which are submitted at regular time intervals, in an attempt to achieve a pre-defined time-weighted average price. These authors take a sample of E-mini S&P 500 futures trades between November 7, 2010, and November 7, 2011. They divide the day into 24 hours, and for every hour, they add the volume traded at each second, irrespective of the minute. Then they plot these aggregate volumes as a surface where the x-axis is assigned to volume per second, the y-axis is assigned to hour of the day, and the z-axis is assigned to the aggregate volume. This analysis allows us to see the distribution of volume within each minute as the day passes, and search for low-frequency traders executing their massive orders on a chronological time-space. The largest concentrations of volume within a minute tend to occur during the first few seconds, for almost every hour of the day. This is particularly true at 00:00–01:00 GMT (around the open of Asian markets), 05:00–09:00 GMT (around the open of U.K. and European equities), 13:00–15:00 GMT (around the open of U.S. equities), and 20:00–21:00 GMT (around the close of U.S. equities).

A useful ML feature may be to evaluate the order imbalance at the beginning of every minute, and determine whether there is a persistent component. This can then be used to front-run large institutional investors, while the larger portion of their TWAP order is still pending.

19.6.4 Options Markets

Muravyev et al. [2013] use microstructural information from U.S. stocks and options to study events where the two markets disagree. They characterize such disagreement by deriving the underlying bid-ask range implied by the put-call parity quotes and comparing it to the actual bid-ask range of the stock. They conclude that disagreements tend to be resolved in favor of stock quotes, meaning that option *quotes* do not contain economically significant information. At the same time, they do find that option *trades* contain information not included in the stock price. These findings will not come as a surprise to portfolio managers used to trade relatively illiquid products, including stock options. Quotes can remain irrational for prolonged periods of time, even as sparse prices are informative.

Cremers and Weinbaum [2010] find that stocks with relatively expensive calls (stocks with both a high volatility spread and a high change in the volatility spread) outperform stocks with relatively expensive puts (stocks with both a low volatility spread and a low change in the volatility spread) by 50 basis points per week. This degree of predictability is larger when option liquidity is high and stock liquidity is low.

In line with these observations, useful features can be extracted from computing the put-call implied stock price, derived from option trades. Futures prices only represent mean or expected future values. But option prices allow us to derive the entire distribution of outcomes being priced. An ML algorithm can search for patterns across the Greek letters quoted at various strikes and expiration dates.

19.6.5 Serial Correlation of Signed Order Flow

Toth et al. [2011] study the signed order flow of London Stock Exchange stocks, and find that order signs are positively autocorrelated for many days. They attribute this observation to two candidate explanations: Herding and order splitting. They conclude that on timescales of less than a few hours, the persistence of order flow is overwhelmingly due to splitting rather than herding.

Given that market microstructure theory attributes the persistency of order flow imbalance to the presence of informed traders, it makes sense to measure the strength of such persistency through the serial correlation of the signed volumes. Such a feature would be complementary to the features we studied in Section 19.5.

19.7   WHAT IS MICROSTRUCTURAL INFORMATION?

Let me conclude this chapter by addressing what I consider to be a major flaw in the market microstructure literature. Most articles and books on this subject study asymmetric information, and how strategic agents utilize it to profit from market makers. But how is information exactly defined in the context of trading? Unfortunately, there is no widely accepted definition of information in a microstructural sense, and the literature uses this concept in a surprisingly loose, rather informal way (López de Prado [2017]). This section proposes a proper definition of information, founded on signal processing, that can be applied to microstructural studies.

Consider a features matrix $X = \{X_t\}_{t=1,\ldots,T}$ that contains information typically used by market makers to determine whether they should provide liquidity at a particular level, or cancel their passive quotes. For example, the columns could be all of the features discussed in this chapter, like VPIN, Kyle's lambda, cancellation rates, etc. Matrix X has one row for each decision point. For example, a market maker may reconsider the decision to either provide liquidity or pull out of the market every time 10,000 contracts are traded, or whenever there is a significant change in prices (recall sampling methods in Chapter 2), etc. First, we derive an array $y = \{y_t\}_{t=1,\ldots,T}$ that assigns a label 1 to an observation that resulted in a market-making profit, and labels as 0 an observation that resulted in a market-making loss (see Chapter 3 for labeling methods). Second, we fit a classifier on the training set (X, y). Third, as new out-of-sample observations arrive $\tau > T$, we use the fit classifier to predict the label $\hat{y}_\tau = E_\tau[y_\tau | X]$. Fourth, we derive the cross-entropy loss of these predictions, L_τ, as described in Chapter 9, Section 9.4. Fifth, we fit a kernel density estimator (KDE) on the array of negative cross-entropy losses, $\{-L_t\}_{t=T+1,\ldots,\tau}$, to derive its cumulative distribution function, F. Sixth, we estimate the microstructural information at time t as $\phi_\tau = F[-L_\tau]$, where $\phi_\tau \in (0, 1)$.

This microstructural information can be understood as the complexity faced by market makers' decision models. Under normal market conditions, market makers produce *informed forecasts* with low cross-entropy loss, and are able to profit from providing liquidity to position takers. However, in the presence of (asymmetrically) informed traders, market makers produce *uninformed forecasts*, as measured by high cross-entropy loss, and they are adversely selected. In other words, microstructural information can only be defined and measured relative to the predictive power of market makers. The implication is that $\{\phi_\tau\}$ should become an important feature in your financial ML toolkit.

Consider the events of the flash crash of May 6, 2010. Market makers wrongly predicted that their passive quotes sitting on the bid could be filled and sold back at a higher level. The crash was not caused by a single inaccurate prediction, but by the accumulation of thousands of prediction errors (Easley et al. [2011]). If market makers had monitored the rising cross-entropy loss of their predictions, they would have recognized the presence of informed traders and the dangerously rising probability of adverse selection. That would have allowed them to widen the bid-ask spread to levels that would have stopped the order flow imbalance, as sellers would no longer have been willing to sell at those discounts. Instead, market makers kept providing liquidity to sellers at exceedingly generous levels, until eventually they were forced to stop-out, triggering a liquidity crisis that shocked markets, regulators, and academics for months and years.

EXERCISES

19.1 From a time series of E-mini S&P 500 futures tick data,
  (a) Apply the tick rule to derive the series of trade signs.
  (b) Compare to the aggressor's side, as provided by the CME (FIX tag 5797). What is the accuracy of the tick rule?

EXERCISES

(c) Select the cases where FIX tag 5797 disagrees with the tick rule.

(i) Can you see anything distinct that would explain the disagreement?

(ii) Are these disagreements associated with large price jumps? Or high cancelation rates? Or thin quoted sizes?

(iii) Are these disagreements more likely to occur during periods of high or low market activity?

19.2 Compute the Roll model on the time series of E-mini S&P 500 futures tick data.

(a) What are the estimated values of σ_u^2 and c?

(b) Knowing that this contract is one of the most liquid products in the world, and that it trades at the tightest possible bid-ask spread, are these values in line with your expectations?

19.3 Compute the high-low volatility estimator (Section 19.3.3.) on E-mini S&P 500 futures:

(a) Using weekly values, how does this differ from the standard deviation of close-to-close returns?

(b) Using daily values, how does this differ from the standard deviation of close-to-close returns?

(c) Using dollar bars, for an average of 50 bars per day, how does this differ from the standard deviation of close-to-close returns?

19.4 Apply the Corwin-Schultz estimator to a daily series of E-mini S&P 500 futures.

(a) What is the expected bid-ask spread?

(b) What is the implied volatility?

(c) Are these estimates consistent with the earlier results, from exercises 2 and 3?

19.5 Compute Kyle's lambda from:

(a) tick data.

(b) a time series of dollar bars on E-mini S&P 500 futures, where

(i) b_t is the volume-weighted average of the trade signs.

(ii) V_t is the sum of the volumes in that bar.

(iii) Δp_t is the change in price between two consecutive bars.

19.6 Repeat exercise 5, this time applying Hasbrouck's lambda. Are results consistent?

19.7 Repeat exercise 5, this time applying Amihud's lambda. Are results consistent?

19.8 Form a time series of volume bars on E-mini S&P 500 futures,

(a) Compute the series of VPIN on May 6, 2010 (flash crash).

(b) Plot the series of VPIN and prices. What do you see?

19.9 Compute the distribution of order sizes for E-mini S&P 500 futures

(a) Over the entire period.

(b) For May 6, 2010.

(c) Conduct a Kolmogorov-Smirnov test on both distributions. Are they significantly different, at a 95% confidence level?

19.10 Compute a time series of daily quote cancellations rates, and the portion of market orders, on the E-mini S&P 500 futures dataset.

(a) What is the correlation between these two series? Is it statistically significant?

(b) What is the correlation between the two series and daily volatility? Is this what you expected?

19.11 On the E-mini S&P 500 futures tick data:

(a) Compute the distribution of volume executed within the first 5 seconds of every minute.

(b) Compute the distribution of volume executed every minute.

(c) Compute the Kolmogorov-Smirnov test on both distributions. Are they significantly different, at a 95% confidence level?

19.12 On the E-mini S&P 500 futures tick data:

(a) Compute the first-order serial correlation of signed volumes.

(b) Is it statistically significant, at a 95% confidence level?

REFERENCES

Abad, D. and J. Yague (2012): "From PIN to VPIN." *The Spanish Review of Financial Economics*, Vol. 10, No. 2, pp.74-83.

Aitken, M. and A. Frino (1996): "The accuracy of the tick test: Evidence from the Australian Stock Exchange." *Journal of Banking and Finance*, Vol. 20, pp. 1715–1729.

Amihud, Y. and H. Mendelson (1987): "Trading mechanisms and stock returns: An empirical investigation." *Journal of Finance*, Vol. 42, pp. 533–553.

Amihud, Y. (2002): "Illiquidity and stock returns: Cross-section and time-series effects." *Journal of Financial Markets*, Vol. 5, pp. 31–56.

Andersen, T. and O. Bondarenko (2013): "VPIN and the Flash Crash." *Journal of Financial Markets*, Vol. 17, pp.1-46.

Beckers, S. (1983): "Variances of security price returns based on high, low, and closing prices." *Journal of Business*, Vol. 56, pp. 97–112.

Bethel, E. W., Leinweber. D., Rubel, O., and K. Wu (2012): "Federal market information technology in the post–flash crash era: Roles for supercomputing." *Journal of Trading*, Vol. 7, No. 2, pp. 9–25.

Carlin, B., M. Sousa Lobo, and S. Viswanathan (2005): "Episodic liquidity crises. Cooperative and predatory trading." *Journal of Finance*, Vol. 42, No. 5 (October), pp. 2235–2274.

Cheung, W., R. Chou, A. Lei (2015): "Exchange-traded barrier option and VPIN." *Journal of Futures Markets*, Vol. 35, No. 6, pp. 561-581.

Corwin, S. and P. Schultz (2012): "A simple way to estimate bid-ask spreads from daily high and low prices." *Journal of Finance*, Vol. 67, No. 2, pp. 719–760.

Cremers, M. and D. Weinbaum (2010): "Deviations from put-call parity and stock return predictability." *Journal of Financial and Quantitative Analysis*, Vol. 45, No. 2 (April), pp. 335–367.

Donefer, B. (2010): "Algos gone wild. Risk in the world of automated trading strategies." *Journal of Trading*, Vol. 5, pp. 31–34.

Easley, D., N. Kiefer, M. O'Hara, and J. Paperman (1996): "Liquidity, information, and infrequently traded stocks." *Journal of Finance*, Vol. 51, No. 4, pp. 1405–1436.

Easley, D., R. Engle, M. O'Hara, and L. Wu (2008): "Time-varying arrival rates of informed and uninformed traders." *Journal of Financial Econometrics*, Vol. 6, No. 2, pp. 171–207.

Easley, D., M. López de Prado, and M. O'Hara (2011): "The microstructure of the flash crash." *Journal of Portfolio Management*, Vol. 37, No. 2 (Winter), pp. 118–128.

Easley, D., M. López de Prado, and M. O'Hara (2012a): "Flow toxicity and liquidity in a high frequency world." *Review of Financial Studies*, Vol. 25, No. 5, pp. 1457–1493.

Easley, D., M. López de Prado, and M. O'Hara (2012b): "The volume clock: Insights into the high frequency paradigm." *Journal of Portfolio Management*, Vol. 39, No. 1, pp. 19–29.

Easley, D., M. López de Prado, and M. O'Hara (2013): *High-Frequency Trading: New Realities for Traders, Markets and Regulators*, 1st ed. Risk Books.

Easley, D., M. López de Prado, and M. O'Hara (2016): "Discerning information from trade data." *Journal of Financial Economics*, Vol. 120, No. 2, pp. 269–286.

Eisler, Z., J. Bouchaud, and J. Kockelkoren (2012): "The impact of order book events: Market orders, limit orders and cancellations." *Quantitative Finance*, Vol. 12, No. 9, pp. 1395–1419.

Fabozzi, F., S. Focardi, and C. Jonas (2011): "High-frequency trading. Methodologies and market impact." *Review of Futures Markets*, Vol. 19, pp. 7–38.

Hasbrouck, J. (2007): *Empirical Market Microstructure*, 1st ed. Oxford University Press.

Hasbrouck, J. (2009): "Trading costs and returns for US equities: Estimating effective costs from daily data." *Journal of Finance*, Vol. 64, No. 3, pp. 1445–1477.

Jarrow, R. and P. Protter (2011): "A dysfunctional role of high frequency trading in electronic markets." *International Journal of Theoretical and Applied Finance*, Vol. 15, No. 3.

Kim, C., T. Perry, and M. Dhatt (2014): "Informed trading and price discovery around the clock." *Journal of Alternative Investments*, Vol 17, No. 2, pp. 68-81.

Kyle, A. (1985): "Continuous auctions and insider trading." *Econometrica*, Vol. 53, pp. 1315–1336.

Lee, C. and M. Ready (1991): "Inferring trade direction from intraday data." *Journal of Finance*, Vol. 46, pp. 733–746.

López de Prado, M. (2017): "Mathematics and economics: A reality check." *Journal of Portfolio Management*, Vol. 43, No. 1, pp. 5–8.

Muravyev, D., N. Pearson, and J. Broussard (2013): "Is there price discovery in equity options?" *Journal of Financial Economics*, Vol. 107, No. 2, pp. 259–283.

NANEX (2011): "Strange days: June 8, 2011—NatGas Algo." NANEX blog. Available at www.nanex.net/StrangeDays/06082011.html.

O'Hara, M. (1995): *Market Microstructure*, 1st ed. Blackwell, Oxford.

O'Hara, M. (2011): "What is a quote?" *Journal of Trading*, Vol. 5, No. 2 (Spring), pp. 10–15.

Parkinson, M. (1980): "The extreme value method for estimating the variance of the rate of return." *Journal of Business*, Vol. 53, pp. 61–65.

Patzelt, F. and J. Bouchaud (2017): "Universal scaling and nonlinearity of aggregate price impact in financial markets." Working paper. Available at https://arxiv.org/abs/1706.04163.

Roll, R. (1984): "A simple implicit measure of the effective bid-ask spread in an efficient market." *Journal of Finance*, Vol. 39, pp. 1127–1139.

Stigler, Stephen M. (1981): "Gauss and the invention of least squares." *Annals of Statistics*, Vol. 9, No. 3, pp. 465–474.

Song, J, K. Wu and H. Simon (2014): "Parameter analysis of the VPIN (volume synchronized probability of informed trading) metric." In Zopounidis, C., ed., *Quantitative Financial Risk Management: Theory and Practice*, 1st ed. Wiley.

Toth, B., I. Palit, F. Lillo, and J. Farmer (2011): "Why is order flow so persistent?" Working paper. Available at https://arxiv.org/abs/1108.1632.

Van Ness, B., R. Van Ness, and S. Yildiz (2017): "The role of HFTs in order flow toxicity and stock price variance, and predicting changes in HFTs' liquidity provisions." *Journal of Economics and Finance*, Vol. 41, No. 4, pp. 739–762.

Wei, W., D. Gerace, and A. Frino (2013): "Informed trading, flow toxicity and the impact on intraday trading factors." *Australasian Accounting Business and Finance Journal*, Vol. 7, No. 2, pp. 3–24.

PART 5

High-Performance Computing Recipes

CHAPTER 20

Multiprocessing and Vectorization

20.1 MOTIVATION

Multiprocessing is essential to ML. ML algorithms are computationally intensive, and they will require an efficient use of all your CPUs, servers, and clusters. For this reason, most of the functions presented throughout this book were designed for asynchronous multiprocessing. For example, we have made frequent use of a mysterious function called `mpPandasObj`, without ever defining it. In this chapter we will explain what this function does. Furthermore, we will study in detail how to develop multiprocessing engines. The structure of the programs presented in this chapter is agnostic to the hardware architecture used to execute them, whether we employ the cores of a single server or cores distributed across multiple interconnected servers (e.g., in a high-performance computing cluster or a cloud).

20.2 VECTORIZATION EXAMPLE

Vectorization, also known as array programming, is the simplest example of parallelization, whereby an operation is applied at once to the entire set of values. As a minimal example, suppose that you need to do a brute search through a 3-dimensional space, with 2 nodes per dimension. The un-vectorized implementation of that Cartesian product will look something like Snippet 20.1. How would this code look if you had to search through 100 dimensions, or if the number of dimensions was defined by the user during runtime?

SNIPPET 20.1   UN-VECTORIZED CARTESIAN PRODUCT

```
# Cartesian product of dictionary of lists
dict0={'a':['1','2'],'b':['+','*'],'c':['!','@']}
for a in dict0['a']:
    for b in dict0['b']:
        for c in dict0['c']:
            print {'a':a,'b':b,'c':c}
```

A vectorized solution would replace all explicit iterators (e.g., For. . .loops) with matrix algebra operations or compiled iterators or generators. Snippet 20.2 implements the vectorized version of Snippet 20.1. The vectorized version is preferable for four reasons: (1) slow nested For. . .loops are replaced with fast iterators; (2) the code infers the dimensionality of the mesh from the dimensionality of dict0; (3) we could run 100 dimensions without having to modify the code, or need 100 For. . .loops; and (4) under the hood, Python can run operations in C or C++.

SNIPPET 20.2   VECTORIZED CARTESIAN PRODUCT

```
# Cartesian product of dictionary of lists
from itertoolsimport izip,product
dict0={'a':['1','2'],'b':['+','*'],'c':['!','@']}
jobs=(dict(izip(dict0,i)) for i in product(*dict0.values()))
for i in jobs:print i
```

20.3   SINGLE-THREAD VS. MULTITHREADING VS. MULTIPROCESSING

A modern computer has multiple CPU sockets. Each CPU has many cores (processors), and each core has several threads. Multithreading is the technique by which several applications are run in parallel on two or more threads under the same core. One advantage of multithreading is that, because the applications share the same core, they share the same memory space. That introduces the risk that several applications may write on the same memory space at the same time. To prevent that from happening, the Global Interpreter Lock (GIL) assigns write access to one thread per core at a time. Under the GIL, Python's multithreading is limited to one thread per processor. For this reason, Python achieves parallelism through multiprocessing rather than through actual multithreading. Processors do not share the same memory space, hence multiprocessing does not risk writing to the same memory space; however, that also makes it harder to share objects between processes.

Python functions implemented for running on a single-thread will use only a fraction of a modern computer's, server's, or cluster's power. Let us see an example of how a simple task can be run inefficiently when implemented for single-thread execution. Snippet 20.3 finds the earliest time 10,000 Gaussian processes of length 1,000 touch a symmetric double barrier of width 50 times the standard deviation.

SNIPPET 20.3 SINGLE-THREAD IMPLEMENTATION OF A ONE-TOUCH DOUBLE BARRIER

```
import numpy as np
#————————————————————————
def main0():
    # Path dependency: Sequential implementation
    r=np.random.normal(0,.01,size=(1000,10000))
    t=barrierTouch(r)
    return
#————————————————————————
def barrierTouch(r,width=.5):
    # find the index of the earliest barrier touch
    t,p={},np.log((1+r).cumprod(axis=0))
    for j in xrange(r.shape[1]): # go through columns
        for i in xrange(r.shape[0]): # go through rows
            if p[i,j]>=width or p[i,j]<=-width:
                t[j]=i
                continue
    return t
#————————————————————————
if __name__=='__main__':
    import timeit
    print min(timeit.Timer('main0()',setup='from __main__ import main0').repeat(5,10))
```

Compare this implementation with Snippet 20.4. Now the code splits the previous problem into 24 tasks, one per processor. The tasks are then run asynchronously in parallel, using 24 processors. If you run the same code on a cluster with 5000 CPUs, the elapsed time will be about 1/5000 of the single-thread implementation.

SNIPPET 20.4 MULTIPROCESSING IMPLEMENTATION OF A ONE-TOUCH DOUBLE BARRIER

```
import numpy as np
import multiprocessing as mp
#————————————————————————
def main1():
    # Path dependency: Multi-threaded implementation
    r,numThreads=np.random.normal(0,.01,size=(1000,10000)),24
    parts=np.linspace(0,r.shape[0],min(numThreads,r.shape[0])+1)
    parts,jobs=np.ceil(parts).astype(int),[]
    for i in xrange(1,len(parts)):
        jobs.append(r[:,parts[i-1]:parts[i]]) # parallel jobs
```

```
    pool,out=mp.Pool(processes=numThreads),[]
    outputs=pool.imap_unordered(barrierTouch,jobs)
    for out_ in outputs:out.append(out_) # asynchronous response
    pool.close();pool.join()
    return
#————————————————————————————————————
if __name__=='__main__':
    import timeit
    print min(timeit.Timer('main1()',setup='from __main__ import main1').repeat(5,10))
```

Moreover, you could implement the same code to multiprocess a vectorized function, as we did with function `applyPtSlOnT1` in Chapter 3, where parallel processes execute subroutines that include vectorized pandas objects. In this way, you will achieve two levels of parallelization at once. But why stop there? You could achieve three levels of parallelization at once by running multiprocessed instances of vectorized code in an HPC cluster, where each node in the cluster provides the third level of parallelization. In the next sections, we will explain how multiprocessing works.

20.4   ATOMS AND MOLECULES

When preparing jobs for parallelization, it is useful to distinguish between atoms and molecules. Atoms are indivisible tasks. Rather than carrying out all these tasks sequentially in a single thread, we want to group them into molecules, which can be processed in parallel using multiple processors. Each molecule is a subset of atoms that will be processed sequentially, by a callback function, using a single thread. Parallelization takes place at the molecular level.

20.4.1   Linear Partitions

The simplest way to form molecules is to partition a list of atoms in subsets of equal size, where the number of subsets is the minimum between the number of processors and the number of atoms. For N subsets we need to find the $N + 1$ indices that enclose the partitions. This logic is demonstrated in Snippet 20.5.

SNIPPET 20.5   THE `linParts` FUNCTION

```
import numpy as np
#————————————————————————————————————
def linParts(numAtoms,numThreads):
    # partition of atoms with a single loop
    parts=np.linspace(0,numAtoms,min(numThreads,numAtoms)+1)
    parts=np.ceil(parts).astype(int)
    return parts
```

It is common to encounter operations that involve two nested loops. For example, computing a SADF series (Chapter 17), evaluating multiple barrier touches (Chapter 3), or computing a covariance matrix on misaligned series. In these situations, a linear partition of the atomic tasks would be inefficient, because some processors would have to solve a much larger number of operations than others, and the calculation time will depend on the heaviest molecule. A partial solution is to partition the atomic tasks in a number of jobs that is a multiple of the number of processors, then front-load the jobs queue with the heavy molecules. In this way, the light molecules will be assigned to processors that have completed the heavy molecules first, keeping all CPUs busy until the job queue is depleted. In the next section, we will discuss a more complete solution. Figure 20.1 plots a linear partition of 20 atomic tasks of equal complexity into 6 molecules.

20.4.2 Two-Nested Loops Partitions

Consider two nested loops, where the outer loop iterates $i = 1, \dots, N$ and the inner loop iterates $j = 1, \dots, i$. We can order these atomic tasks $\{(i,j) | 1 \leq j \leq i, i = 1, \dots, N\}$ as a *lower* triangular matrix (including the main diagonal). This entails $\frac{1}{2}N(N-1) + N = \frac{1}{2}N(N+1)$ operations, where $\frac{1}{2}N(N-1)$ are off-diagonal and N are diagonal. We would like to parallelize these tasks by partitioning the atomic tasks into M subsets of rows, $\{S_m\}_{m=1,\dots,M}$, each composed of approximately $\frac{1}{2M}N(N+1)$ tasks. The following algorithm determines the rows that constitute each subset (a molecule).

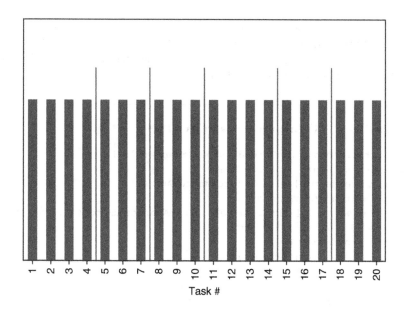

FIGURE 20.1 A linear partition of 20 atomic tasks into 6 molecules

The first subset, S_1, is composed of the first r_1 rows, that is, $S_1 = \{1, \ldots, r_1\}$, for a total number of items $\frac{1}{2}r_1(r_1 + 1)$. Then, r_1 must satisfy the condition $\frac{1}{2}r_1(r_1 + 1) = \frac{1}{2M}N(N + 1)$. Solving for r_1, we obtain the positive root

$$r_1 = \frac{-1 + \sqrt{1 + 4N(N + 1)M^{-1}}}{2}$$

The second subset contains rows $S_2 = \{r_1 + 1, \ldots, r_2\}$, for a total number of items $\frac{1}{2}(r_2 + r_1 + 1)(r_2 - r_1)$. Then, r_2 must satisfy the condition $\frac{1}{2}(r_2 + r_1 + 1)(r_2 - r_1) = \frac{1}{2M}N(N + 1)$. Solving for r_2, we obtain the positive root

$$r_2 = \frac{-1 + \sqrt{1 + 4\left(r_1^2 + r_1 + N(N + 1)M^{-1}\right)}}{2}$$

We can repeat the same argument for a future subset $S_m = \{r_{m-1} + 1, \ldots, r_m\}$, with a total number of items $\frac{1}{2}(r_m + r_{m-1} + 1)(r_m - r_{m-1})$. Then, r_m must satisfy the condition $\frac{1}{2}(r_m + r_{m-1} + 1)(r_m - r_{m-1}) = \frac{1}{2M}N(N + 1)$. Solving for r_m, we obtain the positive root

$$r_m = \frac{-1 + \sqrt{1 + 4\left(r_{m-1}^2 + r_{m-1} + N(N + 1)M^{-1}\right)}}{2}$$

And it is easy to see that r_m reduces to r_1 where $r_{m-1} = r_0 = 0$. Because row numbers are positive integers, the above results are rounded to the nearest natural number. This may mean that some partitions' sizes may deviate slightly from the $\frac{1}{2M}N(N + 1)$ target. Snippet 20.6 implements this logic.

SNIPPET 20.6   THE `nestedParts` FUNCTION

```
def nestedParts(numAtoms,numThreads,upperTriang=False):
    # partition of atoms with an inner loop
    parts,numThreads_=[0],min(numThreads,numAtoms)
    for num in xrange(numThreads_):
        part=1+4*(parts[-1]**2+parts[-1]+numAtoms*(numAtoms+1.)/numThreads_)
        part=(-1+part**.5)/2.
        parts.append(part)
    parts=np.round(parts).astype(int)
    if upperTriang: # the first rows are the heaviest
        parts=np.cumsum(np.diff(parts)[::-1])
        parts=np.append(np.array([0]),parts)
    return parts
```

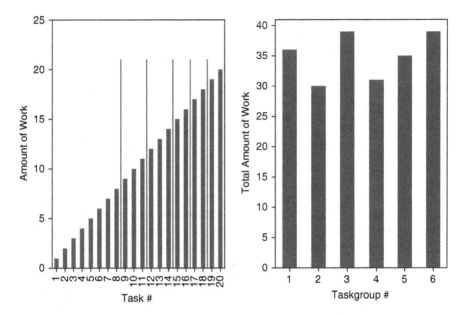

FIGURE 20.2 A two-nested loops partition of atoms into molecules

If the outer loop iterates $i = 1, \ldots, N$ and the inner loop iterates $j = i, \ldots, N$, we can order these atomic tasks $\{(i,j) \mid 1 \leq i \leq j, j = 1, \ldots, N\}$ as an *upper* triangular matrix (including the main diagonal). In this case, the argument upperTriang = True must be passed to function nestedParts. For the curious reader, this is a special case of the bin packing problem. Figure 20.2 plots a two-nested loops partition of atoms of increasing complexity into molecules. Each of the resulting 6 molecules involves a similar amount of work, even though some atomic tasks are up to 20 times harder than others.

20.5 MULTIPROCESSING ENGINES

It would be a mistake to write a parallelization wrapper for each multiprocessed function. Instead, we should develop a library that can parallelize unknown functions, regardless of their arguments and output structure. That is the goal of a multiprocessing engine. In this section, we will study one such engine, and once you understand the logic, you will be ready to develop your own, including all sorts of customized properties.

20.5.1 Preparing the Jobs

In previous chapters we have made frequent use of the mpPandasObj. That function receives six arguments, of which four are optional:

- `func`: A callback function, which will be executed in parallel
- `pdObj`: A tuple containing:
  - The name of the argument used to pass molecules to the callback function
  - A list of indivisible tasks (atoms), which will be grouped into molecules
- `numThreads`: The number of threads that will be used in parallel (one processor per thread)
- `mpBatches`: Number of parallel batches (jobs per core)
- `linMols`: Whether partitions will be linear or double-nested
- `kargs`: Keyword arguments needed by `func`

Snippet 20.7 lists how `mpPandasObj` works. First, atoms are grouped into molecules, using `linParts` (equal number of atoms per molecule) or `nestedParts` (atoms distributed in a lower-triangular structure). When `mpBatches` is greater than 1, there will be more molecules than cores. Suppose that we divide a task into 10 molecules, where molecule 1 takes twice as long as the rest. If we run this process in 10 cores, 9 of the cores will be idle half of the runtime, waiting for the first core to process molecule 1. Alternatively, we could set `mpBatches=10` so as to divide that task in 100 molecules. In doing so, every core will receive equal workload, even though the first 10 molecules take as much time as the next 20 molecules. In this example, the run with `mpBatches=10` will take half of the time consumed by `mpBatches=1`.

Second, we form a list of jobs. A job is a dictionary containing all the information needed to process a molecule, that is, the callback function, its keyword arguments, and the subset of atoms that form the molecule. Third, we will process the jobs sequentially if `numThreads==1` (see Snippet 20.8), and in parallel otherwise (see Section 20.5.2). The reason that we want the option to run jobs sequentially is for debugging purposes. It is not easy to catch a bug when programs are run in multiple processors.[1] Once the code is debugged, we will want to use `numThreads > 1`. Fourth, we stitch together the output from every molecule into a single list, series, or dataframe.

SNIPPET 20.7 THE `mpPandasObj`, USED AT VARIOUS POINTS IN THE BOOK

```
def mpPandasObj(func,pdObj,numThreads=24,mpBatches=1,linMols=True,**kargs):
    '''
    Parallelize jobs, return a DataFrame or Series
    + func: function to be parallelized. Returns a DataFrame
    + pdObj[0]: Name of argument used to pass the molecule
    + pdObj[1]: List of atoms that will be grouped into molecules
    + kargs: any other argument needed by func
```

[1] *Heisenbugs*, named after Heisenberg's uncertainty principle, describe bugs that change their behavior when scrutinized. Multiprocessing bugs are a prime example.

```
Example: df1=mpPandasObj(func,('molecule',df0.index),24,**kargs)
'''
import pandas as pd
if linMols:parts=linParts(len(pdObj[1]),numThreads*mpBatches)
else:parts=nestedParts(len(pdObj[1]),numThreads*mpBatches)
jobs=[]
for i in xrange(1,len(parts)):
    job={pdObj[0]:pdObj[1][parts[i-1]:parts[i]],'func':func}
    job.update(kargs)
    jobs.append(job)
if numThreads==1:out=processJobs_(jobs)
else:out=processJobs(jobs,numThreads=numThreads)
if isinstance(out[0],pd.DataFrame):df0=pd.DataFrame()
elif isinstance(out[0],pd.Series):df0=pd.Series()
else:return out
for i in out:df0=df0.append(i)
return df0.sort_index()
```

In Section 20.5.2 we will see the multiprocessing counterpart to function `processJobs_` of Snippet 20.8.

SNIPPET 20.8   SINGLE-THREAD EXECUTION, FOR DEBUGGING

```
def processJobs_(jobs):
    # Run jobs sequentially, for debugging
    out=[]
    for job in jobs:
        out_=expandCall(job)
        out.append(out_)
    return out
```

20.5.2   Asynchronous Calls

Python has a parallelization library called `multiprocessing`. This library is the basis for multiprocessing engines such as `joblib`,[2] which is the engine used by many `sklearn` algorithms.[3] Snippet 20.9 illustrates how to do an asynchronous call to Python's `multiprocessing` library. The `reportProgress` function keeps us informed about the percentage of jobs completed.

---

[2] https://pypi.python.org/pypi/joblib.

[3] http://scikit-learn.org/stable/developers/performance.html#multi-core-parallelism-using-joblib-parallel.

SNIPPET 20.9   EXAMPLE OF ASYNCHRONOUS CALL TO PYTHON'S MULTIPROCESSING LIBRARY

```
import multiprocessing as mp
#————————————————————————————————————
def reportProgress(jobNum,numJobs,time0,task):
    # Report progress as asynch jobs are completed
    msg=[float(jobNum)/numJobs,(time.time()-time0)/60.]
    msg.append(msg[1]*(1/msg[0]-1))
    timeStamp=str(dt.datetime.fromtimestamp(time.time()))
    msg=timeStamp+' '+str(round(msg[0]*100,2))+'% '+task+' done after '+ \
        str(round(msg[1],2))+' minutes. Remaining '+str(round(msg[2],2))+' minutes.'
    if jobNum<numJobs:sys.stderr.write(msg+'\r')
    else:sys.stderr.write(msg+'\n')
    return
#————————————————————————————————————
def processJobs(jobs,task=None,numThreads=24):
    # Run in parallel.
    # jobs must contain a 'func' callback, for expandCall
    if task is None:task=jobs[0]['func'].__name__
    pool=mp.Pool(processes=numThreads)
    outputs,out,time0=pool.imap_unordered(expandCall,jobs),[],time.time()
    # Process asynchronous output, report progress
    for i,out_ in enumerate(outputs,1):
        out.append(out_)
        reportProgress(i,len(jobs),time0,task)
    pool.close();pool.join() # this is needed to prevent memory leaks
    return out
```

20.5.3   Unwrapping the Callback

In Snippet 20.9, the instruction `pool.imap_unordered()` parallelized `expand-Call`, by running each item in `jobs` (a molecule) in a single thread. Snippet 20.10 lists `expandCall`, which unwraps the items (atoms) in the job (molecule), and executes the callback function. This little function is the trick at the core of the multiprocessing engine: It transforms a dictionary into a task. Once you understand the role it plays, you will be able to develop your own engines.

SNIPPET 20.10   PASSING THE JOB (MOLECULE) TO THE CALLBACK FUNCTION

```
def expandCall(kargs):
    # Expand the arguments of a callback function, kargs['func']
    func=kargs['func']
    del kargs['func']
    out=func(**kargs)
    return out
```

20.5.4   Pickle/Unpickle Objects

Multiprocessing must pickle methods in order to assign them to different processors. The problem is, bound methods are not pickable.[4] The work around is to add functionality to your engine, that tells the library how to deal with this kind of objects. Snippet 20.11 contains the instructions that should be listed at the top of your multiprocessing engine library. If you are curious about the precise reason this piece of code is needed, you may want to read Ascher et al. [2005], Section 7.5.

SNIPPET 20.11   PLACE THIS CODE AT THE BEGINNING OF YOUR ENGINE

```
def _pickle_method(method):
    func_name=method.im_func.__name__
    obj=method.im_self
    cls=method.im_class
    return _unpickle_method,(func_name,obj,cls)
#-----------------------------------------------
def _unpickle_method(func_name,obj,cls):
    for cls in cls.mro():
        try:func=cls.__dict__[func_name]
        except KeyError:pass
        else:break
    return func.__get__(obj,cls)
#-----------------------------------------------
import copy_reg,types,multiprocessing as mp
copy_reg.pickle(types.MethodType,_pickle_method,_unpickle_method)
```

20.5.5   Output Reduction

Suppose that you divide a task into 24 molecules, with the goal that the engine assigns each molecule to one available core. Function processJobs in Snippet 20.9 will capture the 24 outputs and store them in a list. This approach is effective in problems that do not involve large outputs. If the outputs must be combined into a single output, first we will wait until the last molecule is completed, and then we will process the items in the list. The latency added by this post-processing should not be significant, as long as the outputs are small in size and number.

However, when the outputs consume a lot of RAM, and they need to be combined into a single output, storing all those outputs in a list may cause a memory error. It would be better to perform the output reduction operation on the fly, as the results are returned asynchronously by func, rather than waiting for the last molecule to be completed. We can address this concern by improving processJobs. In particular,

[4] http://stackoverflow.com/questions/1816958/cant-pickle-type-instancemethod-when-using-pythons-multiprocessing-pool-ma.

we are going to pass three additional arguments that determine how the molecular outputs must be *reduced* into a single output. Snippet 20.12 lists an enhanced version of `processJobs`, which contains three new arguments:

- `redux`: This is a callback to the function that carries out the reduction. For example, `redux = pd.DataFrame.add`, if output dataframes ought to be summed up.
- `reduxArgs`: This is a dictionary that contains the keyword arguments that must be passed to `redux` (if any). For example, if `redux = pd.DataFrame.join`, then a possibility is `reduxArgs = {'how':'outer'}`.
- `reduxInPlace`: A boolean, indicating whether the `redux` operation should happen *in-place* or not. For example, `redux = dict.update` and `redux = list.append` require `reduxInPlace = True`, since appending a list and updating a dictionary are both in-place operations.

SNIPPET 20.12   ENHANCING `processJobs` TO PERFORM ON-THE-FLY OUTPUT REDUCTION

```
def processJobsRedux(jobs,task=None,numThreads=24,redux=None,reduxArgs={},
                     reduxInPlace=False):
    '''
    Run in parallel
    jobs must contain a 'func' callback, for expandCall
    redux prevents wasting memory by reducing output on the fly
    '''
    if task is None:task=jobs[0]['func'].__name__
    pool=mp.Pool(processes=numThreads)
    imap,out,time0=pool.imap_unordered(expandCall,jobs),None,time.time()
    # Process asynchronous output, report progress
    for i,out_ in enumerate(imap,1):
        if out is None:
            if redux is None:out,redux,reduxInPlace=[out_],list.append,True
            else:out=copy.deepcopy(out_)
        else:
            if reduxInPlace:redux(out,out_,**reduxArgs)
            else:out=redux(out,out_,**reduxArgs)
        reportProgress(i,len(jobs),time0,task)
    pool.close();pool.join() # this is needed to prevent memory leaks
    if isinstance(out,(pd.Series,pd.DataFrame)):out=out.sort_index()
    return out
```

Now that `processJobsRedux` knows what to do with the outputs, we can also enhance `mpPandasObj` from Snippet 20.7. In Snippet 20.13, the new function `mpJobList` passes the three output reduction arguments to `processJobsRedux`.

This eliminates the need to process an outputed list, as mpPandasObj did, hence saving memory and time.

SNIPPET 20.13   ENHANCING mpPandasObj TO PERFORM ON-THE-FLY OUTPUT REDUCTION

```
def mpJobList(func,argList,numThreads=24,mpBatches=1,linMols=True,redux=None,
              reduxArgs={},reduxInPlace=False,**kargs):
    if linMols:parts=linParts(len(argList[1]),numThreads*mpBatches)
    else:parts=nestedParts(len(argList[1]),numThreads*mpBatches)
    jobs=[]
    for i in xrange(1,len(parts)):
        job={argList[0]:argList[1][parts[i-1]:parts[i]],'func':func}
        job.update(kargs)
        jobs.append(job)
    out=processJobsRedux(jobs,redux=redux,reduxArgs=reduxArgs,
                         reduxInPlace=reduxInPlace,numThreads=numThreads)
    return out
```

20.6   MULTIPROCESSING EXAMPLE

What we have presented so far in this chapter can be used to speed-up, by several orders of magnitude, many lengthy and large-scale mathematical operations. In this section we will illustrate an additional motivation for multiprocessing: memory management.

Suppose that you have conducted a spectral decomposition of a covariance matrix of the form $Z'Z$, as we did in Chapter 8, Section 8.4.2, where Z has size TxN. This has resulted in an eigenvectors matrix W and an eigenvalues matrix Λ, such that $Z'ZW = W\Lambda$. Now you would like to derive the orthogonal principal components that explain a user-defined portion of the total variance, $0 \le \tau \le 1$. In order to do that, we compute $P = Z\tilde{W}$, where $\tilde{W}$ contains the first $M \le N$ columns of W, such that $(\sum_{m=1}^{M} \Lambda_{m,m})(\sum_{n=1}^{N} \Lambda_{n,n})^{-1} \ge \tau$. The computation of $P = Z\tilde{W}$ can be parallelized by noting that

$$P = Z\tilde{W} = \sum_{b=1}^{B} Z_b \tilde{W}_b$$

where Z_b is a sparse TxN matrix with only TxN_b items (the rest are empty), $\tilde{W}_b$ is a NxM matrix with only $N_b xM$ items (the rest are empty), and $\sum_{b=1}^{B} N_b = N$. This sparsity is created by dividing the set of columns into a partition of B subsets of columns, and loading into Z_b only the bth subset of the columns. This notion of sparsity may sound a bit complicated at first, however Snippet 20.14 demonstrates how pandas allows us to implement it in a seamless way. Function getPCs receives $\tilde{W}$ through the argument eVec. The argument molecules contains a subset of the file names in fileNames, where each file represents Z_b. The key concept to grasp is that we compute the dot product of a Z_b with the slice of the rows of $\tilde{W}_b$ defined by the columns in Z_b, and that molecular results are aggregated on the fly (redux = pd.DataFrame.add).

SNIPPET 20.14   PRINCIPAL COMPONENTS FOR A SUBSET OF THE COLUMNS

```
pcs=mpJobList(getPCs,('molecules',fileNames),numThreads=24,mpBatches=1,
    path=path,eVec=eVec,redux=pd.DataFrame.add)
#----------------------------------------
def getPCs(path,molecules,eVec):
    # get principal components by loading one file at a time
    pcs=None
    for i in molecules:
        df0=pd.read_csv(path+i,index_col=0,parse_dates=True)
        if pcs is None:pcs=np.dot(df0.values,eVec.loc[df0.columns].values)
        else:pcs+=np.dot(df0.values,eVec.loc[df0.columns].values)
    pcs=pd.DataFrame(pcs,index=df0.index,columns=eVec.columns)
    return pcs
```

This approach presents two advantages: First, because getPCs loads dataframes Z_b sequentially, for a sufficiently large B, the RAM is not exhausted. Second, mpJobList executes the molecules in parallel, hence speeding up the calculations.

In real life ML applications, we often encounter datasets where Z contains billions of datapoints. As this example demonstrates, parallelization is not only beneficial in terms of reducing run time. Many problems could not be solved without parallelization, as a matter of memory limitations, even if we were willing to wait longer.

EXERCISES

20.1 Run Snippets 20.1 and 20.2 with timeit. Repeat 10 batches of 100 executions. What is the minimum elapsed time for each snippet?

20.2 The instructions in Snippet 20.2 are very useful for unit testing, brute force searches, and scenario analysis. Can you remember where else in the book have you seen them? Where else could they have been used?

20.3 Adjust Snippet 20.4 to form molecules using a two-nested loops scheme, rather than a linear scheme.

20.4 Compare with timeit:

(a) Snippet 20.4, by repeating 10 batches of 100 executions. What is the minimum elapsed time for each snippet?

    (b) Modify Snippet 20.4 (from exercise 3), by repeating 10 batches of 100 executions. What is the minimum elapsed time for each snippet?

20.5 Simplify Snippet 20.4 by using `mpPandasObj`.

20.6 Modify `mpPandasObj` to handle the possibility of forming molecules using a two-nested loops scheme with an upper triangular structure.

REFERENCE

Ascher, D., A. Ravenscroft, and A. Martelli (2005): *Python Cookbook*, 2nd ed. O'Reilly Media.

BIBLIOGRAPHY

Gorelick, M. and I. Ozsvald (2008): *High Performance Python*, 1st ed. O'Reilly Media.

López de Prado, M. (2017): "Supercomputing for finance: A gentle introduction." Lecture materials, Cornell University. Available at https://ssrn.com/abstract=2907803.

McKinney, W. (2012): *Python for Data Analysis*, 1st ed. O'Reilly Media.

Palach, J. (2008): *Parallel Programming with Python*, 1st ed. Packt Publishing.

Summerfield, M. (2013): *Python in Practice: Create Better Programs Using Concurrency, Libraries, and Patterns*, 1st ed. Addison-Wesley.

Zaccone, G. (2015): *Python Parallel Programming Cookbook*, 1st ed. Packt Publishing.

CHAPTER 21

Brute Force and Quantum Computers

21.1 MOTIVATION

Discrete mathematics appears naturally in multiple ML problems, including hierarchical clustering, grid searches, decisions based on thresholds, and integer optimization. Sometimes, these problems do not have a known analytical (closed-form) solution, or even a heuristic to approximate it, and our only hope is to search for it through brute force. In this chapter, we will study how a financial problem, intractable to modern supercomputers, can be reformulated as an integer optimization problem. Such a representation makes it amenable to quantum computers. From this example the reader can infer how to translate his particular financial ML intractable problem into a quantum brute force search.

21.2 COMBINATORIAL OPTIMIZATION

Combinatorial optimization problems can be described as problems where there is a finite number of feasible solutions, which result from combining the discrete values of a finite number of variables. As the number of feasible combinations grows, an exhaustive search becomes impractical. The traveling salesman problem is an example of a combinatorial optimization problem that is known to be NP hard (Woeginger [2003]), that is, the category of problems that are at least as hard as the hardest problems solvable is nondeterministic polynomial time.

What makes an exhaustive search impractical is that standard computers evaluate and store the feasible solutions sequentially. But what if we could evaluate and store all feasible solutions at once? That is the goal of quantum computers. Whereas the bits of a standard computer can only adopt one of two possible states ($\{0, 1\}$) at once, quantum computers rely on qubits, which are memory elements that may hold a *linear superposition* of both states. In theory, quantum computers can accomplish this thanks to quantum mechanical phenomena. In some implementations, qubits can support currents flowing in two directions at once, hence providing the desired superposition. This linear superposition property is what makes quantum computers ideally suited for solving NP-hard combinatorial optimization problems. See Williams [2010] for a general treatise on the capabilities of quantum computers.

The best way to understand this approach is through a particular example. We will now see how a dynamic portfolio optimization problem subject to generic transaction cost functions can be represented as a combinatorial optimization problem, tractable to quantum computers. Unlike Garleanu and Pedersen [2012], we will not assume that the returns are drawn from an IID Gaussian distribution. This problem is particularly relevant to large asset managers, as the costs from excessive turnover and implementation shortfall may critically erode the profitability of their investment strategies.

21.3   THE OBJECTIVE FUNCTION

Consider a set on assets $X = \{x_i\}$, $i = 1, \ldots, N$, with returns following a multivariate Normal distribution at each time horizon $h = 1, \ldots, H$, with varying mean and variance. We will assume that the returns are multivariate Normal, time-independent, however not identically distributed through time. We define a trading trajectory as an NxH matrix ω that determines the proportion of capital allocated to each of the N assets over each of the H horizons. At a particular horizon $h = 1, \ldots, H$, we have a forecasted mean μ_h, a forecasted variance V_h and a forecasted transaction cost function $\tau_h [\omega]$. This means that, given a trading trajectory ω, we can compute a vector of expected investment returns r, as

$$r = \text{diag}[\mu' \omega] - \tau [\omega]$$

where $\tau [\omega]$ can adopt any functional form. Without loss of generality, consider the following:

- $\tau_1 [\omega] = \sum_{n=1}^{N} c_{n,1} \sqrt{|\omega_{n,1} - \omega_n^*|}$
- $\tau_h [\omega] = \sum_{n=1}^{N} c_{n,h} \sqrt{|\omega_{n,h} - \omega_{n,h-1}|}$, for $h = 2, \ldots, H$
- ω_n^* is the initial allocation to instrument n, $n = 1, \ldots, N$

$\tau [\omega]$ is an $Hx1$ vector of transaction costs. In words, the transaction costs associated with each asset are the sum of the square roots of the changes in capital allocations, re-scaled by an asset-specific factor $C_h = \{c_{n,h}\}_{n=1,\ldots,N}$ that changes with h. Thus, C_h is an $Nx1$ vector that determines the relative transaction cost across assets.

The Sharpe Ratio (Chapter 14) associated with r can be computed as (μ_h being net of the risk-free rate)

$$SR[r] = \frac{\sum_{h=1}^{H} \mu_h' \omega_h - \tau_h[\omega]}{\sqrt{\sum_{h=1}^{H} \omega_h' V_h \omega_h}}$$

21.4   THE PROBLEM

We would like to compute the optimal trading trajectory that solves the problem

$$\max_{\omega} \; SR[r]$$

$$\text{s.t.} : \sum_{i=1}^{N} |\omega_{i,h}| = 1, \; \forall h = 1, \dots, H$$

This problem attempts to compute a global dynamic optimum, in contrast to the static optimum derived by mean-variance optimizers (see Chapter 16). Note that non-continuous transaction costs are embedded in r. Compared to standard portfolio optimization applications, this is not a convex (quadratic) programming problem for at least three reasons: (1) Returns are not identically distributed, because μ_h and V_h change with h. (2) Transaction costs $\tau_h[\omega]$ are non-continuous and changing with h. (3) The objective function $SR[r]$ is not convex. Next, we will show how to calculate solutions without making use of any analytical property of the objective function (hence the generalized nature of this approach).

21.5   AN INTEGER OPTIMIZATION APPROACH

The generality of this problem makes it intractable to standard convex optimization techniques. Our solution strategy is to discretize it so that it becomes amenable to integer optimization. This in turn allows us to use quantum computing technology to find the optimal solution.

21.5.1   Pigeonhole Partitions

Suppose that we count the number of ways that K units of capital can be allocated among N assets, where we assume $K > N$. This is equivalent to finding the number of non-negative integer solutions to $x_1 + \dots + x_N = K$, which has the nice combinatorial solution $\binom{K+N-1}{N-1}$. This bears a similarity to the classic integer partitioning problem in number theory for which Hardy and Ramanujan (and later, Rademacher) proved an asymptotic expression (see Johansson [2012]). While order does not matter in the partition problem, order is very relevant to the problem we have at hand.

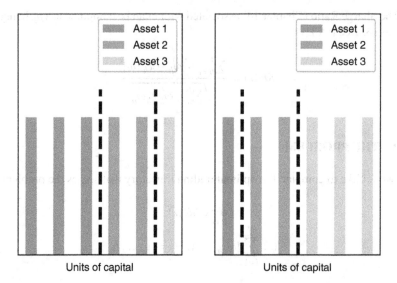

FIGURE 21.1   Partitions $(1, 2, 3)$ and $(3, 2, 1)$ must be treated as different

For example, if $K = 6$ and $N = 3$, partitions $(1, 2, 3)$ and $(3, 2, 1)$ must be treated as different (obviously $(2, 2, 2)$ does not need to be permutated). Figure 21.1 illustrates how order is important when allocating 6 units of capital to 3 different assets. This means that we must consider all distinct permutations of each partition. Even though there is a nice combinatorial solution to find the number of such allocations, it may still be computationally intensive to find as K and N grow large. However, we can use Stirling's approximation to easily arrive at an estimate.

Snippet 21.1 provides an efficient algorithm to generate the set of all partitions, $p^{K,N} = \left\{ \{p_i\}_{i=1,\dots,N} | p_i \in \mathbb{W}, \sum_{i=1}^{N} p_i = K \right\}$, where $\mathbb{W}$ are the natural numbers including zero (whole numbers).

SNIPPET 21.1   PARTITIONS OF k OBJECTS INTO n SLOTS

```
from itertools import combinations_with_replacement
#
def pigeonHole(k,n):
    # Pigeonhole problem (organize k objects in n slots)
    for j in combinations_with_replacement(xrange(n),k):
        r=[0]*n
        for i in j:
            r[i]+=1
        yield r
```

21.5.2   Feasible Static Solutions

We would like to compute the set of all feasible solutions at any given horizon h, which we denote Ω. Consider a partition set of K units into N assets, $p^{K,N}$. For each partition $\{p_i\}_{i=1,\ldots,N} \in p^{K,N}$, we can define a vector of absolute weights such that $|\omega_i| = \frac{1}{K}p_i$, where $\sum_{i=1}^{N} |\omega_i| = 1$ (the full-investment constraint). This full-investment (without leverage) constraint implies that every weight can be either positive or negative, so for every vector of absolute weights $\{|\omega_i|\}_{i=1,\ldots,N}$ we can generate 2^N vectors of (signed) weights. This is accomplished by multiplying the items in $\{|\omega_i|\}_{i=1,\ldots,N}$ with the items of the Cartesian product of $\{-1,1\}$ with N repetitions. Snippet 21.2 shows how to generate the set Ω of all vectors of weights associated with all partitions, $\Omega =$

$$\left\{ \left\{ \tfrac{s_j}{K}p_i \right\} \middle| \{s_j\}_{j=1,\ldots,N} \in \underbrace{\{-1,1\} \text{x} \ldots \text{x} \{-1,1\}}_{N}, \{p_i\}_{i=1,\ldots,N} \in p^{K,N} \right\}.$$

SNIPPET 21.2   SET Ω OF ALL VECTORS ASSOCIATED WITH ALL PARTITIONS

```
import numpy as np
from itertools import product
#————————————————————————
def getAllWeights(k,n):
    #1) Generate partitions
    parts,w=pigeonHole(k,n),None
    #2) Go through partitions
    for part_ in parts:
        w_=np.array(part_)/float(k) # abs(weight) vector
        for prod_ in product([-1,1],repeat=n): # add sign
            w_signed_=(w_*prod_).reshape(-1,1)
            if w is None:w=w_signed_.copy()
            else:w=np.append(w,w_signed_,axis=1)
    return w
```

21.5.3   Evaluating Trajectories

Given the set of all vectors Ω, we define the set of all possible trajectories Φ as the Cartesian product of Ω with H repetitions. Then, for every trajectory we can evaluate its transaction costs and SR, and select the trajectory with optimal performance across Φ. Snippet 21.3 implements this functionality. The object `params` is a list of dictionaries that contain the values of C, μ, V.

SNIPPET 21.3   EVALUATING ALL TRAJECTORIES

```python
import numpy as np
from itertools import product
#————————————————————————————————————————
def evalTCosts(w,params):
    # Compute t-costs of a particular trajectory
    tcost=np.zeros(w.shape[1])
    w_=np.zeros(shape=w.shape[0])
    for i in range(tcost.shape[0]):
        c_=params[i]['c']
        tcost[i]=(c_*abs(w[:,i]-w_)**.5).sum()
        w_=w[:,i].copy()
    return tcost
#————————————————————————————————————————
def evalSR(params,w,tcost):
    # Evaluate SR over multiple horizons
    mean,cov=0,0
    for h in range(w.shape[1]):
        params_=params[h]
        mean+=np.dot(w[:,h].T,params_['mean'])[0]-tcost[h]
        cov+=np.dot(w[:,h].T,np.dot(params_['cov'],w[:,h]))
    sr=mean/cov**.5
    return sr
#————————————————————————————————————————
def dynOptPort(params,k=None):
    # Dynamic optimal portfolio
    #1) Generate partitions
    if k is None:k=params[0]['mean'].shape[0]
    n=params[0]['mean'].shape[0]
    w_all,sr=getAllWeights(k,n),None
    #2) Generate trajectories as cartesian products
    for prod_ in product(w_all.T,repeat=len(params)):
        w_=np.array(prod_).T # concatenate product into a trajectory
        tcost_=evalTCosts(w_,params)
        sr_=evalSR(params,w_,tcost_) # evaluate trajectory
        if sr is None or sr<sr_: # store trajectory if better
            sr,w=sr_,w_.copy()
    return w
```

Note that this procedure selects an globally optimal trajectory without relying on convex optimization. A solution will be found even if the covariance matrices are ill-conditioned, transaction cost functions are non-continuous, etc. The price we pay for this generality is that calculating the solution is extremely computationally intensive. Indeed, evaluating all trajectories is similar to the traveling-salesman problem.

Digital computers are inadequate for this sort of NP-complete or NP-hard problems; however, quantum computers have the advantage of evaluating multiple solutions at once, thanks to the property of linear superposition.

The approach presented in this chapter set the foundation for Rosenberg et al. [2016], which solved the optimal trading trajectory problem using a quantum annealer. The same logic can be applied to a wide range on financial problems involving path dependency, such as a trading trajectory. Intractable ML algorithm can be discretized and translated into a brute force search, intended for a quantum computer.

21.6 A NUMERICAL EXAMPLE

Below we illustrate how the global optimum can be found in practice, using a digital computer. A quantum computer would evaluate all trajectories at once, whereas the digital computer does this sequentially.

21.6.1 Random Matrices

Snippet 21.4 returns a random matrix of Gaussian values with known rank, which is useful in many applications (see exercises). You may want to consider this code the next time you want to execute multivariate Monte Carlo experiments, or scenario analyses.

SNIPPET 21.4 PRODUCE A RANDOM MATRIX OF A GIVEN RANK

```
import numpy as np
#---------------------------------------------
def rndMatWithRank(nSamples,nCols,rank,sigma=0,homNoise=True):
    # Produce random matrix X with given rank
    rng=np.random.RandomState()
    U,_,_=np.linalg.svd(rng.randn(nCols,nCols))
    x=np.dot(rng.randn(nSamples,rank),U[:,:rank].T)
    if homNoise:
        x+=sigma*rng.randn(nSamples,nCols) # Adding homoscedastic noise
    else:
        sigmas=sigma*(rng.rand(nCols)+.5) # Adding heteroscedastic noise
        x+=rng.randn(nSamples,nCols)*sigmas
    return x
```

Snippet 21.5 generates H vectors of means, covariance matrices, and transaction cost factors, C, μ, V. These variables are stored in a `params` list.

SNIPPET 21.5   GENERATE THE PROBLEM'S PARAMETERS

```
import numpy as np
#————————————————————————————————
def genMean(size):
    # Generate a random vector of means
    rMean=np.random.normal(size=(size,1))
    return rMean
#————————————————————————————————
    #1) Parameters
    size,horizon=3,2
    params=[]
    for h in range(horizon):
        x=rndMatWithRank(1000,3,3,0.)
        mean_,cov_=genMean(size),np.cov(x,rowvar=False)
        c_=np.random.uniform(size=cov_.shape[0])*np.diag(cov_)**.5
        params.append({'mean':mean_,'cov':cov_,'c':c_})
```

21.6.2   Static Solution

Snippet 21.6 computes the performance of the trajectory that results from local (static) optima.

SNIPPET 21.6   COMPUTE AND EVALUATE THE STATIC SOLUTION

```
import numpy as np
#————————————————————————————————
def statOptPortf(cov,a):
    # Static optimal porftolio
    # Solution to the "unconstrained" portfolio optimization problem
    cov_inv=np.linalg.inv(cov)
    w=np.dot(cov_inv,a)
    w/=np.dot(np.dot(a.T,cov_inv),a) # np.dot(w.T,a)==1
    w/=abs(w).sum() # re-scale for full investment
    return w
#————————————————————————————————
#2) Static optimal portfolios
w_stat=None
for params_ in params:
    w_=statOptPortf(cov=params_['cov'],a=params_['mean'])
    if w_stat is None:w_stat=w_.copy()
    else:w_stat=np.append(w_stat,w_,axis=1)
tcost_stat=evalTCosts(w_stat,params)
sr_stat=evalSR(params,w_stat,tcost_stat)
print 'static SR:',sr_stat
```

21.6.3 Dynamic Solution

Snippet 21.7 computes the performance associated with the globally dynamic optimal trajectory, applying the functions explained throughout the chapter.

SNIPPET 21.7 COMPUTE AND EVALUATE THE DYNAMIC SOLUTION

```
import numpy as np
#————————————————————————————
#3) Dynamic optimal portfolios
w_dyn=dynOptPort(params)
tcost_dyn=evalTCosts(w_dyn,params)
sr_dyn=evalSR(params,w_dyn,tcost_dyn)
print 'dynamic SR:',sr_dyn
```

EXERCISES

21.1 Using the pigeonhole argument, prove that $\sum_{n=1}^{N} \binom{N}{n} = 2^N - 1$.

21.2 Use Snippet 21.4 to produce random matrices of size $(1000, 10)$, $\texttt{sigma} = 1$ and
 (a) $\texttt{rank} = 1$. Plot the eigenvalues of the covariance matrix.
 (b) $\texttt{rank} = 5$. Plot the eigenvalues of the covariance matrix.
 (c) $\texttt{rank} = 10$. Plot the eigenvalues of the covariance matrix.
 (d) What pattern do you observe? How would you connect it to Markowitz's curse (Chapter 16)?

21.3 Run the numerical example in Section 21.6:
 (a) Use $\texttt{size} = 3$, and compute the running time with $\texttt{timeit}$. Repeat 10 batches of 100 executions. How long did it take?
 (b) Use $\texttt{size} = 4$, and $\texttt{timeit}$. Repeat 10 batches of 100 executions. How long did it take?

21.4 Review all snippets in this chapter.
 (a) How many could be vectorized?
 (b) How many could be parallelized, using the techniques from Chapter 20?
 (c) If you optimize the code, by how much do you think you could speed it up?
 (d) Using the optimized code, what is the problem dimensionality that could be solved within a year?

21.5 Under what circumstances would the globally dynamic optimal trajectory match the sequence of local optima?
 (a) Is that a realistic set of assumptions?
 (b) If not,

(i) could that explain why naïve solutions beat Markowitz's (Chapter 16)?

(ii) why do you think so many firms spend so much effort in computing sequences of local optima?

REFERENCES

Garleanu, N. and L. Pedersen (2012): "Dynamic trading with predictable returns and transaction costs." *Journal of Finance*, Vol. 68, No. 6, pp. 2309–2340.

Johansson, F. (2012): "Efficient implementation of the Hardy-Ramanujan-Rademacher formula," *LMS Journal of Computation and Mathematics*, Vol. 15, pp. 341–359.

Rosenberg, G., P. Haghnegahdar, P. Goddard, P. Carr, K. Wu, and M. López de Prado (2016): "Solving the optimal trading trajectory problem using a quantum annealer." *IEEE Journal of Selected Topics in Signal Processing*, Vol. 10, No. 6 (September), pp. 1053–1060.

Williams, C. (2010): *Explorations in Quantum Computing*, 2nd ed. Springer.

Woeginger, G. (2003): "Exact algorithms for NP-hard problems: A survey." In Junger, M., G. Reinelt, and G. Rinaldi: *Combinatorial Optimization—Eureka, You Shrink!* Lecture notes in computer science, Vol. 2570, Springer, pp. 185–207.

CHAPTER 22

High-Performance Computational Intelligence and Forecasting Technologies

Kesheng Wu and Horst D. Simon

22.1 MOTIVATION

This chapter provides an introduction to the Computational Intelligence and Forecasting Technologies (CIFT) project at Lawrence Berkeley National Laboratory (LBNL). The main objective of CIFT is to promote the use of high-performance computing (HPC) tools and techniques for analysis of streaming data. After noticing the data volume being given as the explanation for the five-month delay for SEC and CFTC to issue their report on the 2010 Flash Crash, LBNL started the CIFT project to apply HPC technologies to manage and analyze financial data. Making timely decisions with streaming data is a requirement for many business applications, such as avoiding impending failure in the electric power grid or a liquidity crisis in financial markets. In all these cases, the HPC tools are well suited in handling the complex data dependencies and providing a timely solution. Over the years, CIFT has worked on a number of different forms of streaming data, including those from vehicle traffic, electric power grid, electricity usage, and so on. The following sections explain the key features of HPC systems, introduce a few special tools used on these systems, and provide examples of streaming data analyses using these HPC tools.

22.2 REGULATORY RESPONSE TO THE FLASH CRASH OF 2010

On May 6, 2010, at about 2:45 p.m. (U.S. Eastern Daylight Time), the U.S. stock market experienced a nearly 10% drop in the Dow Jones Industrial Average, only to recover most of the loss a few minutes later. It took about five months for regulatory agencies to come up with an investigation report. In front of a congressional panel investigating the crash, the data volume (~20 terabytes) was given as the primary reason for the long delay. Since HPC systems, such as those at National Energy Research Scientific Computing (NERSC) center,[1] routinely work with hundreds of terabytes in minutes, we should have no problem processing the data from financial markets. This led to the establishment of the CIFT project with the mission to apply the HPC techniques and tools for financial data analysis.

A key aspect of financial big data is that it consists of mostly time series. Over the years, the CIFT team, along with numerous collaborators, has developed techniques to analyze many different forms of data streams and time series. This chapter provides a brief introduction to the HPC system including both hardware (Section 22.4) and software (Section 22.5), and recounts a few successful use cases (Section 22.6). We conclude with a summary of our vision and work so far and also provide contact information for interested readers.

22.3 BACKGROUND

Advances in computing technology have made it considerably easier to look for complex patterns. This pattern-finding capability is behind a number of recent scientific breakthroughs, such as the discovery of the Higgs particle (Aad et al. [2016]) and gravitational waves (Abbot et al. [2016]). This same capability is also at the core of many internet companies, for example, to match users with advertisers (Zeff and Aronson [1999], Yen et al. [2009]). However, the hardware and software used in science and in commerce are quite different. The HPC tools have some critical advantages that should be useful in a variety of business applications.

Tools for scientists are typically built around high-performance computing (HPC) platforms, while the tools for commercial applications are built around cloud computing platforms. For the purpose of sifting through large volumes of data to find useful patterns, the two approaches have been shown to work well. However, the marquee application for HPC systems is large-scale simulation, such as weather models used for forecasting regional storms in the next few days (Asanovic et al. [2006]). In contrast, the commercial cloud was initially motivated by the need to process a large number of independent data objects concurrently (data parallel tasks).

For our work, we are primarily interested in analyses of streaming data. In particular, high-speed complex data streams, such as those from sensor networks monitoring our nation's electric power grid and highway systems. This streaming workload is not ideal for either HPC systems or cloud systems as we discuss below, but we believe that the HPC ecosystem has more to offer to address the streaming data analysis than the cloud ecosystem does.

Cloud systems were originally designed for parallel data tasks, where a large number of independent data objects can be processed concurrently. The system is thus

---

[1] NERSC is a National User Facility funded by U.S. Department of Energy, located at LBNL. More information about NERSC can be found at http://nersc.gov/.

designed for high throughput, not for producing real-time responses. However, many business applications require real-time or near-real-time responses. For example, an instability event in an electric power grid could develop and grow into a disaster in minutes; finding the tell-tale signature quickly enough would avert the disaster. Similarly, signs of emerging illiquidity events have been identified in the financial research literature; quickly finding these signs during the active market trading hours could offer options to prevent shocks to the market and avoid flash crashes. The ability to prioritize quick turnaround time is essential in these cases.

A data stream is by definition available progressively; therefore, there may not be a large number of data objects to be processed in parallel. Typically, only a fixed amount of the most recent data records are available for analysis. In this case, an effective way to harness the computing power of many central processing units (CPUs) cores is to divide the analytical work on a single data object (or a single time-step) to many CPU cores. The HPC ecosystem has more advanced tools for this kind of work than the cloud ecosystem does.

These are the main points that motivated our work. For a more thorough comparison of HPC systems and cloud systems, we refer interested readers to Asanovic et al. [2006]. In particular, Fox et al. [2015] have created an extensive taxonomy for describing the similarities and differences for any application scenario.

In short, we believe the HPC community has a lot to offer to advance the state-of-the-art for streaming analytics. The CIFT project was established with a mission to transfer LBNL's HPC expertise to streaming business applications. We are pursuing this mission via collaboration, demonstration, and tool development.

To evaluate the potential uses of HPC technology, we have spent time working with various applications. This process not only exposes our HPC experts to a variety of fields, but also makes it possible for us to gather financial support to establish a demonstration facility.

With the generous gifts from a number of early supporters of this effort, we established a substantial computing cluster dedicated to this work. This dedicated computer (named dirac1) allows users to utilize an HPC system and evaluate their applications for themselves.

We are also engaged in a tool development effort to make HPC systems more usable for streaming data analysis. In the following sections, we will describe the hardware and software of the dedicated CIFT machine, as well as some of the demonstration and tool development efforts. Highlights include improving the data handling speed by 21-fold, and increasing the speed of computing an early warning indicator by 720-fold.

22.4   HPC HARDWARE

Legend has it that the first generation of big data systems was built with the spare computer components gleaned from a university campus. This is likely an urban legend, but it underscores an important point about the difference between HPC systems and cloud systems. Theoretically, a HPC system is built with custom

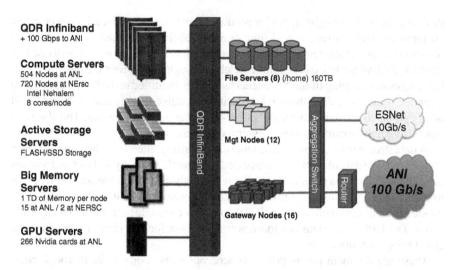

FIGURE 22.1   Schematic of the Magellan cluster (circa 2010), an example of HPC computer cluster

high-cost components, while cloud systems are built with standard low-cost commodity components. In practice, since the worldwide investment in HPC systems is much smaller than that of personal computers, there is no way for manufacturers to produce custom components just for the HPC market. The truth is that HPC systems are largely assembled from commodity components just like cloud systems. However, due to their different target applications, there are some differences in their choices of the components.

Let us describe the computing elements, storage system, and networking system in turn. Figure 22.1 is a high-level schematic diagram representing the key components of the Magellan cluster around year 2010 (Jackson et al. [2010]; Yelick et al. [2011]). The computer elements include both CPUs and graphics processing units (GPUs). These CPUs and GPUs are commercial products in almost all the cases. For example, the nodes on dirac1 use a 24-core 2.2Ghz Intel processor, which is common to cloud computing systems. Currently, dirac1 does not contain GPUs.

The networking system consists of two parts: the InfiniBand network connecting the components within the cluster, and the switched network connection to the outside world. In this particular example, the outside connections are labeled "ESNet" and "ANI." The InfiniBand network switches are also common in cloud computing systems.

The storage system in Figure 1 includes both rotating disks and flash storage. This combination is also common. What is different is that a HPC system typically has its storage system concentrated outside of the computer nodes, while a typical cloud computing system has its storage system distributed among the compute nodes. These two approaches have their own advantages and disadvantages. For example, the concentrated storage is typically exported as a global file system to all computer nodes, which makes it easier to deal with data stored in files. However, this requires a highly capable network connecting the CPUs and the disks. In contrast, the distributed approach could use lower-capacity network because there is some storage that is close to each CPU. Typically, a distributed file system, such as the Google file system (Ghemawat, Gobioff, and Leung [2003]), is layered on top of a cloud computing system to make the storage accessible to all CPUs.

In short, the current generation of HPC systems and cloud systems use pretty much the same commercial hardware components. Their differences are primarily in the arrangement of the storage systems and networking systems. Clearly, the difference in the storage system designs could affect the application performance. However, the virtualization layer of the cloud systems is likely the bigger cause of application performance difference. In the next section, we will discuss another factor that could have an even larger impact, namely software tools and libraries.

Virtualization is generally used in the cloud computing environment to make the same hardware available to multiple users and to insulate one software environment from another. This is one of the more prominent features distinguishing the cloud computing environment from the HPC environment. In most cases, all three basic components of a computer system—CPU, storage, and networking—are all virtualized. This virtualization has many benefits. For example, an existing application can run on a CPU chip without recompiling; many users can share the same hardware; hardware faults could be corrected through the virtualization software; and applications on a failed compute node could be more easily migrated to another node. However, this virtualization layer also imposes some runtime overhead and could reduce application performance. For time-sensitive applications, this reduction in performance could become a critical issue.

Tests show that the performance differences could be quite large. Next, we briefly describe a performance study reported by Jackson et al [2010]. Figure 22.2 shows the performance slowdown using different computer systems. The names below the horizontal axis are different software packages commonly used at NERSC. The left bar corresponds to the Commercial Cloud, the middle bar to Magellan, and the (sometimes missing) right bar to the EC2-Beta-Opt system. The non-optimized commercial

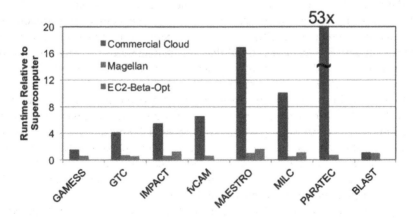

FIGURE 22.2 The cloud ran scientific applications considerably slower than on HPC systems (circa 2010)

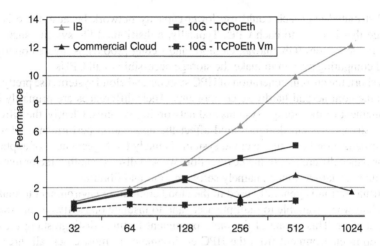

FIGURE 22.3   As the number of cores increases (horizontal axis), the virtualization overhead becomes much more significant (circa 2010)

cloud instances run these software packages 2 to 10 times slower than on a NERSC supercomputer. Even on the more expensive high-performance instances, there are noticeable slowdowns.

Figure 22.3 shows a study of the main factor causing the slowdown with the software package PARATEC. In Figure 2, we see that PARATEC took 53 times longer to complete on the commercial cloud than on an HPC system. We observe from Figure 3 that, as the number of cores (horizontal axis) increases, the differences among the measured performances (measured in TFLOP/s) become larger. In particular, the line labeled "10G- TCPoEth Vm" barely increases as the number of cores grows. This is the case where the network instance is using virtualized networking (TCP over Ethernet). It clearly shows that the networking virtualization overhead is significant, to the point of rendering the cloud useless.

The issue of virtualization overhead is widely recognized (Chen et al. [2015]). There has been considerable research aimed at addressing both the I/O virtualization overhead (Gordon et al. [2012]) as well as the networking virtualization overhead (Dong et al. [2012]). As these state-of-the-art techniques are gradually being moved into commercial products, we anticipate the overhead will decrease in the future, but some overhead will inevitably remain.

To wrap up this section, we briefly touch on the economics of HPC versus cloud. Typically, HPC systems are run by nonprofit research organizations and universities, while cloud systems are provided by commercial companies. Profit, customer retention, and many other factors affect the cost of a cloud system (Armburst et al. [2010]). In 2011, the Magellan project report stated that "Cost analysis shows that DOE centers are cost competitive, typically 3–7 × less expensive, when compared to commercial cloud providers" (Yelick et al. [2010]).

A group of high-energy physicists thought their use case was well-suited for cloud computing and conducted a detailed study of a comparison study (Holzman et al. [2017]). Their cost comparisons still show the commercial cloud offerings as approximately 50% more expensive than dedicated HPC systems for comparable computing tasks; however, the authors worked with severe limitations on data ingress and egress to avoid potentially hefty charges on data movement. For complex workloads, such as the streaming data analyses discussed in this book, we anticipate that this HPC cost advantage will remain in the future. A 2016 National Academy of Sciences study came to the same conclusion that even a long-term lease from Amazon is likely 2 to 3 times more expensive than HPC systems to handle the expected science workload from NSF (Box 6.2 from National Academies of Sciences, [2016]).

22.5 HPC SOFTWARE

Ironically, the real power of a supercomputer is in its specialized software. There are a wide variety of software packages available for both HPC systems and cloud systems. In most cases, the same software package is available on both platforms. Therefore, we chose to focus on software packages that are unique to HPC systems and have the potential to improve computational intelligence and forecasting technologies.

One noticeable feature of the HPC software ecosystem is that much of the application software performs its own interprocessor communication through Message Passing Interface (MPI). In fact, the cornerstone of most scientific computing books is MPI (Kumar et al. [1994], Gropp, Lusk, and Skjellum [1999]). Accordingly, our discussion of HPC software tools will start with MPI. As this book relies on data processing algorithms, we will concentrate on data management tools (Shoshami and Rotem [2010]).

22.5.1 Message Passing Interface

Message Passing Interface is a communication protocol for parallel computing (Gropp, Lusk, and Skjellum [1999], Snir et al. [1988]). It defines a number of point-to-point data exchange operations as well as some collective communication operations. The MPI standard was established based on several early attempts to build portable communication libraries. The early implementation from Argonne National Lab, named MPICH, was high performance, scalable, and portable. This helped MPI to gain wide acceptance among scientific users.

The success of MPI is partly due to its separation of Language Independent Specifications (LIS) from its language bindings. This allows the same core function to be provided to many different programming languages, which also contributes to its acceptance. The first MPI standard specified ANSI C and Fortran-77 bindings together with the LIS. The draft specification was presented to the user community at the 1994 Supercomputing Conference.

Another key factor contributing to MPI's success is the open-source license used by MPICH. This license allows the vendors to take the source code to produce their own custom versions, which allows the HPC system vendors to quickly produce their own MPI libraries. To this day, all HPC systems support the familiar MPI on their computers. This wide adoption also ensures that MPI will continue to be the favorite communication protocol among the users of HPC systems.

22.5.2   Hierarchical Data Format 5

In describing the HPC hardware components, we noted that the storage systems in an HPC platform are typically different from those in a cloud platform. Correspondingly, the software libraries used by most users for accessing the storage systems are different as well. This difference can be traced to the difference in the conceptual models of data. Typically, HPC applications treat data as multi-dimensional arrays and, therefore, the most popular I/O libraries on HPC systems are designed to work with multi-dimensional arrays. Here, we describe the most widely used array format library, HDF5 (Folk et al. [2011]).

HDF5 is the fifth iteration of the Hierarchical Data Format, produced by the HDF Group.[2] The basic unit of data in HDF5 is an array plus its associated information such as attributes, dimensions, and data type. Together, they are known as a data set. Data sets can be grouped into large units called groups, and groups can be organized into high-level groups. This flexible hierarchical organization allows users to express complex relationships among the data sets.

Beyond the basic library for organizing user data into files, the HDF Group also provides a suite of tools and specialization of HDF5 for different applications. For example, HDF5 includes a performance profiling tool. NASA has a specialization of HDF5, named HDF5-EOS, for data from their Earth-Observing System (EOS); and the next-generation DNA sequence community has produced a specialization named BioHDF for their bioinformatics data.

HDF5 provides an efficient way for accessing the storage systems on HPC platform. In tests, we have demonstrated that using HDF5 to store stock markets data significantly speeds up the analysis operations. This is largely due to its efficient compression/decompression algorithms that minimize network traffic and I/O operations, which brings us to our next point.

22.5.3   *In Situ* Processing

Over the last few decades, CPU performance has roughly doubled every 18 months (Moore's law), while disk performance has been increasing less than 5% a year. This difference has caused it to take longer and longer to write out the content of the CPU memory. To address this issue, a number of research efforts have focused on *in situ* analysis capability (Ayachit et al. [2016]).

Among the current generation of processing systems, the Adaptable I/O System (ADIOS) is the most widely used (Liu et al. [2014]). It employs a number of data transport engines that allow users to tap into the I/O stream and perform analytical operations. This is useful because irrelevant data can be discarded in-flight, hence avoiding its slow and voluminous storage. This same *in situ* mechanism also allows it to complete write operations very quickly. In fact, it initially gained attention because of its write speed. Since then, the ADIOS developers have worked with a number of very large teams to improve their I/O pipelines and their analysis capability.

---

[2] The HDF Group web site is https://www.hdfgroup.org/.

Because ADIOS supports streaming data accesses, it is also highly relevant to CIFT work. In a number of demonstrations, ADIOS with ICEE transport engine was able to complete distributed streaming data analysis in real-time (Choi et al. [2013]). We will describe one of the use cases involving blobs in fusion plasma in the next section.

To summarize, *in situ* data processing capability is another very useful tool from the HPC ecosystem.

22.5.4 Convergence

We mentioned earlier that the HPC hardware market is a tiny part of the overall computer hardware market. The HPC software market is even smaller compared to the overall software market. So far, the HPC software ecosystem is largely maintained by a number of small vendors along with some open-source contributors. Therefore, HPC system users are under tremendous pressure to migrate to the better supported cloud software systems. This is a significant driver for convergence between software for HPC and software for cloud (Fox et al. [2015]).

Even though convergence appears to be inevitable, we advocate for a convergence option that keeps the advantage of the software tools mentioned above. One of the motivations of the CIFT project is to seek a way to transfer the above tools to the computing environments of the future.

22.6 USE CASES

Data processing is such an important part of modern scientific research that some researchers are calling it the fourth paradigm of science (Hey, Tansley, and Tolle [2009]). In economics, the same data-driven research activities have led to the wildly popular behavioral economics (Camerer and Loewenstein [2011]). Much of the recent advances in data-driven research are based on machine learning applications (Qiu et al. [2016], Rudin and Wagstaff [2014]). Their successes in a wide variety of fields, such as planetary science and bioinformatics, have generated considerable interest among researchers from diverse domains. In the rest of this section, we describe a few examples applying advanced data analysis techniques to various fields, where many of these use cases originated in the CIFT project.

22.6.1 Supernova Hunting

In astronomy, the determination of many important facts such as the expansion speed of the universe, is performed by measuring the light from exploding type Ia supernovae (Bloom et al. [2012]). The process of searching the night sky for exploding supernovae is called synoptic imaging survey. The Palomar Transient Factory (PTF) is an example of such a synoptic survey (Nicholas et al. [2009]). The PTF telescopes scan the night sky and produce a set of images every 45 minutes. The new image is compared against the previous observations of the same patch of sky to determine

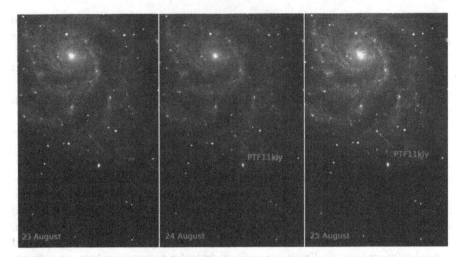

FIGURE 22.4   Supernova SN 2011fe was discovered 11 hours after first evidence of explosion, as a result of the extensive automation in classification of astronomical observations

what has changed and to classify the changes. Such identification and classification tasks used to be performed by astronomers manually. However, the current number of incoming images from the PTF telescopes is too large for manual inspection. An automated workflow for these image processing tasks has been developed and deployed at a number of different computer centers.

Figure 22.4 shows the supernova that was identified earliest in its explosion process. On August 23, 2011, a patch of the sky showed no sign of this star, but a faint light showed up on August 24. This quick turnover allowed astronomers around the world to perform detailed follow-up observations, which are important for determining the parameters related to the expansion of the universe.

The quick identification of this supernova is an important demonstration of the machine learning capability of the automated workflow. This workflow processes the incoming images to extract the objects that have changed since last observed. It then classifies the changed object to determine a preliminary type based on the previous training. Since follow-up resources for extracting novel science from fast-changing transients are precious, the classification not only needs to indicate the assumed type but also the likelihood and confidence of the classification. Using classification algorithms trained on PTF data, the mislabeling of transients and variable stars has a 3.8% overall error rate. Additional work is expected to achieve higher accuracy rates in upcoming surveys, such as for the Large Synoptic Survey Telescope.

22.6.2 Blobs in Fusion Plasma

Large-scale scientific exploration in domains such as physics and climatology are huge international collaborations involving thousands of scientists each. As these

collaborations produce more and more data at progressively faster rates, the existing workflow management systems are hard-pressed to keep pace. A necessary
solution is to process, analyze, summarize, and reduce the data before it reaches the
relatively slow disk storage system, a process known as in-transit processing (or in-
flight analysis). Working with the ADIOS developers, we have implemented the ICEE
transport engine to dramatically increase the data-handling capability of collaborative
workflow systems (Choi et al. [2013]). This new feature significantly improved the
data flow management for distributed workflows. Tests showed that the ICEE engine
allowed a number of large international collaborations to make near real-time collaborative decisions. Here, we briefly describe the fusion collaboration involving KSTAR.

KSTAR is a nuclear fusion reactor with fully superconducting magnets. It is
located in South Korea, but there are a number of associated research teams around
the world. During a run of a fusion experiment, some researchers control the physics
device at KSTAR, but others may want to participate by performing collaborative
analysis of the preceding runs of the experiment to provide advice on how to config-
ure the device for the next run. During the analysis of the experimental measurement
data, scientists might run simulations or examine previous simulations to study parametric choices. Typically, there may be a lapse of 10 to 30 minutes between two suc-
cessive runs, and all collaborative analyses need to complete during this time window
in order to affect the next run.

We have demonstrated the functionality of the ICEE workflow system with two
different types of data: one from the Electron Cyclotron Emission Imaging (ECEI)
data measured at KSTAR, and the other involving synthetic diagnostic data from the
XGC modelling. The distributed workflow engine needs to collect data from these
two sources, extract a feature known as blobs, track the movement of these blobs,
predict the movement of the blobs in the experimental measurements, and then provide advices on actions to be performed. Figure 22.5 shows how the ECEI data is
processed. The workflow for the XGC simulation data is similar to what is shown in
Figure 22.5, except that the XGC data is located at NERSC.

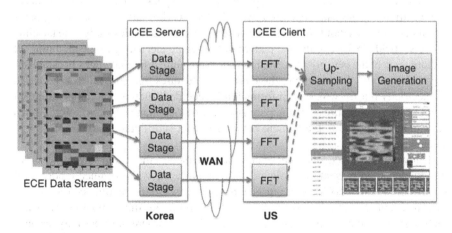

FIGURE 22.5   A distributed workflow for studying fusion plasma dynamics

To be able to complete the above analytical tasks in real-time, effective data management with ICEE transport engine of ADIOS is only part of the story. The second part is to detect blobs efficiently (Wu et al. [2016]). In this work, we need to reduce the amount of data transported across wide-area networks by selecting only the necessary chunks. We then identify all cells within the blobs and group these cells into connected regions in space, where each connected region forms a blob. The new algorithm we developed partitions the work into different CPU cores by taking full advantage of the MPI for communication between the nodes and the shared memory among the CPU cores on the same node. Additionally, we also updated the connected component label algorithm to correctly identify blobs at the edge, which were frequently missed by the earlier detection algorithms. Overall, our algorithm was able to identify blobs in a few milliseconds for each time step by taking full advantage of the parallelism available in the HPC system.

22.6.3   Intraday Peak Electricity Usage

Utility companies are deploying advanced metering infrastructure (AMI) to capture electricity consumption in unprecedented spatial and temporal detail. This vast and fast-growing stream of data provides an important testing ground for the predictive capability based on big data analytical platforms (Kim et al. [2015]). These cutting-edge data science techniques, together with behavioral theories, enable behavior analytics to gain novel insights into patterns of electricity consumption and their underlying drivers (Todd et al. [2014]).

As electricity cannot be easily stored, its generation must match consumption. When the demand exceeds the generation capacity, a blackout will occur, typically during the time when consumers need electricity the most. Because increasing generation capacity is expensive and requires years of time, regulators and utility companies have devised a number of pricing schemes intended to discourage unnecessary consumption during peak demand periods.

To measure the effectiveness of a pricing policy on peak demand, one can analyze the electricity usage data generated by AMI. Our work focuses on extracting baseline models of household electricity usage for a behavior analytics study. The baseline models would ideally capture the pattern of household electricity usage including all features except the new pricing schemes. There are numerous challenges in establishing such a model. For example, there are many features that could affect the usage of electricity but for which no information is recorded, such as the temperature set point of an air-conditioner or the purchase of a new appliance. Other features, such as outdoor temperature, are known, but their impact is difficult to capture in simple functions.

Our work developed a number of new baseline models that could satisfy the above requirements. At present, the gold standard baseline is a well-designed randomized control group. We showed that our new data-driven baselines could accurately predict the average electricity usage of the control group. For this evaluation, we use a well-designed study from a region of the United States where the electricity usage is the highest in the afternoon and evening during the months of May through August.

Though this work concentrates on demonstrating that the new baseline models are effective for groups, we believe that these new models are also useful for studying individual households in the future.

We explored a number of standard black-box approaches. Among machine learning methods, we found gradient tree boosting (GTB) to be more effective than others. However, the most accurate GTB models require lagged variables as features (for example, the electricity usage a day before and a week before). In our work, we need to use the data from year T-1 to establish the baseline usage for year T and year T + 1. The lagged variable for a day before and a week before would be incorporating recent information not in year T-1. We attempted to modify the prediction procedure to use the recent predictions in place of the actual measured values a day before and a week before; however, our tests show that the prediction errors accumulate over time, leading to unrealistic predictions a month or so into the summer season. This type of accumulation of prediction errors is common to continuous prediction procedures for time series.

To address the above issue, we devised a number of white-box approaches, the most effective of which, known as LTAP, is reported here. LTAP is based on the fact that the aggregate variable electricity usage per day is accurately described by a piecewise linear function of average daily temperature. This fact allows us to make predictions about the total daily electricity usage. By further assuming that the usage profile of each household remains the same during the study, we are able to assign the hourly usage values from the daily aggregate usage. This approach is shown to be self-consistent; that is, the prediction procedure exactly reproduces the electricity usage in year T–1, and the predictions for the control group in both year T and T + 1 are very close to the actual measured values. Both treatment groups have reduced electricity usages during the peak-demand hours, and the active group reduced the usage more than the passive group. This observation is in line with other studies.

Though the new data-driven baseline model LTAP predicts the average usages of the control group accurately, there are some differences in predicted impact of the new time-of-use pricing intended to reduce the usage during the peak-demand hours (see Figure 22.6). For example, with the control group as the baseline, the active group reduces its usage by 0.277 kWh (out of about 2 kWh) averaged over the peak-demand hours in the first year with the new price and 0.198 kWh in the second year. Using LTAP as the baseline, the average reductions are only 0.164 kWh for both years. Part of the difference may be due to the self-selection bias in treatment groups, especially the active group, where the households have to explicitly opt-in to participate in the trial. It is likely that the households that elected to join the active group are well-suited to take advantage of the proposed new pricing structure. We believe that the LTAP baseline is a way to address the self-selection bias and plan to conduct additional studies to further verify this.

22.6.4   The Flash Crash of 2010

The extended time it took for the SEC and CFTC to investigate the Flash Crash of 2010 was the original motivation for CIFT's work. Federal investigators needed to

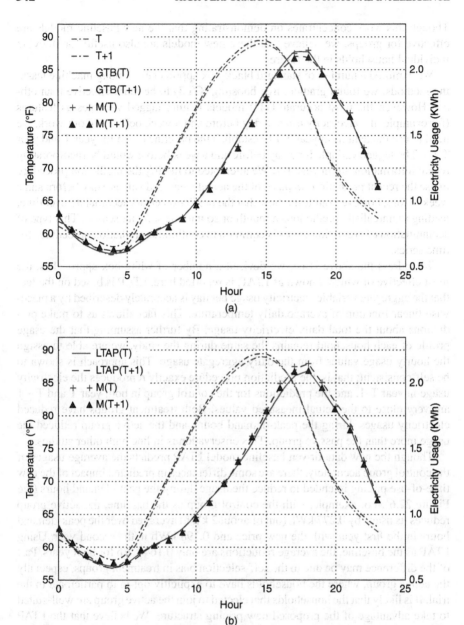

FIGURE 22.6 Gradient tree boosting (GBT) appears to follow recent usage too closely and therefore not able to predict the baseline usage as well as the newly develop method named LTAP. (a) GTB on Control group. (b) LTAP on Control group. (c) GTB on Passive group. (d) LTAP on Passive group. (e) GTB on Active group. (f) LTAP on Active group

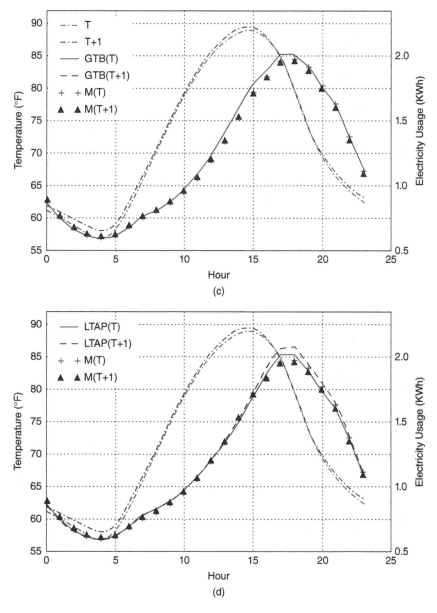

FIGURE 22.6   *(Continued)*

sift through tens of terabytes of data to look for the root cause of the crash. Since
CFTC publicly blamed the volume of data to be the source of the long delay, we
started our work by looking for HPC tools that could easily handle tens of terabytes.
Since HDF5 is the most commonly used I/O library, we started our work by applying
HDF5 to organize a large set of stock trading data (Bethel et al. [2011]).

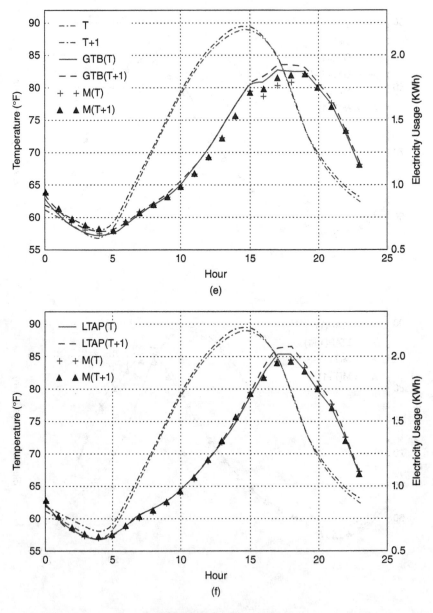

FIGURE 22.6   *(Continued)*

Let us quickly review what happened during the 2010 Flash Crash. On May 6, at about 2:45 p.m. (U.S. Eastern Daylight Time), the Dow Jones Industrial Average dropped almost 10%, and many stocks traded at one cent per share, the minimum price for any possible trade. Figure 22.7 shows an example of another extreme case, where shares of Apple (symbol AAPL) traded at $100,000 per share, the maximum

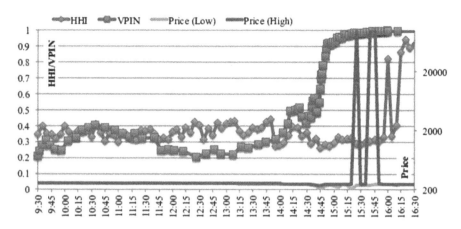

FIGURE 22.7   Apple Stock price on May 6, 2010, along with HHI and VPIN values computed every 5 minutes during the market hours

possible price allowed by the exchange. Clearly, these were unusual events, which undermined investors' faith and confidence in our financial markets. Investors demanded to know what caused these events.

To make our work relevant to the financial industry, we sought to experiment with the HDF5 software, and apply it to the concrete task of computing earlier warning indicators. Based on recommendations from a group of institutional investors, regulators, and academics, we implemented two sets of indicators that have been shown to have "early warning" properties preceding the Flash Crash. They are the Volume Synchronized Probability of Informed Trading (VPIN) (Easley, Lopez de Prado, and O'Hara [2011]) and a variant of the Herfindahl-Hirschman Index (HHI) (Hirschman [1980]) of market fragmentation. We implemented these two algorithms in the C++ language, while using MPI for inter-processor communication, to take full advantage of the HPC systems. The reasoning behind this choice is that if any of these earlier warning indicators is shown to be successful, the high-performance implementation would allow us to extract the warning signals as early as possible so there might be time to take corrective actions. Our effort was one of the first steps to demonstrate that it is possible to compute the earlier warning signals fast enough.

For our work, we implemented two versions of the programs: one uses data organized in HDF5 files, and another reads the data from the commonly used ASCII text files. Figure 22.8 shows the time required to process the trading records of all S&P 500 stocks over a 10-year timespan. Since the size of the 10-year trading data is still relatively small, we replicated the data 10 times as well. On a single CPU core (labeled "Serial" in Figure 22.8), it took about 3.5 hours with ASCII data, but only 603.98 seconds with HDF5 files. When 512 CPU cores are used, this time reduces to 2.58 seconds using HDF5 files, resulting in a speedup of 234 times.

On the larger (replicated) dataset, the advantage of HPC code for computing these indices is even more pronounced. With 10 times as much data, it took only about 2.3

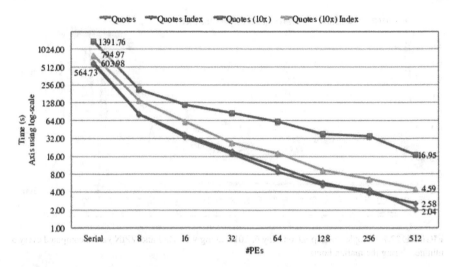

FIGURE 22.8 Time to process 10-year worth of SP500 quotes data stored in HDF5 files, which takes 21 times longer when the same data is in ASCII files (603.98 seconds versus approximately 3.5 hours)

times longer for the computer to complete the tasks, a below-linear latency increase. Using more CPU makes HPC even more scalable.

Figure 22.8 also shows that with a large data set, we can further take advantage of the indexing techniques available in HDF5 to reduce the data access time (which in turn reduces the overall computation time). When 512 CPU cores are used, the total runtime is reduced from 16.95 seconds to 4.59 seconds, a speedup of 3.7 due to this HPC technique of indexing.

22.6.5 Volume-synchronized Probability of Informed Trading Calibration

Understanding the volatility of the financial market requires the processing of a vast amount of data. We apply techniques from data-intensive scientific applications for this task, and demonstrate their effectiveness by computing an early warning indicator called Volume Synchronized Probability of Informed Trading (VPIN) on a massive set of futures contracts. The test data contains 67 months of trades for the hundred most frequently traded futures contracts. On average, processing one contract over 67 months takes around 1.5 seconds. Before we had this HPC implementation, it took about 18 minutes to complete the same task. Our HPC implementation achieves a speedup of 720 times.

Note that the above speedup was obtained solely based on the algorithmic improvement, without the benefit of parallelization. The HPC code can run on parallel machines using MPI, and thus is able to further reduce the computation time.

The software techniques employed in our work include the faster I/O access through HDF5 described above, as well as a more streamlined data structure for storing the bars and buckets used for the computation of VPIN. More detailed information is available in Wu et al. [2013].

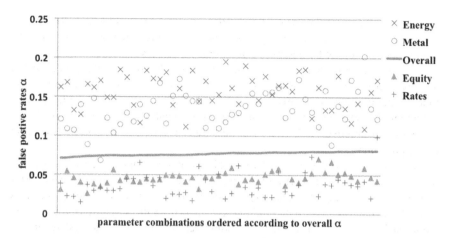

FIGURE 22.9 The average false positive rates (α) of different classes of futures contracts ordered according to their average.

With a faster program to compute VPIN, we were also able to explore the parametric choices more closely. For example, we were able to identify the parameter values that reduce VPIN's false positive rate over one hundred contracts from 20% to only 7%, see Figure 22.9. The parameter choices to achieve this performance are: (1) pricing the volume bar with the median prices of the trades (not the closing price typically used in analyses), (2) 200 buckets per day, (3) 30 bars per bucket, (4) support window for computing VPIN = 1 day, event duration = 0.1 day, (5) bulk volume classification with Student t-distribution with $v = 0.1$, and (6) threshold for CDF of VPIN = 0.99. Again, these parameters provide a low false positive rate on the totality of futures contracts, and are not the result of individual fitting.

On different classes of futures contracts, it is possible to choose different parameters to achieve even lower false positive rates. In some cases, the false positive rates can fall significantly below 1%. Based on Figure 22.9, interest rate and index futures contracts typically have lower false positive rates. The futures contracts on commodities, such as energy and metal, generally have higher false positive rates.

Additionally, a faster program for computing VPIN allows us to validate that the events identified by VPIN are "intrinsic," in the sense that varying parameters such as the threshold on VPIN CDF only slightly change the number of events detected. Had the events been random, changing this threshold from 0.9 to 0.99 would have reduced the number of events by a factor of 10. In short, a faster VPIN program also allows us to confirm the real-time effectiveness of VPIN.

22.6.6 Revealing High Frequency Events with Non-uniform Fast Fourier Transform

High Frequency Trading is pervasive across all electronic financial markets. As algorithms replace tasks previously performed by humans, cascading effects similar to the 2010 Flash Crash may become more likely. In our work (Song et al. [2014]), we brought together a number of high performance signal-processing tools to improve our understanding of these trading activities. As an illustration, we summarize the Fourier analysis of the trading prices of natural gas futures.

Normally, Fourier analysis is applied on uniformly spaced data. Since market activity comes in bursts, we may want to sample financial time series according to an index of trading activity. For example, VPIN samples financial series as a function of volume traded. However, a Fourier analysis of financial series in chronological time may still be instructive. To this purpose, we use a non-uniform Fast Fourier Transform (FFT) procedure.

From the Fourier analysis of the natural gas futures market, we see strong evidences of High Frequency Trading in the market. The Fourier components corresponding to high frequencies are (1) becoming more prominent in the recent years and (2) are much stronger than could be expected from the structure of the market. Additionally, a significant amount of trading activity occurs in the first second of every minute, which is a tell-tale sign of trading triggered by algorithms that target a Time-Weighted Average Price (TWAP).

Fourier analysis on trading data shows that activities at the once-per-minute frequency are considerably higher than at neighboring frequencies (see Figure 22.10). Note that the vertical axis is in logarithmic scale. The strength of activities at once-per-minute frequency is more than ten times stronger than the neighboring frequencies. Additionally, the activity is very precisely defined at once-per-minute, which indicates that these trades are triggered by intentionally constructed automated events. We take this to be strong evidence that TWAP algorithms have a significant presence in this market.

We expected the frequency analysis to show strong daily cycles. In Figure 22.10, we expect amplitude for frequency 365 to be large. However, we see the highest

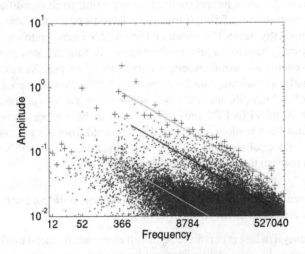

FIGURE 22.10 Fourier spectrum of trading prices of natural gas futures contracts in 2012. Non-uniform FFT identifies strong presence of activities happening once per day (frequency = 366), twice per day (frequency = 732), and once per minute (frequency = 527040 = 366*24*60).

amplitude was for the frequency of 366. This can be explained because 2012 was a leap year. This is a validation that the non-uniform FFT is capturing the expected signals. The second- and third-highest amplitudes have the frequencies of 732 and 52, which are twice-a-day and once-a-week. These are also unsurprising.

We additionally applied the non-uniform FFT on the trading volumes and found further evidence of algorithmic trading. Moreover, the signals pointed to a stronger presence of algorithmic trading in recent years. Clearly, the non-uniform FFT algorithm is useful for analyzing highly irregular time series.

22.7 SUMMARY AND CALL FOR PARTICIPATION

Currently, there are two primary ways to construct large-scale computing platforms: the HPC approach and the cloud approach. Most of the scientific computing efforts use the HPC approach, while most of the business computing needs are satisfied through the cloud approach. The conventional wisdom is that the HPC approach occupies a small niche of little consequence. This is not true. HPC systems are essential to the progress of scientific research. They played important roles in exciting new scientific discoveries including the Higgs particle and gravitational waves. They have spurred the development of new subjects of study, such as behavioral economics, and new ways of conducting commerce through the Internet. The usefulness of extremely large HPC systems has led to the 2015 National Strategic Computing Initiative.[3]

There are efforts to make HPC tools even more useful by accelerating their adoption in business applications. The HPC4Manufacturing[4] effort is pioneering this knowledge transfer to the U.S. manufacturing industry, and has attracted considerable attention. Now is the time to make a more concerted push for HPC to meet other critical business needs.

In recent years, we have developed CIFT as a broad class of business applications that could benefit from the HPC tools and techniques. In decisions such as how to respond to a voltage fluctuation in a power transformer and an early warning signal of impending market volatility event, HPC software tools could help determine the signals early enough for decision makers, provide sufficient confidence about the prediction, and anticipate the consequence before the catastrophic event arrives. These applications have complex computational requirements and often have a stringent demand on response time as well. HPC tools are better suited to meet these requirements than cloud-based tools.

In our work, we have demonstrated that the HPC I/O library HDF5 can be used to accelerate the data access speed by 21-fold, and HPC techniques can accelerate the computation of the Flash Crash early-warning indicator VPIN by 720-fold. We have developed additional algorithms that enable us to predict the daily peak electricity

---

[3] The National Strategic Computing Initiative plan is available online at https://www.whitehouse.gov/ sites/whitehouse.gov/files/images/NSCI%20Strategic%20Plan.pdf. The Wikipedia page on this topic (https://en.wikipedia.org/wiki/National_Strategic_Computing_Initiative) also has some useful links to additional information.

[4] Information about HPC4Manufacturing is available online at https://hpc4mfg.llnl.gov/.

usage years into the future. We anticipate that applying HPC tools and techniques to other applications could achieve similarly significant results.

In addition to the performance advantages mentioned above, a number of published studies (Yelick et al. [2011], Holzman et al. [2017]) show HPC systems to have a significant price advantage as well. Depending on the workload's requirement on CPU, storage, and networking, using a cloud system might cost 50% more than using a HPC system, and, in some cases, as much as seven times more. For the complex analytical tasks described in this book, with their constant need to ingest data for analysis, we anticipate the cost advantage will continue to be large.

CIFT is expanding the effort to transfer HPC technology to private companies, so that they can also benefit from the price and performance advantages enjoyed by large-scale research facilities. Our earlier collaborators have provided the funds to start a dedicated HPC system for our work. This resource should make it considerably easier for interested parties to try out their applications on an HPC system. We are open to different forms of collaborations. For further information regarding CIFT, please visit CIFT's web page at http://crd.lbl.gov/cift/.

22.8 ACKNOWLEDGMENTS

The CIFT project is the brainchild of Dr. David Leinweber. Dr. Horst Simon brought it to LBNL in 2010. Drs. E. W. Bethel and D. Bailey led the project for four years.

The CIFT project has received generous gifts from a number of donors. This work is supported in part by the Office of Advanced Scientific Computing Research, Office of Science, of the U.S. Department of Energy under Contract No. DE-AC02-05CH11231. This research also uses resources of the National Energy Research Scientific Computing Center supported under the same contract.

REFERENCES

Aad, G., et al. (2016): "Measurements of the Higgs boson production and decay rates and coupling strengths using pp collision data at $\sqrt{s} = 7$ and 8 TeV in the ATLAS experiment." *The European Physical Journal C*, Vol. 76, No. 1, p. 6.

Abbott, B.P. et al. (2016): "Observation of gravitational waves from a binary black hole merger." *Physical Review Letters*, Vol. 116, No. 6, p. 061102.

Armbrust, M., et al. (2010): "A view of cloud computing." *Communications of the ACM*, Vol. 53, No. 4, pp. 50–58.

Asanovic, K. et al. (2006): "The landscape of parallel computing research: A view from Berkeley." *Technical Report UCB/EECS-2006-183*, EECS Department, University of California, Berkeley.

Ayachit, U. et al. "Performance analysis, design considerations, and applications of extreme-scale in situ infrastructures." Proceedings of the International Conference for High Performance Computing, Networking, Storage and Analysis. IEEE Press.

Bethel, E. W. et al. (2011): "Federal market information technology in the post Flash Crash era: Roles for supercomputing." Proceedings of WHPCF'2011. ACM. pp. 23–30.

Bloom, J. S. et al. (2012): "Automating discovery and classification of transients and variable stars in the synoptic survey era." *Publications of the Astronomical Society of the Pacific*, Vol. 124, No. 921, p. 1175.

Camerer, C.F. and G. Loewenstein (2011): "Behavioral economics: Past, present, future." In *Advances in Behavioral Economics*, pp. 1–52.

Chen, L. et al. (2015): "Profiling and understanding virtualization overhead in cloud." *Parallel Processing (ICPP)*, 2015 44th International Conference. IEEE.

Choi, J.Y. et al. (2013): ICEE: "Wide-area in transit data processing framework for near real-time scientific applications." 4th SC Workshop on Petascale (Big) Data Analytics: Challenges and Opportunities in Conjunction with SC13.

Dong, Y. et al. (2012): "High performance network virtualization with SR-IOV." *Journal of Parallel and Distributed Computing*, Vol. 72, No. 11, pp. 1471–1480.

Easley, D., M. Lopez de Prado, and M. O'Hara (2011): "The microstructure of the 'Flash Crash': Flow toxicity, liquidity crashes and the probability of informed trading." *Journal of Portfolio Management*, Vol. 37, No. 2, pp. 118–128.

Folk, M. et al. (2011): "An overview of the HDF5 technology suite and its applications." Proceedings of the EDBT/ICDT 2011 Workshop on Array Databases. ACM.

Fox, G. et al. (2015): "Big Data, simulations and HPC convergence, iBig Data benchmarking": 6th International Workshop, WBDB 2015, Toronto, ON, Canada, June 16–17, 2015; and 7th International Workshop, WBDB 2015, New Delhi, India, December 14–15, 2015, Revised Selected Papers, T. Rabl, et al., eds. 2016, Springer International Publishing: Cham. pp. 3–17. DOI: 10.1007/978-3-319-49748-8_1.

Ghemawat, S., H. Gobioff, and S.-T. Leung (2003): "The Google file system," *SOSP '03: Proceedings of the nineteenth ACM symposium on operating systems principles*. ACM. pp. 29–43.

Gordon, A. et al. (2012): "ELI: Bare-metal performance for I/O virtualization." *SIGARCH Comput. Archit. News*, Vol. 40, No. 1, pp. 411–422.

Gropp, W., E. Lusk, and A. Skjellum (1999): *Using MPI: Portable Parallel Programming with the Message-Passing Interface*. MIT Press.

Hey, T., S. Tansley, and K.M. Tolle (2009): *The Fourth Paradigm: Data-Intensive Scientific Discovery*. Vol. 1. Microsoft research Redmond, WA.

Hirschman, A. O. (1980): *National Power and the Structure of Foreign Trade*. Vol. 105. University of California Press.

Holzman, B. et al. (2017): "HEPCloud, a new paradigm for HEP facilities: CMS Amazon Web Services investigation. *Computing and Software for Big Science*, Vol. 1, No. 1, p. 1.

Jackson, K. R., et al. (2010): "Performance analysis of high performance computing applications on the Amazon Web Services Cloud. *Cloud Computing Technology and Science (CloudCom)*. 2010 Second International Conference. IEEE.

Kim, T. et al. (2015): "Extracting baseline electricity usage using gradient tree boosting." IEEE International Conference on Smart City/SocialCom/SustainCom (SmartCity). IEEE.

Kumar, V. et al. (1994): *Introduction to Parallel Computing: Design and Analysis of Algorithms*. Benjamin/Cummings Publishing Company.

Liu, Q. et al., (2014): "Hello ADIOS: The challenges and lessons of developing leadership class I/O frameworks." *Concurrency and Computation: Practice and Experience*, Volume 26, No. 7, pp. 1453–1473.

National Academies of Sciences, Engineering and Medicine (2016): *Future Directions for NSF Advanced Computing Infrastructure to Support U.S. Science and Engineering in 2017–2020*. National Academies Press.

Nicholas, M. L. et al. (2009): "The Palomar transient factory: System overview, performance, and first results." *Publications of the Astronomical Society of the Pacific*, Vol. 121, No. 886, p. 1395.

Qiu, J. et al. (2016): "A survey of machine learning for big data processing." *EURASIP Journal on Advances in Signal Processing*, Vol. 2016, No. 1, p. 67. DOI: 10.1186/s13634-016-0355-x

Rudin, C. and K. L. Wagstaff (2014) "Machine learning for science and society." *Machine Learning*, Vol. 95, No. 1, pp. 1–9.

Shoshani, A. and D. Rotem (2010): "Scientific data management: Challenges, technology, and deployment." *Chapman & Hall/CRC Computational Science Series*. CRC Press.

Snir, M. et al. (1998): *MPI: The Complete Reference. Volume 1, The MPI-1 Core*. MIT Press.

Song, J. H. et al. (2014): "Exploring irregular time series through non-uniform fast Fourier transform." Proceedings of the 7th Workshop on High Performance Computational Finance, IEEE Press.

Todd, A. et al. (2014): "Insights from Smart Meters: The potential for peak hour savings from behavior-based programs." Lawrence Berkeley National Laboratory. Available at https://www4.eere.energy.gov/seeaction/system/files/documents/smart_meters.pdf.

Wu, K. et al. (2013): "A big data approach to analyzing market volatility." *Algorithmic Finance*. Vol. 2, No. 3, pp. 241–267.

Wu, L. et al. (2016): "Towards real-time detection and tracking of spatio-temporal features: Blob-filaments in fusion plasma. *IEEE Transactions on Big Data*, Vol. 2, No. 3, pp. 262–275.

Yan, J. et al. (2009): "How much can behavioral targeting help online advertising?" Proceedings of the 18th international conference on world wide web. ACM. pp. 261–270.

Yelick, K., et al. (2011): "The Magellan report on cloud computing for science." U.S. Department of Energy, Office of Science.

Zeff, R.L. and B. Aronson (1999): *Advertising on the Internet*. John Wiley & Sons.

Index

Page numbers followed by *f* or *t* refer to figure or table, respectively.

Investment strategies (*Continued*)
profit-taking and stop-loss limits in,
170–171, 172, 211
risk in. *See* Strategy risk
structural breaks and, 249
trade-off between precision and
frequency in, 212–213, 212*f*
trading rules and algorithms in,
169–170
Investment strategy failure probability,
216–218
algorithm in, 217
implementation of algorithm in,
217–218
probabilistic Sharpe ratio (PSR)
similarity to, 218
strategy risk and, 216–217

K-fold cross-validation (CV), 103–109
description of, 103–104, 104*f*
embargo on training observations in,
107–108, 108*f*
leakage in, 104–105
mean decrease accuracy (MDA)
feature with, 116
overlapping training observations in,
109
purging process in training set for
leakage reduction in, 105–106,
107*f*
when used, 104
Kyle's lambda, 286–288, 288*f*

Labeling, 43–55
daily volatility at intraday estimation
for, 44–45
dropping unnecessary or
under-populated labels in, 54–55
fixed-time horizon labeling method
for, 43–44
learning side and size in, 48–50
meta-labeling and, 50–53
quantamental approach using, 53–54

triple-barrier labeling method for,
45–46, 47*f*
Labels
average uniqueness over lifespan of,
61–62, 61*f*
class weights for underrepresented
labels, 71–72
estimating uniqueness of, 60–61
Lawrence Berkeley National Laboratory
(LBNL, Berkeley Lab), 18, 329,
331
Leakage, and cross-validation (CV),
104–105
Leakage reduction
bagging for, 105
purging process in training set for,
105–106, 107*f*
sequential bootstraps for, 105
walk-forward timefolds method for,
155
Lempel-Ziv (LZ) estimator, 265–269
Leverage, in backtesting, 196
Limit prices, in bet sizing, 145–148
Log loss scoring, in hyper-parameter
tuning, 133–134, 135*f*
Log-uniform distribution, 132–133
Look-ahead bias, 152

Machine learning (ML), 3
finance and, 4, 14
financial machine learning separate
from, 4
HRP approach using, 221, 224
human investors and, 4, 14
prejudices about use of, 16
Machine learning asset allocation,
223–244. *See also* Hierarchical
Risk Parity (HRP) approach
Monte Carlo simulations for,
234–236, 235*f*–236*f*, 242–244
numerical example of, 231–233, 232*f*,
233*f*, 233*t*
quasi-diagonalization in, 224, 229,
233*f*